Words of Pr
the First E

"… a very fine addition to any sci-fi fan's bookshelf… It is certainly unique, and certainly not similar, and in terms of analysis one of the finest pieces of work I have read, not just about *The Prisoner*, but Telefantasy in general."

Rick Davy, *The Unmutual* website, July 2013

"… a delightfully written and well-researched study… an excellent book that breaks new ground in the study of one of the most remarkable TV series ever made."

Robert Fairclough, *Adventures in Time and Space* website, August 2013

"… the author skilfully draws together a pattern of connections that demonstrate how certain programmes may have been influenced, in some way, by the classic 60s show… [His] obvious love for intelligent TV really draws you in, and… it left me with a list of shows that I really must track down and watch."

Rosie Marsh, *The Crack* magazine, July 2013

The extensive referencing and footnotes "give the book a tone of both respect and authority, as well as being a fine tribute to the author's research… Unique, as the title suggests, and unhesitatingly recommended."

Roger Goodman, *PrizBiz*, July 2013

"I did… find the long essay on *Blake's 7* interesting, and I enjoyed the chapter on *Joe 90!*"

Tony Jones, *Starburst* magazine, June 2013

"… might be immensely useful for anyone studying a course in comparable Prisonerology".

Darren Humphries Ebooks, June 2013

Unique But Similar

the
Prisoner
compared

Andrew K. Shenton

This paperback edition published July 2017 by Miwk Publishing Ltd.
Miwk Publishing, 45a Bell Street, Reigate, Surrey RH2 7AQ

ISBN 978-1-908630-81-0

A CIP catalogue record for this book is available from the British Library.

Cover illustrations / book design and layout by Robert Hammond.

Typeset in Albertus Medium and Utopia.

www.miwkpublishing.com
This product was lovingly Miwk made.

Contents

The Author... 7

Acknowledgements... 9

Introduction: This Book in Context... 13

Part A: Overview... 31

Section I: Some Preliminary Thoughts on
Comparisons Without and Within... 33

Section II: Stepping Into Various Worlds Beyond The Village... 45

Part B: The Individual Comparisons... 79

Chapter One: Endless Sunny Days and Rain-making
The Prisoner and *Look and Read – Cloud Burst*... 81

Chapter Two: A Tale of Two Villages
The Prisoner and *Children of the Stones*... 95

Chapter Three: Two Perspectives on the Loss of Individual Identity
The Prisoner and *Doctor Who – The Faceless Ones*... 111

Chapter Four: Individuals and Champions
The Prisoner and *The Champions – The Interrogation*... 127

Chapter Five: Sunshine and Shadow
The Prisoner and *The Twilight Zone*... 137

Chapter Six: Villages and Houses
The Prisoner and *Rod Serling's Night Gallery – The House*... 157

Chapter Seven: Sixes and Sevens
The Prisoner and *The Omega Factor*... 167

Chapter Eight: The Unnamed and the Unidentified
The Prisoner and *UFO*... 191

Chapter Nine: The Individual and the "Team"
The Prisoner and *Blake's 7*... 219

Chapter Ten: Fight and Flight
The Prisoner and *Logan's Run*... 255

Chapter Eleven: A Village Like No Other and a School That is Different
The Prisoner and *Codename Icarus*... 269

Chapter Twelve: Two Struggles Against Oppression
The Prisoner and *Knights of God*... 279

Chapter Thirteen: The Incarcerated Individual, the Boy Hero and the
Whitehall Mandarin – Their Common Tactics of Subversion
The Prisoner – Hammer Into Anvil, Joe 90 – See You Down There and
Yes, Prime Minister – Man Overboard... 289

Chapter Fourteen: The Journey That Never Was... Another Weapon in the
Armoury of Deception *The Prisoner – The Chimes of Big Ben* and *Mission:
Impossible – The Train*... 297

Epilogue... 307

Appendix: The Works Examined... 309

The Author

Dr Andrew K. Shenton is a former Lecturer in the School of Computing, Engineering and Information Sciences at Northumbria University. Over the last 20 years, he has written extensively on such diverse subjects as research methods, librarianship, information behaviour, education, science fiction and cricket, and he now has to his name over 200 published pieces. He has won significant awards for several of them. Andrew's work has been cited in books, reports, journal articles and conference papers, and formed recommended reading for modules of university courses that have included PhD programmes. He currently divides his time between writing, mentoring students and working in a high school in north-east England. In March 2014, he received a higher doctorate for his published research in library and information science.

The author's fascination with *The Prisoner* began some 35 years ago when he started reading about the programme in books such as the first volume of Starlog's *TV Episode Guides* and the seminal *Encyclopedia of Science Fiction*, edited by Peter Nicholls. Like many SF fans of his generation, Andrew watched *The Prisoner* for the first time when the fledgling Channel 4 broadcast it in 1983–84. By this stage he was well aware of the show's legendary reputation and the episodes more than lived up to his expectations. His earliest attempt to write about *The Prisoner* came soon after he had seen the final episode, when he prepared for his school magazine a review of *Fall Out* entitled *Six Into One Won't Go*. Ultimately, however, fearing ridicule from his peers, whom he felt would mock his attempt to give serious consideration to such an unconventional production and one which, at the time of his writing, was over 15 years old, he lacked the courage to submit the work and it remains unpublished. Had he possessed a little more of Number Six's uncompromising individualism, he might well have made a different decision! For many years, Andrew has been an avid collection of *Prisoner* materials, including video cassettes, DVDs, CDs, books and magazine articles. His assessments of *Prisoner* episodes are not always consistent with the established wisdom. Andrew's personal favourites are *Many Happy Returns, Hammer Into Anvil* and *Do Not Forsake Me Oh My Darling*.

Acknowledgements

Thanks are due to a number of people without whose input this book would never have been conceived, written or published. Whilst watching *The Prisoner* for the first time in the mid 1980s, I spent many happy hours discussing the episodes with my teenaged pals Gavin Davy and Michael Reid, very often as we trekked to and from school. Had it not been for their willingness to dissect the programme with me and, in particular, seek answers to the fundamental question "What's it all about?" I doubt that I would have spent so long considering the series. My ideas would probably have remained in my head and gone uncommunicated. My memories of those debates, now so many years ago, served me admirably when preparing the material for *Unique But Similar*.

It is often said that advances in scholarship are achieved by "standing on the shoulders of giants", in other words by building on the academic contributions of our predecessors. Whilst I cannot forecast that, in the years to come, this new edition of *Unique But Similar* will come to be regarded as a seminal work on *The Prisoner*, I can certainly applaud the role that past commentators on the series have played in furnishing me with source material for the book and in stimulating my own ideas.

I also owe a substantial debt of gratitude to all those who have procured for me copies of some of the sources that are cited here. Without their help, I would have been unable to see many of them. Locally, Naomi Hay-Gibson and the staff of Northumbria University Library and Newcastle City Library have given me invaluable assistance in this respect. Beyond north-eastern England, I must acknowledge the efforts of Louise Weston, of the BBC Written Archives Centre, who mailed to me a copy of the *Radio Times* article on *The Omega Factor*.

The role of Roger Goodman during the preparation of this book has been unique. Not only has Roger himself contributed to the knowledge base that relates to *The Prisoner* by interviewing Patrick McGoohan and editing an excellent book on the series; he has also, through his business, provided access to a wide range of information sources that pertain to the programme.

Thanks must be extended to Rick Davy. He has always proved very receptive to my work on *The Prisoner* and it was he who offered me an outlet for my early comparative essays in the form of his website *The Unmutual*. After learning of my intention to collate these essays, revise their content and add more material to form a book, Rick has been unstinting in his support and encouragement. His ideas for marketing the work have been particularly welcome.

I appreciate, too, the critical assessments of reviewers who read and offered their opinions on the first edition of *Unique But Similar*. Where these writers raised what I believe to be legitimate issues, I have attempted to address their concerns in this new edition. I feel that their comments have contributed much to my ability to enhance the original version of the work.

The publishers have exceeded all my expectations. As well as adopting a positive attitude to the project from the outset, they have offered prudent and constructive advice on how the work could be improved. The finished book would have been substantially weaker had the manuscript not received such meticulous attention.

My sincerest thanks go to all of you.

Dedication

This book is dedicated to my parents and greatest teachers, Ken and Joan Shenton. Without their constant support, especially in my early years, I would never have acquired the academic skills necessary to write *Unique But Similar*. The book is for them, with love and eternal gratitude.

Introduction:
This Book in Context

It seems truly extraordinary that *The Prisoner* has stimulated so much discussion over such a long period when one considers that the series consists of just 17 episodes and occupies only around 14 hours of total screen time. It may, however, be argued that the mystique resulting from *The Prisoner's* relatively brief production life has contributed to the programme's long-term appeal. Certainly, the impact that can be made by a short series was well understood by Patrick McGoohan. When asked in an interview if he would have welcomed the opportunity to make more episodes and address further themes, he responded negatively, declaring that he would have preferred fewer than the actual 17 instalments. In McGoohan's own words, "Less would have been more. More enigmatic." (p. 8)[1]

Some impression of the degree of critical comment on the programme comes from Rupert Booth's remark, "More words have been written about the seventeen episodes than are contained within the episodes themselves." (p. 223)[2] During the last 30 years, over a dozen substantial non-fiction works dealing in some way with the series have been published. With a spate of new books appearing as recently as 2010[3] and fresh impetus coming from the 2009 revival, interest in *The Prisoner* shows little sign of waning.

In view of the volume of literature, and in particular, the statement made nearly 15 years ago in the *Encyclopedia of Television* that "every aspect of the series has been subjected to scrutiny", (p. 1830)[4] a reader seeing *Unique But Similar* for the first time may well ask if yet another book about the programme is necessary, and whether the work can be considered to fill any real gap in terms of what has already been written about the series. Indeed, one of Roger Langley's most recent publications, *The Prisoner Dialogue Decodes*, which appeared in 2014, concludes on a note of such striking finality that one could be forgiven for thinking that the last pronouncements on *The Prisoner* have already been made. In his "Village Postscript" at the end of the volume, Langley asserts that his book "has revealed all that can be known about *The Prisoner*'s central character and the place in which he was held, its methods and reasons". (p. 99) Langley believes that the different approach that has been taken in his work, which concentrates especially on the series' dialogue, "closes the doors, or bars, on the creation of a final dossier". (p. 99)[5] Since this statement is made by a man who must be rated as one of the most knowledgeable experts on the programme, anyone contemplating the task of writing a new book about *The Prisoner* may fear that their contribution will be no more than limited. Certainly for Langley, research in relation to major areas of the programme can go no further.

It is a measure of the advanced state of discussion surrounding *The Prisoner* that, for years now, commentators have pored over the minutiae of the individual episodes and constructed far-reaching arguments on the basis of "evidence" that may be limited to one particular instalment. Let us take a case in point. Drawing inspiration from *Do Not Forsake Me Oh My Darling*, the author of the *Complete Encyclopedia of Television Programs: 1947–1979* asserts that the abduction of The Prisoner, who, it is maintained, may be assumed to be *Danger Man*'s John Drake, resulted from the way in which he had handled an assignment involving Professor Seltzman. These events were not, however, seen in *The Prisoner* and it is difficult from the dialogue within the relevant episode to establish a clear picture of what exactly took place in the previous meeting between the two men. Summarising the developments that led up to The Prisoner's kidnapping, the *Encyclopedia* nonetheless states quite unequivocally,

> Assigned to locate a missing scientist, secret agent John Drake permits him to defect to Russia when he discovers the nature of the doctor's work: to complete a deadly mind transference device. Returning to England and reprimanded for his actions, Drake resigns, feeling it is a matter of principal. (p. 376)[6]

One might not have been surprised if this explanation had appeared in an "opinion" or "comment" column of a *Prisoner* fanzine; it is rather more unexpected that it is presented as undisputed fact in a published encyclopedia of television programmes. Although the stance taken in the book is a minority view, Richard Meyers gives the argument sufficient credence to report it in his work on "TV detectives". He does, however, mistakenly assert that *A Change of Mind* is the episode in which the evidence is apparent.[7] The possibilities offered by an early encounter between the hero and Seltzman in providing a motivation for The Prisoner's resignation continue to intrigue to this day and would be resurrected in the audio version of the show developed by Big Finish and inaugurated in January 2016.

It would be erroneous, of course, to believe that the *Encyclopedia's* interpretation is the only explanation that has been put forward in response to one of *The Prisoner's* key questions – why does the hero resign? Other writers have constructed their own theories, again drawing on material from individual episodes. Given McGoohan's statement that "if there are any answers to *The Prisoner*, they are in the final episode", (p. 115)[8] it is not surprising that various commentators have formed responses to the resignation issue based on what has been witnessed in *Fall Out*. Gary Gerani and Paul H. Schulman, for example, confidently assert that Number Six's resignation was motivated by his determination "to imprison himself, thereby demonstrating that each man is his own warden, conforming to society's design only by his own commands", (p. 124) as well as by his desire to protest against the repressive behaviour of the intelligence services.[9] Nevertheless, McGoohan himself was reluctant to give clear cut answers to the question and has merely commented that his character, "resigns as a matter of choice. He shouldn't have to answer to anyone. It's entirely his prerogative, his God-given right as an individual, to proceed in any way he sees fit." (p. 179)[10]

It would appear that *Prisoner* script editor George Markstein, however, had his own, very specific ideas about what lay behind the hero's resignation. According to his close friend James Follett, Markstein envisaged that, in his younger days, the man we would come to know as Number Six had submitted a proposal on how retired secret agents who posed a security risk might be treated by their own side. His idea was to create a retirement centre where former agents could live out their final years in comfort but under close surveillance. Some time later, the hero discovered that his plan had been put into practice but as an interrogation centre and prison camp, rather than in the benign way he had intended. Outraged, he resigned, certain that he would be brought to The Village. His hope was to learn more about how his proposal had been implemented and devise a method of destroying it.[11] Follett explains that The Prisoner's expression on waking in The Village was not meant to be one of bewilderment, then – "it was recognition!"[12]

Elaborating on her claim that a "considerable amount of academic attention [has been] given to television fantasy dramas", Catherine Johnson observes that much of the scholarship surrounding *The Prisoner* is concerned with the "fan culture" it has engendered. (p. 1)[13] This is not the focus of *Unique But Similar*, however. Perhaps the most fundamental difference between this book and all its predecessors is that here the author is as concerned with other television productions as he is with *The Prisoner* itself. Specifically, the work concentrates on those programmes, or individual episodes thereof, which bear some kind of significant resemblance to McGoohan's creation, and discusses the common ground that can be identified.

So as to appreciate the distinctiveness of the book when set against others that pertain to *The Prisoner*, it is necessary to spend a few moments reviewing the literature in existence. This is especially important since many of the books involved are themselves extensively cited in *Unique But Similar*. One of the key features of this volume on *The Prisoner* is that, unlike a lot of the others, it makes no attempt to discuss each of the instalments in turn. Such an "episode guide" treatment has been a recurrent characteristic of books devoted to the programme from the earliest up to those that have appeared in recent years, and indeed it seems to have become the norm in volumes devoted to any particular series.

The Prisoner has attracted interest from viewers of very different philosophical and political persuasions. In the late 1970s, *The Encyclopedia of Science Fiction* recognised that the programme enjoyed a substantial following among liberals.[14] Much more recently, M. Keith Booker has noted how Number Six's defeats seem "to suggest the ultimate impossibility of a single man overcoming the authority of an oppressive society", (p. 94) and can be construed to form a Leftist agenda that proposes the need for collective action, although in *Checkmate*, the hero's efforts to escape after assembling a team also result in failure. Booker feels, too, however, that McGoohan's political vision is essentially anti-authoritarian in the Right wing libertarian sense,[15] and it may be no coincidence that some of the earliest academic articles on the series were indeed written by libertarians. One such paper is Chris R. Tame's *Different Values: An Analysis of Patrick McGoohan's The Prisoner* (published in *New Libertarian Review*, issue 34/35, September 1974). In it, Tame himself draws attention to previous work about the series by fellow libertarians:

- Page, G. W. The Prisoner. *Metro Magazine*, 1 (1), November 1968.
- Chamberlain, F. R. Individualism comes to television. *The Individualist*, 2 (3/4), March/April 1970.

A significant weakness of the early pieces on *The Prisoner* is that since they were written before repeat screenings and video recordings of the episodes could be seen, many were produced after only one viewing of the show. Consequently, mistakes could easily be made; there was no opportunity for verification through rewatching, and interpretations may have been formed on the basis of little more than first impressions.[16] It is illuminating to contrast these circumstances with the context in which Chris Gregory wrote *Be Seeing You... Decoding The Prisoner* in the mid 1990s. At one point in his text he acknowledges, "This book... could never have been written in this form without the use of a VCR." (p. 184)[17] Tame himself is remarkably honest when appraising *Different Values* in a 1983 postscript to a reproduced version of his original work. He concedes,

> Since writing this essay I have seen *The Prisoner* several times again. Moreover, a number of interviews with its principal creators have taken place that enable one to make a more accurate evaluation of many aspects of the series. In the light of these facts I believe my view of the final episode expressed above is incorrect. (p. 6)[18]

In truth, there are further major errors in Tame's article – the episode *Dance of the Dead* is referred to more than once as *Carnival of Death* and the character played by Leo McKern is described as "the first Number 2". (p. 4)[19] Nevertheless, written at a time when *The Prisoner* was still a source of confusion and bemusement to many, the piece exhibits a commendable degree of insight and understanding. The paper has drawn praise from noted *Prisoner* commentator David Stimpson, who feels that parts of Tame's analysis "hit the nail on the head".[20]

Reviewing merchandise associated with the show, Robert Fairclough describes *The Prisoner Program Guide* (written by Neil McLean and David Stansfield and published by the Ontario Educational Communications Authority in 1976) and *The Prisoner Puzzle* (written by Susan Nobel and Diana Goldsborough and published by the Ontario Educational Communications Authority in 1978) as "the first publications to treat the programme seriously as a work of art". (p. 131)[21] Today, these booklets, written from a teaching and learning standpoint to support classroom investigations into *The Prisoner*, seem odd curiosities. Consisting of no more than 30 pages and 21 pages respectively, they clearly cannot be considered substantial works, although they are similar to many of the later *Prisoner* books in that much of their content is devoted to sequential consideration of the individual episodes. As in *Unique But Similar*, there is a strong comparative element in these booklets. The *Program Guide* encourages students to make links between, for example, the first episode of *The Prisoner, Arrival*, and spy stories, such as John le Carré's *The Spy Who Came in From the Cold* and Len Deighton's *Funeral in Berlin*, whilst in *The Prisoner Puzzle*, the final instalment, *Fall Out*, is likened to the last chapter of *Alice Through the Looking Glass*. It is, however, striking that, in both booklets, few of the creative works highlighted in connection with *The Prisoner* are television series. One possible explanation is that, at the time of their writing, television was still in its relative infancy as compared with literature and cinema. Indeed, in 1979, not long after the two booklets had appeared, David Owen asserted, "Television science fiction is a less fully developed genre than its cinematic counterpart." (p. 24)[22] Despite the fact that *The Prisoner* has been examined so minutely over the last 30 years, in particular, even today some of the issues raised in the OECA booklets may well surprise readers seeing the works for the first time, and the links made may seem either tenuous or insightful depending on one's viewpoint. For example, most readers are unlikely to look, without prompting, for similarities between The Prisoner's early experiences in The Village and a child's first day at school. Nevertheless, many years after the publication of *The Prisoner Program Guide* Jon E. Lewis and Penny Stempel would pursue the school theme further by remarking on the parallels between Number Six's Village costume and the uniform of an English public school.[23]

The appearance of factual books on *The Prisoner* has been by no means regular during the 50 years since the programme was initially broadcast. It was not until some two decades after *The Prisoner*'s original showing, in fact, that the first major and commercially published non-fiction books on the series started to be seen. The time gap may seem counterintuitive, as one might have assumed that interest in *The Prisoner* would be at its peak during the period when the show was being broadcast for the first time and immediately afterwards. Perhaps some insight into why there was such a lengthy time lapse may be gained from Ted C. Rypel's comments regarding the lack of contemporary information available on the original version of *The Outer Limits*. There was little, he notes, "beyond a few stills and exploitative mentions in the sensationalistic monster mags of the day. Nobody did books about TV shows back then." (p. 11)[24]

The situation with respect to the timing of factual publications associated with *The Prisoner* is certainly very different from that pertaining to another British cult favourite, *Blake's 7*. The last episode of that show was originally broadcast in December 1981 and within a year the first significant information book about the series – *Terry Nation's Blake's 7: The Programme Guide* by Tony Attwood (W. H. Allen, 1982) – had appeared.[25] The reader should be aware, too, that volumes such as *The Making of Star Trek* by Stephen E. Whitfield and Gene Roddenberry (Ballantine, 1968) and Tim Heald's *The Making of Space: 1999 – A Gerry Anderson Production* (Ballantine, 1976) were written at such an early date that the authors were unable to present episode guides that cover all the instalments which would ultimately form the entirety of each series.[26] Similarly, both editions of *The Making of Doctor Who* by Terrance Dicks and Malcolm Hulke (first edition: Pan, 1972; second edition: Tandem, 1976) were published while the programme in question was still in production. The distribution over time of *Prisoner* literature, meanwhile, not only provides one of the most telling indicators of the longevity of the cult that surrounds the series but also reflects the fact that serious critical appraisal of the show was somewhat belated in its arrival.[27]

Despite its novelty at the time of its first appearance, one of the early published volumes, *The Official Prisoner Companion* by Matthew White and Jaffer Ali (Sidgwick and Jackson, 1988), has been the target of strong criticism in various quarters. Reflecting some years later on how the book had been received, Anthony McKay wrote, "This sketchily researched paperback was universally panned by fans of the series because of several glaring factual errors and its fascination with shallow philosophical questions requiring long nonsensical answers."[28] Andrew Pixley was equally unimpressed and levels similar charges against the work, although the episode guide, which forms the core of the book, largely escapes his condemnation.[29] Perhaps most seriously, the work drew complaint from McGoohan himself, who commented, "Everything [the writers] claimed that I said, apart from two things, is inaccurate." (p. 219)[30]

Another book heavily oriented around an episode guide is Dave Rogers's *The Prisoner and Danger Man* (Boxtree, 1989), whose story synopses, Pixley considers, are so detailed that they "are almost mini-novels". (p. 129)[31] Steven Ricks feels that the book's value has diminished with time, arguing that it would "have been ideal before the advent of video". (p. 32)[32] In reminiscences that will, no doubt, resonate with longstanding *Prisoner* fans the world over, Langley recalls the problems that arose in the early years even when enthusiasts were simply intent on understanding the plot developments within an instalment they had seen some time previously. He writes,

> ... making sense of them depended upon one's ability to remember what had happened in the episode and the order in which the events occurred. This was at a time when people had difficulty in remembering which No. 2 came from which episode and which blonde actress appeared in which story. (p. 121)[33]

Given this background, it is easy to appreciate how useful the Rogers book would have been in an earlier era and, even today, it remains an invaluable work of reference for any enthusiast wishing to check a particular plot detail or refamiliarise themselves with the minutiae of a certain episode without watching the whole instalment again. A more vividly illustrated work, although one giving a similarly high priority to an in-depth episode-by-episode approach, is *The Prisoner: A Televisionary Masterpiece* by Alain Carrazé and Hélène Oswald (Virgin, 1990).

The comments made by Ricks remind us that, over the last 30 years, the authors of non-fiction books on television series such as *The Prisoner* have had to take on a challenge that has become very familiar to writers of tie-in novelisations over the same period. Discussing the Target *Doctor Who* range, David J. Howe notes how the direct script-to-book conversions increasingly came to be viewed by readers as unsatisfactory. The first such *Doctor Who* volumes were written in the era before the widespread use of domestic video recorders and the novelisations gave fans the opportunity to "relive" the original adventures. However, when VHS tapes of the serials became available readers began to want books that "extrapolated from or presented a different slant on the source material". (p. 49)[34] The importance of early novelisations effectively forming surrogates for the episodes involved is acknowledged by Chris Bentley, too. Writing about the 1970s *Space: 1999* book adaptations, he asserts, "in the days before every home had a video recorder, episode novelisations were the only way for television aficionados to experience the stories of their favourite programmes again in the years between repeat screenings". (p. 172)[35] It should perhaps be added at this point that the twelve-volume series of *Star Trek* "fotonovels", which appeared in 1977 and 1978, fulfilled a similar role in the eyes of many Trekkies. In the same way, within non-fiction books detailed synopses of the individual episodes would once have formed a key resource but, in the modern era, with enthusiasts able to watch each instalment whenever they wish, such a limited treatment of the material is likely to be dismissed as unnecessary duplication. Typically, greater analytical insight or background detail on each episode's production is demanded.

A notable development in the last 20 years has been the publication of books either concentrating on a certain aspect of *The Prisoner* or written from a particular angle. The specificity of their territory may prompt the general reader to assume that works of this type may be limited in their circulation to channels associated with fan outlets, such as appreciation societies, but of late, they have been released by mainstream publishers. Gregory's *Be Seeing You... Decoding The Prisoner* (John Libbey Media, 1997) formed one of the first commercially published volumes to appraise the series from an academic perspective. It has much in common with such books as John Tulloch and Manuel Alvarado's *Doctor Who: The Unfolding Text* (Macmillan, 1983), Toby Miller's *The Avengers* (British Film Institute, 1997) and Peter Wolfe's *In the Zone: The Twilight World of Rod Serling* (Bowling Green State University Popular Press, 1997) in that each presents a scholarly analysis of a major science fiction/fantasy television series. Unlike the authors of these other books, however, Gregory chooses to base his study mainly around an instalment-by-instalment discussion – a decision that did not find universal favour. Peter Dunn, for example, feels that, for much of the book, the text amounts to no more than "another dreary episode guide",[36] although other parts of it present themed essays that bring together evidence from different episodes. In contrast, another scholarly book that takes a (broadly) chronological approach to the individual stories that make up an overall saga, James Chapman's *Inside the TARDIS: The Worlds of Doctor Who* (I. B. Tauris, 2006), avoids the pitfall of rehashing the plots of stories with which readers are already familiar by giving greater attention to analysis and comment than to narrative.

The true novelty of Gregory's approach in *Be Seeing You* lies in his attempt to understand the stages in the overall *Prisoner* saga in terms of an existing framework from elsewhere, specifically the separation–initiation–return sequence delineated by Joseph Campbell.[37] Dunn believes that such a perspective is altogether too pretentious, with the so-called "return" element actually consisting of "a cowboy romp, an *Avengers* pastiche, one really thought-provoking episode, and a final hodge podge of ideas flung together by McGoohan whilst he was tired and emotional".[38] Dunn makes further substantial criticisms; specifically he highlights the considerable degree of speculation on Gregory's part and the lack of input from those actually involved in the show.[39] It is certainly true that the book has by no means received unanimous praise but, as an early attempt to provide an academic examination of *The Prisoner*, it is still significant.

Many other commercially published, scholarly analyses of *The Prisoner* followed *Be Seeing You*. In the first few years of 21st century, there were noteworthy book chapter essays by, among others, Piers D. Britton and Simon J. Barker,[40] M. Keith Booker,[41] Mark Bould,[42] Sue Short[43] and Douglas L. Howard.[44] In each of these instances, the main text is complemented by an impressive set of references and/or footnotes. It may be no coincidence that all these detailed scholarly investigations are recent and their temporal distribution is indicative of a wider trend; commenting in 2007, Graham Sleight, who as editor of the international science fiction journal *Foundation* would seem well placed to offer a knowledgeable overview of developments in the genre, recognised that academic writing on SF has "expanded enormously over the last couple of decades". (p. 4)[45]

Beyond the realm of learned scholarship, various books have adopted as their foci individual aspects of *The Prisoner*. These include the people involved in the making of the show (see S. J. Gillis's *The Gillis Guide to The Prisoner*, SJG Communications Services, 1997), the role within the series of George Markstein (see *George Markstein and The Prisoner*, edited by Roger Goodman, pandqmedia, 2014), Portmeirion locations that are of special relevance to fans (see Catherine Nemeth Frumerman's *On the Trail of The Prisoner*, PrizBiz, 2003) and diagrams/plans associated with life in The Village (see Tim Palgut's *The Prisoner: The Village Files*, Titan, 2003). The emergence of these books may be seen as an indicator that, at least in some areas, the literature on *The Prisoner* has started to gain ground on that of other cult SF series which ran for longer and consisted of more episodes. For example, Frumerman's book can be regarded as roughly equivalent to the *Doctor Who* guides *Travel Without the TARDIS* (Jean Airey and Laurie Haldeman, Target, 1986) and *Doctor Who: On Location* (Richard Bignell, Reynolds and Hearn, 2001). More recent evidence of this strand within publishing can be seen in the form of *The Avengers: On Location* (Chris Bentley, Reynolds and Hearn, 2007). Other books about where *The Prisoner* was filmed have followed. They include two by Langley – *Portmeirion in The Prisoner and its History* (2nd edition, 2011) and *The Prisoner Located* (2013). The later book is appreciably wider in scope, as it covers such territory as studio sets and location filming beyond Portmeirion.

Palgut's *The Village Files*, meanwhile, is descended from the same lineage as such longstanding titles as *The Star Trek Blueprints* (Franz Joseph, Ballantine, 1975), *Star Trek: The Star Fleet Technical Manual* (Franz Joseph, Ballantine, 1975), the *Moonbase Alpha Technical Notebook* (Geoffrey Mandell and David Hirsch, Starlog, 1977), *The Doctor Who Technical Manual* (Mark Harris, Severn House, 1983) and *The Horizon Blake's 7 Technical Manual* (published in three parts by Horizon in 1988, 1990 and 1992 respectively). *The Village Files* may also be compared to the "Gerry Anderson" books, *Gerry Anderson's Supermarionation Cross-sections* (Graham Bleathman, Carlton, 2000), *Thunderbirds FAB Cross-sections* (Graham Bleathman, Carlton, 2000), *International Rescue, Thunderbirds: TB1-TB5, Tracy Island and Associated Rescue Vehicles – Agents' Technical Manual* (Sam Denham and Graham Bleathman, Haynes, 2012) and *Inside the Worlds of Gerry Anderson: Featuring Cross-section Artworks* (Graham Bleathman, Egmont, 2014).

The diagrams in *The Village Files* are imaginatively presented as a set of top secret documents within a "manual" that has been entrusted to the reader. A similarly creative scenario has been developed by Leslie Glen when assembling his quiz book *The Prisoner Interrogations* (St. Inan's Press, 2012). Whereas comparable works, such as those relating to the original series of *Doctor Who*[46] and *The Twilight Zone*,[47] are conventional in their approaches, Glen's book is inspired by the principles of psychometric testing and incorporates six "interrogations", each of which consists of 17 questions.

Many of the items featured in *The Village Files* would be subjected to further scrutiny in the richly illustrated partworks production *The Prisoner: The Official Fact File* (De Agostini, 2005–2006), which appeared just a few years later. Lots of the entities examined in the Titan book would figure in the *Fact File* sections on "technology", "transport" or "locations". Additional sections included an episode guide, an alphabetical run-down of *Prisoner* characters and a study of the real world, 1960s context of the programme. As it provides an A to Z sweep of a particular television series from the first episode to the last, the *Fact File*'s "characters" section is similar to *Doctor Who: The Universal Databank* (Jean-Marc Lofficier, Doctor Who Books, 1992), the "lexicon" element of the *Star Trek Concordance* (Bjo Trimble, Titan, 1995) and the "Index" chapter of *Terry Nation's Blake's 7: The Programme Guide* (Tony Attwood, W. H. Allen, 1982), although, as its name indicates, the territory of the *Fact File*'s section is restricted to people in the series. Further coverage of the characters in McGoohan's programme can be found in Langley's booklet, *The Prisoner Who's Who?* (2012)

Roger Goodman's book about George Markstein is worthy of particular comment. Produced by the same team that was responsible for *On the Trail of The Prisoner*, this work is undoubtedly one of the most important volumes about the series that has appeared since the publication of the first edition of *Unique But Similar* in 2013 and it sheds much light on the role of an individual whose contribution to the early development of the *Prisoner* series has long been a matter of debate.[48]

Ian Rakoff's *Inside The Prisoner: Radical Film and Television in the 1960s* (Batsford, 1998) remains unique in documenting the series from the perspective of a member of the crew responsible for it, although, as Ricks observes, it digresses somewhat into discussion of other projects on which the writer worked.[49] It is a measure of how far appreciation and understanding of *The Prisoner* have developed in the last 30 years that, although in what has come to be termed almost universally as "the Goodman interview", McGoohan expressed grave reservations as to the value of the commercial publication of the programme's scripts, suspecting that many people "wouldn't understand what they were about",[50] today one of the most acclaimed works relating to the series is the two-volume *The Prisoner: The Original Scripts*, edited and annotated by Robert Fairclough (Reynolds and Hearn, 2005 and 2006). Its appearance should also be seen, however, as indicative of a general vogue in terms of the publication of television scripts that was prevalent in the late 1990s and early 2000s. Rick Davy lauds the first book of scripts as "the ultimate tome of *Prisoner* information",[51] and the second as "arguably the most important, and most complete, *Prisoner* book ever published (especially when placed alongside Volume 1)".[52]

Despite the evidence that points to an increasing specialisation in the literature, broader texts have continued to appear as well. Fairclough's own *The Prisoner: The Official Companion to the Classic TV Series* (Carlton, 2002) provides a very colourful and wide-ranging investigation, and again an episode guide lies at its core. Steven Paul Davies's work *The Prisoner Handbook: An Unauthorized Companion* (Boxtree, 2002) includes what may be regarded as the classic ingredients of a general *Prisoner* non-fiction text – consideration of the programme's origins, information about the Portmeirion location, an account of the production of the series, an episode-by-episode breakdown, discussion of the programme's themes and possible meanings and an exploration of the fan culture that surrounds the show. A particularly detailed and penetrating study, *Fall Out: The Unofficial and Unauthorised Guide to The Prisoner*, by Alan Stevens and Fiona Moore (Telos, 2007), is unusual in breaking off periodically from an episode guide treatment to present related, individual essays. In this respect, it may be compared to the six-volume *About Time* work on *Doctor Who*,[53] and its detail is comparable to that of other Telos books dealing with major British SF series produced during the period covered by *Unique But Similar*, namely *Blake's 7*,[54] *Survivors*,[55] *Space: 1999*,[56] *Sapphire and Steel*[57] and *The Avengers*.[58] The content of *Fall Out*'s chapter on "illustrious predecessors" to *The Prisoner* and, especially, the section on television series within the chapter *Out of The Village: The Influence of The Prisoner on Later Popular Culture* are of special relevance to *Unique But Similar* in that here Stevens and Moore explore links between *The Prisoner* and other shows. Their latter analysis is reminiscent of Wesley Britton's *Influence of The Prisoner* section which appears in a text devoted not to the series exclusively but rather the genre of "Spy Television" (Praeger, 2004). As these essays occupy only a few pages, they amount to minor components in the overall books, however, whereas the area addressed forms the essential territory of *Unique But Similar*.

No review of *Prisoner* literature would be complete without reference to the variety of mini-guides, many of which have been produced chiefly by fans for fans. Some, like Ricks's *The Prisoner: I am Not a Number! A Series Guide* (TR 7,

2000), have received considerable praise, with Davy acclaiming this particular work as "superb".[59] Before its publication, Ricks had acquired an impressive reputation among *Prisoner* enthusiasts for his efforts in creating a range of illuminating documentaries for VHS video cassette.[60] In terms of the scope of *Unique But Similar*, the most relevant tape is *The Prisoner Inspired*, which discusses events, plays and books that may have influenced McGoohan's thinking and, in addition, productions that could themselves have drawn ideas from the programme. In the former capacity, the importance of George Orwell's *Nineteen Eighty-four*, Franz Kafka's *The Trial* and Bridget Boland's *The Prisoner* is acknowledged but the television connections that are explored tend to be limited to advertisements that incorporate imagery from the series. Another programme that is discussed at length in *Unique But Similar* – *Yes, Prime Minister* – has also been compared to *Nineteen Eighty-four*. Armando Iannucci feels that both have influenced the public's perception with regard to the role of the state.[61] Although Graham McCann draws no such parallel between George Orwell's novel and *Yes Minister/Yes, Prime Minister*, he does believe that the latter forms one of the very few television programmes that have changed the way viewers look at the world.[62]

The importance of the early *Prisoner* booklets should not be underestimated. As they predated the first mainstream books on the programme and appeared well before the World Wide Web gained a foothold in homes, schools, universities and public libraries, at the time of their appearance they formed something of an oasis of information on *The Prisoner* in a landscape that was otherwise largely desert. Beyond the material made available by appreciation societies through newsletters and fanzines, there was little widely accessible information other than what was offered in articles on the programme found in magazines more broadly devoted to fantasy and SF, and *Prisoner* entries in reference books such as SF encyclopedias, guides to a variety of SF series on television and A to Zs of the whole range of TV shows. Documenting the *Prisoner* booklets that had been published before their own work, White and Ali draw attention to Max Hora's *Portmeirion Prisoner Production* (Number Six, 1985), the same author's *Village World* (Six of One, 1987) and Langley's *The Making of The Prisoner* (Escape, 1985).[63] Another early booklet – Hora's *The Prisoner of Portmeirion* (Number Six, 1985) – is the only "recommended reading" on *The Prisoner* that John Javna offers in his 1988 volume on memorable science fiction television programmes. (p. 142)[64] Both Hora and Langley have played a key role within *Prisoner* fan circles for many years. Hora's *The Prisoner of Portmeirion* ran to a second edition (published in 1989 and with later reprints), whilst in more recent times, Langley has written some considerably more substantial volumes. In 2010, his 1999 work *The Prisoner in Portmeirion* was revised and expanded to form *The Making of The Prisoner*, published by Escape. Another of Langley's newer books, *The Pris6ner From the Inside: Plots, Scripts, Background* (Escape, 2010), is of similar size. It cites material from various existing *Prisoner* books, offers critical comment on and background to the episodes and makes comparisons with other creative works. In the past few years, Langley has also, however, produced briefer works devoted to highly specific aspects of the programme. These include *The Prisoner 1967 Press Conference* (2011), *The Prisoner Original 60s Publicity Material* (2012) and *The Prisoner Dialogue Decodes* (2014).

There can be no doubt that, at the time of writing, today's *Prisoner* fans are well served by the amount and, increasingly, the variety of literature relating to the series. So much has now been said that any author contemplating writing a new book is faced with the challenging task of finding a novel angle on the series. Since *Unique But Similar* explores a series of productions that may be said to share some sort of similarity with *The Prisoner* and discusses the identified common ground in detail, it can be understood to be part of recent trends towards an increasing specialisation in *Prisoner* literature. I am confident that the book offers a certain originality, although it is, of course, ultimately readers, commentators on *The Prisoner* and reviewers who will decide how far the writer is justified in making such a claim.

References and Notes

1. Interview With Patrick McGoohan. In: Carrazé, A. and Oswald, H. The Prisoner: A televisionary masterpiece. Virgin: London, 1990, pp. 6–8.
2. Booth, R. Not a number: Patrick McGoohan – A life. Supernova: Twickenham, 2011.
3. Langley, R. The making of The Prisoner. Escape, 2010a; Langley, R. The Pris6ner from the inside: Plots, scripts, background. Escape, 2010b; Langley, R. The Prisoner series guide, 2nd ed. 2010c.
4. Berger, A. A. The Prisoner: British spy and science fiction series. In: Newcomb, H. (ed.) Encyclopedia of television, volume 3 M–R, 2nd ed. Fitzroy Dearborn: New York, 2004, pp. 1829–1830.
5. Langley, R. The Prisoner dialogue decodes. 2014.

There have, of course, been previous attempts to draw a metaphorical line under The Prisoner. It may seem remarkably premature today but as long ago as January 1984 presenter Saul Reichlin began the documentary Six Into One: The Prisoner File by announcing his intention of solving The Prisoner's conundrums for once and for all in his programme. Only weeks later, in March – some four years before the appearance of the first major book on the series – the front cover of issue

67 of the magazine Starburst purported to offer within the pages that followed "the last word on The Prisoner" when it publicised a new article by Jon Abbott. The following year, McGoohan chose to conclude an interview with Barrington Calia for New Video by commenting to his interlocutor, "We put to rest the final Prisoner interview." The transcript appears in the Summer/Fall 1985 edition of the magazine and is reproduced in The Official Prisoner Companion (pages 177–181).

6. Terrace, V. Complete encyclopedia of television programs: 1947–1979. Thomas Yoseloff Ltd: London, 1980.

7. Meyers, R. TV detectives. A. S. Barnes & Co.: San Diego, California, 1981.

8. Quoted in: White, M. and Ali, J. The official Prisoner companion. Sidgwick and Jackson: London, 1988.

9. Gerani, G. and Schulman, P. H. Fantastic television: A pictorial history of sci-fi, the unusual and the fantastic from the '50s to the '70s. Titan: London, 1987. Reprint of 1977 work.

10. Talking With McGoohan. In: White, M. and Ali, J. op. cit., pp. 175–181.

11. Sanders, J. "The Prisoner" ending revealed! 7 January 2009. URL: http://jasonsanders.wordpress.com/2009/01/07/the-prisoner-ending-revealed/ (accessed: 23 February 2017).

12. Follett, J. There's no mystery. In: Goodman, R. (ed.) George Markstein and The Prisoner. pandqmedia: Berwyn, Denbighshire, 2014, p. 97.

13. Johnson, C. Telefantasy. BFI: London, 2005.

14. Brosnan, J. and Nicholls, P. The Prisoner. In: Nicholls, P. (ed.) The encyclopedia of science fiction: An illustrated A to Z. Granada: St. Albans, 1979, pp. 475–476.

15. Booker, M. K. Strange TV: Innovative television series from The Twilight Zone to The X-Files. Greenwood: Westport, Connecticut, 2002.

16. An illuminating discussion of the difficulties inherent in writing about television series when the author has no access to the programmes themselves can be found in: Lucanio, P. and Coville, G. American science fiction television series of the 1950s. McFarland: Jefferson, North Carolina, 1998, pp. 1–4. The authors take the view that the episodes form "the primary sources", (p. 1) and in instances where they are unavailable for viewing errors may be made by even well intentioned writers who are not careless or intent on fabrication.

17. Gregory, C. Be seeing you... Decoding The Prisoner. John Libbey Media: Luton, 1997.

18. Tame, C. R. Different values: An analysis of Patrick McGoohan's The Prisoner. Libertarian Reprints, 1, 1983. Reprint of 1974 work. URL: http://www.libertarian.co.uk/lapubs/libre/libre001.pdf (accessed: 23 February 2017).

19. Ibid.

20. Stimpson, D. Different Values, 10 February 2012. URL: http://david-stimpson.blogspot.co.uk/2012/02/different-values.html (accessed: 23 February 2017).

21. Fairclough, R. The Prisoner: The official companion to the classic TV series. Carlton: London, 2002.

22. Suarès, J.-C., Siegel, R. and Owen, D. Fantastic planets. Reed Books: Danbury, New Hampshire, 1979.

23. Lewis, J. E. and Stempel, P. Cult TV: The essential critical guide. Pavilion Books: London, 1993.

24. Schow, D. J. and Rypel, T. C. The Outer Limits at 50. Creature Features: Burbank, California, 2014.

25. Oliver, M. B. Blake's 7: The merchandise guide – Unofficial and unauthorised. Telos: Prestatyn, 2012.

26. The Star Trek book by Whitfield and Roddenberry would seem to be a significant exception to Rypel's "rule" that books about television programmes were not written in the 1960s.

27. The fact that various parallels can be drawn, however, between the distribution of literature surrounding The Prisoner and that of other television programmes of a similar era adds weight to Rypel's argument in relation to the general dearth of books about 1960s TV series. In his volume The Avengers, Dave Rogers suggests that no book devoted to the show had appeared until his own work was published in 1983, some 14 years after the series' demise. Yet, over the last 30 years, more than a dozen further volumes on The Avengers have appeared. A very similar pattern pertains to The Twilight Zone. The first significant non-fiction book on that show was not published until 1982. Yet, between 1987 and 2017, at least ten other major volumes about The Twilight Zone have come out. In addition, during the same period, scripts of individual episodes have been published commercially and biographies of creator Rod Serling have been written. These developments again mirror the situation with regard to Prisoner literature as here, too, sets of scripts have been released in book form and biographies of Patrick McGoohan are available.

28. McKay, A. Review: The Prisoner Video Companion. DWB, 108, December 1992, p. 25.

29. Pixley, A. Guide to the TV guides. In: Leigh, G. (ed.) The DWB compendium: The best of the first 100 issues. DreamWatch Publishing: Brighton, 1993, pp. 127–129.

30. Quoted in: Booth, R. op. cit.

31. Pixley, A. op. cit.

32. Ricks, S. The Prisoner: I am not a number! A series guide. TR 7: Borehamwood, 2000.

33. Langley, R. op. cit. 2010b.

34. Howe, D. J. The Target book: A history of the Target Doctor Who books. Telos: Tolworth, 2007.

35. Bentley, C. Afterword. In: Tubb, E. C. Earthbound. Century 21 Books, 2003, pp. 171–174.

36. Dunn, P. Review: Decoding The Prisoner. The Unmutual. URL: http://www.theunmutual.co.uk/reviewsdecoding.htm (accessed: 23 February 2017).

37. Campbell, J. The hero with a thousand faces. Fontana: London, 1993.

38. Dunn, P. op. cit.

39. Dunn, P. op. cit.

40. Britton, P. D. and Barker, S. J. Reading between designs: Visual imagery and the generation of meaning in The Avengers, The Prisoner, and Doctor Who. University of Texas Press: Austin, Texas, 2003, pp. 94–130.

41. Booker, M. K. op. cit., pp. 71–96.

42. Bould, M. This is the modern world: The Prisoner, authorship and allegory. In: Bignell, J. and Lacey, S. (eds.) Popular television drama: Critical perspectives. Manchester University Press: Manchester, 2005, pp. 93–109.

43. Short, S. Countering the counterculture: The Prisoner and the 1960s. In: Cook, J. R. and Wright, P. (eds.) British science fiction television: A hitchhiker's guide. I. B. Tauris: London, 2006, pp. 71–92; Short, S. Cult telefantasy series: A critical analysis of The Prisoner, Twin Peaks, The X-Files, Buffy the Vampire Slayer, Lost, Heroes, Doctor Who and Star Trek. McFarland: Jefferson, North Carolina, 2011, pp. 13–32.

44. Howard, D. L. The Prisoner. In: Lavery, D. (ed.) The essential cult TV reader. University Press of Kentucky: Lexington, Kentucky, 2010, pp. 189–200.

45. Sleight, G. Editorial. Foundation, 101 [volume 36], Winter 2007, pp. 3–4.

46. Robinson, N. The Doctor Who quiz book. Target: London, 1981; Robinson, N. The second Doctor Who quiz book. Target: London, 1983; Robinson, N. The third Doctor Who quiz book. Target: London, 1985; Robinson, N. Doctor Who crossword book. Target: London, 1982; Heath, A. Doctor Who brain-teasers and mind-benders. Target: London, 1984.

47. DeVóe, B. Trivia from The Twilight Zone. BearManor Media: Albany, Georgia, 2004.

48. Even the label that should be attached to the capacity in which Markstein worked on The Prisoner has been the subject of disagreement. Although he is credited as the programme's script editor in the on-screen titles and in many of the leading books on the show (notably Stevens and Moore's Fall Out and Fairclough's Official Companion), Markstein himself preferred to think of himself as the "story editor", who was responsible for such fundamentals as the ethos and spirit of the series, as well as generating plot ideas. (see Not a number: Patrick McGoohan – A Life, p. 171) The use of this title to define Markstein's contribution is not limited to the man himself; James Follett also describes the role of Markstein as that of "story editor", (see George Markstein and The Prisoner, p. 97) and the back cover of the book that includes Follett's reminiscences refers to Markstein in these terms, too.

49. Ricks, S. op. cit.

50. McGoohan, P. On the trail of The Prisoner: Roger Goodman talks to Patrick McGoohan. CD. PrizBiz, 2007. Audio recording of 1979 interview.

51. Davy, R. Review: The Prisoner – The Original Scripts, Volume 1. The Unmutual. URL: http://www.theunmutual.co.uk/reviewsscripts1.htm (accessed: 23 February 2017).

52. Davy, R. Review: The Prisoner – The Original Scripts, Volume 2. The Unmutual. URL: http://www.theunmutual.co.uk/reviewsscripts2.htm (accessed: 23 February 2017).

53. Wood, T. and Miles, L. About time: The unauthorized guide to Doctor Who: 1963–1966 – Seasons 1 to 3. Mad Norwegian Press: Des Moines, Iowa, 2006; Wood, T. and Miles, L. About time: The unauthorized guide to Doctor Who: 1966–1969 – Seasons

4 to 6. Mad Norwegian Press: Des Moines, Iowa, 2006; Miles, L. and Wood, T. About time: The unauthorized guide to Doctor Who: 1970–1974 – Seasons 7 to 11. Mad Norwegian Press: Metairie, Los Angeles, 2004; Miles, L. and Wood, T. About time: The unauthorized guide to Doctor Who: 1975–1979 – Seasons 12 to 17. Mad Norwegian Press: Metairie, Los Angeles, 2004; Miles, L. and Wood, T. About time: The unauthorized guide to Doctor Who: 1980–1984 – Seasons 18 to 21. Mad Norwegian Press: Metairie, Los Angeles, 2005; Wood, T. About time: The unauthorized guide to Doctor Who: 1985–1989 – Seasons 22 to 26, the TV movie. Mad Norwegian Press: Des Moines, Iowa, 2007.

54.   Stevens, A. and Moore, F. Liberation: The unofficial and unauthorised guide to Blake's 7. Telos: Tolworth, 2003.

55.   Cross, R. and Priestner, A. The end of the world? The unofficial and unauthorised guide to Survivors. Telos: Tolworth, 2005.

56.   Wood, R. E. Destination Moonbase Alpha: The unofficial and unauthorised guide to Space: 1999. Telos: Prestatyn, 2010.

57.   Callaghan, R. Assigned! The unofficial and unauthorised guide to Sapphire and Steel. Telos: Prestatyn, 2010.

58.   Richardson, M. Bowler hats and kinky boots: The unofficial and unauthorised guide to The Avengers. Telos: Bromley, 2014.

59.   Davy, R. Review: The Prisoner Series Guide. The Unmutual. URL: http://www.theunmutual.co.uk/reviewsguide.htm (accessed: 23 February 2017).

60.   The Prisoner Investigated Vol. 1. VHS video cassette. TR 7 Productions: Borehamwood, 1990; The Prisoner Investigated Vol. 2. VHS video cassette. TR 7 Productions: Borehamwood, 1990; The Prisoner In-depth Tape 1. VHS video cassette. TR 7 Productions: Borehamwood, 1991; The Prisoner In-depth Tape 2. VHS video cassette. TR 7 Productions: Borehamwood, 1992; The Prisoner In-depth Tape 3. VHS video cassette. TR 7 Productions: Borehamwood, 1992; The Prisoner In-depth Tape 4. VHS video cassette. TR 7 Productions: Borehamwood, 1993; The Prisoner In-depth Tape 5. VHS video cassette. TR 7 Productions: Borehamwood, 1993; The Prisoner In-depth Tape 6. VHS video cassette. TR 7 Productions: Borehamwood, 1994; The Prisoner Inspired. VHS video cassette. TR 7 Productions: Borehamwood, 1992; The Prisoner in Production. VHS video cassette. TR 7 Productions: Borehamwood, 1993; The Prisoner in Conclusion. VHS video cassette. TR 7 Productions: Borehamwood, 1994; The Prisoner on Location. VHS video cassette. TR 7 Productions: Borehamwood, 1996.

61.   Jay, A. and Lynn, J. The Yes Minister miscellany. Biteback: London, 2009.

62.   McCann, G. A very courageous decision: The inside story of Yes Minister. Aurum: London, 2014.

63.   White, M. and Ali, J. op. cit.

64.   Javna, J. The best of science fiction TV: The critics' choice from Captain Video to Star Trek, from The Jetsons to Robotech. Titan: London, 1988.

PART A
Overview

SECTION I:
Some Preliminary Thoughts on Comparisons Without and Within

Unique But Similar is not a book that aims to unravel the meaning(s) of *The Prisoner*. Many analyses of this kind have been carried out already and, if we subscribe to Rupert Booth's view of the series, such attempts are ill-advised. According to Booth, "The ongoing quest for answers from *The Prisoner* is pointless. Its purpose was never to provide answers but to provoke questions." (p. 223)[1]

This is, instead, a book of *Prisoner* comparisons. Essentially, it considers the similarities that can be detected between Patrick McGoohan's programme and other television productions. Attention is focused entirely on the 1960s version of *The Prisoner*; it is not concerned with the twenty-first century revival. It must also be emphasised from the outset that the book does not seek to identify programmes that have influenced or been influenced by *The Prisoner*, directly or indirectly. This is not, therefore, a work concerned with cause and effect. It simply explores common features.

As there are so many series that may be compared to *The Prisoner*, the decision has been taken to restrict the overall time period to works produced up to and including 1987 – the year of the programme's 20th anniversary. By limiting the scope of the study in this way, the author has gained the additional benefit of avoiding the temptation to compare *The Prisoner* with relatively recent television productions that have also come to be regarded as groundbreaking – specifically programmes such as *Twin Peaks, Nowhere Man, Lost, Life on Mars* and *Persons Unknown*. Many efforts have already been made to draw parallels between these series and *The Prisoner*. Indeed, a comparison of *The Prisoner* and *Lost* has formed the focus of a whole article by Joanne Morreale.[2]

It is the contention of the author that, although in the era covered by *Unique But Similar*, *The Prisoner* had neither achieved the widespread critical acclaim nor exerted the degree of influence that it enjoys today, it is still possible to identify various shows from the pre-1988 period that share with *The Prisoner* common concepts, plot elements or messages. The fact that so many comparisons of this type can be made should not surprise the reader. After all, when asked if he noticed similarities between the modern version of *Battlestar Galactica* and *Blake's 7*, Chris Boucher has commented, "If you look hard enough you can see patterns and resemblances everywhere." (p. 171)[3] Certainly, some rather arbitrary comparisons can be drawn. In seeking to illustrate this problem, Tony Jones makes the point that it is possible to link such seemingly disparate creative works as *Fall Out* and the Genesis album *The Lamb Lies Down on Broadway*.[4] Of course, thematic connections between *The Prisoner* and popular music extend far and wide. The loss of individual identity – an issue so integral to McGoohan's programme – is especially apparent in Malvina Reynolds's *Little Boxes*. Famously performed by artists such as Pete Seeger and Nina and Frederik, the song includes lyrics which refer to people who are alike in nature, inhabit identical houses and lead similar lives.[5]

Although we may well believe that one of the main reasons why *The Prisoner* remains so celebrated today is that it was able to make a virtue out of being an enigma, the series is by no means alone in this respect. In modern music especially, many works have been lauded on the basis of their obscure allusions. The final studio album of the great Swedish group Abba is a case in point. While Abba are frequently regarded as one of the quintessential mainstream pop acts, *The Visitors* is, in the words of Andrew Oldham, Tony Calder and Colin Irwin, "mysterious and thoroughly confusing". (p. 93)[6] The authors recount how the work was "widely believed to be an album of hidden meanings". (p. 184)[7] Yet, it may be no coincidence that, as the group's biographer Carl Magnus Palm recognises, "for many of their most ardent admirers, *The Visitors* is Abba's crowning achievement", (p. 64)[8] despite the fact that it did not enjoy the level of sales success associated with some of their earlier efforts.[9] If Abba's previous albums were characterised by a *Danger Man*-like accessibility and offered mass appeal, *The Visitors* made *Prisoner*esque demands of the listener and attracted an appreciation of the kind that is more consistent with a "cult" following.

In exploring Boucher's argument that resemblances may be seen everywhere, we can detect **some** common ground between *The Prisoner* and particular cinema films that substantially predate the series. The 1943 movie *Sherlock Holmes Faces Death*, starring Basil Rathbone and Nigel Bruce, may be viewed as comparable to the *Checkmate* episode of *The Prisoner* – in each production we see chess involving human pieces take place within an enclosed community that includes various people who have performed similar jobs in the past. Nevertheless, in virtually all other respects the two works are entirely different. Other plot elements that we may associate with *The Prisoner* are found in an even older film – *Lost Horizon* – from 1937. Here, too, the man who becomes the story's key protagonist has been the holder of a high profile and trusted position within his country. He is the target of a kidnapping at the beginning of the drama and soon finds himself in an apparently idyllic place populated by people of various nationalities. Newcomers are kitted out in distinctive attire virtually as soon as they arrive. Despite the community's remote location, the English language is spoken by many of the inhabitants. Surrounded by mountains, it is, seemingly, a world of its own, although the High Lama entertains hopes that one day, everywhere on Earth will take on Shangri-La's characteristics. The outward appearance is one of perfection; yet by no means all the people are content and some see themselves as no better than prisoners even though their lives are made very comfortable. The day-to-day leader, Chang, is largely uninformative in relation to key issues. The hero is offered the chance to lead but he eventually attempts to escape.[10] These are, however, plot features that link *Lost Horizon* to *The Prisoner* somewhat superficially and, in truth, there are many obvious differences and even contrasts. In particular, the simple, utopian environment of Shangri-La seems, for the most part, genuinely free from greed and materialism, whilst The Village clearly suffers from some of the worst excesses of modern society. Furthermore, whereas there is no indication by the end of *The Prisoner* that Number Six has any desire to return to The Village, *Lost Horizon* concludes with the hero journeying back to Shangri-La.

So as to avoid concentrating on the kind of tenuous connections that exist between *The Prisoner* and the Sherlock Holmes film, and the former and *Lost Horizon*, the decision was taken to ensure that the chapters which follow address either

- television productions whose content shares a **fundamental** similarity with one of the key themes of *The Prisoner* or the main plotline within one particular episode,

or

- situations where a **wide range** of similarities between McGoohan's programme and another show can be detected.

Although 11 of the 14 chapters of *Unique But Similar* relate to productions that first appeared on television after the original transmission of *The Prisoner*, it would be erroneous to believe that the book is concerned with the legacy of McGoohan's series. Any investigation of that kind would have to explore how far the similarities between *The Prisoner* and the shows examined here were the result of the former's **influence**, rather than merely being coincidental. Where there is an absence of clear evidence to reveal a cause and effect relationship, it is all too easy to slip into the dangerous realm of inference and begin from the position that because two productions share significant elements, the later work is likely to have derived inspiration from the earlier one when, in fact, the more recent author may not actually have even been aware of the existence of the preceding work. Any reader who has substantial personal experience of writing for publication will be aware of the tendency among commentators and reviewers to read into their work ideas that the author never intended and reach conclusions that are entirely unsound. Let us briefly consider a pertinent illustration. In discussing the problem of "incorrect speculations", Peter Dunn highlights a claim made in one source that Ken Kesey's novel *One Flew Over the Cuckoo's Nest* was "quite possibly a direct influence" on the thinking of Roger Parkes when he wrote the *Prisoner* episode *A Change of Mind*. Dunn goes on, though, to report how Parkes himself has unequivocally denied any such link. The author revealed that *The Manchurian Candidate* was, in fact, "the main influence".[11]

This is not meant to be an iconoclastic book. It is not the author's aim within any particular chapter to present a case that leads the reader to jettison any belief they may have that *The Prisoner* was unique and, consequently, important. Rather, the purpose of the work lies in demonstrating, through the totality of the 14 chapters, that the programme can legitimately be compared with other television series of roughly the same temporal period, in ways that often escape attention. We may well conclude that it is the combination of all the various ingredients in *The Prisoner* that renders the programme special. Even in this sense we must be somewhat cautious, however. If anything is examined sufficiently minutely, we may say that it is the blend of its elements that make it original. This is a challenge that has exercised for decades scholars such as PhD students who are required to demonstrate in their work that they have made a unique contribution to knowledge. Another perspective would be to say that although many of *The Prisoner*'s key themes are addressed in other television series as well, ideas that are intrinsic to the whole nature of

McGoohan's programme are evident only in isolated instalments of the other shows.

Unique But Similar is intended in style to be rigorous but readable. In reviewing the literature pertaining to the classic US anthology series *The Twilight Zone*, Don Presnell and Marty McGee suggest that much academic writing suffers from a "droning, arcane tone", (p. 2)[12] and certainly there can be no doubt that high levels of theory, philosophical discussion and Media Studies jargon can alienate both the fan and the general reader. This work attempts to avoid these pitfalls, whilst still endeavouring to offer a scholarly treatment.

Much of *Unique But Similar* is devoted to **direct** comparisons between *The Prisoner* and other television productions which are in some significant way (or ways) similar. On occasions, however, comments are also made in relation to what we may term **peripheral** programmes – series that come to mind as a result of some link with the work that is being compared to *The Prisoner*. In Chapter Ten, for example, *The New People* is briefly mentioned, not as a result of any specific connection to *The Prisoner* but because of the similarity of its theme to that of the principal series under examination in the chapter – *Logan's Run*. If the shows that have been directly compared to *The Prisoner* are deemed to be one step removed from McGoohan's in terms of their treatment in this book, then peripheral programmes are effectively two steps distant. Whilst some readers may consider these references needless digressions, it was felt by the author that they were important in providing background to the television landscape of the time.

Before looking at the links between *The Prisoner* and other television productions, it would seem appropriate to explore patterns within *The Prisoner*'s own episodes. In academia, such an approach is common – and entirely logical. After all, it is sensible to understand a phenomenon in terms of its own intrinsic characteristics before investigating how it compares with other related phenomena. The rest of Section I is thus concerned with what we may term an orientating "micro-analysis" before attention is turned to a more macro level.

One way of understanding the episodes of any television series lies in summarising their features in accordance with the types defined in a typology, which, in its totality, covers the entire range. A typology may be created by comparing the series' episodes with one another in order to pinpoint areas of similarity and difference. Similarities are highlighted by the fact that certain episodes adhere to one particular type, while broad differences are apparent in the presentation of a set of separate types; more minor differences are addressed in discussions of the scope of each type.

At the heart of many such typologies devoted to a particular television series lies the claim noted by Christopher Booker that every story is essentially a variation on one of seven fundamental scenarios, or sometimes a similar observation is made in terms of five or six plots.[13] We may conclude that a television programme's episodes can likewise be categorised on the basis of a small number of groups. Even though the original version of *Doctor Who* ran for some 26 years and embraced over 150 individual serials, it is possible to arrange all the stories under a limited number of headings. Consider for a moment how easy it is to pigeonhole many of them instantly according to the very rough categories listed below. Some of the serials can be described in more than one of these ways.

- Pure historicals;[14]
- Encounters in the past with alien beings;
- Adventures on contemporary Earth;
- Portrayals of future Earth;
- Contacts in space;
- Intrigue on alien worlds;
- Threats in other dimensions.

Paul Smith proposes a less extensive set of divisions. His typology is based largely on the story varieties of "Historical", "Monster" and "Futuristic" but he acknowledges that the placing of each serial in a particular category is "slightly subjective" and some do not fit into any of his main groups.[15] Lance Parkin, meanwhile, distinguishes between *Doctor Who* serials that form challenging, intellectual television, romps through history, satires, monster shows and silly, fun adventures.[16] Other typologies have been formulated by members of the production staff themselves. For example, Malcolm Hulke, who was a key figure in the development of *Doctor Who* in the late 1960s and early 1970s, remarked to fellow writer Terrance Dicks that the plot possibilities during the early Jon Pertwee period in which The Doctor was exiled to Earth were basically restricted to tales of alien invasion and mad scientists.[17]

The labels given to some *Doctor Who* story types have become commonly quoted by fans. The phrase "base under siege", for example, is employed especially frequently. Indeed, it is a measure of how widely the expression has been adopted that a *Google* search carried out by the author in March 2015 revealed that some 6,830 web documents contained the search terms "base under siege" and "Doctor Who". Tat Wood and Lawrence Miles view *The Web of Fear* as a prime example of this form of serial.[18] In exploring instances of the "Threat and Disaster" school of science fiction within *Doctor Who* (p 66), James Chapman summarises the essential features of the "base under siege" scenario

– in an isolated, confined outpost, a small group of people confronts an alien invader. A threat to the "known" world comes from an "unknown" source (p. 66); once discovered, the intruder endangers both the base and humanity in general, until it is defeated by scientific knowledge and human ingenuity.[19]

Typologies may be constructed on the basis of the different aims of the writers, too. In discussing the episodes comprising the original version of *The Twilight Zone*, Tony Albarella highlights "message" scripts, "idea" stories and hybrids that aim to blend the two styles. (p. 461)[20]

The Prisoner's episodes can also be divided into a small number of groups. This section will present three. Each of the types outlined below refers to one of the hero's key aims, and episodes may be categorised on the basis of the most prevalent aim(s) in the individual instalments; there are, of course, many other typologies that can be defined – some more intricate and abstract than others.

- **Escape.** Here Number Six tries to leave The Village. Occasionally, his efforts are carefully planned over a prolonged period, as in *The Chimes of Big Ben*, whereas other attempts, such as that in *The Schizoid Man*, emerge from an opportunity that he tries to seize spontaneously. Some of his bids for freedom are solo ventures, notably in *Many Happy Returns*, but in *The Chimes of Big Ben*, Number Six hatches a plan with Nadia, and in *Checkmate*, he systematically seeks to recruit fellow dissidents. One of The Prisoner's more indirect attempts at escape is made in *Dance of the Dead* – here he is intent on smuggling out of The Village a message via a dead body that he floats in the sea. In several instances, Number Six's escape is initially permitted by the leaders, yet he eventually finds himself back in his prison after being apparently on the brink of victory. In *Arrival*, this is a ploy by Number Two to emphasise to the newcomer that The Village is escape-proof and in *The Chimes of Big Ben*, Number Six is led to believe he has secured freedom in order that he might then reveal information about his decision to resign. It is only in *Many Happy Returns* and the final instalment, *Fall Out*, that Number Six actually leaves the physical confines of The Village. M. Keith Booker suggests that, even in the former, however, there are signs "that the entire escape was engineered by his captors as a way of breaking his spirits by raising his hopes, only to dash them". (p. 46)[21]

- **Self-preservation.** Many episodes are devoted to schemes by Number Two to break The Prisoner, who is subjected to a variety of ordeals, one of the most sadistic of which is shown at the beginning of *Dance of the Dead*. In such encounters, Number Six's priorities are to remain intact mentally and physically, and to prevent himself from revealing his secrets. As *The Prisoner: The Official Fact File* points out, however, for much of *Dance of the Dead*

Number Two's aims are simply to coerce him into accepting his Village identity and ensure that, as far as the outside world is concerned, he is dead.[22] Alain Carrazé and Hélène Oswald feel that the episode ends in one of The Prisoner's worst defeats. They write, "never has his situation seemed so hopeless". (p. 116)[23] Although the plans executed by Number Two vary over the course of the series, the leader's use of drugs, in particular, is a recurring feature. They are much in evidence in *A. B. and C.*, *A Change of Mind* and *Living in Harmony*. *A. B. and C.* also provides a rare instance of a plot in which Number Two is willing to risk the life of his adversary if it means that he is able to extract the information he seeks. The increasing desperation on the part of Number Two to break The Prisoner reaches a climax in the last but one episode, *Once Upon a Time*. Here The Village's chief administrator is allowed one week to use the highly dangerous Degree Absolute method. Attacks on Number Six's identity are made more than once – most obviously in *The Schizoid Man* and *Do Not Forsake Me Oh My Darling* – although in the latter case Number Six is merely a pawn to bring Professor Seltzman to The Village. In *The Chimes of Big Ben*, meanwhile, more mundane trickery is used to undermine the hero's sense of place. The campaign against Number Six is much less drastic in some episodes, such as *The Girl Who Was Death*, in which Number Two hopes that Number Six will give clues regarding his resignation motives when he reads The Village's children a bedtime story.

- **Subversion**. The series abounds with instances in which Number Six hijacks schemes by Number Two for his own ends or otherwise exploits situations in The Village to turn the tables on his opponent. In *The General*, he puts an end to "Speedlearn" and in *It's Your Funeral*, he prevents the assassination of the retiring Number Two. In some stories, Number Six not only thwarts the authorities' plans but also wins decisive victories himself. Two of the most significant are gained in *Hammer Into Anvil*, in which Number Six wreaks vengeance of his own on Number Two, and in *A Change of Mind*, where he turns the mob mentality of the Villagers against their master. Nevertheless, such dramatic turnarounds are rare and several attempts end in failure. Indeed, in *Free For All*, Number Six's campaign for the office of Number Two ends in a physical battering, whilst in *The General*, Number Six is unsuccessful in transmitting The Professor's subversive message and in *The Schizoid Man*, he is unable to grasp an opportunity to escape after foiling Number Two's attempt to make him doubt his own identity.

Although this typology embraces only three categories of story, it would seem sufficiently comprehensive to accommodate the plots of all 17 *Prisoner* episodes. Roger Langley draws attention to the atypical nature of *It's Your Funeral*. Highlighting such characteristics as the lack of an attempt to wrest secrets from Number Six and the absence of any effort by the hero to escape, he concludes that "the episode has none of the usual *Prisoner* hallmarks". (p. 111)[24] Yet, since the hero foils the authorities' scheme to kill the outgoing Number Two, it can unhesitatingly be placed in the "subversion" category and if we examine the remaining stories that may be given the same label we can see how *It's Your Funeral* shares some similarities with certain other instalments. From a classification perspective, *Dance of the Dead* is perhaps more problematic. As Langley recognises, the episode lacks a straightforward plotline and is, in his words, a "sequence of events woven together: carnival, illicit radio, dead body, condemned man… trial and incorporeal machine". (p. 75)[25] Still, the fundamental *Prisoner* themes of escape and self-preservation are also in evidence.

Episode title \ Story type	Escape	Self-preservation	Subversion	Victor
Arrival	•			Number Two
The Chimes of Big Ben	•	•		Number Two
				Number Six
A. B. and C.		•		Number Six
Free For All			•	Number Two
The Schizoid Man		•		Number Six
	•			Number Two
The General			•	Number Six
Many Happy Returns	•			Number Two
Dance of the Dead	•	•		Number Two
Checkmate	•			Number Two
Hammer Into Anvil			•	Number Six
It's Your Funeral			•	Number Six
A Change of Mind		•		Number Six
Do Not Forsake Me Oh My Darling		•		Professor Seltzman
Living in Harmony		•		Number Six
The Girl Who Was Death		•		Number Six
Once Upon a Time				Number Six
Fall Out	•			Number Six

Another way of understanding *The Prisoner*, at least on a superficial level, is to interpret each episode as a duel – usually cerebral rather than physical – between Number Six and Number Two, the most obvious manifestation of authority within The Village. Matthew White and Jaffer Ali suggest that much can be learned by identifying the victories of Number Six and those of his opponents.[26] The table above lists the 17 instalments, indicates the type of story in relation to the groups defined above and states who may ultimately be considered victorious. In this context, "Number Two" is defined loosely as those who run The Village.

If the episodes are sequenced in their original broadcast order, it is apparent that most of Number Six's successes lie in the second half of the series, thus reflecting an overall shift in the balance of power between the two sides, a trend that culminates in Number Six's crushing psychological triumph in the penultimate episode, *Once Upon a Time*. However, in *Do Not Forsake Me Oh My Darling*, whilst Number Six's mind is returned to his original body, the key event is that of Professor Seltzman's escape from The Village, a move made possible by his remarkable mind-swapping machine and his ability to manipulate it in a way that Number Two never considered a possibility. Thus, as Max Hora argues, the victory here belongs more to Professor Seltzman than to Number Six.[27]

References and Notes

1. Booth, R. Not a number: Patrick McGoohan – A life. Supernova: Twickenham, 2011.
2. Morreale, J. Lost, The Prisoner, and the end of the story. Journal of Popular Film and Television, 38 (4), 2010, pp. 176–185.
3. Chris Boucher Interview, April 2010. In: Oliver, M. B. Blake's 7: The merchandise guide – Unofficial and unauthorised. Telos: Prestatyn, 2012, pp. 162–171.
4. Jones, T. Review: Unique But Similar: The Prisoner Compared. Starburst, 29 June 2013. URL: http://www.starburstmagazine.com/reviews/book-reviews-latest-literary-releases/5644-book-review-unique-but-similar-the-prisoner (accessed: 23 February 2017).
5. Little Boxes was, in fact, a song mentioned by Patrick McGoohan himself more than once during the making of The Prisoner. When he asked Wilfred Josephs to compose the theme music for his new programme, McGoohan suggested that he draw inspiration from Little Boxes, Beethoven's Choral Symphony and another composition which Josephs considered "equally esoteric". (see The Prisoner Investigated Vol. 1) Much later, Little Boxes was one of five pieces that McGoohan tentatively proposed might be heard during the early scene in Fall Out where The Prisoner walks past several juke boxes down the rock-faced corridor on his way to

meeting The President and the assembled congregation. (see The Prisoner: The Original Scripts – Volume 2)

6. Oldham, A., Calder, T. and Irwin, C. Abba: The name of the game. Sidgwick and Jackson: London, 1995.

7. Ibid.

8. Palm, C. M. Abba: The complete guide to their music. Omnibus Press: London, 2005.

9. Writing in Abba Gold: The Complete Story, John Tobler quotes statistics that give some insight into the response of the record-buying public to The Visitors. In highlighting the album's "short UK chart life", (p. 98) Tobler notes that whereas Super Trouper – the Abba album that immediately preceded it – spent some 43 weeks in the charts, the figure for The Visitors was a mere 21 weeks.

10. Unique But Similar is not the first book to connect Lost Horizon with a major work of science fiction television. In Saints and Avengers: British Adventure Series of the 1960s, James Chapman draws parallels between this film and The Champions. Specifically, he notes their shared interest in lost civilisations and even gives his essay on The Champions the title Return From Shangri-La. Chapman recognises, however, that in the television programme, "The existence of the lost civilisation is merely a plot device which serves to provide the heroes... with their special powers." (p. 177) Indeed, the community is barely seen at all and nothing is learnt of the lifestyle or culture of its people.

11. Dunn, P. Review: Decoding The Prisoner. The Unmutual. URL: http://www.theunmutual.co.uk/reviewsdecoding.htm (accessed: 23 February 2017).

12. Presnell, D. and McGee, M. A critical history of television's The Twilight Zone, 1959–1964. McFarland: Jefferson, North Carolina, 1998.

13. Booker, C. The seven basic plots: Why we tell stories. Continuum: London, 2005.

14. Lance Parkin suggests that the "Historical" category can itself be subdivided. Specifically, he defines three subtypes: "Educational" stories, "You Can't Change History" serials and "History is Wrong" adventures (Time Unincorporated: The Doctor Who Fanzine Archives – Vol.1, pages 104 and 105).

15. Smith, P. Time and space visualiser: The story and history of Doctor Who as data visualisations. Wonderful Books: London, 2013.

16. Parkin, L. Time unincorporated: The Doctor Who fanzine archives – Vol. 1. Mad Norwegian Press: Des Moines, Iowa, 2009.

17. The U.N.I.T. Family: Part One. Doctor Who: Inferno. DVD. BBC, 2006.

18. Wood, T. and Miles, L. About time: The unauthorized guide to Doctor Who: 1966–1969 – Seasons 4 to 6. Mad Norwegian Press: Des Moines, Iowa, 2006.

19. Chapman, J. Inside the TARDIS: The worlds of Doctor Who. I. B. Tauris: London, 2006.

20. Albarella, T. (ed.) As timeless as infinity: The complete Twilight Zone scripts of Rod Serling – Volume ten. Gauntlet: Colorado Springs, Colorado, 2013.

21. Booker, M. K. Science fiction television. Praeger: Westport, Connecticut, 2004.

22. The Prisoner: The Official Fact File. De Agostini, 2005–2006.

The aims of Number Two here bring to mind the appearance of the hearse in The Prisoner's standard title sequence. It would appear that the figure who emerges from this car, and is dressed as an undertaker, is responsible for the hero's abduction. If, in Dance of the Dead, Number Two is intent on ensuing that The Prisoner now has no life beyond his existence in The Village, then the death-related imagery we see in the usual opening title sequence would seem very apt.

23. Carrazé, A. and Oswald, H. The Prisoner: A televisionary masterpiece. Virgin: London, 1990.

24. Langley, R. The Pris6ner from the inside: Plots, scripts, background. Escape, 2010.

25. Ibid.

26. White, M. and Ali, J. The official Prisoner companion. Sidgwick and Jackson: London, 1988.

27. Hora, M. The Prisoner of Portmeirion, 2nd ed. Number Six Publications, 1995.

SECTION II:
Stepping into Various Worlds Beyond The Village

Some 20 years after *The Prisoner*'s first showing on British television, the entry for the programme in *The ITV Encyclopedia of Adventure* concluded, "There has been nothing like it before or since." (p. 372)[1] Not long afterwards, Jacques Sternberg made a very similar observation, commenting, "*The Prisoner* seems to have inspired no other work of the same kind."[2] Sternberg's attitude to the series is, in fact, neatly encapsulated in the title of his essay, *The Prisoner, Pioneer Without Heirs*. It is not unusual to see such arguments in critical comment on the programme. Indeed, exploring its legacy in terms of its impact on subsequent television, James Chapman expressed the same opinion nearly 15 years after the assessments of Sternberg and the *ITV Encyclopedia*.[3]

Although Peter Wright, too, feels that *The Prisoner* "exerts little influence over subsequent productions", he asserts that its "paranoid ambience" is evident in the 1981 *ITV Playhouse* production *Sin With Our Permission*. (p. 294)[4] *The Encyclopedia of TV Science Fiction* also sees "strong overtones of *The Prisoner*" in this work – surveillance is again constant and the hero, "in true Number Six style", discovers that the fururistic town in which the drama is set is actually an escape-proof prison. The *Encyclopedia* further suggests that the Head of the Information Department is "a strong Number Two-type character". (p. 569)[5]

Sue Short views *The Prisoner* as a trendsetter of sorts and summarises a range of what she describes as "features that recur in subsequent telefantasy". (p. 25)

Specifically, she cites,

> ... the subversion of expectation rendered by mixing generic
> signifiers; high production values; a measure of playfulness
> (including baroque excesses, dream sequences, and extravagant
> ruses); allusions made to familiar tropes (referencing other media,
> fairy tales, and popular culture); a refusal to "pander" to audiences
> (with complex plotting and unanswered questions); and an
> insistent ambiguity. (p. 25)[6]

Still, the aforementioned beliefs of Sternberg[7] and Chapman[8] in relation to the
novelty and unique nature of *The Prisoner* remain widely held to this day in
many quarters. As recently as August 2015, the *Radio Times* magazine described
the programme as an "absolute original" and "a genre all of its own: the
conceptual, allegorical adventure mystery". (p. 24)[9]

It is a peculiar anomaly, then, that a particularly strong strand within critical
comment on the series in recent years has seen authors identify **similarities**
between *The Prisoner* and other creative works. One of the most significant
books on *The Prisoner* includes an especially wide-ranging analysis of the links
between the programme and later manifestations of popular culture.[10] Some
writers have sought to explore either how certain works may have had some
impact on *The Prisoner* in terms of plot and theme or how others may have been
inspired by it but there have also been instances where commentators have
been content merely to highlight areas of similarity, and the question of whether
or not the common features are intentional has gone unaddressed. The parallels
that can be drawn between *The Prisoner* and the US television production *Twin
Peaks* recur in much of the literature,[11] as do connections between McGoohan's
series and the much later *Wayward Pines*.[12] An important outlet for essays
written from such a comparative standpoint has been *The Projection Room*
section within Rick Davy's website *The Unmutual*. At the time of writing (i.e.
February 2017), fourteen such articles can be accessed from this area.[13]

The earliest comparisons of *The Prisoner* and other works predate the
modern Internet age very substantially, however. As long ago as the late 1970s,
in fact, Susan Nobel and Diana Goldsborough wrote of how two *Prisoner*
episodes brought to mind classical texts. Specifically, they noted "strong
parallels" between *Many Happy Returns* and *The Odyssey*, and the "distinct
similarity" between *Dance of the Dead* and the myth of Orpheus in the
Underworld. (p. 11)[14] These ideas are undoubtedly more valid than one of the
first speculative comparisons, made while *The Prisoner* was in production and

which quickly proved to be largely ill-founded. The ITC press book for the show comments on the frequency with which links between his programme and *The Fugitive* were suggested to Patrick McGoohan in the early days.[15] With hindsight, many fans will find such comparisons laughable, although there is a certain unity between Number Six and Richard Kimble. Alan Armer, who produced *The Fugitive*, describes the show's hero as "a single guy fighting the world for something [he believes] in" and intent on finding truth. Envisioning the protagonist as "the classic Western hero", Armer admires the simple purity of his one-man struggle. The Prisoner can, of course, also be appreciated in these terms.[16]

Just a few years later, another lone battle would be fought by reporter Carl Kolchak, hero of *Kolchak: The Night Stalker*, as he explored various supernatural and – occasionally – extraterrestrial incidents in contemporary America. Even reference books that offer no more than brief overviews of the series often comment on the solitary nature of Kolchak's quest. *The Encyclopedia of TV Science Fiction*, for example, records, "Barely tolerated by his ulcer-ridden editor, and despised by the cops and politicians, Kolchak works a lonely beat, his only companions a camera and a tape recorder into which he narrates his findings." (p. 216)[17] There are parallels, too, with the character of David Vincent in *The Invaders*, which, like *The Fugitive*, was produced by Armer. *The Encyclopedia of Fantasy* notes how Kolchak "is continually thwarted in his efforts to prove his theories... and all his proofs conveniently disappear at the end of each episode".[18] Vincent's investigations into aliens among us meet with a similar fate just as frequently.

The pages that follow in this book present 14 essays, four of which first appeared, in different forms, on *The Unmutual* site. Of the ten remaining, one was originally published as an article within the peer reviewed science fiction journal *Foundation*, and the other nine (which here provide Chapters Four, Five, Eight, Nine, Ten, Eleven, Twelve, Thirteen and Fourteen) have been specially written for *Unique But Similar*. The essays which constitute the final two chapters are unique in the work since, whereas all the preceding pieces focus on the whole *Prisoner* saga, one particular instalment comes under scrutiny in each of these parts. Although all the essays are united here as chapters within a book, when those making up Chapters One, Two, Three, Six and Seven were written they were conceived as individual entities and were not intended to form an integrated whole. In preparing this material for publication in *Unique But Similar*, the author made various amendments. Where appropriate, new observations were added, comments within the original text that had become dated were removed or altered and, so as to promote consistency across the individual chapters, a common format was introduced for all the references.

Although some readers may find the multitude of superscript numbers that punctuate the text intrusive, the references, in fact, form an integral element of the work. Not only do they endow the text with greater academic rigour generally; they also enable the reader to explore further the evidence that the writer has used when forming his arguments. It must conceded, however, that the extensive use of references and direct quotations is not to the taste of all readers, some of whom find treatments of popular television programmes written from a scholarly perspective dry and far removed from the light reads to which they may be accustomed. David J. Howe, Mark Stammers and Stephen James Walker are critical of one of the early books to offer an academic discourse on a popular science fiction programme, describing *Doctor Who: The Unfolding Text* as "complex and hard-going for the lay-person to read". (p. 157)[19] Even today, nearly thirty-five years after the publication of this item, there remains a tendency in some quarters to equate works of this kind with stodgy "textbooks".

The source material cited in *Unique But Similar* varies greatly in format, focus and degree of academic rigour but much of it falls into one of six categories:

- quick reference volumes – encyclopedias of television programmes, science fiction or science fiction television productions;
- specialist works, whose territory varies in scale from science fiction television as a body to individual series;
- biographies and autobiographies relating to people closely associated with the television programmes featured;
- popular magazines, such as *Radio Times*;
- scholarly journals and professional periodicals, for example *Foundation*, *Media History* and the *School Librarian*;
- fan magazines and websites.

Since the publication of the first edition of *Unique But Similar* in June 2013, further chapters have been written, all the original material has been re-examined with a view to ensuring that the text remains pertinent and up-to-date, new arguments have been added and further evidence incorporated. The author has also attempted to address some of the issues raised by critics who reviewed the original book. In this respect, I have taken a similar perspective to that of Rodney Marshall when he wrote the second edition of *Subversive Champagne: Beyond Genre in The Avengers*. In his preface, Marshall explains how he has responded to the constructive criticisms made of his book on a French *Avengers* website.[20] The new version of *Unique But Similar* is almost twice as long as the first edition.

Whilst all the creative works with which *The Prisoner* is compared here are television productions, the variety in their scope is marked. In some instances, it is the whole programme that is under examination (as is the case with *Children of the Stones*, *The Omega Factor*,[21] *UFO*, *Blake's 7*, *Logan's Run*, *Codename Icarus* and *Knights of God*). Elsewhere, the focus lies on one serial within an overall show – this is true of the *Doctor Who* adventure *The Faceless Ones* and the *Look and Read* component *Cloud Burst*. In other chapters, a single episode of a programme is being analysed. Several of these – the *Night Gallery* segment *The House*, the *Joe 90* instalment *See You Down There*, and the *Yes, Prime Minister* story *Man Overboard* – last no more than half an hour. More details of all the works under investigation can be found in the Appendix.

Perhaps the most obvious similarity between a particular episode of *The Prisoner* and an individual instalment of another series involves the former's *A. B. and C.* and *Counterstrike's Nocturne*. Since it is generally agreed that the script of one of these was consciously redeveloped by the writer, Anthony Skene, to form the basis of the other episode, the relationship between them was deemed too close to justify a comparison of the kind that is intended in this book. Moreover, the key aspects of overlap have already been outlined in *The Prisoner: The Official Fact File*.[22] There is, however, a divergence of opinion in terms of which script formed the original source material. *The Encyclopedia of TV Science Fiction* asserts unequivocally that the script for *Nocturne* "was a reworking of Skene's own... for *The Prisoner* episode *A, B & C*". (p. 101)[23] In introducing the script for the *Prisoner* story in his well received two-volume collection, Robert Fairclough reports a similar sequence of events,[24] and publications such as *The Official Fact File*,[25] Alan Morton's substantial reference book on SF, fantasy and horror television[26] and one of Roger Langley's more recent works on *The Prisoner*[27] all make the same claim. Yet, Fairclough himself offers a rather different account in his *Official Companion* to *The Prisoner*. Specifically, he writes,

> The origins of *A.B. and C.* lie in Anthony Skene's first script for the BBC science fiction series *Counterstrike*... Although the series was not transmitted until 1969, *Counterstrike* had a long development – the initial scripts were written in 1966. Skene's script, *Nocturne*, was rewritten for *The Prisoner* when the production of *Counterstrike* stalled. (p. 48)[28]

Although it may seem fertile ground for comparison, no attempt is made in *Unique But Similar* to draw parallels between *The Prisoner* and certain episodes of *Danger Man*. By and large, the book aims to avoid retreading old ground, and significant links between *The Prisoner* and appropriate episodes of McGoohan's previous series have been covered at length elsewhere, notably by Alan Stevens and Fiona Moore.[29] In a lighter vein, more trivial connections have been outlined by Catherine Nemeth Frumerman, who offers intriguing insights into how *Danger Man* anticipated *The Prisoner's* attention to the number six and penny farthing bicycles.[30]

Readers may well be struck by the contrasting nature of the programmes that are featured in this book. They include a situation comedy, children's drama, material for schools, family-friendly viewing and adult fantasy. The diversity reflects the fact that there are strong similarities between individual features of *The Prisoner* and those of many other creative works. Readers may be somewhat surprised to see that three of the programmes discussed in detail in this book are aimed very much at children, and a fourth, i.e. *Doctor Who*, although regarded by this author as a family programme, is popularly perceived as a show predominantly directed at young people. The children's productions explored here are not isolated cases by any means. It is possible to argue that *The Prisoner* and *Mr Benn*, for example, also share important similarities. Both deal with the exploits of an eponymous character who, without possessing any special powers in the style of a comic book superhero, seems to command unlimited personal skills and seldom suffers from a shortage of ideas when faced with practical problems. Each is seen on various occasions to assume a leadership role in relation to others. Every week, the two protagonists find themselves immersed in a fantasy situation within a setting that is – at least ostensibly – very different from the environment with which they are accustomed. Each works for freedom and, in some instances, they find themselves in conflict with others as they attempt to subvert unjust schemes. Farah Mendlesohn raises the possibility that Mr. Benn's adventures may not be "real", (p. 247)[31] and the question of whether or not Number Six's tribulations within The Village take place only within the hero's head is one to which we will return again and again in this book. Of course, there are major differences between the programmes, too. Most notably, Mr Benn himself forms an archetypal hero, whereas The Prisoner's aggressive individualism frequently renders him a much less sympathetic character. Tess Read suggests that Mr Benn's key personality traits are those of "kindness, thoughtfulness and compassion". (p. 10)[32] These qualities are less immediately evident in Number Six.

Echoes of *Prisoner* themes can also be found in children's literature. The mid 1970s saw the appearance of a four-volume collection of SF written for young people and published by Armada.[33] The second anthology included one of most poetic stories of its type ever written – Chris Parr's *The South Gate Sea*.[34] Although its true province is that of the wellbeing of the natural environment, the story's references to a futuristic school in which pupils and teachers alike are known by numbers and a classroom culture that emphasises rote learning and the knowledge of facts, rather than the development of understanding, are unlikely to be missed by *Prisoner* fans.

Even putting aside the similarities between *The Prisoner* and *The South Gate Sea*, it is noticeable how many of the creative works to which *The Prisoner* is compared in *Unique But Similar* fall into the SF category. This perhaps reflects a significant characteristic of the genre itself. According to Buck Houghton, producer of the first three seasons of *The Twilight Zone*, "[SF] is a limited field, and you can't write in it without stepping on somebody's former idea." (p. 194)[35] Houghton's argument is consistent with the stances taken by one of his successors as *Twilight Zone* producer, Bert Granet,[36] and the series' creator, Rod Serling. The latter had, on several occasions, to defend himself against accusations that he had stolen a particular plot from elsewhere. In one such instance, he commented,

> In all areas of science fiction... it is rare that we do a [*Twilight Zone*] show in which at least ten people do not accost us, waving material of their own, and accuse us of plagiarism, conscious or otherwise... when you deal in this kind of storytelling, you automatically handle certain ideas in precisely the same manner that other science fictionaires do. (p. 692)[37]

It is interesting to note that *The Encyclopedia of Science Fiction* asserts that by the mid 1960s (i.e. the point when the final season of *The Twilight Zone* was first broadcast), genre science fiction "had reached a crisis point in both England and America... far too many writers were creating endless and sometimes mindless variations on the same few traditional SF themes". (p. 424)[38] From a *Prisoner* perspective, further evidence of the conceptual limitations within science fiction can be found in the similarities that Mark Ward detects between, firstly, *Do Not Forsake Me Oh My Darling* and the *Out of the Unknown* episode *This Body is Mine* and, secondly, *The Schizoid Man* and another instalment of *Out of the Unknown – Welcome Home*.[39] The first two stories are linked by a mind-swap theme, and the last two by issues surrounding the hero's perception of his personal identity.[40] Nevertheless, it should be acknowledged that by no means everyone would support the argument that science fiction is a very restricted genre. As editor of various SF anthology books for young people in the 1970s, Richard Davis is well placed to appreciate the diversity of material within the field. He maintains, "Its subjects, its themes, its points of view, are limitless as the universe itself; unlike mainstream fiction it is not subject to the laws of our own space and time." (p. 9)[41]

The question of whether *The Prisoner* can really be considered to constitute an SF programme generates much debate. John Javna indicates that McGoohan would not himself describe *The Prisoner* in this way, and quotes a 1967 interview in which he insisted he was dealing with "a contemporary subject... not science fiction. I hope that will be recognized by the audience." (p. 48)[42] Some 12 years later, in the Goodman interview, McGoohan emphatically restated his position on the matter, remarking, "I don't think it's got anything to do with science fiction whatsoever."[43] Nevertheless, Rupert Booth suggests that McGoohan was happy to allow the inclusion of such SF elements as Rover, mind-swapping and identical doubles on the basis that they facilitated the series' allegorical dimension by freeing the narrative from the constraints of reality.[44] Brian J. Woodman cites further elements that bring science fiction to mind, notably futuristic sets, automated doors and other "strange scientific inventions". (p. 946)[45]

There is, though, a prominent school of thought among commentators that regards *The Prisoner* as no more than "peripheral" SF at most. In *Science Fiction: The Illustrated Encyclopedia*, the claim is made, "This bizarre series is perhaps British SF television's flagship, despite being itself only fringe SF." (p. 300)[46] Furthermore, although coverage of it can be found in a variety of major reference books on SF and SF television,[47] in their guide to "cult TV" John E. Lewis and Penny Stempel place their *Prisoner* entry in a section devoted to "crime and mystery".[48] Elsewhere, discussion on *The Prisoner* in even wide-ranging essays on science fiction and fantasy television is sometimes conspicuous by its absence. Mark Siegel's article about the subject, for example, makes no mention of *The Prisoner*, and it goes uncited in the 24-show "videography" that follows, even though the programme's most passionate enthusiasts could, no doubt, present a compelling case that it amply demonstrates one of the characteristics which Siegel feels is exhibited by the best science fiction and fantasy television – such series "can offer dramatic and exciting metaphorical structures that... help us to see ourselves and our world in a fresh and constructive way". (p. 102)[49] Much obviously depends in terms of categorisation on what the individual viewer makes of *The Prisoner* but undoubtedly there are many instances in which particular plot elements found in certain episodes are consistent with wider genre themes and, as *The Ultimate Encyclopedia of Science Fiction* declares, even if the SF devices "may appear to be marginal... they are vital to the construction of the imaginary edifice". (p. 140)[50]

The debt that *The Prisoner* owes to particular SF scenarios is perhaps best understood by considering a case in point. *Di Fate's Catalog of Science Fiction Hardware*, which provides an extensive overview of possible science and technology in the future, concludes a discussion of the development of information provision by postulating that, one day, knowledge will be able to pass directly from "storage computers to the human brain", whilst the individual is unconscious or hypnotised. (p. 115)[51] The eminent scientist Arthur C. Clarke also notes the use that speculative authors and artists have made of machines that may be termed "mechanical educators". These "could impress on the brain, in a matter of a few minutes, knowledge and skills which might otherwise take a lifetime to acquire". (p. 182)[52] Few works of SF offer so memorable a manifestation of such a gadget as the *Prisoner* episode *The General*, with the subliminator device assuming the role of Clarke's "mechanical educator".

An alternative school of thought posits that *The Prisoner* is actually an example of "New Wave science fiction" (p. 48) – its concern lies not with technology but rather with social issues that arise in a speculative situation.[53] In marked contrast to McGoohan's interpretation, *Prisoner* script editor George Markstein has, in fact, gone on record as saying that, for him, the show is "a form of science fiction" that deals with "people here". (p. 83)[54] Other, less senior personnel who worked on the programme saw the the show in a similar way. Ian Rakoff recounts that to junior technicians like himself *The Prisoner* "appeared to be an enigmatic, contemporary science fiction series". (p. 24)[55]

M. Keith Booker maintains that there are multiple strands within the science fiction dimension of *The Prisoner*. He, too, believes that the futuristic technologies in evidence "are more important for what they tell us about the here and now than about far places and distant futures" and points to how they echo rumours of "existing real-world capabilities". (p. 81) He also explains that the *Prisoner* episodes *A. B. and C.* and *Living in Harmony* foreshadow the "cyberpunk" science fiction of the 1980s and 1990s, in which the virtual reality provided by computer simulations becomes indistinguishable from actual reality.[56]

Even when we disregard the clear science fiction elements within *The Prisoner*, we can draw parallels between some of the programme's less fanciful plot components and one of SF's most potent images. Langley equates the land that adjoins The Village and into which citizens are not allowed to venture with the territory outside the futuristic domed cities we see so often in SF films.[57] It is an indication of the popularity of the domed city concept in speculative situations that the second volume in the Usborne *World of the Future* series of three books, which concentrates entirely on "future cities", shows a large depiction of this kind of environment prominently on the front cover.[58] The other two volumes in the range are devoted to such fundamentals as "robots" and "star travel". In television, domed cities are a particular feature of the opening episodes of *Logan's Run* and *Blake's 7* – two shows that are investigated at length in *Unique But Similar*. Whether the community inhabits The Village or a domed city, there is, in the words of Langley, an interest in "what lies beyond", (p. 126)[59] and indeed it is not long before we see The Prisoner, Logan and Blake in areas where access to the ordinary citizen is not permissible.

A criticism often levelled against certain episodes of *The Twilight Zone*, in particular, is that even by the end of the instalment involved, no attempt has been made to offer any real basis for the events depicted. In *And When The Sky Was Opened*, for example, three astronauts who have returned to Earth after an expedition into space vanish one by one. Their disappearances are not explained. For Marc Scott Zicree, this omission is a significant problem. He writes, "*And When the Sky Was Opened* is a flawed episode… it sets up the question 'What is going on here?' – then fails to satisfactorily answer it. In this case, an answer isn't even attempted." (p. 63)[60] Commentators who adopt such a view would, no doubt, take an equally dismissive attitude to the reluctance of *The Prisoner's* writers to account satisfactorily for the "preposterous" events that take place in The Village. According to James Gunn, science fiction deals rationally with the fantastic,[61] and the conclusion may be drawn that where no rational basis presented, the creative territory is one of fantasy. If we adhere to this line of thought, we may be tempted to see both *And When The Sky Was Opened* and *The Prisoner* as fantasies, rather than science fiction. Critical reaction to another episode of *The Twilight Zone* adds weight to this stance. Drawing attention to the lack of a time machine and, instead, the use of a "visual allusion to *Through the Looking Glass*" to establish the situation in which the hero finds himself back in his home town some twenty-five years earlier, Zicree indicates that the classic instalment *Walking Distance* "makes no pretense at being science fiction… it's clearly a fantasy". (p. 43)[62] In truth, though, the division between fantasy and science fiction is frequently more hazy than we may wish to acknowledge. As Siegel points out, even in such an archetypal science fiction programme as *Star Trek*, the details of how advanced technologies such as phasers and faster-than-light drives work are not explained.[63]

Whilst today *The Prisoner* is justly lauded as an innovative series, it would be unwise to believe that it was the first British television programme to combine to a significant degree elements of SF with components from other genres. Indeed, the opening words on that part of the inlay sheet appearing on the back of the DVD package of *Undermind*, which was released in July 2012 as the first edition of this book was being prepared, proudly proclaim, "Crime drama meets science fiction in this chilling and intriguing ABC series... first broadcast in 1965."[64] More independent reviews, such as the entries in *The Encyclopedia of TV Science Fiction*[65] and the *Radio Times Guide to Science Fiction*,[66] attest to *Undermind*'s status as an unusual television hybrid – one that was screened over two years before *The Prisoner*. *The Avengers* is, of course, another crime drama that incorporated science fiction elements and more will be said about this programme later in this section. Other hybrids from a similar period as *The Prisoner* – specifically the late 1960s – featured no science fiction ingredients whatsoever. The original version of *Randall and Hopkirk (Deceased)*, for example, combined elements of humour, supernatural fantasy and the detective genre. According to Tise Vahimagi, the series "operated in some unique area between *Blythe Spirit*-type comedy and pulp private-eye violent drama". (p. 54)[67]

As they read this book, many people whose interests extend beyond the series will surely find themselves recognising similarities between *The Prisoner* and other creative works with which they are familiar. *The Official Fact File* notes how fans of The Beatles identify common ground between the group's feature film *Help!* and the *Prisoner* episode *The Girl Who Was Death*, and the text goes on to cite various shared features.[68] There are situations, too, where more fleeting similarities may be detected between *The Prisoner* and other productions. In some instances, parallels may be drawn on the basis of a single speech made by one of the characters. In *Do Not Forsake Me Oh My Darling*, Number Two suggests that, once the secrets of a groundbreaking, mind-swapping machine have been acquired, the security of no country will be safe against The Village's espionage methods since, when diplomatic exchanges of agents take place, the bodies of spies who are returned may contain the minds of Village agents. In the early *Outer Limits* story *The Hundred Days of the Dragon*, an Oriental power attempts to infiltrate the US via a ploy that also uses a revolutionary process in order to exploit the trusted status of key personnel. Here, though, an agent's mind is not moved elsewhere; rather, a fluid has been developed that renders the body of an individual malleable, thereby allowing an Oriental agent to assume the physical appearance of the supreme politician in a rival country. It would be ill-advised, however, to make a comparison between the two productions without offering a significant caveat. The inquiring viewer may well wonder how far both the events which unfold in *Do*

Not Forsake Me Oh My Darling and the episode's portrayal of The Village are faithful to the original concept of *The Prisoner*. Chris Gregory is concerned that, in this instalment, the role of The Village "is reduced to that of a SPECTRE-like organisation, competing for 'secrets' with other 'world powers'". (p. 146)[69] It is certainly difficult to reconcile this tendency with the more allegorical dimension of The Village that emerges elsewhere in the series. For Rupert Booth, another problem of consistency emerges with the episode – "the 'mind-swap' plotline veers a little too much towards *Star Trek*-style sci-fi" and seems incongruous "even in the advanced world of The Village". (p. 202)[70]

It is possible, however, to make other links between *The Prisoner* and *The Hundred Days of the Dragon*. Whilst various writers argue that Curtis, who appears in *The Schizoid Man*, is – or may be – some sort of clone of the hero,[71] James Van Hise maintains that the man has been "altered to look exactly like Number Six". (p.119)[72] Van Hise's interpretation may give rise to speculation that the Village authorities have used a technique somewhat similar to that employed by the oriental scientists in·*The Hundred Days of the Dragon*.

Undoubtedly, some readers of *Unique But Similar* will have already seen analyses that draw comparisons between *The Prisoner* and television programmes from the pre-1988 era which are not discussed at length here. An essay devoted to links between *The Prisoner* and *1990*, for example, has long been available from *The Unmutual* website,[73] and comparisons between McGoohan's show and other famous series abound. Robert Sellers believes that *The Prisoner* and *Man in a Suitcase* parallel "each other in terms of theme – two solitary men in an alien environment, railing against a system they hold to be unjust and oppressive". (p. 115) Sellers reports, too, how the shows were made by different factions that had emerged from the production team previously responsible for *Danger Man*.[74] Certain similarities can be detected between Sellers's *Prisoner – Man in a Suitcase* analysis and Rick Davy's comparison of the former and *Callan*. Davy summarises that both the Edward Woodward series and *The Prisoner* concentrate on "one man's fight against the powers that be, [with him] steadfastly sticking to his own morals and beliefs". (p. 44)[75] For Lewis and Stempel, the heroes of the two programmes were "outsiders" and very much products of the anti-Establishment days of the late 1960s.[76]

In a brief examination in his book on "spy television", Wesley Britton sees several pertinent commonalities between *The Prisoner* and *The Avengers*, and highlights a magazine article that would appear more concerned with fanciful conjecture linking the two series.[77] Toby Miller also refers to this piece, describing the journal in which it appeared as a US "personal-opinion-and-natter-zine" dedicated to *The Avengers*. (p. 151)[78] A useful starting point for making comparisons between *The Prisoner* and *The Avengers* lies in *The Ultimate Encyclopedia of Science Fiction*'s comment that each programme took "TV surrealism to unprecedented extremes". (p. 140)[79] Like *The Prisoner*, *The Avengers* was a television hybrid with a strong science fiction element. In addition, Lauren Humphries-Brooks draws attention to its ingredients of spy drama, the detective genre, parody and satire.[80] The "fun" strand is especially apparent in the closing minutes of *The Grave-diggers*, which are presented in a form reminiscent of silent films, in a scene that features speeded up action, melodramatic piano music, imminent danger, a damsel in distress, scheming villains, a dashing hero and, ultimately, a "close shave" rescue. Marshall highlights how several of the Emma Peel episodes of *The Avengers* "playfully mock" such establishments as merchant banks, marriage bureaux, London hotels and golf clubs (p. 160),[81] whilst, in a slightly more abstract vein, *The Prisoner* ridicules, for example, modern art (in *The Chimes of Big Ben*), democratic processes (in *Free For All*) and rote methods of education (in *The General*).

It is revealing to note, too, how some of the ideas that have been applied by authors to one of these series in reviews are equally valid in relation to the other. For example, Marshall highlights how Harold Pinter has commented with regard to his own plays that "underneath what is being said, something else is being said". Marshall feels that this statement is also true in relation to *The Avengers'* "subversively surreal suppression of realism". (p. 193)[82] Given that *The Prisoner* can be seen to function as an allegory or metaphor, Pinter's observation is highly appropriate when considering this series as well.

More specifically, in presenting their guide to the episodes of *The Avengers* and *The New Avengers*, Paul Cornell, Martin Day and Keith Topping detect a host of links between elements within individual instalments of the first show and *The Prisoner*. A few observations, such as the presence of a penny farthing bicycle in an exhibition in *The Bird Who Knew Too Much*, seem somewhat tenuous, although others are much more substantial. In discussing *Room Without a View*, the authors point to the *Prisoner*esque situations in which people are gassed, disappear suddenly and are taken to what would seem to be a faraway place. It may also be noted that the victims hold important positions; they possess invaluable information and brainwashing is a key theme in the story. There are marked similarities between the "*Prisoner*" plot features that Cornell, Day and Topping identify in *Room Without a View* and those they detect in *Epic*. Here, too, Emma Peel is gassed and abducted. On this occasion, she awakens in what initially appears to be her own flat. In recounting details within the two instalments as evidence of *Prisoner – Avengers* links, Cornell, Day and

Topping cover similar ground to that which Britton would tread a few years later.[83] He adds, however, that the two series "employed mind-switching machines and both had their leads fight duplicates of themselves". (p. 108)[84] In terms of other dastardly plots hatched against key protagonists, we can draw parallels between *A. B. and C.* and the *Avengers* episodes *Too Many Christmas Trees* and *Death's Door.* As Bernard Ginez points out, dream manipulation is a feature of both these Emma Peel stories.[85]

Murdersville, another Emma Peel instalment from the same season as *Epic*, again bears some significant resemblances to *The Prisoner*. Here the heroine finds herself in a superficially idyllic village but all is not what it seems. The inhabitants are evasive and behave strangely. Emma is soon the victim of a conspiracy to make her doubt her own sanity. In time, she is taken captive and learns that she can trust no-one other than her fellow prisoners, all of whom have chosen to take a stand against the will of the majority. As in McGoohan's series, leadership in the village comes from an unexpected source, in this case a corrupt, yet outwardly respectable, doctor. Whilst Cornell, Day and Topping do not connect these features with *The Prisoner*, they do note that the helicopter used to pursue Emma when she escapes "is very *Prisoner*esque". (p. 222)[86] Daniel O'Brien sees links, too, between *The Prisoner* and the later *Avengers* episode *Pandora*. He reports how, in the latter, Tara King is kidnapped, drugged, imprisoned and brainwashed. She attempts unsuccessfully to escape and is misled by captors who pose as friends.[87]

With regard to creative personnel, for Alain Carrazé and Jean-Luc Putheaud, Patrick McGoohan and *The Avengers'* Brian Clemens share a certain equivalence in that, according to the authors, each "had the skill and invention to turn a brilliant idea into a timeless series". (p. 9)[88] Even as long ago as 1979, Richard Holliss felt it appropriate to contrast how well both *The Prisoner* and *The Avengers* had withstood the test of time in comparison with the early episodes of *Doctor Who*. Holliss attributes this success to the fact that each programme "uses sf more casually not stilting episodes with outdated special effects and limited budgets". (p. 12)[89] Although another significant factor may be that both *The Prisoner* and the last two seasons of *The Avengers* were made in colour, as opposed to black and white, Philip Sandifer maintains that because of its much inferior production values, "*Doctor Who* in the 1960s never had an episode that looked half as good as *The Prisoner* looked, even ignoring the color issue." (pp. 374–375)[90]

Connections can be made in terms of characters, too. Just as Number Six may be thought of as the ultimate individual, John Steed may be regarded as a model English gentleman. In each series, the protagonists remain something of a mystery. *Prisoner* fans have speculated for years on Number Six's background, and there is a comparable lack of certainty in relation to Steed's employers. In a memorable simile, Andrew Pixley comments, "Trying to pin down details on the people Steed works for is like trying to snare a shadow." (p. 311)[91] Both Steed and Number Six inhabit a fantasy world. In *The Prisoner* this is, of course, The Village, whilst *The Avengers* presents a quintessential Britain. In Clemens's words, the land depicted in his show is one "of bowlers and brollies, of charm and muffins for tea, a Britain long since gone – if it ever really existed!" (p. 9)[92] In *The Avengers* and *The Prisoner*, the heroes' enemies are ill-defined. One of the great mysteries in the latter is the nature of the side that runs The Village, and Chapman cites several episodes of *The Avengers* in which neither the identity of the hostile enemy powers nor the reason for the invasion they plot is disclosed. Chapman muses, "the threat to national security has... been reduced to an abstract level completely devoid of political ideology". (p. 79)[93] In some instalments, other fundamentals also go unaddressed. In *Dead Man's Treasure*, which, according to James Speirs, is a favourite among fans of the programme,[94] Steed and Emma take part in a car rally in order to recover top secret papers. The precise nature of the documents remains a mystery throughout the episode.

There are, however, important differences in emphasis between *The Prisoner* and *The Avengers*. Referring to particular instalments so as to buttress his argument, Miller outlines how a staple *Avengers* plot formula involves "an invitation to an isolated country estate, psychological torture, a sense of powerlessness, and then a turnaround". (p. 71)[95] Whilst we may argue that the last three elements also emerge in *The Prisoner*, the fact that McGoohan's character is kidnapped, rather than merely lured to The Village, provides a clear difference between *The Prisoner*'s premise and one of the archetypal *Avengers* scenarios. The recurring pattern identified by Miller is echoed, at least in part, by Andrew Cartmel, who refers to surreal episodes "where some sinister mastermind is tampering with the sanity of Steed and Mrs Peel". (p. 66)[96] Instalments such as *Too Many Christmas Trees*, *The House That Jack Built* and *The Joker* quickly spring to mind in this context. At first sight, *The Prisoner* may seem generically similar, with in this case Number Six cast as the series hero and Number One his arch adversary. The mental disintegration theme is especially apparent in episodes like *The Schizoid Man*, *Living in Harmony* and *Once Upon a Time*. Ultimately, however, Number One is not revealed as an *Avengers*-style criminal mastermind at all, and McGoohan's real intent is shown to have been altogether more abstract and cerebral. As McGoohan acknowledges, when the last episode defied expectations and, instead of seeing the "ultimate evil villain", viewers "got Number 6's alter ego they were none too happy. They, the majority, felt cheated." (p. 7)[97]

Perhaps the best assessment of the unexpected nature of the revelation is offered by Alain Carrazé and Hélène Oswald. Through the use of a quotation from Martin Buber, they note that the answer to the question of Number One's identity is given on a level that is different from that on which the question was formulated.[98] The revelation that Number One is actually The Prisoner is consistent with the "theme of the self" that Sue Thornham and Tony Purvis note is well established in science fiction literature. Pointing to examples that date back to the nineteenth century and which include *The Strange Case of Dr. Jekyll and Mr. Hyde*, the authors define this type of story thus: "the threat to the self is internal, in the form of self-alienation or splitting of identity, caused by the excessive desire for knowledge, reason or control". (p. 103)[99] *Prisoner* fans may wish to muse on these ideas in order to devise for themselves a satisfactory explanation for the seemingly schizophrenic nature of the hero's personality. The splitting of the self into "good" and "bad" parts is not, however, confined to science fiction. In terms of detective fiction, for example, Matthew Sweet maintains that Professor Moriarty may be interpreted as "the dark side of Holmes to some extent".[100]

Catherine Johnson detects similarities between *The Prisoner* and the original series of *Star Trek*. Specifically, she observes how each show employs a format that is sufficiently fluid to allow experimentation within its narrative structure. The tendency of episodes of *The Prisoner* to draw on themes from various forms of literature, film and television will be discussed later and, in a *Star Trek* connection, Johnson isolates individual instalments that make use of such genres as crime mystery, spy, Western and gangster,[101] although the predominant genre is, of course, science fiction.[102] Three of these forms, in fact, figure very significantly in particular instalments of McGoohan's series. The hybrid nature of *The Prisoner* is so pronounced that *Sci-Fi Chronicles* elects to categorise the programme as "spy-fi" (p. 261) – it is, the book tells us, an espionage thriller that features impossible technologies.[103] If we accept the argument that McGoohan and his fellow writers used *The Prisoner* as means of making their views known on various contemporary issues, there are also clear parallels to be drawn between their thinking and that of *Star Trek*'s Gene Roddenberry, who has recalled, "I realised that by creating a separate world... I could make statements about sex, religion, Vietnam, unions, politics and intercontinental missiles." (p. 385)[104] Similar comments may be made of Rod Serling's work for *The Twilight Zone*. Arlen Schumer refers to to his "meditations on a wide spectrum of philosophic concerns, from the political to the metaphysical", (p. 22)[105] whilst Serling's widow Carol points out how, "through parable and allusion, [Serling] could make social comment and confront issues". (p. 163)[106]

Stevens and Moore see connections between *The Prisoner* and another landmark work of science fiction television – the *Quatermass* saga. Specifically, they comment on how *Quatermass II*

> dealt with paranoia and fear focused around the idea of an alien force taking over British bureaucracy, with the added concern that it was difficult to tell who was working for whom... *Quatermass and the Pit...* is in part about the power of denial and the influence of the darker aspects of the human psyche. (p. 21)[107]

The way in which *The Prisoner* reflected real life 1960s concerns will be discussed at several points in *Unique But Similar*, *Quatermass* creator Nigel Kneale has explained how his serials were also a product of their time. The 1950s, Kneale maintains, is often regarded as a decade of "paranoia" and "perhaps stories like mine were a sort of controlled paranoia – inoculation against the real horrors".[108] For many viewers, such "surrogate terror" was highly effective and the *Quatermass* serials long remained in the memory. The actress and model Twiggy, for example, recalls that whilst watching *Quatermass and the Pit*, "I'd be in my pyjamas, hiding behind the sofa, scared to death. It made a huge impression."[109] Mark Elstob, who at the time of writing, plays Number Six in Big Finish's audio reimagining of *The Prisoner*, sees parallels between McGoohan's role in relation to the original series and Nigel Kneale's with regard to *Quatermass*. For Elstob, *Quatermass* is one of the few shows that "bears the imprimatur of its creator" so obviously as does *The Prisoner*. He continues, "Whoever the leading actors or the directors or producers might have been, one always hears Nigel Kneale's pessimistically intelligent and dramatic voice."[110]

A production that commentators link more frequently with *The Prisoner* is *Sapphire and Steel*. Writing in 2006, Wright suggests that with the possible exception of McGoohan's programme, *Sapphire and Steel* "remains the most perplexing British television science fiction series to date". (p. 192)[111] According to Steven Savile, in presenting conundrums that lacked easy answers, or indeed any answers at all, *Sapphire and Steel* formed "a worthy successor to *The Prisoner*," (p. 87)[112] and *The Ultimate Encyclopedia of Science Fiction* maintains that it aspired to attract a similar kind of cult following through a "make-it-up-as-you-go exercise in stylized surrealism". (p. 152)[113]

Both programmes formed easy targets for critics who expected television drama to follow accepted rules. In exploring how *The Champions* and *Randall and Hopkirk (Deceased)* were received in the late 1960s, Chapman highlights "the inability of British television critics to accept fantasy on its own terms and to insist upon judging it by the criteria of conventional drama". (p. 208)[114] Reactions of derision and dismay were probably particularly inevitable in some quarters to *The Prisoner*, given that, like many episodes of *The Twilight Zone*, it portrayed a world in which anything was possible. *Sapphire and Steel*, meanwhile, presented protagonists whose abilities were ill-defined and, on occasion, able to recover seemingly hopeless situations. It should be stressed, however, that the telefantasy programmes cited were not the first works to ignite a debate as to what constitutes "fair" storytelling. Vanessa Wagstaff and Stephen Poole draw attention to how, as long ago as the mid 1920s, fierce controversy was provoked in this regard by Agatha Christie's early novel *The Murder of Roger Ackroyd*.[115]

For Wright, the equivocal nature of *Sapphire and Steel* stimulates "speculative and interpretive viewing" and "creative discussion and invention". (p. 192)[116] Undoubtedly, both *The Prisoner* and *Sapphire and Steel* are highly original and challenge those watching. Whilst some dismissed the latter as "drivel"[117] and "self-indulgent nonsense", (p. 301)[118] others revelled in the opportunity to "try to comprehend the incomprehensible".[119] *The Prisoner* provoked a similar range of responses at the time and both programmes are more highly acclaimed now than when they were first broadcast. Each was concluded with a final scene which is remembered as particularly enigmatic. Sellers regards the ending of the final *Sapphire and Steel* story, in which the heroes seem to be trapped adrift in space, apparently forever, as controversial and "deliberately ambiguous". (p. 267)[120] It is important, however, to draw a fundamental distinction between the closing moments of the last *Sapphire and Steel* adventure and *Fall Out*. McGoohan did not intend *The Prisoner* to continue after this episode. Indeed, he has gone on record as saying, "The original concept was completely expressed during its television run." (p. 179)[121] In contrast, writing in 1992, the creator of *Sapphire and Steel*, P. J. Hammond, anticipated, "when the Earth is threatened once more, [the protagonists] could be released from their prison to carry on with their assigned task – repairing the holes in time". (p. 4)[122]

Steve O'Brien views *Sapphire and Steel* as "a peculiarly English expression of science fiction". (p. 360)[123] Referring to the inspiration for the series coming from J. B. Priestley's time plays, O'Brien writes, "*An Inspector Calls* provides a pitch-perfect template for this claustrophobic, paranoid melodrama". (p. 360)[124] If we accept the argument that *The Prisoner* effectively satirises the idiosyncrasies and eccentricities of life in and the institutions of Britain, then we may regard the programme as similarly peculiar to our island. I will return to this issue in Chapter Nine. We should be mindful, too, of Sandifer's argument that *The Prisoner*'s core themes amounted to "specific anxieties within British culture: the focus on mind control and social conditioning". (p. 298) For Sandifer, these issues had so little resonance in the US that a programme such as *The Prisoner* would never be made there.[125]

The science fiction/fantasy television films *Artemis 81* and *Red Shift* – the latter an entry in the BBC's much respected *Play for Today* series – were broadcast at around the same time as *Sapphire and Steel* and provoked similar degrees of bafflement among critics. *Red Shift* is disconcertingly episodic, with the action shifting between contrasting settings. Specifically, the story revolves around counterpart characters inhabiting the times of the Romans, the English Civil War and the present respectively, whilst in *Artemis 81*, the events we witness take place in such diverse locations as an alien planet, a North Sea ferry, a ruined tower and an Oxford library. Undoubtedly, the disjointed nature of *Red Shift*'s narratives and the abstract links between them disorientated many viewers, as did the various convolutions and obscurities that permeated the three-hour long *Artemis 81*. Like *The Prisoner* and *Sapphire and Steel*, both productions offered the individual little explicit information with which to work and gave few easy answers to basic questions. Much fell on the viewer to construct their own understanding from what they were watching. It was a challenge that proved too much for some. The *Daily Mail* went so far as to describe *Artemis 81* as "almost incomprehensible" (p, 531),[126] and Hazel Holt believed that *Red Shift*'s "time shifts became a meaningless jumble". (p. 2)[127]

In some instances the ideas of individual *Prisoner* writers provide clear links between McGoohan's programme and subsequent television productions. The influence of *Prisoner* stalwarts Terence Feely and David Tomblin on Gerry Anderson's *UFO* will be discussed in Chapter Eight and it is surely no coincidence that one of the stories presented in Anderson's later series *Space: 1999* which particularly evokes themes associated with *The Prisoner* was also written by Feely. Speaking on *The Prisoner In-depth Tape 6*, Feely explains that, for him, *The Prisoner* was especially concerned with the manipulation of the public. He talks at length about the importance of independent thought and the need for people not to accept the world that is presented to them by others.[128] It is useful to bear in mind this background when considering his second season *Space: 1999* story *The Bringers of Wonder*.

In this unique two-parter, aliens arrive on the Moon and employ telepathic control to convince the Alphans that they are close relatives and friends who are intent on taking them back home to Earth. Through illusory methods, the invaders set about manipulating the humans' actions for their own advantage. Ultimately, their plan involves using the Alphans to blow up the Moon's nuclear waste dumps so that the aliens can feed on the radiation which will be released. This will, of course, destroy the humans. Only one man, the base's commander, John Koenig, sees through the deception and is aware of the aliens' true nature. Parallels with *The Prisoner* are striking. In each case, for the most part a single individual battles against seemingly insurmountable forces. Whilst the hero's adversaries aim to impose a façade that is reassuring and benign, and endeavour to offer an artificial happiness in order to maintain control, he alone is able to look beyond the apparent situation and see what is really happening. He can trust no-one and seems paranoid to all those around him. In *The Bringers of Wonder*, the real enemies are the invading aliens who are determined to condition everyone on the base but Koenig's colleagues cannot be relied upon either, since the aliens' control over them means that they ignore his warnings and, for much of the story, assume he must be mentally ill. The commander is, however, no "superman" in the mould of Number Six. His ability to resist the aliens' illusions stems not from his innate attributes. Rather, it is an unexpected side effect of an electronic "brain massage" treatment that he has received from an Alphan machine at the beginning of the story. Koenig is also dissimilar to Number Six in that he is an authority figure within his community and it is the aliens' telepathic control of his colleagues that results in him having to fight the will of the majority on this occasion. The theme of mass manipulation is evident, too, in *Devil's Planet*. In this late second season episode, the planet Ellna is uninhabitable but the leader of the people on the planet's penal colony, Entra, maintains a pretence in which this knowledge is kept from virtually all the others. Again, it is Koenig who helps them to see what is actually happening.

A sequence of events similar to that which we see in *Bringers of Wonder* emerges in the first season episode *Guardian of Piri*, although here there is no *Prisoner – Space: 1999* authorship link. Scripted by Christopher Penfold, this earlier instalment sees the Alphans invited to spend their lives in a state of eternal happiness on the planet of Piri. Only Koenig realises that, in truth, the Alphans are being offered no more than a living death. In a state of blissful joy, the Moonbase personnel reject his orders, accept the false information presented to them and make plans to leave Alpha for their "new world". Their minds are actually being controlled by the Guardian of Piri, which strives to make the Alphans "perfect" and suitable for the Pirian world. Instructed by The Servant of The Guardian to kill Koenig, his colleagues turn on him like an angry mob. Koenig realises, however, that the original Pirians perished as a result "of total apathy". The planet is now dead and, ultimately, Koenig is able to break the Guardian's hold over his people by destroying The Servant. Like *The Bringers of Wonder* and *Devil's Planet*, *Guardian of Piri* addresses many *Prisoner* themes, notably indoctrination, the importance of non-conformism and the need for freedom of thought. As Robert E. Wood recognises, it has much to say, too, about the nature of man.[129]

Parallels can also be drawn between *The Bringers of Wonder* and Anthony Terpiloff's first season episode *Collision Course*. Here, again, Koenig struggles to convince his colleagues of the wisdom of his arguments when the base is threatened. Thinking that he must be suffering from the hallucinatory and disorientating effects of radiation sickness, even his most trusted friends plot to deceive him. On this occasion, however, they are not victims of an alien plot. They simply cannot accept his instructions, which are based on faith rather than rational explanation. To a certain extent, the roles we see in *The Bringers of Wonder* are reversed in *Collision Course*. In Feely's story, Koenig alone knows that action must be taken against the alien invaders, whilst in *Collision Course*, he understands that the best option lies in doing nothing and it is the other Alphans who favour decisive measures. In both cases, Koenig's stance is eventually vindicated.

Like Feely, the aforementioned David Tomblin was an important figure in the history of *Space: 1999*. Wood points to the "very surrealistic elements" within one of the four episodes he directed – *Another Time, Another Place* (p. 92),[130] whilst John Kenneth Muir highlights the same instalment's "thought-provoking" and "very mysterious" nature. Muir adds that here "answers were intentionally left clouded in order to encourage viewer speculation". (p. 39)[131] All these characteristics are very much associated with *The Prisoner*, too. More specifically, just as Number Six encounters his twin in *The Prisoner*, in *Another Time, Another Place*, we meet various Alphan doppelgängers.

Finally in terms of *Prisoner* – *Space: 1999* connections, it may be difficult for fans of the former to watch the bouncing balls that appear in the latter's episode *The AB Chrysalis* without thinking of Rover. In this case, the spheres are numbered alien voice probes, rather than community enforcers, however. Neil McLean and David Stansfield suggest that since what they call the "White Ball" seen in *The Prisoner* is an "archetype" of the kind postulated by psychologist Carl Jung, "it should recur frequently in one form or another". (p. 27)[132] Readers familiar with the *Space: 1999* instalment may well wonder whether the appearance of the spheres here was inspired by *The Prisoner*, whether in each instance the round shape is being used for a particular symbolic purpose or whether the similarity between the two productions is entirely coincidental.

These issues may also be raised in relation to the *Tomorrow People* story *The Living Skins*, in which sinister alien Ballboids threaten Earth. The weather balloon-like nature of the Ballboids makes resemblances to Rover all the more obvious. In addition, as Marshall notes, "surreal, *Prisoner*-esque balloons" are evident in one of the alien forests we see in *Blake's 7*, (p. 296) specifically in the first season episode *The Web*.[133] Their presence is never explained.

Occasionally, commentators who view *The Prisoner* as an innovator in its particular area identify counterparts in other genres, which, they believe, made comparable attempts to break an established mould. A similar argument is sometimes posited by those seeking to promote such shows. Publicity material that accompanied the DVD release of *The Strange World of Gurney Slade*, for example, declares, "Both firmly of its time and spectacularly ahead of it, [the programme] is to television comedy what *The Prisoner* has become to television drama – brilliantly inventive, startlingly surreal and unlike anything previously seen on television."[134]

It should also be recognised that sources which discuss in turn a series of works on the basis that they share a common theme effectively invite comparison between them simply by covering each under a common heading. In exploring "50 years of cult fantasy and science fiction" television, Savile scrutinises *The Prisoner*, together with *The X-Files* and *Torchwood*, within a chapter devoted to paranoia,[135] and in the *Archive on 4* radio documentary *Very British Dystopias*, *The Prisoner* is analysed alongside such works for television as the 1954 adaptation of *Nineteen Eighty-four*, the *Quatermass* serials, *1990* and the classic *Edge of Darkness*.[136] Although in both Savile's book and the radio programme the featured productions are examined independently, any reader/listener familiar with the works under consideration may well be tempted to draw parallels between them. A comparative attitude of this kind would, in fact, seem a distinct possibility when the individual interacts with any source whose territory is specific and well defined, and where various TV programmes are investigated. Direct comparisons between *The Prisoner* and, in particular, *Nineteen Eighty-four* have, of course, been made for many years. Elaborating on his claim, made in a 1974 essay, that the system of social control in place within The Village "is the trend of the present and the society of the future", Chris R. Tame, recognises that just as *Nineteen Eighty-four* provides a portrayal "of the political essentials of 1948", The Village incorporates fundamental features of own society. (p. 2)[137]

Booker's study of "strange TV" is especially noteworthy. In addressing programmes that "produce a kind of cognitive estrangement that encourages viewers to look at the world in new and different ways, rather than merely act as passive consumers of the television signal and the consumerist messages that it inevitably carries", (p. 2) the author concentrates his attention on *The Twilight Zone, The Prisoner, Twin Peaks* and *The X-Files*. By uniting his coverage of each of these series under the "strange TV" heading, he encourages readers to draw comparisons between them and, in his concluding comments, he recognises the post-modern characteristics of all of them. Specifically, he isolates "fragmentation of narratives and characters, multiplicity in style and genre, and the collapse of traditional categorical boundaries of all kinds". (p. 152)[138]

Let us consider briefly a fundamental relationship between two productions featured in some depth in the *Archive on 4* programme – *The Prisoner* and *Edge of Darkness*. Although the documentary makes no direct connections between them, they are, in fact, linked not only by their dystopian nature but also by the prominence of paranoia within their plots. Paranoia is such a major theme within *The Prisoner* that we will return to it time and time again in *Unique But Similar* and even some of the broadest overviews of the show refer to *The Prisoner*'s preoccupation with this state of mind.[139] For example, in *The Encyclopedia of Science Fiction*'s entry entitled "television", which offers a brief history of the key developments and the productions of significance, Peter Nicholls and John Brosnan introduce their comments on *The Prisoner* with the observation that the show was "equally reliant on evoking total paranoia" as *The Invaders* in the US. (p. 1207)[140] John Caughie, meanwhile, devotes much attention within his study of *Edge of Darkness* to that serial's "paranoid narrative". In particular, he considers how the story demonstrates a classic characteristic of paranoia – "while you have some difficulty identifying precisely who your enemy is, you have even more difficulty working out who your friends are". (p. 82) He goes on to highlight how *Edge of Darkness*'s narrative "conspires to heighten our bafflement, our sense of things out of control leaving deductive reason with no purchase". (p. 88)[141] The viewer's uncertainty is increased by other characteristics noted by Sandifer, namely the lack of exposition that is offered and the careful controls that are imposed on the audience's knowledge and expectations.[142] How often have *Prisoner* fans experienced similar barriers when watching their favourite series?

On some occasions, commentators explore the development of a significant theme by specifying, within certain temporal boundaries, particular works that exhibit it. Although a production of special interest to the reader, such as *The Prisoner*, may lie outside the indicated timeframe, in instances where its territory is clearly embraced by the concept(s) in question, readers may naturally identify for themselves links between the cited productions and the work of major interest to them. For example, in discussing the *Doctor Who* serial

The Sun Makers, Chapman recognises its concern with "individuals being processed by an oppressive, bureaucratic state", and notes that this motif "was a recurring feature of 1970s SF". (p. 129) In his view, the concept informed the dystopian futures depicted in the films *THX 1138*, *Sleeper* and *Logan's Run*.[143] Given that *The Prisoner* was made in the 1960s, it is inevitable that Chapman does not mention the programme, yet no doubt many *Prisoner* fans would be quick to detect similarities between, on one hand, their favourite series and, on the other, the productions referred to by Chapman.[144] Indeed the television version of *Logan's Run* is covered at length in this book.

The Introduction to the first edition of *Unique But Similar* closed with the observation that it is probably true to say that the number of links fans can make between *The Prisoner* and other creative works is limited only by the range of their cultural experience. The appearance of this second edition can be taken as testimony to the accuracy of that claim. At no point during the writing of the first edition was the author confident that he had set down all the appropriate *Prisoner* comparisons that he would ever wish to make. Nevertheless, he could not have envisaged at that point that, within a mere four years, an expanded edition would appear and include another four essays. The temporal scope of the book has not been broadened in any way – it is still concerned with television programmes from the period up to 1987 that share some measure of similarity with McGoohan's series.

References and Notes

1.   Rogers, D. The ITV encyclopedia of adventure. Boxtree: London, 1988.

2.   Sternberg, J. The Prisoner, pioneer without heirs. In: Carrazé, A. and Oswald, H. The Prisoner: A televisionary masterpiece. Virgin: London, 1990, p. 16.

3.   Chapman, J. Saints and Avengers: British adventure series of the 1960s. I. B. Tauris: London, 2002.

4.   Wright, P. British television science fiction. In: Seed, D. (ed.) A companion to science fiction. Blackwell: Oxford, 2005, pp. 289– 305.

5.   Fulton, R. The encyclopedia of TV science fiction. Boxtree: London, 1990.

6.   Short, S. Cult telefantasy series: A critical analysis of The Prisoner, Twin Peaks, The X-Files, Buffy the Vampire Slayer, Lost, Heroes, Doctor Who and Star Trek. McFarland: Jefferson, North Carolina, 2011.

7.   Sternberg, J. op. cit.

8.   Chapman, J. op. cit.

9.   Graham, A. Happy birthday ITV! Radio Times, 22–28 August 2015, pp. 20–25.

10.   Stevens, A. and Moore, F. Fall out: The unofficial and unauthorised guide to The

Prisoner. Telos: Tolworth, 2007.

11. See, for example: Brosnan, J. and Nicholls, P. The Prisoner. In: Clute, J. and Nicholls, P. (eds.) The encyclopedia of science fiction, 2nd ed. Orbit: London, 1993, pp. 962–963; Gregory, C. Be seeing you... Decoding The Prisoner. John Libbey Media: Luton, 1997; Chapman, J. op. cit.; Savile, S. Fantastic TV: 50 years of cult fantasy and science fiction. Plexus: London, 2010.

12. See, for example: Lowry, B. TV review: "Wayward Pines". Variety, 24 April 2015. URL: http://variety.com/2015/tv/reviews/tv-review-wayward-pines-1201478560/# (accessed: 23 February 2017); Knox-Smith, M. Wayward Pines: The Prisoner updated? MikesFilmTalk, 8 June 2015. URL: http://www.mikesfilmtalk.com/2015/06/08/wayward-pines-the-prisoner-updated/ (accessed: 23 February 2017).

13. The Projection Room – The Prisoner Compared. The Unmutual. URL: http://www.theunmutual.co.uk/projection.htm (accessed: 23 February 2017).

14. Nobel, S. and Goldsborough, D. The Prisoner puzzle. Ontario Educational Communications Authority: Toronto, Ontario, 1978.

15. Reproduced in: Langley, R. (ed.) The Prisoner original 60s publicity material. 2012.

16. The Peacemaker DVD Audio Commentary. The Invaders: The Believers box. CBS/Paramount, 2009.

17. Fulton, R. op. cit.

18. Cotter, B. Kolchak: The Night Stalker. In: Clute, J. and Grant, J. (eds.) The encyclopedia of fantasy. Orbit: London, 1997, p. 546.

19. Howe, D. J., Stammers, M. and Walker, S. J. Doctor Who: The eighties. Doctor Who Books: London, 1996.

20. Marshall, R. Subversive champagne: Beyond genre in The Avengers. 2014a.

21. Throughout this book, the name of Jack Gerson's series is written as The Omega Factor, although in the on-screen opening and closing credits of the programme the title is always shown as The Ωmega Factor.

22. The Prisoner: The Official Fact File. De Agostini, 2005–2006.

23. Fulton, R. op. cit.

24. Fairclough, R. (ed.) The Prisoner: The original scripts – Volume 1. Reynolds and Hearn: Richmond, London, 2005.

25. The Prisoner: The Official Fact File. op. cit.

26. Morton, A. The complete directory to science fiction, fantasy and horror television series: A comprehensive guide to the first 50 years 1946 to 1996. Other Worlds Books: Peoria, Illinois, 1997.

27. Langley, R. The Pris6ner from the inside: Plots, scripts, background. Escape, 2010a.

28. Fairclough, R. The Prisoner: The official companion to the classic TV series. Carlton: London, 2002.

29. Stevens, A. and Moore, F. op. cit.

30. Frumerman, C. N. On the trail of The Prisoner: A walking guide to Portmeirion's Prisoner sites. PrizBiz, 2003.
31. Mendlesohn, F. The inter-galactic playground: A critical study of children's and teens' science fiction. McFarland: Jefferson, North Carolina, 2009.
32. Read, T. Mr Benn's little book of life. Arrow: London, 2001.
33. Davis, R. (ed.) Armada sci-fi 1. Armada: London, 1975a; Davis, R. (ed.) Armada sci-fi 2. Armada: London, 1975b; Davis, R. (ed.) Armada sci-fi 3. Armada: London, 1976; Davis, R. (ed.) SF 4. Armada: London, 1977.
34. Parr, C. The south gate sea. In: Davis, R. (ed.) op. cit. 1975b, pp. 22–44.
35. Quoted in: Zicree, M. S. The Twilight Zone companion. Bantam: New York, 1982.
36. Bert Granet Interview. In: Stanyard, S. T. Dimensions behind The Twilight Zone: A backstage tribute to television's groundbreaking series. ECW Press: Toronto, Ontario, 2007, pp. 122–129.
37. Quoted in: Grams Jr., M. The Twilight Zone: Unlocking the door to a television classic. OTR Publishing: Churchvillle, Maryland, 2008.

Given that Serling had to defend himself against charges of plagiarism so frequently, it is ironic that several plot ideas which underpinned Twilight Zone stories would re-emerge in various guises in the years to come. One of the most striking examples can be seen in the graphic novel Switch Face by Jonny Zucker and Kev Hopgood. In both the book and the Twilight Zone story The Four of Us are Dying, an individual who can change his facial appearance at will assumes the look of other people for his own amusement and benefit but the ability ultimately proves his undoing when, having taken on the likeness of a man he sees in a street poster in order to flee from pursuers, he finds himself mistaken for the actual person and is held accountable for that man's crimes. It is entirely possible that Jonny Zucker and George Clayton Johnson – the writer of the short story on which The Four of Us are Dying was based – conceived the two works entirely independently but the similarities between them are inescapable.

38. Nicholls, P. New wave. In: Nicholls, P. (ed.) The encyclopedia of science fiction: An illustrated A to Z. Granada: St. Albans, 1979, pp. 424–425.
39. Ward, M. Out of the Unknown: A guide to the legendary BBC series. Kaleidoscope: Bristol, 2004.

A related Prisoner – Out of the Unknown connection pertains to authorship. Welcome Home was written by Moris Farhi, who also contributed a script to The Prisoner – The Outsider, an ultimately unused submission commissioned in 1966. Readers wishing to see Farhi's Prisoner script in full will find it in: Fairclough, R. (ed.) op. cit., 2005, pp. 433–465. Farhi's recollections of his work on the programme can be heard in: The Prisoner In-depth Tape 5. VHS video cassette. TR 7 Productions: Borehamwood, 1993.

There are also echoes of Fall Out's duality of man theme in the Out of the

Unknown story Deathday. However, whereas in the final episode of The Prisoner Number Six wrestles with the darker side of his personality, in Brian Hayles's Out of the Unknown script a wife killer is troubled by a figure who is ultimately revealed to be a manifestation of his "conscience" that has been created by his own sense of guilt.

Michael Ferguson, who directed the Out of the Unknown episode The Yellow Pill, has made his own connections between this instalment and The Prisoner. In the documentary Return of the Unknown found in the Out of the Unknown DVD box set, Ferguson suggests that in his eyes, the two are united by their surrealism and the theme of "the mind being not quite where it thinks it is".

Links between The Prisoner and Out of the Unknown extend beyond authorship and plot, and into music, too. Just a few years after an extract from Roger Roger's Lunar Landscape had been used in one of the scenes where The President is delivering his speech on revolt in Fall Out, part of the same piece was adopted as the theme music for the fourth season episodes of Out of the Unknown. The full composition can be heard on: Original Music From The Prisoner: Volume Two. CD. Silva Screen, 1991.

40. Anyone wishing to watch This Body is Mine, Welcome Home and Deathday for themselves will find the episodes available on the Out of the Unknown DVD package.
41. Davis, R. (ed.) Space 2. Beaver: London, 1980. Reprint of 1974 work.
42. Javna, J. The best of science fiction TV: The critics' choice from Captain Video to Star Trek, from The Jetsons to Robotech. Titan: London, 1988.
43. McGoohan, P. On the trail of The Prisoner: Roger Goodman talks to Patrick McGoohan. CD. PrizBiz, 2007. Audio recording of 1979 interview.
44. Booth, R. Not a number: Patrick McGoohan – A life. Supernova: Twickenham, 2011.
45. Woodman, B. J. Escaping genre's village: Fluidity and genre mixing in television's The Prisoner. Journal of Popular Culture, 38 (5), August 2005, pp. 939–956.
46. Clute, J. Science fiction: The illustrated encyclopedia. Dorling Kindersley: London, 1995.
47. See, for example: Fulton, R. op. cit.; Clute, J. and Nicholls, P. (eds.) op. cit.; Clute, J. op. cit.; Phillips, M. and Garcia, F. Science fiction television series: Episode guides, histories, and casts and credits for 62 prime time shows, 1959 through 1989. McFarland: Jefferson, North Carolina, 1996; Pringle, D. (ed.) The ultimate encyclopedia of science fiction: The definitive illustrated guide. Carlton: London, 1996; Fane-Saunders, K. (ed.) Radio Times guide to science fiction. BBC Worldwide: London, 2001.
48. Lewis, J. E. and Stempel, P. Cult TV: The essential critical guide. Pavilion Books: London, 1993.
49. Siegel, M. Science fiction and fantasy TV. In: Rose, B. G. (ed.) TV genres: A handbook

and reference guide. Greenwood: Westport, Connecticut, 1985, pp. 91–106.

50. Pringle, D. (ed.) op. cit.

51. Di Fate, V. and Summers, I. Di Fate's catalog of science fiction hardware. Sidgwick and Jackson: London, 1980.

52. Clarke, A. C. Profiles of the future: An inquiry into the limits of the possible, Millennium edition. Indigo: London, 2000.

53. Javna, J. op. cit.

54. Where The Secret Agent Is Whisked Away. In: Goodman, R. (ed.) George Markstein and The Prisoner. pandqmedia: Berwyn, Denbighshire, 2014, pp. 78–95.

55. Rakoff, I. Inside The Prisoner: Radical television and film in the 1960s. Batsford: London, 1998.

56. Booker, M. K. Strange TV: Innovative television series from The Twilight Zone to The X-Files. Greenwood: Westport, Connecticut, 2002.

57. Langley, R. The making of The Prisoner. Escape, 2010b.

58. Gatland, K. and Jefferis, D. The world of the future: Future cities – Homes and living into the 21st century. Usborne: London, 1979.

59. Langley, R. op. cit. 2010b.

60. Zicree, M. S. op. cit.

61. Stableford, B. and Nicholls, P. Definitions of SF. In: Nicholls, P. (ed.) op. cit., pp. 159–161.

62. Zicree, M. S. op. cit.

63. Siegel, M. op. cit.

64. Undermind: The Complete Series. DVD. Network, 2012.

65. Fulton, R. op. cit.

66. Fane-Saunders, K. (ed.) op. cit.

67. Vahimagi, T. TV zone. Starburst, 4 (3) [issue 40], 1981, pp. 54–55.

68. The Prisoner: The Official Fact File. op. cit.

69. Gregory, C. op. cit.

70. Booth, R. op. cit.

71. See, for example: McLean, N. and Stansfield, D. The Prisoner program guide. Ontario Educational Communications Authority: Toronto, Ontario, 1976; White, M. and Ali, J. The official Prisoner companion. Sidgwick and Jackson: London, 1988; Frumerman, C. N. op. cit.

72. Van Hise, J. Sci fi TV: From The Twilight Zone to Deep Space Nine – The authoritative, magnificently opinionated guide to the first fabulous fifty years. HarperPrism: New York, 1993.

73. Hobson, A. Nineteen Eighty-four plus six. The Unmutual, 2008. URL: http://www.theunmutual.co.uk/compares1990.htm (accessed: 23 February 2017).

74. Sellers, R. Cult TV: The golden age of ITC. Plexus: London, 2006.

75. Davy, R. So who was George Markstein? In: Goodman, R. (ed.) op. cit., pp. 20–52.

76. Lewis, J. E. and Stempel, P. op. cit.
77. Britton, W. Spy television. Praeger: Westport, Connecticut, 2004.
78. Miller, T. The Avengers. British Film Institute: London, 1997.
79. Pringle, D. (ed.) op. cit.
80. Humphries-Brooks, L. Foreword. In: Marshall, R. (ed.) Mrs Peel: we're needed: The Technicolor world of Emma Peel – The Avengers on film, Volume 2, 2014b, pp. 9–13.
81. Marshall, R. op. cit. 2014a.
82. Marshall, R. op. cit. 2014a.
83. Cornell, P., Day, M. and Topping, K. The Avengers dossier: The definitive unauthorised guide. Virgin: London, 1998.
84. Britton, W. op. cit.
85. Ginez, B. Review: Too Many Christmas Trees. In: Marshall, R. (ed.) Bright horizons: The monochrome world of Emma Peel – The Avengers on film, Volume 1, 2014c, pp. 81–88.
86. Cornell, P., Day, M. and Topping, K. op. cit.
87. O'Brien, D. SF: UK – How British science fiction changed the world. Reynolds and Hearn: Richmond, London, 2000.
88. Carrazé, A. and Putheaud, J-L. The Avengers companion. Titan: London, 1997.
89. Holliss, R. The Avengers. Starburst, 2 (1) [issue 13], 1979, pp. 12–16.
90. Sandifer, P. TARDIS eruditorum: An unofficial critical history of Doctor Who – Volume 6, The Peter Davison and Colin Baker years. Eruditorum Press, 2015.
91. Pixley, A. The Avengers files. Reynolds and Hearn: Richmond, London, 2004.
92. Clemens, B. Foreword. In: Rogers, D. The complete Avengers. Boxtree: London, 1989, p. 9.
93. Chapman, J. op. cit.
94. Speirs, J. Review: Dead Man's Treasure. In: Marshall, R. (ed.) op. cit. 2014b, pp. 232–244.
95. Miller, T. op. cit.
96. Cartmel, A. Through time: An unauthorised and unofficial history of Doctor Who. Continuum: London, 2005.
97. Interview With Patrick McGoohan. In: Carrazé, A. and Oswald, H. The Prisoner: A televisionary masterpiece. Virgin: London, 1990, pp. 6–8.
98. Carrazé, A. and Oswald, H. op. cit.
99. Thornham, S. and Purvis, T. Television drama: Theories and identities. Palgrave Macmillan: Basingstoke, 2005.
100. The Search for Sherlock Holmes. DVD. Demand DVD, 2014.
101. Johnson, C. Telefantasy. BFI: London, 2005.
102. David Gerrold goes so far as to argue that ten different creative forms are evident in the original series of Star Trek – high comedy, satire, farce, tragedy, psycho-case study, morality fable, soap opera, theology, melodrama and high camp. He

concludes, "Star Trek is the most flexible format for a television series ever to have been postulated for commercial network broadcasting" (see The World of Star Trek (second edition), p. 35).

103. Haley, G. (ed.) Sci-fi chronicles: A visual history of the galaxy's greatest science fiction. Aurum: London, 2014.

104. Quoted in: Fulton, R. op. cit.

105. Schumer, A. Visions from the Twilight Zone. Chronicle: San Francisco, California, 1990.

106. Serling, C. Carol Serling on Rod Serling. In: Schumer, A. op. cit., pp. 162–163.

107. Stevens, A. and Moore, F. op. cit.

108. The Quatermass Memoirs. CD. BBC, 2006.

109. Watchlist: Twiggy. Radio Times. 4–10 October 2014, p. 162.

110. Briggs, N. The Prisoner: A personal view. In: The Prisoner Full Cast Audio Drama: Volume One. Big Finish, 2016.

111. Wright, P. Echoes of discontent: Conservative politics and Sapphire and Steel. In: Cook, J. R. and Wright, P. (eds.) British science fiction television: A hitchhiker's guide. I. B. Tauris: London, 2006, pp. 192–218.

112. Savile, S. op. cit.

113. Pringle, D. (ed.) op. cit.

114. Chapman, J. op. cit.

115. Wagstaff, V, and Poole, S. Agatha Christie: A reader's companion. Aurum: London, 2004.

An Agatha Christie novel that may be more likely to bring to mind themes associated with The Prisoner is The Seven Dials Mystery. In this connection, too, allegations of "unfair" storytelling have been made. The New York Times, for example, adjudged, in a contemporary review, that the author had "rather overstepped the bounds of what should be permitted to a writer of detective stories. She has held out information which the reader should have had." (quoted in: Agatha Christie: A Reader's Companion, p. 54)

Given that a television adaptation of The Seven Dials Mystery was broadcast in 1981 – well within the temporal boundaries of Unique But Similar – the plot of the book is of significant interest here. The television production is largely very faithful to Christie's novel. As in The Prisoner, characters are identified by numbers, rather than by their names. In McGoohan's programme, this allows the true identity of the hero to be concealed from the viewer, and it is not until an advanced stage of the Christie book that we learn the real names of each numbered member of the Seven Dials Club.

The question of Number One's identity is an enigma that exercises the viewer's attention for much of the Prisoner saga, and a similar air of uncertainty surrounds Number Seven in The Seven Dials Mystery. Number One is invariably absent from the day-to-day life of The Village, and Number Seven is not to be seen when the members of the Seven Dials Club are attending to their routine business. Like Number One in The Prisoner, he is literally unmasked in a shocking moment late in the drama. Number Seven is revealed to be a police superintendent already familiar to us and who has appeared in a previous Christie novel – The Secret of Chimneys.

The nature and purpose of those who "run" The Village are, of course, left unclear, and in The Seven Dials Mystery, the intentions of the eponymous group are initially ill-defined, too, although in this case the matter is resolved in the novel's conclusion. The Seven Dials Club would seem at first to be a sinister secret society but we ultimately discover that it is actually concerned with serving the country.

In her Introduction to the 2001 Agatha Christie Signature Edition of The Seven Dials Mystery, Val McDermid explains that, by presenting outlandish protagonists in the story, Christie draws attention to their inherently ridiculous nature. We may make the same comment about the caricatures we meet in The Prisoner. According to Gregory, the Colonel who appears in The Chimes of Big Ben is "something of a 'cartoon' version of a British secret service boss". (see Be Seeing You... Decoding The Prisoner, p. 73)

More fundamentally, McDermid points out how The Seven Dials Mystery is effectively a parody which, despite having "all the ingredients of the classic 1920s thriller", (p. 7) subverts the genre, and we will see in Chapter Eight of Unique But Similar that certain episodes of The Prisoner are pastiches as well – two, in particular, incorporate major elements from the spy and Western genres. If these additions seem somewhat incongruous intrusions, there are also instances in which features of conventional drama are more subtly integrated into the Prisoner narrative. Gregory notes how in A. B. and C., Number Six's break-in to a Village laboratory via a heating system grid gives the episode the apparent air of an action/adventure series, which contrasts with the programme's "subversive attempt to change the parameters of television itself". (Be Seeing You... Decoding The Prisoner, p. 79)

116. Wright, P. op. cit.
117. Nicholls, P. Sapphire and Steel. In: Clute, J. and Nicholls, P. (eds.) op. cit., p. 1048.
118. Clute, J. op. cit.
119. Peel, J. Sapphire and Steel: Time on their hands. Fantasy Empire, Collector's Edition 2, 1983.
120. Sellers, R. op. cit.
121. Talking With McGoohan. In: White, M. and Ali, J. op. cit., pp. 175–181.
122. Hammond, P. J. Sapphire and Steel. Virgin: London, 1992. Reprint, with new introduction, of 1979 work.
123. O'Brien, S. Sapphire and Steel. In: Haley, G. (ed.) op. cit., p. 360.

124. Ibid.

125. Sandifer, P. TARDIS eruditorum: An unofficial critical history of Doctor Who – Volume 3, Jon Pertwee. Eruditorum Press: Danbury, Connecticut, 2013.

126. Quoted in: Fulton, R. op. cit.

127. Quoted in: Rolinson, D. The boundary's undefined: Red Shift. In: viewers' booklet. Red Shift. DVD. British Film Institute, 2014, pp. 1– 4.

128. The Prisoner In-depth Tape 6. VHS video cassette. TR 7 Productions: Borehamwood, 1994.

129. Wood, R. E. Destination Moonbase Alpha – The unofficial and unauthorised guide to Space: 1999. Telos: Prestatyn, 2010.

130. Ibid.

131. Muir, J. K. Exploring Space: 1999 – An episode guide and complete history. McFarland: Jefferson, North Carolina, 1997.

132. McLean, N. and Stansfield, D. op. cit.

133. Marshall, R. Blake's 7: A critical guide to series 1–4. Out There Publications, 2015.

134. Network. The Strange World of Gurney Slade: The complete series, 2011. URL: http://www.networkdvd.net/product_info.php?products_id=1392 (accessed: 11 December 2012).

135. Savile, S. op. cit.

136. Archive On 4: Very British Dystopias. BBC Radio 4. 15 June 2013.

137. Tame, C. R. Different values: An analysis of Patrick McGoohan's The Prisoner. Libertarian Reprints, 1, 1983. Reprint of 1974 work. URL: http://www.libertarian.co.uk/lapubs/libre/libre001.pdf (accessed: 23 February 2017).

138. Booker, M. K. op. cit.

139. See, for example: Brosnan, J. and Nicholls, P. The Prisoner. In: Clute, J. and Nicholls, P. (eds.) op. cit., pp. 962–963.

140. Nicholls, P. and Brosnan, J. Television. In: Clute, J. and Nicholls, P. (eds.) op. cit., pp. 1205–1209.

141. Caughie, J. Edge of Darkness. British Film Institute: London, 2007.

142. Sandifer, P. op. cit. 2015.

143. Chapman, J. Inside the TARDIS: The worlds of Doctor Who. I. B. Tauris: London, 2006.

144. Nevertheless, in issue 27 of In-Vision, Andrew Pixley draws attention to a major difference in the mood within the The Prisoner and The Sun Makers. He observes that in the latter, the atmosphere "is repressive from the word go, unlike the mock gaiety of… the Village of The Prisoner, where the ruling power maintains a façade of satisfaction and harmony". (p. 4)

Other Doctor Who stories that feature the hero's fourth incarnation and which have been linked with The Prisoner by commentators include The Masque of

Mandragora and The Android Invasion. The former's connection is almost entirely restricted to the use of Portmeirion location filming, in this case to represent late 15th century Italy. Prisoner fans may be disappointed when viewing The Masque of Mandragora that more is not seen of some of Portmeirion's most instantly identifiable buildings and architectural features. Lawrence Miles and Tat Wood go so far as to suggest that the Portmeirion we see in The Prisoner is "almost unrecognisable" when we watch the Doctor Who story. (see About Time: The Unauthorized Guide to Doctor Who: 1975–1979 – Seasons 12 to 17, p. 98) This is perhaps not surprising, however, given Richard Bignell's observation that the location filming had "to be very carefully planned and shot to ensure that none of the buildings in other [i.e. non-Renaissance] architectural styles or any other modern features" were evident. (see Doctor Who: On Location, p. 133) It is maybe an indication of the relatively low profile of Portmeirion in the context of the finished serial that whereas many books dealing with The Prisoner feature images of the village on the front, neither of the two covers of the Masque of Mandragora novelisation reproduced in The Target Book – David J. Howe's guide to the Doctor Who book adaptations – depicts any part of Portmeirion at all. Still, Miles and Wood report in the About Time work cited above that in the eyes of some Doctor Who fans, Portmeirion's close association with The Prisoner "ruins" its value as a location for the filming of The Masque of Mandragora. (p. 98) Such a view may, though, have come about only over time. One must remember that when the BBC production team visited Portmeirion in May 1976 the Prisoner cult was nowhere near the size it is today. The Six of One appreciation society had not, in fact, even come into existence by this point.

In Who's Next: An Unofficial and Unauthorised Guide to Doctor Who, meanwhile, Mark Clapham, Eddie Robson and Jim Smith suggest that The Android Invasion strives "to capture the atmosphere of The Prisoner". (p. 198) The authors do not elaborate on their claim, although it would appear that they are alluding to the surrealism and strangeness that arise in a village which, on a superficial level, is highly attractive. In the words of Terrance Dicks's novelisation of the serial, it "looked like the cover-photograph on a 'Holidays in Britain' travel brochure". (p. 15) Yet, neither the village seen in The Android Invasion nor that in The Prisoner is what it seems. The purposes of those who run each place are sinister; key locations are subject to surveillance and important protagonists are placed under analysis. Clapham, Robson and Smith are not alone in being reminded of The Prisoner when watching The Android Invasion. Readers keen to see the comments made by other writers on the similarities are referred to the websites Adventures With the Wife in Space (http://wifeinspace.com/2012/05/the-android-invasion/), The Greenman (http://thesnufkin.blogspot.co.uk/2013/11/top-five-pubs-in-doctor-who.html) and The Doctor Who Ratings Guide (http://www.pagefillers.com/dwrg/andri.htm).

PART B
The Individual Comparisons

CHAPTER ONE
Endless Sunny Days
and Rain-making

This chapter is a revised and expanded version of an essay that originally appeared
in *The Projection Room* section of the website *The Unmutual*.

At first glance the "cult" 1960s series, *The Prisoner*, and the now largely forgotten
serial, *Cloud Burst*, produced in the mid 1970s, appear to share few similarities.
The former was a prime-time drama programme made for a mass audience,
whilst the latter formed one of the stories within *Look and Read*, the long-
running BBC series for schools, the main purpose of which was to instruct
youngsters in the use of the English language, rather than to entertain. This
educational aim is emphasised by the fact that in each of the ten episodes of
Cloud Burst the drama was complemented by a didactic teaching segment that
formed a significant part of the broadcast.

One man fulfilled several important roles in both *The Prisoner* and *Cloud
Burst*. This is particularly true of the former, which is frequently seen, of course,
as the brainchild of Patrick McGoohan. In addition to being executive producer
and star of the show, McGoohan wrote three episodes and directed five.
Furthermore, *The Prisoner* was made by McGoohan's own production company,
Everyman. Chris Gregory refers to the "unique chance" afforded to McGoohan
"to take 'authorial' control over the series and to turn it into a vehicle for his own
very personal vision", (p. 2)[1] and Robert Sellers goes so far as to suggest that
McGoohan's power over the programme was such that he was able to run a
"creative dictatorship" on the set. (p. 127)[2] It is not hard to see why, at the press
conference which launched *The Prisoner* in September 1967, one of the

reporters felt the series could be called *The Pat McGoohan Show*.[3] Some of those involved in the making of *The Prisoner* have expressed similar views. Pat Jackson, who directed four episodes, observes, "Patrick had almost complete total control over it… Without Patrick's vision, *The Prisoner* would never have existed." (pp. 158–159)[4]

Although Richard Carpenter's influence on *Cloud Burst* was less marked and the role of producer Sue Weeks was considerable, his importance should not be underestimated. By the time he wrote *Cloud Burst*, Carpenter already had a proven track record in *Look and Read*, having contributed the earlier serial *The Boy From Space*. He would also write the next, *The King's Dragon*. Perhaps most famous for *Catweazle*, Carpenter would, in time, be responsible, too, for such series as *The Ghosts of Motley Hall* and *Robin of Sherwood*. As well as writing *Cloud Burst*, Carpenter narrated parts of the story and presented the teaching element within each episode. These personal appearances gave him the opportunity to provide viewers with some insight into his thinking when writing the story.

Both *The Prisoner* and *Cloud Burst* can be understood on a range of levels. On the most superficial plane, each can be enjoyed as a tale of action and adventure, with *The Prisoner* following one man's efforts to escape his captors and regain his freedom, and *Cloud Burst* featuring a plot to hold the country to ransom using a fantastic new invention. Closer examination reveals, however, that there are many more themes within the episodes of these programmes. On the grandest scale, *The Prisoner* has often been interpreted as a comment on the relationship between the individual and society, and as a study of the nature of mankind. Although some of the issues tackled by *Cloud Burst* are much less philosophical and esoteric, they are still substantial. Many take the form of contrasts: good and evil, positive and negative applications of science, altruism and terrorism, and loyalty and treachery. The same can be said of a lot of the major themes within *The Prisoner*. Among the "oppositions" isolated by Steven Paul Davies are those of willpower and force, escape and entrapment, and trust and deception. (p. 136)[5] Chris R. Tame, meanwhile, highlights the conflicts of "the Man versus the State, Autonomy and Individualism versus Regimentation and Conformity, [and] the Individual versus the Collective". (p. 2)[6]

Perhaps surprisingly, several of the issues addressed by the productions are, in fact, the same. For example, both may be seen to be concerned with the "duality" of man. In *Fall Out*, the final episode of *The Prisoner*, it is shown that the person in overall charge of The Village in which Number Six is incarcerated is The Prisoner himself. One explanation for this revelation is that the two characters are intended to represent different sides of the same individual. A similar theme may be identified in *Cloud Burst*. The hero, Ram Pandit, wants to use his new invention, a "rain-gun", for the benefit of mankind, specifically to alleviate starvation by bringing rain to the dry land of India, whilst his evil twin brother, Ravi, seeks to exploit the machine as a weapon for his own ends. Again, the two characters may be interpreted as different sides of the same person, especially as actor Renu Setna played both Ram and Ravi. Indeed, in one of the many plot twists, it is implied at the end of the third episode, *Rav 1*, that the theft of a "firing program", which is necessary for the rain-gun to be used, may have been masterminded by Ram himself. The theme of contrasting identities also emerges in the personality of Mrs Green. Ostensibly she is Ram's faithful housekeeper, yet she is ultimately shown to be working with Ravi.

A second thematic similarity between *The Prisoner* and *Cloud Burst* lies in their exploration of the nature of science. As Matthew White and Jaffer Ali,[7] Chris Gregory[8] and Steven Paul Davies[9] have all observed, the use made of technology is a key issue in *The Prisoner*, and in *Cloud Burst*, the matter of how the rain-gun should be employed is central to the entire serial. During his personal appearance in episode seven, *To The Mill!*, Carpenter specifically draws attention to this theme and invites his young viewers to suggest other machines that may be put to "good" and "bad" uses. In an interview reported by Jane Killick, Carpenter has indicated that nuclear energy was foremost in his mind.[10] In *The Prisoner*, the use made of science is perhaps most directly addressed in the episode *Do Not Forsake Me Oh My Darling*. M. Keith Booker points out that here Professor Seltzman's mind transfer machine is, like other advanced technologies in evidence in The Village, shown in a negative light – each is put to sinister use by the authorities for mind control and manipulation.[11] The moral dimension is succinctly encapsulated in the following conversation that takes place between Seltzman, who is being held in The Village, and his captor, Number Two (extract from *The Prisoner: A Televisionary Masterpiece*, p. 164):

SELTZMAN: How [Rutherford] must regret having split the atom.

NUMBER TWO: Yes... almost as bad as splitting the identity of two human beings. Unlike all the king's men, only you can put them together again.

SELTZMAN: Don't rely on it.

NUMBER TWO: Why make this stand now? You must have known what you were doing when you invented the wretched process.

SELTZMAN: Only people like you make it wretched.[12]

A similar dialogue, again involving a villain and a captured scientist, appears in the *To The Mill!* episode of *Cloud Burst*. The following passage is taken from pages 30–31 of the pupil's pamphlet, with the events told from Ravi's perspective:

"Inside my control room, I told Ram my plans.

'You could have been rich if you had worked for me,' I told him.

'Yes, but you wanted me to make new guns and rockets, Ravi. Guns and rockets to make you rich.

I will never work on anything that can kill,' said Ram.

'But that's just what you have done,' I said."[13]

The loss of individual identity is another theme within both productions. In *The Prisoner*, virtually everyone in The Village is referred to simply by a number, and a similar pattern emerges with Ravi's team in *Cloud Burst*. Ravi himself is addressed at various points as "Number One", and Mrs Green as "Number Three". The other member of the team is only ever known as "Number Two". In both productions, numbered badges enable the viewer to identify individual characters. Although in *Cloud Burst* the use of numbers in place of people's names is very limited and is quite different in scale from the situation in *The Prisoner*, where a whole society consists of individuals known solely by numbers, in each case the dehumanising use of numbers is applied to a sinister group which the hero is resisting.

In both *The Prisoner* and *Cloud Burst*, the representation of people via numbers is also a ploy to conceal from viewers the true identities of particular individuals. In the former, we never learn The Prisoner's real name, and in the latter the actual identity of Number Three is not revealed until the closing scene of the final episode. The attempts made to prevent the viewer from learning the truth on occasions lead to a certain awkwardness in both programmes. Gregory notes the "farcical" results that arise in the *Prisoner* episode *Do Not Forsake Me Oh My Darling*. (p. 142)[14] Here, in scenes outside The Village, The Prisoner's fiancée makes inquiries about his whereabouts without ever using his actual name. Similarly, in *Cloud Burst*, the figure with the motorcycle is always shown wearing a crash helmet, even when this is hardly appropriate to the situation. The fact that her face is invariably obscured by a visor in such circumstances does, however, increase the atmosphere of menace. The use of her designation as "Number Three", which eliminates the need for Ravi to refer to her as "Mrs Green", works rather more successfully and is consistent with practices within Ravi's team, as we never learn the real name of Number Two.

Not only do certain general themes emerge across both series; *The Prisoner* and *Cloud Burst* include more specific plot events that are comparable. In both productions, the hero comes face-to-face with his identical double. Robert Fairclough notes how, in the former's *Schizoid Man* episode, Number Six "literally becomes his own worst enemy" in a story based on the "fantasy cliché of the 'evil double'" (p. 54)[15] John Kenneth Muir shows how this scenario has "been a staple of genre TV for decades. Nearly every [major] sci-fi protagonist… has faced this situation at least once." (p. 129) In the period covered by *Unique But Similar*, Muir cites instances in the *Star Trek* episodes *What are Little Girls Made of?*, *The Enemy Within* and *Whom Gods Destroy*, the *Seed of Destruction* instalment of *Space: 1999* and *Ardala's Return*, a first season adventure for *Buck Rogers in the 25th Century*.[16] In *The Schizoid Man* and *Cloud Burst*, one twin impersonates the other. In the former, Curtis attempts to destabilise The Prisoner by pretending to be him, then later Number Six reverses the roles in order to mount an escape attempt, whilst in Richard Carpenter's story, the evil Ravi twice poses as Ram.

In the closing stages of *Cloud Burst* and *The Prisoner*, a villain is unmasked and, on both occasions, the revealed figure is familiar yet entirely unexpected to the first-time viewer. In *The Prisoner*, the person in question is Number One, the identity of whom the hero has been striving to learn throughout the series.[17] In *Cloud Burst*, the true nature of Number Three is rather more incidental. For much of the story, viewers had been encouraged to think of Number Three as simply "the man on the motorbike" and were not led to question the individual's identity further. Ultimately, however, Number Three is shown to be Mrs Green in order to provide a final twist ending.

Both climaxes prompt the viewer to reassess the events that they have witnessed. In *The Prisoner*, we may well consider from a fresh perspective why The Village's authorities have been reluctant to damage Number Six physically and why he often seems to have been treated as a special case. Various commentators argue that another clue of significance has been offered, too. Week after week, during the opening title sequence, The Prisoner demands, "Who is Number One?" On each occasion, he receives the same response – "You are Number Six." Viewers are immediately inclined to assume that his captors are simply being evasive. They react to a question that has been put to them by making an unrelated assertion but we can equally justifiably interpret the reaction as a direct answer – "**You** are, Number Six."[18] Furthermore, *The Oxford Dictionary of English Proverbs* reminds us that in popular parlance "number one" is a term frequently employed to mean oneself.[19]

It is also worth taking a moment to revisit as a whole the events of the *Prisoner* episodes *The Schizoid Man*, *Checkmate* and *Fall Out*. In the third of these, we witness a surreal variation on the conflict between contrasting twins.

With hindsight, the Village authorities' use of a double in *The Schizoid Man* would seem an eerie precursor of what is to come… In *Checkmate*, meanwhile, The Rook betrays The Prisoner after reaching the conclusion that since Number Six demonstrates the air of authority characteristic of the Village guardians, he must himself be a supporter of the establishment. If The Prisoner really is Number One, then, in retrospect, The Rook's assessment is far more accurate than we would have suspected when we first watched the instalment.

By the end of *Cloud Burst*, we know that it was help from Mrs Green that enabled Ravi to steal Ram's plans for the rain-gun, and the housekeeper's ability to turn off Ram's computer despite her claim to be technologically ignorant is seen in a new and sinister light. The revelation also explains why, after Number Three was given instructions to "get rid of those kids" in episode five, *In the Hut*, the first person to arrive on the scene was Mrs Green. We may remember, too, that although Number Three was often seen in conversation with others, on only one occasion did we actually hear the character speak, and even then the voice was distorted because it was heard over a radio. Another clue is reported by the observant Ben Clarke. He notes that actress Anne Ridler, who played both Mrs Green and Number Three, receives a credit in the episodes' closing titles even when the former character has not been seen.[20]

The exposing of the motorcyclist provides the final answer to a series of questions that viewers may ask about who can be trusted in *Cloud Burst*. The trust issue may, of course, be raised in relation to *The Prisoner* as well. It permeates a range of episodes and it is especially apparent in *Arrival*, *The Chimes of Big Ben*, *Many Happy Returns* and *Checkmate*. In *Cloud Burst*, the integrity of several characters is questioned during the ten episodes. Long before the treachery of Mrs Green is revealed, it seems at one point that Ram himself may be in league with the sinister "man on the motorbike" (at the climax of the third instalment, *Rav 1*) and on another occasion, it is suggested that Ram's colleague, Dick Turner, may be the menacing motorcyclist (in the cliffhanger of *In the Hut*). However, these suspicions prove, in time, to be unjustified. There are further similarities in the ways in which the writers of the two productions play with viewers' expectations. In the *Prisoner* episode *The General*, for example, the eponymous character is shown to be a computer and a comparable disclosure is made in the *Cloud Burst* instalment *Ram Pandit*. Here a computer is revealed to be the third member of the research team, whom Ram and Dick keep "imprisoned" in their laboratory.

Parallels can be drawn, too, between *The General* and the *Twilight Zone* episode *The Old Man in the Cave*. In both cases, viewers are led to believe that the titular character is a human mastermind of crucial importance to the community and, initially at least, each is treated by citizens and leaders alike with a reverence that might be reserved for a deity. Eventually, though, they are shown to be no more than electronic tools and both machines are ultimately destroyed as a result of either human ingenuity or a physical battering. A similar fate befalls Scapina in the *New Avengers* story *Complex*. For much of this episode viewers are made to think that Scapina is an enemy master spy but ultimately the name is revealed to apply to a state-of-the-art security building whose nerve centre is an advanced computer. Scapina, we learn, is actually an acronym for Special Computerised Automated Project In North America, and what had been assumed to be Scapina's codename, X 41, is, in fact, simply an identifier for the design plans. In the final moments, New Avenger Purdey sabotages the building by causing a fire that triggers Scapina's sprinkler system and the water, in turn, ruins the electrical circuitry. Whilst, in the *Prisoner* story, The General is an instrument of the Village authorities and merely forms a component within yet another of their schemes, and in *The New Avengers*, Scapina is an espionage device for a rival world power, The Old Man in the Cave is essential to the community's basic survival. In all four productions, the "unmasking" of the machine provides a powerful plot twist. The viewer's surprise at this revelation in the instalments of *The Twilight Zone* and *The Prisoner* is not shared by the community's leader, who has obviously been aware of the truth for some time. In *The General, The Old Man in the Cave* and *Complex*, the unexpected disclosure takes place near the end of the story, whilst in *Cloud Burst* it happens as early as the climax of the second episode.

There is some uncertainty as to the times when *The Prisoner* and *Cloud Burst* are set. It is generally assumed that the former takes place in the present day, although this is never stated explicitly. The ITC press book for the series suggests that the events we witness could be happening "today or tomorrow".[21] Still, the themes within the programme are evidently meant to be highly generic and not tied to a particular period of time. A date on a wall chart (in the *To The Mill!* episode) implies that the events in *Cloud Burst* may be taking place in 1980, some six years after the story was originally broadcast, yet it is possible that the chart is simply referring to a projected situation forecast for 1980. Certainly, there is no dialogue to indicate that *Cloud Burst* is set in the future and overall the environment in which the action takes place is highly characteristic of the mid 1970s. It is, however, unequivocally established that all the events in *Cloud Burst* happen within two days, whereas in *The Prisoner*, it would appear that over a year separates the title character's initial incarceration and his escape from The Village at the end of *Fall Out*.

Both programmes feature futuristic inventions that seem incongruous with their general settings. In *The Prisoner*, these include "Speedlearn" technology, a mind-swapping device, truth machines and hardware that enables a person's dreams to be manipulated and represented as pictures on a viewing screen. In *Cloud Burst*, the invention takes the form of the rain-gun. As Muir recognises, the theme of weather control has fascinated writers of television science fiction for many years.[22] Before *Cloud Burst*, the subject had been addressed in the television series *Flash Gordon* (in the story *The Rains of Death*), *Fireball XL5* (in *The Day the Earth Froze*), *The Avengers* (in *A Surfeit of H_2O*), *Doctor Who* (in *The Moonbase* and *The Seeds of Death*) and *The Invaders* (in *Storm*). Lillian Biermann Wehmeyer notes that in children's literature weather control forms a significant element within Peter Dickinson's novel *The Weathermonger*.[23] This book may well be of particular interest to fans of television science fiction because, together with *Heartsease* and *The Devil's Children*, it formed a trilogy that was adapted as the ten-part BBC serial *The Changes* in the mid 1970s.

The plot of *Cloud Burst* is especially reminiscent of the *Avengers* story as here, too, a new rain-making machine forms a weapon when in the hands of an unscrupulous scientist intent on personal gain. The author's thinking is similar, too. In discussing *A Surfeit of H_2O* as recently as June 2014, scriptwriter Colin Finbow commented how in the episode "a reliable way to create rain [was] like so many of our inventions for good" one that "someone would surely use... for evil ends". (p. 364)[24] The theme of the use of new technology to reduce global famine so prevalent in *Cloud Burst* is also apparent in the *Doctor Who* serial *The Enemy of the World*. Jean-Marc Lofficier explains how, in this Patrick Troughton adventure, an orbital "suncatcher" harnesses solar energy and beams it to barren parts of the Earth in order to transform them into productive arable land.[25] The machine is not, however, featured in the story to any real degree. Whilst there is much futuristic technology in The Village within *The Prisoner*, in *Cloud Burst* it is limited to the rain-gun. In both programmes, other elements of technology are typical of the period in which the drama was made. Indeed, now antiquated computers figure prominently in *The Prisoner* (notably in the episode *The General*) and *Cloud Burst*. Plots to put new technology to sinister use are defeated in both programmes by human ingenuity. In the *Prisoner* story *Do Not Forsake Me Oh My Darling*, the captured scientist, Professor Seltzman, not only uses his mind-swapping machine to return The Prisoner's brain to its correct body but he is also able to exploit his device to effect his own escape. In the conclusion of the final episode of *Cloud Burst*, *Fire the Rockets!*, Jenny's model plane is employed as an improvised missile to sabotage Ravi's rain-gun and foil his scheme to flood the Fens. Much will be made in subsequent chapters of the circularity of *The Prisoner*'s plot. T. J. Worthington notes that

Cloud Burst also exhibits this characteristic since the model plane that is used to bring an end to Ravi's plans effectively "started everything off" – it was a search for the toy by Jenny and Tim that first brought the children into contact with Ram.[26]

Little is revealed of the motivations of particular characters in *The Prisoner* and *Cloud Burst*. Indeed, one of the biggest mysteries within the 17 episodes of *The Prisoner* is why the hero of the series resigned from his top secret post. It is his continual refusal to discuss this matter that results in his long-term imprisonment in The Village. In the same way, in *Cloud Burst* it is never apparent why Mrs Green has betrayed Ram and joined forces with Ravi.

Portrayals of women are generally negative throughout both programmes. Many critics have noted this to be the case in *The Prisoner*. White and Ali write that the "untrustworthiness of women" is a key theme within the series, (p. 21)[27] and Gregory highlights the "fear and suspicion" with which women are treated. (p. 199)[28] Gregory further suggests that females within *The Prisoner* fall into one of four categories: "authority figures", "temptresses", "dupes" or "innocent victims". (p. 205–206)[29] Booker goes so far as to argue that women are typically "Number Six's worst antagonists in the series". (p. 90)[30] Just three females are involved in the plot of *Cloud Burst*, the most prominent of whom is the girl, Jenny. Her mother, Mrs Barber, is mentioned in the third episode, *Ravi 1*, yet never actually appears, and Mrs Green, the only woman seen on-screen, is ultimately revealed to be collaborating with the story's villain. Whereas the adult male characters tend to be scientists, the sole woman is ostensibly a humble housekeeper. Nevertheless, Jenny emerges as a bright and resourceful girl, even though in the early stages of the story she seems less adventurous than her brother, Tim, who of the two is keener to learn more about the house that they notice when they are searching for Jenny's model plane. In *The Signal*, she realises much more quickly than Tim that the man who is apparently Ram Pandit is not all that he appears to be. Furthermore, many of the children's best ideas come from Jenny. In the penultimate episode, *Escape!*, it is she who suggests creating a diversion that she and Tim may use in their attempt to free Ram and Dick Turner but it is Tim who effects it, and in the conclusion of *Cloud Burst*, it is Jenny who thinks of utilising her model plane to sabotage Ravi's scheme.

One area in which major differences emerge between the two productions lies in the involvement of children within the plot. Youngsters are largely absent from *The Prisoner*. In fact, as Fairclough notes, only in the closing moments of the episode *The Girl Who Was Death* do any children appear.[31] Youngsters certainly have a more prominent role within *Cloud Burst*, and this reflects the audience at which the serial was targeted. Nevertheless, it should be recognised that McGoohan has gone on record as saying that, since *The Prisoner* was designed to be a family oriented programme, he intended children to be among his viewers.[32] In *Cloud Burst*, meanwhile, the opportunity is clearly presented for viewers to identify with Jenny and Tim, who are two of the first people viewers meet at the beginning of the opening episode, *Out of Control*. In both the television serial and the pupil's pamphlet, Richard Carpenter uses the children, along with himself, Ravi and Dick Turner, as characters who narrate the story of *Cloud Burst*. Both Jenny and Tim figure significantly in the plot itself. Although the real hero of the tale is Ram, the children play major roles in the action by rescuing him from imprisonment by Ravi and by providing the idea that enables Ravi's plot to be defeated.

The on-screen conclusions of both *The Prisoner* and *Cloud Burst* avoid a neat resolution to the drama and imply that there are further events to come. The whole of the final episode of *The Prisoner* is, of course, highly controversial and open to different interpretations, although it is now widely believed that the way in which the last scene repeats what the viewer has already witnessed implies that the themes of the programme, if not the actual events, will recur. In the same way, in *Cloud Burst*, whilst Ravi's scheme to flood the Fens is thwarted, he evades capture and appears free to commit further crimes in the future. Nevertheless, Richard Carpenter's closing voice-over narration offers a more satisfying conclusion than the on-screen action provides: "And so Ravi had been stopped. No-one knew where he went, and he was never seen again. But because of Jenny and her plane there was no cloud burst. No rain. No floods. The Fens were safe."

Barrington Calia highlights a demonstrative emphasis in the method of acting employed by McGoohan. Specifically, Calia comments that he brings to Number Six's every action a defiant quality.[33] Booker takes a similar view, pointing to the character's theatrical and artificial histrionics, his "exaggerated rolling R's and stentorian proclamations that seem to belong more on the stage than in the real world". (p. 84)[34] Watching *Cloud Bust* at home today, we can detect a degree of exaggeration in the acting in this production, too. Clarke draws attention to how, even at the height of excitement in the serial's climax, characters talk slowly and deliberately. Here, however, the style was determined by pragmatic concerns. Clarke points out that *Look and Read* was intended to be watched by substantial groups of children in large school halls, and it was important that the dialogue was clearly audible to all the viewers.[35]

As the Introduction to *Unique But Similar* has indicated, over the past 25 years, *The Prisoner* has been subjected to minute analysis and has been scrutinised in a wealth of books, articles and video cassettes. The long-running appreciation society *Six of One* exists to ensure that this brief piece of 60s drama is never forgotten. Whereas to this day *The Prisoner* is frequently repeated on television and all 17 episodes have been released on both VHS video cassette and DVD, for over 25 years between the autumn term of 1977 and June 2003 *Cloud Burst* was not broadcast. Until its belated repeat screenings on the digital channel CBBC, there was little opportunity either for the drama to find a new audience or for nostalgic adults who remembered the programme fondly from their primary school days to revisit it. *Cloud Burst* has never been made available on video cassette or DVD, and unlike some of the later *Look and Read* stories, it has not been adapted into a full-length novel. Apart from recordings of the twenty-first century transmissions made by eager fans, the only real lasting reminders of the story are websites devoted to the *Look and Read* programme and the 48-page pupil's pamphlet produced for schools. Surprisingly, mention of *Cloud Burst* is made in the pocket-sized *Rough Guide to Cult TV;* a one sentence synopsis is offered in a short final section on "strange TV shows", (p. 373) although it seems here to be regarded as a standalone drama. There is no indication that it is part of a wider educational series and it is the only *Look and Read* serial featured.[36]

One of the explanations frequently advanced for the continuing popularity of *The Prisoner* is that its themes remain as pertinent today as when the show was made in the 1960s. In particular, Davies draws attention to the modern-day relevance of issues pertaining to constant surveillance and the increasing amounts of administration and bureaucracy in everyday life, both of which were prominent concerns in *The Prisoner.*[37] The series is by no means unique among television programmes, of course, in retaining its topicality today. The original version of *Survivors*, which deals with the aftermath of a situation in which the world's population is decimated by a deadly virus, is similarly durable. Carolyn Seymour starred in the first season of the show and has commented, "It's so relevant now, more than ever… These days, we rely so much on computers for the infrastructure of everything and that would just fall down now without them." She goes on to identify a modern, real world disease comparable to the virus that wreaks such havoc in *Survivors*. "Imagine what it would be like if Ebola came here – that's where *Survivors* is." (p. 18)[38]

Despite the fact that many of today's forty- and fifty-somethings who watched it as youngsters would probably struggle to remember it now, similar comments may be made of *Cloud Burst*. Indeed, the current speed of technological progress increases the importance of issues surrounding the use to which new science and technology are put, and the devastation caused by the ever more familiar floods throughout the world render a "rain-gun" perhaps a more chilling invention now than in the 1970s. Moreover, in today's post-September 11th era, the thought that such a device could be used as a weapon of mass destruction by a group of terrorists appears significantly more credible than 40 years ago.

References and Notes

1. Gregory, C. Be seeing you... Decoding The Prisoner. John Libbey Media: Luton, 1997.
2. Sellers, R. Cult TV: The golden age of ITC. Plexus: London, 2006.
3. Langley, R. The Prisoner 1967 press conference. 2011.

   It is difficult to identify other individuals who have been able to exercise the same degree of creative control over their television series as McGoohan was allowed to exert over The Prisoner. Nevertheless, whilst the level of freedom granted to McGoohan in relation to The Prisoner was undoubtedly far greater than the scope given to Darren McGavin to shape Kolchak: The Night Stalker, McGavin's involvement in Kolchak certainly went far beyond simply starring in and narrating each episode. McGavin is frequently described as the programme's executive producer, although he is not identified as such in the programme's on-screen credits. The titles do indicate, though, that the show was "produced in association" with McGavin's company, Francy Productions, and unit manager Ralph Sariego has recalled how McGavin "wanted to control everything. He wanted to be involved with every aspect of production." (quoted in: Science Fiction Television Series: Episode Guides, Histories, and Casts and Credits for 62 Prime Time Shows, 1959 through 1989, p. 162)

4. Dixon, W. W. All my films are personal: An interview with Pat Jackson. Journal of Popular Film and Television, 39 (4), 2011, pp. 150–161.
5. Davies, S. P. The Prisoner handbook: An unauthorized companion. Boxtree: London, 2002.
6. Tame, C. R. Different values: An analysis of Patrick McGoohan's The Prisoner. Libertarian Reprints, 1, 1983. Reprint of 1974 work. URL: http://www.libertarian.co.uk/lapubs/libre/libre001.pdf (accessed: 23 February 2017).
7. White, M. and Ali, J. The official Prisoner companion. Sidgwick and Jackson: London, 1988.
8. Gregory, C. op. cit.
9. Davies, S. P. op. cit.
10. Killick, J. Richard Carpenter: A Catweazle start. TV Zone, 46, September 1993, pp. 17–19.

11. Booker, M. K. Strange TV: Innovative television series from The Twilight Zone to The X-Files. Greenwood: Westport, Connecticut, 2002.

12. Carrazé, A. and Oswald, H. The Prisoner: A televisionary masterpiece. Virgin: London, 1990.

13. Carpenter, R. Cloud Burst. British Broadcasting Corporation: London, 1974.

14. Gregory, C. op. cit.

15. Fairclough, R. The Prisoner: The official companion to the classic TV series. Carlton: London, 2002.

16. Muir, J. K. Exploring Space: 1999 – An episode guide and complete history. McFarland: Jefferson, North Carolina, 1997.

17. It is well known that when The Prisoner was being made McGoohan took a secretive attitude to how it would be resolved. McGoohan himself admits, "I didn't want it to be overanalyzed like everything else, so I revealed the conclusion no sooner than I had to." (see Talking With McGoohan, The Official Prisoner Companion, p. 181) This lack of openness led to considerable speculation on the part of the production staff. In The Prisoner Investigated Vol. 1, propsman Mickey O'Toole comments that there was a general feeling that The Butler would be shown to be Number One. The ITC Prisoner press book, in fact, suggests this as a distinct plot possibility. (see The Prisoner Original 60s Publicity Material) Nevertheless, the revelation of the villain's actual identity in Fall Out did not come as a shock to everyone. Lewis Greifer, writer of the episode The General, says in The Prisoner In-depth Tape 5 that he expected Number One to be unmasked as either McGoohan himself or a God-like/Freudian figure.

18. See, for example: White, M. and Ali, J. op. cit.; Lewis, J. E. and Stempel, P. Cult TV: The essential critical guide. Pavilion Books: London, 1993; Phillips, M. and Garcia, F. Science fiction television series: Episode guides, histories, and casts and credits for 62 prime time shows, 1959 through 1989. McFarland: Jefferson, North Carolina, 1996; Britton, W. Spy television. Praeger: Westport, Connecticut, 2004.

The claim that, with hindsight, the opening title sequence effectively signposted the series' greatest revelation weeks before Number One was unmasked as The Prisoner himself in Fall Out is not supported by everyone, however. For an alternative view, the reader is referred to: Sandifer, P. TARDIS eruditorum: An unofficial critical history of Doctor Who – Volume 2, Patrick Troughton. 2012, pp. 132–133.

19. Wilson, F. P. (ed.) The Oxford dictionary of English proverbs, 3rd ed. Clarendon Press: Oxford, 1974.

20. Clarke, B. Look and Read: Cloud Burst. Broadcast for Schools.co.uk, 31 December 2011.
URL: http://www.broadcastforschools.co.uk/site/Look_and_Read/Cloud_Burst (accessed: 23 February 2017).

21. Reproduced in: Langley, R. (ed.) The Prisoner original 60s publicity material. 2012.

22. Muir, J. K. A critical history of Doctor Who on television. McFarland: Jefferson, North Carolina, 1999.

23. Wehmeyer, L. B. Images in a crystal ball: World futures in novels for young people. Libraries Unlimited: Littleton, Colorado, 1981.

24. Marshall, R. (ed.) Bright horizons: The monochrome world of Emma Peel – The Avengers on film, Volume 1, 2014.

25. Lofficier, J-M. Doctor Who: The universal databank. Doctor Who Books: London, 1992.

26. Worthington, T. J. Peep-peep, Pandit and 'papers. offthetelly.co.uk, 2009. URL: http://www.offthetelly.co.uk/oldott/www.offthetelly.co.uk/index545b.html?page_id=753 (accessed: 23 February 2017).

27. White, M. and Ali, J. op. cit.

28. Gregory, C. op. cit.

29. Gregory, C. op. cit.

30. Booker, M. K. op. cit.

31. Fairclough, R. op. cit.

32. Talking With McGoohan. In: White, M. and Ali, J. op. cit., pp. 175–181.

33. Ibid.

34. Booker, M. K. op. cit.

35. Clarke, B. op. cit.

36. Simpson, P. (ed.) The rough guide to cult TV: The good, the bad and the strangely compelling. Rough Guides: London, 2002.

37. Davies, S. P. op. cit.

38. Quoted in: Smith, K. Only the strong survive. Vortex, 76, June 2015, pp. 16–18.

CHAPTER TWO
A Tale of
Two Villages

This chapter is a revised and expanded version of an essay that originally appeared in *The Projection Room* section of the website *The Unmutual*.

The previous chapter began by contrasting *The Prisoner* with the *Look and Read* serial *Cloud Burst*. Areas of similarity between the former and *Children of the Stones*, a seven-part HTV serial made for youngsters some ten years later, are more immediately apparent. Indeed, in his review of a DVD release of the programme, Michael S. Gant goes so far as to describe *Children of the Stones* as "*The Prisoner* for tweeners".[1] Nevertheless, any comparison should perhaps begin by acknowledging the most fundamental differences – the shows were not only made for different audiences but at different times and by different television companies and production teams. Only Peter Graham Scott, who produced and directed *Children of the Stones*, and who also directed the *Prisoner* story *The General*, appears to have worked in a significant capacity on both programmes. Still, actors-turned-writers were heavily involved in the development of the two works. Jeremy Burnham, co-creator and co-writer of *Children of the Stones*, had been a noted film and television actor in the 1950s and 1960s and, by the mid 1970s, he had made his mark in writing too, having contributed to such series as *The Avengers* and *Paul Temple*. Co-author Trevor Ray had also initially come to prominence through acting and, although his experience of writing for television was less than that of Burnham, he had worked in a script-editing capacity on *Doctor Who* and *Paul Temple*. Like Ray, Patrick McGoohan, the man who, obviously, had the greatest creative input into

The Prisoner, was hitherto best known for his acting – most specifically his portrayal of John Drake in *Danger Man*. Even as recently as the late 1990s, in fact, Chris Gregory suggested that McGoohan's "reputation as an 'author' rests with *The Prisoner* alone". (p. 197)[2]

McGoohan and Burnham/Ray appear to have been able to exercise a considerable degree of control over the production of their respective programmes. The substantial role played by McGoohan in the making of *The Prisoner* was highlighted in Chapter One, and Gareth Thomas, co-star of *Children of the Stones*, has recalled how Burnham and Ray were heavily involved in the production of the HTV programme. In particular, Thomas has reported their frequent presence during the recording of the episodes and has recollected that very few changes were made to their scripts as they were being filmed.[3]

With regard to structure and plot, there are many similarities between *Children of the Stones* and *The Prisoner*. On a fundamental level, both may be considered serials, yet they are of different kinds. John Tulloch and Manuel Alvarado believe *The Prisoner* to be an "episodic serial". Here, they explain, the viewer "has to see all the episodes encompassed within... to understand fully the narrative structure and closure". (p. ix)[4] The same description may be applied to *Children of the Stones*. However, in the 1960s serial, most of the 17 episodes can be enjoyed as fairly self-contained stories, especially since a résumé of the overall premise is provided as part of the title sequence of most of the instalments. The order in which the episodes should be seen has been the subject of great conjecture over the years,[5] and the fact that there is no universally agreed running order suggests that episodes two to 15 may be watched virtually interchangeably. Such an argument has been cogently expressed by Gregory.[6] In contrast, the later instalments of *Children of the Stones* are not easily understood without seeing the previous parts.

The essentials of the plots of *The Prisoner* and *Children of the Stones* are remarkably alike. In each case, the serial begins with the hero(es) arriving in a village that seems a world in itself, each with its own rites and customs. During the course of the episodes, the main characters learn more about the place and its people. The inhabitants who are not warders can be categorised into two groups – those who have become blissfully happy in the village and live in a trance-like state, and others who are much less at ease. In each village, leadership is provided by a dominating figure who is served by a shadowy butler and lives in some isolation within a building much more splendid than the houses of the other villagers. The leader uses advanced scientific equipment to aid the suppression of the village inhabitants and it soon becomes apparent to the heroes that they are not expected to leave. Rebelling against the artificial happiness imposed on the rest of the village, they resist efforts to "treat" them. The potential value of the protagonists to their communities is recognised and they are offered roles of great importance. After initial, ineffective escape attempts, in the final episode they are successful in leaving their respective villages by road and appear to liberate the other inhabitants, at least temporarily. Still, the overall battle has not been won...

In *The Prisoner* and *Children of the Stones*, the villages are superficially idyllic, with the weather fine and warm seemingly day after day. As Catherine Nemeth Frumerman writes, in The Prisoner's Village "it always seemed to be summertime". (p. 12)[7] Yet, in both places sinister plots are hatched by authority figures, and the inhabitants are reduced to a state of mindless conformity. They are rendered passive and unable to respond for themselves. In *Children of the Stones*, this "world empty of feeling", as it is described in the penultimate episode by one of the heroes, has been the result of a systematic process by the maverick astronomer, Raphael Hendrick, to subjugate all inhabitants of Milbury to his will, a scheme that appears akin to the "instant social conversion" method employed by the authorities in the *Prisoner* story *A Change of Mind*. Indeed, Hendrick's plan "to extract... man's ability to think for himself, the quality that makes him human", as one of his antagonists describes it, closely matches the objectives of the Village authorities in *The Prisoner*. In a similar vein, the way in which the Milbury youngsters are fast-tracked to working with advanced mathematical concepts in *Children of the Stones* is somewhat reminiscent of the "Speedlearn" programme featured in the *Prisoner* instalment *The General*.

In each series, the villagers acknowledge each other in highly idiosyncratic fashion (with "Be seeing you!" in *The Prisoner* and "Happy day!" in *Children of the Stones*). This is testimony not only to the unique nature of each place but also to the lack of individual expression among the inhabitants. In addition, the phrase may be considered a clear indication on the part of the inhabitant that they accept their society's norms. The distinctiveness of each village is further emphasised by other unusual customs. In particular, strange variations are introduced in existing pastimes. In *The Prisoner*, a game of chess with human pieces is played on the village lawn (in *Checkmate*), whilst in *Children of the Stones*, we see a modified morris dance, and a variation on the ancient "clipping the church" ritual is used to welcome newly-treated villagers to the brethren. Even some of the dialogue spoken within one of the serials would appear equally appropriate in the other. For example, in the penultimate instalment, in response to the imposed happiness brought about by Hendrick, the hero of *Children of the Stones* retorts with the *Prisoner*esque soundbite "There can be no happiness without free will."

Nevertheless, key differences emerge in the plots of the two programmes. Although each concentrates primarily on events involving a newcomer or pair of newcomers, the circumstances leading to their arrival in the respective villages are very different. In *Children of the Stones*, astrophysicist Adam Brake and his son, Matthew, come to Milbury voluntarily, in order that the former can undertake research work for Adam's university, whilst in *The Prisoner*, the hero is kidnapped from his home so that representatives of the abductors may learn the reason for his resignation from an important and top secret post. Subsequently, whilst Adam and Matthew become fairly well integrated into the life of the village, with the boy attending the local school and Adam forming close relationships with other inhabitants, especially the museum curator, Margaret, in *The Prisoner*, the new arrival never settles and trusts few fellow residents. Even though an atmosphere of menace is apparent in both villages from the outset, in *Children of the Stones*, it is only gradually that the true extent of the villagers' slavery to Hendrick emerges, whereas in *The Prisoner*, a mood of violence and enforced conformity is evident from the first episode. Furthermore, whilst escape is a key theme within *The Prisoner*, especially in the first half of the saga, in *Children of the Stones*, it is not until the penultimate instalment that Adam and Matthew try to leave Milbury.

The leadership provided by Hendrick is quite different from that of Number Two in *The Prisoner*. The latter is himself merely following the orders of a superior, the largely unseen Number One, but Hendrick appears accountable to nobody. His scheme for control of Milbury is clearly his own and he has gained his power by harnessing the cosmic forces he has discovered. Moreover, unlike Number Two, he is not intent on extracting secrets from others. Apparently viewing himself as a kind of quasi-religious figure, he seems to occupy no official position of outright leadership in Milbury, other than being lord of the manor and a local Justice of the Peace. He is aided only by his butler, Link. Number Two, in contrast, has the might of the authorities behind The Village available to him. He has at his disposal a team of underlings and a wealth of surveillance and security equipment that enable him to maintain order. Both Hendrick and Number Two exploit computer-based technology in order to execute their schemes. Matthew White and Jaffer Ali note how the size of some of this hardware dates the *Prisoner* episode *The General* quite markedly,[8] and a similar criticism may be made of Hendrick's computer in *Children of the Stones*.

The conclusions of *The Prisoner* and *Children of the Stones* are highly enigmatic and leave the viewer with a sense of unease. The ominous closing scene in each production leads to the suspicion that the events which have been witnessed may occur again. In the former, it would appear that The Prisoner has not truly escaped from The Village, and in the HTV serial, whilst the viewer may be confident that Adam and his son are finally free, it seems that the Hendrick character, now in the guise of Sir Joshua Litton, a newcomer to Milbury, may make another attempt to take control of the village and instil "happiness" in all the inhabitants. The impression of recursion is reinforced by the title of the final episode, *Full Circle*. Dialogue in the *Children of the Stones* novelisation theorises that the events of the serial have taken place before and will happen again as part of some "predestined" order. (p. 159)[9]

Several commentators have speculated that some – or even all – of what has been depicted in *The Prisoner* may be understood to be simply a "bad dream",[10] and a similar suggestion may be offered to explain the happenings in *Children of the Stones*, especially since, in the climax of the last instalment, Matthew's question "Did it happen, or didn't it?" draws a non-committal answer from Adam.[11] Around the time that *The Prisoner* was made, other notable television shows also offered stories whose plots may be understood in terms of being dreams. This is true, for example, of the *Twilight Zone* episodes *King Nine Will Not Return*[12] and *I Am the Night – Color Me Black*,[13] the *Doctor Who* serial *The Mind Robber*[14] and the *Space: 1999* instalment *Missing Link*.[15] As in *The Prisoner* and *Children of the Stones*, however, the evidence in support of the dream argument in these instances is by no means conclusive. The dénouement of *King Nine Will Not Return* is especially enigmatic. Initially, it appears that a desert adventure we have witnessed has taken place only in the protagonist's mind but ambiguity is added when sand is found in one of his shoes. The resolution of the *Twilight Zone* episode *The Arrival* also gives rise to different interpretations. It is generally accepted that the events portrayed are no more than a hallucination, yet in both the trailer for the story and his closing narration writer Rod Serling presents an alternative explanation – the plane forming the subject of the drama is a ghostly airborne equivalent of the *Flying Dutchman* ship.[16]

James Chapman maintains that *The Mind Robber*, too, may be "read" in "various ways". (p. 71)[17] Andrew Cartmel feels that rather than seen as a dream, the events depicted may perhaps be regarded as a hallucination resulting from the TARDIS crew inhaling mercury vapour after a malfunction within the ship.[18] In the *Time Shift: Fantasy Sixties* television documentary it is hypothesised that the surrealism of the adventure may have been heavily influenced by the drug culture of the period.[19] This viewpoint is consistent with the frequent use of the word "trippy" in discussions of *The Mind Robber*, and one of the possibilities raised by Chapman is indeed that the drama which unfolds is a psychedelic experience.[20] Although many writers would, no doubt, hesitate before making a definitive pronouncement on what exactly *The Mind Robber* involves, Tat Wood unequivocally labels it "the 'hallucination' story" (p. 104) but even he offers no firm statement on the origin of the illusion.[21]

Various commentators who maintain that the events we witness in *The Mind Robber* and *The Prisoner* amount to no more than dreams have postulated that certain elements may be symbolic of characters who have caused upset or danger to the protagonists in the past. Neil McLean and David Stansfield posit that it may be possible to interpret the Number Two in *Hammer Into Anvil* as "a memory of an unpleasant colleague", (p. 19)[22] although those taking this view may be reading too much into the fact that the same actor – Patrick Cargill – plays Number Two in this episode and had already appeared in *Many Happy Returns* as Thorpe, a senior official in the British intelligence service. As Gregory points out, "there is no evidence to suggest that the two roles are intended to be the same". (p. 118)[23] Paul Cornell, Martin Day and Keith Topping, meanwhile, report that the white robots and tin soldiers which appear in *The Mind Robber*'s Land of Fiction have been thought by some to be the "subconscious representations of the Cybermen and the Quarks" in the minds of The Doctor's companions, Jamie and Zoe. (p. 94)[24] Like *The Prisoner*, *The Mind Robber* has been the subject of criticism from viewers who believe that creative storytelling should be supported by rational explanation. Steve Adamski is especially condemnatory of the frequency with which a particular threat in *The Mind Robber* is neutralised by the main characters simply convincing themselves that, since they are in a Land of Fiction, the being responsible for the danger does not actually exist.[25]

The Prisoner and *Children of the Stones* are both often regarded as works of science fiction. Indeed, there are entries for each in *The Encyclopedia of TV Science Fiction*.[26] Certainly, scientific ideas and SF themes, especially ESP, are prevalent in both but it may be said that each is no more than "borderline" SF and the two programmes actually transcend genre. In the case of *The Prisoner*, such a stance is supported by the fact that, in the episode *Living in Harmony*, the basic scenario is reworked into a Western format. Instances in which SF series have transplanted their heroes into Western settings abound. Over a period of less than 20 years, scenarios of this kind emerged in such diverse programmes as *Fireball XL5* (1875), *Doctor Who* (*The Gunfighters*), *The Time Tunnel* (*Billy the Kid*), *Star Trek* (*Spectre of the Gun*), *Joe 90* (*Lone-handed 90*) and *Man From Atlantis* (*Shoot-out at Land's End*). *The Prisoner*'s use of the Western environment differs considerably from that of these works, however, since, rather than merely providing an unexpected location for another adventure in the range, *Living in Harmony* presents in a new context the concepts inherent in the series' central premise. After listing various elements common to the Western episode and more conventional "Village" instalments, Gregory concludes that *Living in Harmony* "appears to be McGoohan's way of demonstrating to the viewers that *The Prisoner* needs to be 'read' allegorically to be understood, in that its basic situation can be reproduced in a completely different generic setting". (p. 147)[27] For Brian J. Woodman, *Living in Harmony* is an example of how the mixing of genres can take place even within an individual episode of *The Prisoner*, rather than merely across the series as a whole.[28]

Douglas L. Howard suggests that *The Prisoner* may be variously understood to be "science fiction", a "spy thriller", a "subversive political commentary" or "an allegory about the struggle of the individual against the armies of social conformity". (p. 189)[29] This last description could be pertinently applied to *Children of the Stones*, too, since, as the *Radio Times* magazine recalls, the work addresses "issues of individuality and community assimilation". (p. 137)[30] Undoubtedly, like *The Prisoner*, *Children of the Stones* can be interpreted in more ways than one. It may also be deemed to be a serial dealing primarily in mystery, folklore, the supernatural or mysticism. In addition, Thomas has highlighted how the mood of relaxation among the treated villagers is reminiscent of 1960s "hippy culture".[31]

Much of the action in both serials occurs in a small number of stock locations within the featured village. In *The Prisoner*, these include The Green Dome, home to Number Two, Number Six's house and the Stone Boat and its environs, whilst in *Children of the Stones*, the village museum, the cottage in which Adam and Matthew are staying and Hendrick's residence, the stately Highfield House, are similarly important. For all their "fantastic" feel, *The Prisoner* and *Children of the Stones* were both at least partly filmed in real life settings, with villages in Britain effectively doubling for fictitious places. In the former, the North Wales holiday resort of Portmeirion was used as The Village, whilst for the latter, Avebury in Wiltshire was transformed into Milbury. Both locations are responsible for much of the atmosphere and with it the effectiveness of the productions.[32]

Relationships emerge as a major theme in each serial. In *The Prisoner*, the distance that Number Six places between himself and other members of the community emphasises his individuality, and the frequency with which he is betrayed by others establishes The Village as a place where no-one can be trusted. The relationship between Number Six and The Village is clearly central to the whole series, as it is designed to mirror the wider relationship between man and society with which the programme is especially concerned. Many of the relationships in *Children of the Stones* are rather more personal. Most notably, they are those that involve Adam and his son, and Adam and the museum curator, Margaret. Nevertheless, the heroes of both serials steadfastly avoid any romantic entanglements. Thomas has attributed Adam's attitude towards Margaret to the fact that the children's or, in his words, "kidult" nature of the programme prevented his character from developing a sexual relationship with her,[33] and similar concern for his audience at least partly determined McGoohan's principles governing Number Six's sexual conduct. McGoohan has justified the character's behaviour on the grounds that he was aiming to produce a show suitable for family viewing.[34]

Despite the importance of interpersonal relationships in *The Prisoner* and *Children of the Stones*, traditional family structures are entirely absent in both communities. This is perhaps not surprising in *The Prisoner*, given that virtually all The Village's inhabitants would seem to be either "warders", who are responsible for maintaining order in the community, or "inmates" who have been kidnapped and forced to make new lives in The Village. The situation in Milbury is rather more puzzling, however. All the families in evidence are of the single-parent, same-sex variety. Although odd in itself, this situation is especially unusual in view of the fact that the programme was made as far back as 1976 when one-parent families were far less common than they are today. The only family groups that feature in the story at all are Adam and his son, Matthew; Margaret and her daughter, Sandra; the village doctor, Lyle, and his boy, Kevin; and Browning, a farmer, and his son, Jimmo. The dialogue makes clear that Adam and Margaret have been widowed but the fates of the wives of Lyle and Browning are never established. Curiously, no partners of any other characters in the story are seen. The significance of this pattern is not explained, yet it could be that Hendrick allows no Milbury resident to have any companion other than those in his wider brethren.

In each serial, there are obvious opportunities for viewer identification. For years, fans of *The Prisoner* have empathised with Number Six and in the Goodman interview, McGoohan explains how he would like to think that enthusiasts saw in his character elements of rebellion that they recognised in themselves but which they had been unable to show or demonstrate to the extent that they are exhibited by the hero.[35] In *Children of the Stones*, meanwhile, the young viewer is intended to relate to the boy, Matthew, who draws his father into the story. The teamwork between them is a key element within the plot. In fact, *The Rough Guide to Cult TV* suggests that the seriousness with which Adam responds to his son's ideas, some of which appear quite fanciful to the rational academic, may have been a vital part of the programme's popular appeal to youngsters.[36] Stewart Lee sees how many of the issues at the heart of the plot could find resonance with young viewers. Reflecting on his own experience, he comments, "despite its fantastic subject material, *Children of the Stones* seemed to address my own real childhood concerns about conformity, fitting in and an abstract fear of the unknown".[37]

If *Children of the Stones* is understood as a serial whose story is rooted fundamentally in youngsters' real life situations and issues, it is perhaps appropriate to place it in the same category as another popular SF ITV programme for children which ran in the 1970s – *The Tomorrow People*. For Steve O'Brien, this was a series "rich in metaphor". (p. 79)[38] We should note in this context how Elizabeth Adare, one of its principal stars, sees a similarity between the way in which the eponymous youngsters "break out" into the next stage of human evolution and how, in adolescence, real world individuals shed the child state and take their first steps into adulthood.[39] Parallels can also be drawn between the relevance of *Children of the Stones* to Lee's anxieties in terms of "fitting in" and the opinion of *Tomorrow People* creator Roger Price, who wrote or co-wrote all but one of the original 22 stories, that his show "touched the feeling of 'not quite belonging' that many, maybe even most, kids have". (pp. 79–80)[40]

It may be said that *The Prisoner* provided a platform to enable McGoohan to express his personal opinions on a variety of contemporary issues. Robert Fairclough, in fact, goes so far as to describe the programme as "McGoohan's rage against modern society".[41] Notwithstanding *The Tomorrow People*'s science fiction – and even comic book-like – premise, it has been argued that the real life views of Roger Price permeated his show, too. Nicholas Young, who played John, the only Tomorrow Person to remain throughout the eight seasons, feels that in various instances, Price's political prejudices, against authority in particular, were obvious and his attitudes formed strong subtexts of the episodes.[42]

Whilst the sympathies of most of those watching *The Prisoner* are more likely to lie with Number Six than with the Village authorities and we may well take issue with the more brutal tactics of oppression that we witness, it may also be said that if all citizens behaved in a similar way to the hero, society could not exist. This is recognised, in fact, by McGoohan. He notes how, if every man pursued the same aim as Number Six and attempted to be "completely free" or "utterly himself", "society would be overrun by rampant extremists and there would be anarchy". (p. 6)[43] Another contrast within *The Prisoner* is noted by M. Keith Booker – for all our sympathies with Number Six's plight, the audience is "maneuvered into a position of sharing the desire of his captors to discover his secrets". (p. 84)[44] It may be appropriate, then, to see the hero's struggle not in black and white terms but rather as a grey area, and this perspective will be considered further in Chapter Nine, in which *The Prisoner* is compared with *Blake's 7*. Stewart Lee points to an ambivalence in *Children of the Stones* which is essentially similar. The serial would seem, he claims, to be "more complex and ambiguous than perhaps the writers intended. Were we invited to be a little sympathetic to the Druid Hendrick and his attempts to mould a better tomorrow? Were the rationalists leaving the time-locked villagers to their fate really the heroes of the piece?"[45] The appeal of Hendrick is particularly apparent in the *Children of the Stones* novelisation. Here Adam considers Hendrick's charm to be "a good deal more than skin deep" and at one point we are told he "could not help liking the man". (p. 124)[46]

Like *The Prisoner*, today *Children of the Stones* is much admired. Lee describes it as "one of the most extraordinary television series of the 70s".[47] It is an indication of its continuing appeal that, as late as October 2012, BBC Radio 4 broadcast a documentary devoted to what *Radio Times* described as the serial's "enduring impact and legacy". (p. 137)[48] Both *Children of the Stones* and *The Prisoner* have been released on video cassette and DVD more than once, and each has been subjected to further work and updating many years after the making of the original serial. A new version of *The Prisoner* was broadcast in 2009, and in the 2012 radio documentary, Burnham revealed that he was just about to complete work on a *Children of the Stones* sequel, set 25 years later.[49] This follow-up, *Return to the Stones*, was published as a Kindle ebook in November 2012 and in traditional hardback form in July 2013.[50]

References and Notes

1. Gant, M. S. Movies: Children of the Stones. Metroactive, 2010. URL: http://www.metroactive.com/metro/01.21.09/dvd-children-of-the-stones-0903.html (accessed: 23 February 2017).

2. Gregory, C. Be seeing you... Decoding The Prisoner. John Libbey Media: Luton, 1997.

3. Interview With Gareth Thomas. Children of the Stones. DVD. Second Sight, 2002.

4. Tulloch, J. and Alvarado, M. Doctor Who: The unfolding text. Macmillan: London, 1983.

5. The sequencing issue is pursued in such sources as: White, M. and Ali, J. The official Prisoner companion. Sidgwick and Jackson: London, 1988; The Prisoner Inspired. VHS video cassette. TR 7 Productions: Borehamwood, 1992; Hora, M. The Prisoner of Portmeirion, 2nd ed. Number Six Publications, 1995; Gregory, C. op. cit.; Stevens, A. and Moore, F. Fall out: The unofficial and unauthorised guide to The Prisoner. Telos: Tolworth, 2007.

6. Gregory, C. op. cit.

7. Frumerman, C. N. A cooler shade of George Markstein. In: Goodman, R. (ed.) George Markstein and The Prisoner. pandqmedia: Berwyn, Denbighshire, 2014, pp. 10–17.

8. White, M. and Ali, J. op. cit.

9. Burnham, J. and Ray, T. Children of the Stones. Fantom Publishing, 2013. Reprint of 1977 work.

10. Including: Hora, M. op. cit.; Gregory, C. op. cit.; O'Brien, D. SF: UK – How British science fiction changed the world. Reynolds and Hearn: Richmond, London, 2000; Davies, S. P. The Prisoner handbook: An unauthorized companion. Boxtree: London, 2002; Sandifer, P. TARDIS eruditorum: An unofficial critical history of Doctor Who – Volume 2, Patrick Troughton. 2012.

11. Another late 1970s children's programme in which the action is sometimes assumed to consist mainly of dreams is the animated Jamie and the Magic Torch. After retiring to bed for the night, the hero shines his torch on the carpet and finds a gateway to a land in which he experiences various surreal adventures. It is left to the viewer to decide whether the events "really" happen or whether they take place only in Jamie's head.

12. Brode, D. and Serling, C. Rod Serling and The Twilight Zone: The 50th anniversary tribute. Barricade Books: Fort Lee, New Jersey, 2009.

13. Ibid.

14. Cornell, P., Day, M. and Topping, K. Doctor Who: The discontinuity guide. Doctor Who Books: London, 1995; Richards, J. Doctor Who: The legend – 40 years of time travel. BBC: London, 2003; Chapman, J. Inside the TARDIS: The worlds of Doctor Who. I. B. Tauris: London, 2006; Wood, T. and Miles, L. About time: The unauthorized guide to Doctor Who: 1966–1969 – Seasons 4 to 6. Mad Norwegian Press: Des Moines, Iowa, 2006.

It is perhaps worth noting that the events seen in the Doctor Who serial The Deadly Assassin have also been interpreted as a "bad dream". According to Jan Vincent-Rudzki, "What must have happened is that at the end of The Hand of Fear [the previous story] the Doctor was knocked out when the TARDIS took off and had a crazy mixed up nightmare about Gallifrey." (quoted in: Doctor Who: The Television Companion, p. 313) Yet, this view should be seen within the context of the author's scathing assessment of The Deadly Assassin, rather than a serious theory as to the nature of the plot.

15. Wood, R. E. Destination Moonbase Alpha: The unofficial and unauthorised guide to Space: 1999. Telos: Prestatyn, 2010; Ogland, P. (ed.) Space: 1999 – Episode by episode, commentary and analysis by Online Alpha. Lulu Press: Raleigh, North Carolina, 2014.

There are more parallels that can be drawn between this Space: 1999 instalment and The Prisoner. If we dismiss the "dream" theory and accept the interpretation of

John Kenneth Muir in Exploring Space: 1999 – An Episode Guide and Complete History, the story begins with Koenig's "soul" being removed from his body after a spaceship crash and taken to another world. (p. 39) In order to help him adjust to the new environment, the Commander is presented with a replica of familiar and reassuring surroundings, namely his quarters on Moonbase Alpha, whilst he is scrutinised by a host who is intent on acquiring "information". Here an alien anthropologist seeks to learn more about the human species through a series of experiments.

16. Reproduced in: Grams Jr., M. The Twilight Zone: Unlocking the door to a television classic. OTR Publishing: Churchvillle, Maryland, 2008.
17. Chapman, J. op. cit.
18. Cartmel, A. Through time: An unauthorised and unofficial history of Doctor Who. Continuum: London, 2005.
19. Time Shift: Fantasy Sixties. BBC4. 16 April 2005.
20. Chapman, J. op. cit.

The Mind Robber is not the only Doctor Who story from the latter half of the 1960s to be described as "psychedelic". The word has been frequently applied to aspects of The War Games, too. For example, when giving his assessment of this serial in his book Dimensions in Time and Space, Mark Campbell praises the "psychedelic sets". (p. 74) Since The Mind Robber, The War Games and The Prisoner, which is also, of course, often labelled "psychedelic", all date from the same period, it is difficult to avoid the conclusion that they were very much products of their time. For Sandifer, of the two shows – Doctor Who and The Prisoner – it was the former that explored this territory first, however. (see TARDIS Eruditorum: An Unofficial Critical History of Doctor Who – Volume 2, Patrick Troughton)

21. Wood, T. The empire of the senses: Narrative form and point-of-view in Doctor Who. In: Butler, D. (ed.) Time and relative dissertations in space: Critical perspectives on Doctor Who. Manchester University Press: Manchester, 2007, pp. 89–107.

Even if we accept the theory that much of what we witness in The Mind Robber takes place only in the characters' minds, we should appreciate that this was not the first Doctor Who story to incorporate a hallucination element to a significant degree. As early as the first season, The Velvet Web episode of The Keys of Marinus featured an adventure in the City of Morphoton that consisted almost entirely of illusions. We are told initially that the City is home to perhaps the most contented people in the universe and their every need is fulfilled. Not long after The Doctor and his friends arrive, however, it emerges that illusions are being fed to the travellers via a Mesmeron device and somno-discs placed on their foreheads. When Barbara's treatment fails after her disc has become dislodged, she uncovers the deception and is "invited" to see the community's physicians on the pretence that she must be sick. It also becomes apparent that serving girls who wait on the visitors are actually deeply hypnotised. Mind control is a theme common to both The Prisoner and this particular Doctor Who serial and just as the Village authorities exercise complete domination over the citizens, the Brains of Morphoton subjugate all the humans within the City to their will. In both cases, people are manipulated and the real nature of the environment is concealed. In truth, The Village is little more than a prison, whilst the City of Morphoton is filthy and decaying.

22. McLean, N. and Stansfield, D. The Prisoner program guide. Ontario Educational Communications Authority: Toronto, Ontario, 1976.

23. Gregory, C. op. cit.

There are other situations, too, in The Prisoner where the use of the same actor/actress in different episodes can lead to contrasting interpretations. For example, one may take the view that William Lyon Brown plays the same person on three separate occasions in the series. He is seen as the undertaker in the opening title sequence, a shadowy agent in Do Not Forsake Me Oh My Darling and a doctor in Dance of the Dead. Perhaps he is one of The Village's most versatile operatives... The Prisoner: The Official Fact File, however, connects only the first two roles directly, asserting that the undertaker and the agent in Do Not Forsake Me Oh My Darling are one and the same. The Fact File then speculates, "The sinister man also appears to be one of The Village's set of doubles, identical to the Doctor who interrogates the Prisoner in his bedroom before the annual Carnival."

24. Cornell, P., Day, M. and Topping, K. op. cit.

Comparisons can also be drawn between the possible aims of Mind Robber writer Peter Ling and those of The Prisoner's Patrick McGoohan. In particular, each production may be understood as a reaction to a real world situation in the television industry. In The Encyclopedia of TV Science Fiction, Roger Fulton reports that some have suggested that The Prisoner may be regarded as McGoohan's way of "resigning" from his role as secret agent John Drake in Danger Man. The Mind Robber, meanwhile, with its emphasis on the treadmill that results from the constant need to produce new fiction, is viewed by Brian J. Robb as "a satire of Doctor Who's own serialised storytelling, even down to the production-line nature of telling an ongoing story". (see Timeless Adventures: How Doctor Who Conquered TV, pp. 85–86)

25. Bradbury, K. C. (ed.) Portal to infinity: An independent and unauthorized guide to BBC TV's Doctor Who. 1st Books, 2004.

26. Fulton, R. The encyclopedia of TV science fiction. Boxtree: London, 1990.

27. Gregory, C. op. cit.

28. Woodman, B. J. Escaping genre's village: Fluidity and genre mixing in television's The Prisoner. Journal of Popular Culture, 38 (5), August 2005, pp. 939–956.

29. Howard, D. L. The Prisoner. In: Lavery, D. (ed.) The essential cult TV reader. University Press of Kentucky: Lexington, Kentucky, 2010, pp. 189–200.

30. Thursday Radio. Radio Times, 29 September–5 October 2012, pp. 136–137.

31. Interview With Gareth Thomas. op. cit.

32. While it is rare for distinctive real world locations to be so integral to science fiction television productions as Avebury is to Children of the Stones and Portmeirion is to The Prisoner, the HTV serial's use of a circle of standing stones will, no doubt, bring to mind for many Doctor Who fans the Tom Baker adventure The Stones of Blood, which incorporated location footage of Rollright Stones in Oxfordshire.

33. Interview With Gareth Thomas. op. cit.

34. Talking With McGoohan. In: White, M. and Ali, J. op. cit., pp. 175–181.

35. McGoohan, P. On the trail of The Prisoner: Roger Goodman talks to Patrick McGoohan. CD. PrizBiz, 2007. Audio recording of 1979 interview.

36. Simpson, P. (ed.) The rough guide to cult TV: The good, the bad and the strangely compelling. Rough Guides: London, 2002.

37. Happy Days: The Children Of The Stones. BBC Radio 4. 4 October 2012.

38. O'Brien, S. The Tomorrow People. SFX, 239, October 2013, pp. 78–81.

39. Beyond Tomorrow: Interviews With The Cast Of The Tomorrow People. DVD. Fantom Films, 2005.

40. Quoted in: O'Brien, S. op. cit.

41. Fairclough, R. Unique But Similar: The Prisoner Compared – Review. Adventures in time and space, 16 August 2013.
    URL: http://rob-fairclough.blogspot.co.uk/2013/08/unique-but-similar-prisoner-compared.html (accessed: 23 February 2017).

42. The Final Jaunt. The Tomorrow People: The complete series. DVD. Revelation Films, 2006.

43. Interview With Patrick McGoohan. In: Carrazé, A. and Oswald, H. The Prisoner: A televisionary masterpiece. Virgin: London, 1990, pp. 6–8.

44. Booker, M. K. Strange TV: Innovative television series from The Twilight Zone to The X-Files. Greenwood: Westport, Connecticut, 2002.

45. Happy Days: The Children Of The Stones. op. cit.

46. Burnham, J. and Ray, T. op. cit.

47. Happy Days: The Children Of The Stones. op. cit.

48. Thursday Radio. op. cit.

49. Happy Days: The Children Of The Stones. op. cit.

50. There are strong parallels between the final moments of the Children of the Stones television serial and the last page of Jeremy Burnham's sequel. In both cases, a new arrival in Milbury makes his first appearance in the story and is intent on buying a house in the village. His arrival is ominous and would seem to indicate that old battles must be fought once more… The mood of the final part of Return to the Stones may remind us of that prevalent at the end of Fall Out, too – in each instance, just when it would seem that we are about to enjoy a "happy" ending to what has

often been a harrowing tale, a dark edge is introduced by unexpected events that are sinister in their implication.

CHAPTER THREE
Two Perspectives on the Loss of Individual Identity

This chapter is a revised and expanded version of an essay that originally appeared in *The Projection Room* section of the website *The Unmutual.*

The subject of individual identity was explored in a wide range of fantasy and science fiction productions in the late 1960s. Clearly, the issue was of central concern in *The Prisoner,* and the matter was also addressed in a quite different context in the *Doctor Who* serial *The Faceless Ones.* Broadcast in April and May 1967, *The Faceless Ones* was transmitted only months before the opening episode of *The Prisoner* was first shown on UK television. Essentially, it deals with a scheme by aliens to steal the identities of human beings by making duplicate bodies of kidnapped young holiday makers. Beyond the theme of individual identity, however, on cursory examination there may appear to be little commonality in the plots of this serial and *The Prisoner.* Certainly, it seems that no previous author has made any significant comparison of the two. Nevertheless, several writers see parallels between the *Doctor Who* tale and the *Danger Man* episode *Colony Three.* Paul Cornell, Martin Day and Keith Topping feel that the former may have been influenced by the latter but they do not indicate any specific areas of similarity.[1] Meanwhile, Tat Wood and Lawrence Miles report that in both cases "the sleepers are tested on their knowledge of whatever person they're pretending to be". (p. 93)[2] An indirect link between *The Faceless Ones* and *The Prisoner* lies in the fact that a host of commentators make connections between *Colony Three* and *The Prisoner.*[3] In addition, close inspection reveals a surprising number of rather more concrete similarities between Patrick McGoohan's series and the Patrick Troughton *Doctor Who* adventure.

An argument can be made that both *The Faceless Ones* and *The Prisoner* take place in contemporary times, specifically 1960s Earth. Indeed, in the former's last episode the date of the story is confirmed as 20th July 1966. One of the key differences is that *The Faceless Ones* is predominantly set in a real life airport, whilst The Village is presented as a fantasy world far removed from normality. As The Prisoner himself comments warily to Number Twelve in *The General*, "Nothing's impossible in this place." People are seldom treated as individuals with their own characteristics in either The Village or the airport. In the former, such dehumanisation is achieved through the constant use of numbers to represent people and the application of a range of other techniques specifically developed to promote conformity and integration. John Kenneth Muir notes how, in *The Faceless Ones*, the airport setting is particularly appropriate for a story about the loss of individual identity. He muses,

> ... what better place to comment on the dehumanization of the individual than a center for mass transport, where hundreds of people are herded into lines, treated as numbers, and met with disdain and dull indifference by overburdened officials? Who has not felt like just 'a face in the crowd' while standing in line on an escalator or behind a metal detector? (p. 142)[4]

The Village may be regarded as the ultimate manifestation of "Big Brother" society. In the words of the original synopsis created to provide an overview of *The Prisoner*, surveillance in The Village is "constant. Television cameras record every move and activity both indoors and outside. Every type of modern electronic surveillance system is used to keep tabs on everyone."[5] Comparable spying methods are evident in *The Faceless Ones*. Asserting that many plot twists within the serial "involve people seeing things... on TV monitors", Wood and Miles suggest that this serial is "the most surveillance-minded... so far in the series". (p. 87)[6] Philip Sandifer, too, considers surveillance to be "one of the dominant themes of the story". (p. 77)[7]

Although we may think today that the exploration of contemporary concerns surrounding surveillance within the context of such speculative series as *Doctor Who* and *The Prisoner* must have been quite innovative at the time, they were not by any means the first television programmes of their type to tackle the subject. Some years earlier, the *O.B.I.T.* episode of *The Outer Limits* had examined the divisive effects of surveillance in everyday life. Just as *The Prisoner* investigated the tension between the right of the individual to freedom and that of the state to maintain order, *Outer Limits* writer Meyer Dolinsky was intrigued by another societal issue – surveillance may be presented as a means of promoting a free society but it may actually lead to fear, suspicion and witch-hunts of a kind that, in truth, undermine personal freedom.[8] For James Van Hise, any debate about the validity of the intrusion of government surveillance on people's private lives is, however, obscured in *O.B.I.T.* by the benefit that that "the machine involved unmasks a deadly alien in our midst. [The story] thus skirts over the real issue and misdirects us." (p. 41)[9] Whilst it is true that the surveillance equipment does indeed achieve some good in exposing an alien plot to take over the Earth, there can be no doubt that *O.B.I.T.* also unequivocally establishes how the same machinery can lead to distrust and demoralisation.[10] It seems that Dolinsky would return to the theme of surveillance a few years later in the *Invaders* episode *Vikor*, which, according to Mark Phillips and Frank Garcia, he co-wrote under the name Michael Adams.[11] Here the hero tricks the aliens by using one of their own listening devices to provide false information and bring their latest scheme to an end. Less than two years after *O.B.I.T.* was first shown in America, the *Out of the Unknown* instalment *The Dead Past* addressed similar themes in Britain. Again, it is envisioned that the irresistible opportunities for surveillance which are offered by advanced technology may undermine cohesion within society. In this case, the prospect is raised that housewives will spy on their husbands or neighbours, businessmen on their competitors and employers on their workers.

Abduction is a further key theme in *The Prisoner* and *The Faceless Ones*. In the former, the eponymous character is kidnapped apparently because of the information he carries in his head, and in the latter young people are being taken to provide bodies whose duplicates will give identities to members of an alien race that have lost their own in a massive explosion. Questions of trust are also pivotal in both productions. Number Six's attempts to discover who is an inmate like himself and who is a warder form a major plot development which is particularly evident in the *Checkmate* story and, as the aliens attempt to infiltrate Gatwick Airport in *The Faceless Ones*, it is only gradually that The Doctor realises a method of learning who on the airport staff is genuine and who an impostor.

Paranoia is a term that has been used in connection with the plots of each drama. In a broad overview of *The Prisoner*, *The Encyclopedia of Science Fiction* refers to the show's "obsessive evocations of a whole range of fantasies of paranoia", (p. 963)[12] and, explaining their own use of the word in relation to *The Faceless Ones*, David J. Howe, Mark Stammers and Stephen James Walker

highlight how "any character could suddenly be revealed to be a... 'duplicate'".
(p. 93)[13] Paranoia is a theme that was very much in evidence in various other
60s SF television productions, and is especially associated with *The Invaders* in
the US and *Undermind* in Britain. In the penultimate episode of *The Invaders* –
The Pursued – paranoia reaches its peak when even a newspaper delivery boy is
revealed to be an alien agent. *The Prisoner*, however, differs from *The Invaders*,
Undermind and the *Doctor Who* serial since, in McGoohan's series, those who
have infiltrated the society in question and who effectively represent danger to
the hero are supporters of the ruling régime, whereas in the other productions,
their aims are far more subversive.[14] Despite this contrast, a similar mood of
mystery permeates *The Prisoner* and *The Invaders*. As Darryl Cox points out, in
the latter, "you never truly see who the aliens 'are', any more than you find out
who's running the Village".[15]

Games of bluff feature prominently in *The Prisoner* and *The Faceless Ones*.
Such a ruse is central to the plot of *Hammer Into Anvil*, as well as to the
conclusion of *The Schizoid Man*. In the former, The Prisoner seeks to destroy
Number Two in an act of revenge and in the latter he is intent on engineering an
opportunity to escape but in *The Faceless Ones*, The Doctor and the airport
authorities are playing for time in order to give those looking for the missing
humans greater opportunity to conduct their search.

We learn very little in both *The Prisoner* and the *Doctor Who* serial about the
perpetrators of the abductions. The issue of which side runs The Village has long
been the subject of supposition and, as Cox recognises, is never resolved in the
programme. In *The Faceless Ones*, The Doctor terms the alien race
"Chameleons", yet it would seem that this could be a descriptive label rather
than their actual name. As Wood and Miles note, the aliens never speak of
themselves in this way,[16] although the travel firm that provides a cover for their
kidnapping operation is known as "Chameleon Youth Tours" and, in the last
episode, their base is referred to as "Chameleon Headquarters" on several
occasions. Given that the aliens would appear to have taken on their
chameleon-like nature only since their own identities were obliterated in the
explosion, it seems unlikely that the race has always been known as
"Chameleons". None of the individual aliens is ever named and even their
leader is addressed simply as "The Director".[17] This anonymity emphasises the
absence of personal identities. So, too, does the fact that the duplicates lack the
regional accents of the human originals. Viewers do not see the aliens' home
planet and the satellite from which they are directing their operations is, again,
left unnamed.

The Prisoner's messages with regard to the nature of man and the relationship between the individual and society have been debated for years. Rather less attention has been attached to the philosophical arguments underpinning *The Faceless Ones*. Mark Clapham, Eddie Robson and Jim Smith venture some way into this territory by suggesting that the implication of the plot "seems to be that, without a physical form that we can recognise as ourselves, we cease to function". (p. 91)[18] Within *The Prisoner*, such a notion is most apparent in the episode *The Schizoid Man*, in which the Village authorities attempt to alter Number Six's particular characteristics so that he will begin to doubt his sanity, and in *Do Not Forsake Me Oh My Darling* other clear similarities between the *Doctor Who* story and *The Prisoner* emerge. Here, however, through the use of Professor Seltzman's machine, The Prisoner's mind is transplanted into the actual body of another person, rather than merely being accommodated in a duplicate. Still, as Catherine Nemeth Frumerman recognises, twins or clones form a recurring theme in *The Prisoner*. She notes that they can be seen in *Arrival, Free For All, The Schizoid Man* and *Fall Out*.[19] It is an indication of the prevalence of clones/doubles in *Doctor Who* that Justin Richards and Andrew Martin devote some three pages of their *Book of Lists* to instances in the series where such characters are evident. In fact, *The Faceless Ones* forms only one of thirty *Doctor Who* stories cited by the authors that employ such a plot device.[20]

Sue Thornham and Tony Purvis refer to the "deviant" self alongside "the double" when discussing "themes of the self" and "themes of the other" in science fiction. (pp. 103–104)[21] If we amalgamate the "deviant" self and "double" within one broad category, then the overarching construct can be seen to include The Valeyard, who prosecuted The Sixth Doctor in *The Trial of a Time Lord*. In a particularly *Prisoner*-like revelation, The Valeyard is shown, in the final phase of the story, to be the hero's darker side, between his twelfth and thirteenth incarnations. Although when discussing the roots of *The Trial of a Time Lord*, Cornell, Day and Topping do not connect the serial with the revelation surrounding Number One in *Fall Out*, they do detect a theme that is common to the second phase of the same story and the *Prisoner* episode *A Change of Mind*.[22] The authors do not elaborate but given the story's mind transfer theme, it would seem that they may have confused this instalment with *Do Not Forsake Me Oh My Darling*.[23]

The disclosure surrounding The Valeyard's identity somewhat echoes a theory that has been put forward in relation to the climax of the earlier *Doctor Who* story *The Armageddon Factor* – the concluding adventure in the *Key to Time* season. According to David J. Howe and Stephen James Walker, the dénouement "could be interpreted as suggesting that the two Guardians [i.e.

the Black, who is evil, and the White, who is good] are really just two sides of the same individual". (p. 361)[24] It is true that what initially appears to be the White Guardian is seen to metamorphose into the Black, although we may take the view that this is simply because the Black Guardian has been impersonating his White counterpart. The final chapter of Terrance Dicks's novelisation, which is almost entirely faithful to the ending of the television serial, does nothing to dispel the possibility that there is a duality to The Guardian. Here, too, a "white robed, white bearded figure" with a "benign smile" (p. 123) quickly becomes a "leering scowling demon". (p. 125)[25] In addition, a certain ambiguity arises from the fact that in the closing credits of part six of the television version, the being we have been led to believe was the Black Guardian is identified merely as "The Guardian". In truth, however, a **range** of questions emerges from the resolution of *The Armageddon Factor*. One of the most fundamental is whether the White Guardian even exists.[26]

Colin Gordon and Wanda Ventham appear in both *The Faceless Ones* and *The Prisoner*. Whilst Ventham has a relatively minor role in the latter's episode *It's Your Funeral*, Colin Gordon plays major parts in *The Prisoner* and *The Faceless Ones*. In each instance, he is an autocratic leader who shows little humour or even tolerance of others. We do not learn his name in either *The Faceless Ones* or *The Prisoner*. In the *Doctor Who* story, he portrays the manager of Gatwick Airport and is usually referred to simply as "The Commandant". If we assume that The Village in *The Prisoner* represents the ultimate bureaucratic society, then by extension, Number Two may be considered the ultimate bureaucrat, and a similar label can be attached to the airport Commandant, who frequently pronounces to others on matters involving security, procedures and regulations.[27] In a moment which, with hindsight, can be viewed with some irony given his later appearances as Number Two in *The Prisoner*, in the opening instalment of *The Faceless Ones* one of the airport staff refers to him as "Number One". Since for much of the *Prisoner* episode *A. B. and C.* the Number Two played by Gordon is under pressure from an unseen superior whom viewers are led to assume must be Number One, this reference is particularly humorous, albeit unintentionally. Even when The Commandant introduces himself to characters he has not previously met, he never reveals his actual name and this serves to reinforce the mood of anonymity within the airport that has been highlighted by Muir. Perhaps the conclusion to be drawn here is that our world is not as dissimilar to that of the Chameleons as we may wish to think. Nevertheless, in an apparent in-joke centring on the identity of the actor, in Terrance Dicks's novelisation The Commandant is given the name Charles Gordon.[28]

Anonymity does not extend only to the airport manager and the aliens in *The Faceless Ones*. The real name of the eponymous character in *Doctor Who* is, of course, one of the show's ongoing enigmas,[29] Indeed, it is one of 14 "unanswerable questions" pertaining to the series that are posed by Jacqueline Rayner in *Doctor Who: The Official Quiz Book*. (p. 371)[30] On several occasions, though, the hero assumes the alias Dr John Smith. Jean-Marc Lofficier lists seven different stories during the Second and Third Doctor eras in which the Time Lord refers to himself in this way.[31] Similarly, the hero of *The Prisoner* introduces himself as Peter Smith on meeting Mrs Butterworth in the episode *Many Happy Returns* but few viewers take this name seriously and debates over whether he is intended to be John Drake, from *Danger Man*, rage.[32] Roger Langley, in fact, notes with some irony that during the course of the series viewers find out more about The Village than they do about Number Six.[33]

It is perhaps difficult from our modern day, twenty-first century perspective to appreciate the true extent to which The Doctor was a figure of mystery in 1967. In order to gain some sense of the context of the time, we should remind ourselves that it was not until two years later that major revelations surrounding the Time Lords and The Doctor's departure from his home planet would emerge in Patrick Troughton's final adventure. As Wood writes, "For the first few years, until *The War Games*, the Doctor was as mysterious as any world visited." (p. 104)[34]

The durations of *The Prisoner* and the *Doctor Who* serial in terms of their numbers of episodes are often the subject of comment. McGoohan has indicated more than once that he would have liked to have produced only seven instalments of *The Prisoner*,[35] and *The Faceless Ones* has been criticised by writers such as Howe[36] and Clapham, Robson and Smith[37] for being overlong. Undoubtedly, the dénouements of both productions fell short of many viewers' expectations. Dave Rogers reports, "During and immediately after *Fall Out* had been transmitted, the ATV duty officer logged well over 150 calls from a confused public". (p. 138)[38] Even one of the *Prisoner* directors, Peter Graham Scott, admits that he found *Fall Out* "a bit of a mess" and suggests that McGoohan used its intellectual and unconventional nature to exact "revenge" on Lew Grade, the Head of ATV, who, Scott claims, had pressurised McGoohan to an extreme degree in his work. Faced with such a bizarre conclusion, Grade would surely find it difficult to sell the series.[39] For some, the sixth episode of *The Faceless Ones* was also an anti-climax. In an ending that Mark Campbell describes as "lame", (p. 49)[40] the serial concludes with the aliens resigned to living their lives without individual identities and The Doctor making only a vague offer to help their scientists.

In the time straight after the original transmission of the two productions, neither received any great popular acclaim. Robert Fairclough refers to the "lukewarm reaction" with which *The Prisoner* met, (p. 523)[41] and for many years, *The Faceless Ones* attracted little attention. Although the serial was viewed by an average audience of 7.38 million, a figure that places it comfortably in the top half of the Patrick Troughton *Doctor Who* serials in terms of viewing statistics,[42] the W. H. Allen novelisation, which in 2000 David J. Howe and Arnold T. Blumberg found to be the sole item of merchandise associated with this particular story,[43] did not appear until December 1986, almost 20 years after the serial was broadcast. Moreover, in a *DWB* poll of *Doctor Who* fans carried out in 1991, *The Faceless Ones* failed to appear at all in a ranked list of the programme's leading 133 serials.[44] Nevertheless, both dramas have been the subject of considerable interest in the twenty-first century. Not only has *The Prisoner* been examined in a detailed partworks production[45] and a range of new books on the series has been published in the last 15 years[46] but, in 2005, the series attained fifth position in an *SFX* poll to find the top 50 greatest UK SF and fantasy television shows.[47] It is an measure of how far attitudes have shifted over time that whilst James Chapman lauds the influence on popular television of *Danger Man*, which in his words "turned the secret agent adventure series into a prominent vehicle for the economic and cultural export of Britishness" (p. 51),[48] in 2015, *The Prisoner* appeared on a *Radio Times* list of 60 memorable ITV shows, whereas *Danger Man* was not included.[49]

The Faceless Ones, too, has undergone something of a critical reappraisal. Unlike *The Prisoner*, the serial no longer exists in its entirety in the archives. Still, in 2002, all six parts were released in audio form on compact disc. In the following year, the two surviving episodes appeared on VHS video cassette. Reviews of *The Faceless Ones* from around this time onwards have generally been complimentary. Campbell, for example, awards the serial a rating of 80%, adjudging the script to be "ambitious" and the production itself "well-made". (p. 49)[50] In a further generally positive assessment, Clapham, Robson and Smith describe *The Faceless Ones* as "a hugely impressive attempt to stretch the series' format", (p. 91)[51] and Keith Bradbury even goes so far as to urge his readers, "Don't miss this one!" (p. 86)[52] More recently, in a poll conducted by the *Doctor Who Magazine* in 2014, the serial registered a higher overall position than such critically acclaimed adventures as *The Awakening*, *Black Orchid* and *The Celestial Toymaker*.[53]

References and Notes

1. Cornell, P., Day, M. and Topping, K. Doctor Who: The discontinuity guide. Doctor Who Books: London, 1995.

    It is something of an oddity that, although Cornell, Day and Topping make no direct reference to The Prisoner when discussing The Faceless Ones, despite indicating that there are links between the Doctor Who serial and Colony Three, the same authors do highlight how the story that immediately preceded The Faceless Ones, namely The Macra Terror, "foreshadows a lot of [The Prisoner's] imagery". (p. 73) Cornell, Day and Topping also draw attention to the fact that this serial's writer, Ian Stuart Black, "was one of the creators of Danger Man and heard Patrick McGoohan's ideas on a number of occasions". (p. 73) The Prisoner – Macra Terror link is pursued by Tat Wood and Lawrence Miles, too. They write ruefully, "It's often been noted that [The Macra Terror] would probably have a better reputation if ITC hadn't investigated the same themes for fourteen hours of screen-time and with a much bigger budget later on in the same year. But the existence of The Prisoner at least demonstrates that Ian Stuart Black was tapping into something which worried a lot of people". (see About Time: The Unauthorized Guide to Doctor Who: 1966–1969 – Seasons 4 to 6, p. 84) Writing in Doctor Who: The Television Companion, David J. Howe and Stephen James Walker point to the fact some commentators see parallels between The Macra Terror and the works of Franz Kafka and George Orwell in that all are concerned with the themes of indoctrination, propaganda and unquestioning obedience to authority. These are also, of course, areas that are very much associated with The Prisoner. Other more specific links with The Macra Terror emerge, too; menace lurks behind a façade of gaiety, and real control of the community that is depicted lies in an unexpected source. Whilst many of the published comparisons of the two productions are found in books devoted to Doctor Who, one of the most insightful observations comes from Prisoner expert Robert Fairclough. In his Adventures in Time and Space website (http://rob-fairclough.blogspot.co.uk/2013/08/unique-but-similar-prisoner-compared.html), he notes, "the Doctor and friends expose the oppressive forces behind a holiday camp-type Earth colony, complete with parades, slogans, chirpy radio jingles and a corrective hospital". By highlighting these elements, Fairclough ensures that similarities between The Macra Terror and The Prisoner are obvious to his readers.

    In his biography of Patrick McGoohan, Rupert Booth also draws attention to "a possible cross-pollination of ideas" in relation to McGoohan and Black, and writes that the "thematic similarity [between the two productions] is startling". (p. 148) He identifies, for example, how Number Six in The Prisoner and The Doctor in The Macra Terror play similar roles – both are disharmonious rebels intent on ending an oppressive regime and freeing others. They question what they are told and neither follows instructions blindly. (see Not a Number: Patrick McGoohan – A Life)

    In volume two of TARDIS Eruditorum: An Unofficial Critical History of Doctor

Who, Philip Sandifer addresses the Prisoner – Macra Terror link, too. Although he goes so far as to suggest that the first twenty minutes of Arrival, which see the hero exploring what would appear to be a holiday camp, seem "largely like a remake of The Macra Terror", (p. 133) he argues that the Doctor Who serial "was made too late to have an influence on The Prisoner". (p. 134) On the contrary, in fact, Sandifer postulates that it was Ian Stuart Black's thinking that was affected by hearing about the production of The Prisoner. Sandifer also points to the surrealism associated with the "giant crabs in a holiday camp" scenario prevalent in The Macra Terror. (p. 322) The Prisoner's forays into surrealism are, of course, well acknowledged, and the contrast within The Macra Terror's central premise would seem to meet the criterion which Prisoner writer Terence Feely believes must be satisfied by surrealist work – it juxtaposes two entirely disparate objects or concepts that are never normally found together. (see The Prisoner In-depth Tape 6)

Sandifer briefly links The Prisoner and a wide range of other Doctor Who stories. In this connection, he notes how both the Prisoner instalment Living in Harmony and the Doctor Who adventure The Gunfighters combine classic British-style drama and the American Western, and goes on to highlight, in relation to The Prisoner, the plot themes of The Rescue, the "absurd presentationalist techniques" of The Web Planet, the original conception of The Celestial Toymaker and the "postmodern narrative techniques" of The Chase. (p. 135) Although all these serials are from the era of the First Doctor, Sandifer writes how another Patrick Troughton adventure – The Enemy of the World – can be compared to The Prisoner in that it portrays "a Village-like structure" within a "James Bond"-style story. (p. 144) As in The Prisoner's Village, fundamental truths are concealed from the citizens.

Doctor Who viewers would witness deception on a comparable scale six years later in the adventure Invasion of the Dinosaurs. In this instance, a large group of people are made to believe that they are en route to another planet in a spaceship, whereas the craft is actually merely a mock-up and they will instead be travelling back to Earth's past via a time machine. This serial's treatment of themes such as propaganda, brainwashing (in the guise of "re-education"), rebellion against the norm, paranoia and personal betrayal will also be of interest to Prisoner fans. Just as Number Six learns to trust no-one, in the words of Cornell, Day and Topping, there are parts of Invasion of the Dinosaurs "when it seems that almost everybody's a traitor". (see Doctor Who: The Discontinuity Guide, p. 160) Furthermore, in two different scenes, the villains of the story learn of The Doctor's presence in key locations through the use of surveillance devices. In the most Prisoneresque moment of the serial, after The Doctor and his companion Sarah have been arrested for looting, they are brought before a military representative and are addressed solely by their identification numbers. The Doctor responds by reminding the soldier, "We do have names, you know."

One of the traitors in Invasion of the Dinosaurs is played by Noel Johnson, who, some eight years earlier, had taken on a significant role in the Out of the Unknown story Thirteen to Centaurus, the plot of which bears some striking similarities to the later Doctor Who serial. In this instalment, the authorities exercise a high degree of surveillance over the crew of what, again, initially seems to be a spaceship on a journey to another planet. The apparent travellers are subjected to propaganda and conditioning to ensure that they remain content during what they believe will be a long voyage. It eventually emerges, however, that the journey is really no more than a charade and the spaceship is a mock-up. As in The Prisoner, while most of the people are ignorant of the true reality, an intelligent independent thinker soon begins asking inconvenient questions. Scheming and manipulative himself, he evades conditioning and ultimately turns the tables on the authorities.

2. Wood, T. and Miles, L. About time: The unauthorized guide to Doctor Who, 1966–1969, seasons 4 to 6. Mad Norwegian Press: Des Moines, Iowa, 2006.

3. See, for example: Lewis, J. E. and Stempel, P. Cult TV: The essential critical guide. Pavilion Books: London, 1993; Fairclough, R. The Prisoner: The official companion to the classic TV series. Carlton: London, 2002; Stevens, A. and Moore, F. Fall out: The unofficial and unauthorised guide to The Prisoner. Telos: Tolworth, 2007; Howard, D. L. The Prisoner. In: Lavery, D. (ed.) The essential cult TV reader. University Press of Kentucky: Lexington, Kentucky, 2010, pp. 189–200; Short, S. Cult telefantasy series: A critical analysis of The Prisoner, Twin Peaks, The X-Files, Buffy the Vampire Slayer, Lost, Heroes, Doctor Who and Star Trek. McFarland: Jefferson, North Carolina, 2011.

4. Muir, J. K. A critical history of Doctor Who on television. McFarland: Jefferson, North Carolina, 1999.

5. Reproduced in: Langley, R. (ed.) The Prisoner original 60s publicity material. 2012.

6. Wood, T. and Miles, L. op. cit.

7. Sandifer, P. TARDIS eruditorum: An unofficial critical history of Doctor Who – Volume 2, Patrick Troughton. 2012.

8. Schow, D. J. and Frentzen. J. The Outer Limits: The official companion. Ace: New York, 1986.

9. Van Hise, J. Sci fi TV: From The Twilight Zone to Deep Space Nine – The authoritative, magnificently opinionated guide to the first fabulous fifty years. HarperPrism: New York, 1993.

10. As the second edition of Unique But Similar was in preparation, O.B.I.T. attracted a new wave of attention. With statements made in the Snowden case revealing a higher degree of intrusive US government surveillance than many American citizens thought possible, various commentators noted the prescience of this particular Outer Limits episode. See, for example: O.B.I.T.: A Warning From The Past. Occupy Hobart News, 4 November 2013. URL: http://www.occupy-hobart.org/obit (accessed: 15 May 2014); Gizzi, J. Libertarians: Snowden debate foretold 50 years ago in "Outer Limits" episode. Newsmax, 25 December 2013. URL: http://www.newsmax.com/Newsfront/snowden-libertarians-outer-limits-obit/2013/12/25/id/543772/ (accessed: 23 Fenruary 2017).

11. Phillips, M. and Garcia, F. Science fiction television series: Episode guides, histories, and casts and credits for 62 prime time shows, 1959 through 1989. McFarland:

Jefferson, North Carolina, 1996

12. Brosnan, J. and Nicholls, P. The Prisoner. In: Clute, J. and Nicholls, P. (eds.) The encyclopedia of science fiction, 2nd ed. Orbit: London, 1993, pp. 962–963.

13. Howe, D. J., Stammers, M. and Walker, S. J. Doctor Who: The sixties. Doctor Who Books: London, 1992.

14. Not only is the strategy of infiltration common to the aliens in The Invaders and the Village authorities in The Prisoner. In The Experiment, for example, the former also employ against their adversaries machines designed to impose their will on others and treatments to suppress their victims' memories. We see the use of drugs and/or processes that inflict hallucinations in The Innocent and Dark Outpost; in Quantity: Unknown, an alien duplicitously poses as an ally; The Invaders seek to condition human behaviour in The Possessed; dream manipulation figures significantly in The Pit. Perhaps most strikingly, in The Leeches, the aliens kidnap important men and drain their brains of information.

15. Cox, D. Reviews & ratings for The Invaders: Edge of the 60's. IMDb, 9 August 2001. URL: http://www.imdb.com/title/tt0061265/reviews-3 (accessed: 23 February 2017).

16. Wood, T. and Miles, L. op. cit.

17. Fans of The Invaders will, no doubt, identify parallels between this situation and how in the episode The Ransom the important alien whom David Vincent takes prisoner is referred to by another of his kind as simply "The Leader". Curiously, when the protagonist apparently returns in the later episode The Peacemaker Vincent suddenly begins referring to him as Ryder, although at no point in the story is this name used by any of the invaders. It would certainly seem that the Leader in the earlier episode and Ryder in the later are intended to be the same character; on seeing Vincent in The Peacemaker The Leader alludes to a previous encounter between them and in a subsequent scene Vincent refers to this event, too. One wonders whether since the alien is played on both occasions by Alfred Ryder, the name that is bestowed upon him in The Peacemaker was a result of mere convenience.

18. Clapham, M., Robson, E. and Smith, J. Who's next: An unofficial and unauthorised guide to Doctor Who. Virgin: London, 2005.

19. Frumerman, C. N. On the trail of The Prisoner: A walking guide to Portmeirion's Prisoner sites. PrizBiz, 2003.

20. Richards, J. and Martin, A. Doctor Who: The book of lists – The Doctor Who trivia buff's essential companion. BBC: London, 1997.

21. Thornham, S. and Purvis, T. Television drama: Theories and identities. Palgrave Macmillan: Basingstoke, 2005.

22. Cornell, P., Day, M. and Topping, K. op. cit.

23. Cornell, Day and Topping are not the first to be under the misapprehension that the events we witness in Do Not Forsake Me Oh My Darling take place in A Change of Mind. It was pointed out in the Introduction that Richard Meyers – who was writing some fourteen years before Cornell, Day and Topping – makes the same

error when seeking to explain the reasons for The Prisoner's resignation. It is easy to understand how such a mistake can be made. Elaborating on his assertion that many Prisoner episodes "have the wrong titles", Jonathan Morris goes so far as to suggest that "A Change of Mind" would reflect much more accurately the plot of the mind-swap episode than does its actual title, "Do Not Forsake Me Oh My Darling", which, he argues, would be better suited to the Western instalment (see A Change of Mind, Cult TV, DVD, & lovely stuff: News, reviews & fun, 18 June 2014, http://www.bbc.co.uk/cult/classic/prisoner/episodeguide/eleven.shtml).

The titles of various Doctor Who stories, too, have been subjected to ridicule by fans. In The Book of Lists referenced above, Richards and Martin cite 17 Doctor Who productions whose names they believe are inappropriate and explain the reasons for their objections. Unlike Morris, however, the writers do not suggest using one story's title in place of the title actually given to another.

24. Howe, D. J. and Walker, S. J. Doctor Who: The television companion – The official BBC guide to every TV story. BBC: London, 1998.
25. Dicks, T. Doctor Who and the Armageddon Factor. W. H. Allen: London, 1980.
26. Clapham, M., Robson, E. and Smith, J. op. cit.
27. It is appropriate to note at this point that in the radio programme The Enthusiasts: The Whovians (BBC Radio 4, 11 December 1985), the claim is made that the Daleks, too, can be considered to represent "officialdom". Readers wanting to pursue this issue further should listen to the second CD in the package Doctor Who at the BBC (BBC Audiobooks, 2003). If we accept the Daleks-as-bureaucrats interpretation, we may see certain parallels between The Doctor and Number Six. Each is cast as a renegade individual who is intent on resisting strong coercive forces bent on imposing rigid conformity.

     For Muir, various opponents of The Doctor, in fact, can be understood as representing "personal identity either sublimated or destroyed", whilst the hero stands for individuality. Muir points to The Doctor's "out-of-fashion clothes and unique genius" as evidence of his one-of-a-kind status. Muir concludes his argument with the observation that Doctor Who can "be viewed as an examination not only of political revolution and a response to the forces of establishment, but the ultimate triumph of the individual over the more impressive resources and power of 'Big Brother.'" (see A Critical History of Doctor Who on Television, p. 142) In contrast, fans of The Prisoner will note that no such decisive victory for their hero seems remotely forthcoming.
28. Dicks, T. Doctor Who: The Faceless Ones. W. H. Allen: London, 1986.
29. For detailed essays on The Doctor's name, the reader should consult: Wood, T. and Miles, L. About time: The unauthorized guide to Doctor Who: 1963–1966 – Seasons 1 to 3. Mad Norwegian Press: Des Moines, Iowa, 2006, pp. 279 and 281; Sandifer, P. TARDIS eruditorum: An unofficial critical history of Doctor Who – Volume one, William Hartnell, 2nd ed. Eruditorum Press, 2013, pp. 357–359.
30. Rayner, J. Doctor Who: The Official Quiz Book. BBC, 2014.
31. Lofficier, J-M. Doctor Who: The universal databank. Doctor Who Books: London,

1992.

32. See, for example: White, M. and Ali, J. The official Prisoner companion. Sidgwick and Jackson: London, 1988; Rogers, D. The Prisoner and Danger Man. Boxtree: London, 1989; Gregory, C. Be seeing you... Decoding The Prisoner. John Libbey Media: Luton, 1997; Sellers, R. Cult TV: The golden age of ITC. Plexus: London, 2006; Stevens, A. and Moore, F. op. cit.; Booth, R. Not a number: Patrick McGoohan – A life. Supernova: Twickenham, 2011; Goodman, R. (ed.) George Markstein and The Prisoner. pandqmedia: Berwyn, Denbighshire, 2014; Lewin, R. The Prisoner. In: Haley, G. (ed.) Sci-fi chronicles: A visual history of the galaxy's greatest science fiction. Aurum: London, 2014, p. 261.

33. Langley, R. The Prisoner dialogue decodes. 2014.

34. Wood, T. The empire of the senses: Narrative form and point-of-view in Doctor Who. In: Butler, D. (ed.) Time and relative dissertations in space: Critical perspectives on Doctor Who. Manchester University Press: Manchester, 2007, pp. 89–107.

35. See, for example: McGoohan, P. On the trail of The Prisoner: Roger Goodman talks to Patrick McGoohan. CD. PrizBiz, 2007. Audio recording of 1979 interview; Interview With Patrick McGoohan. In: Carrazé, A. and Oswald, H. The Prisoner: A televisionary masterpiece. Virgin: London, 1990, pp. 6–8.

36. Howe, D. J., Stammers, M. and Walker, S. J. Doctor Who: The handbook – The Second Doctor. Virgin: London, 1997.

37. Clapham, M., Robson, E. and Smith, J. op. cit.

38. Rogers, D. op. cit.

39. Time Shift: Fantasy Sixties. BBC4. 16 April 2005.

40. Campbell, M. Dimensions in time and space. Steven Scott: London, 2003.

41. Fairclough, R. (ed.) The Prisoner: The original scripts – Volume 2. Reynolds and Hearn: Richmond, London, 2006.

42. Howe, D. J., Stammers, M. and Walker, S. J. op. cit. 1997.

43. Howe, D. J. and Blumberg, A. T. Howe's transcendental toybox. Telos/ATB Publishing, 2000.

44. 1991 Doctor Who Series Survey Results. DWB, 96, December 1991, pp. 10–13.

45. The Prisoner: The Official Fact File. De Agostini, 2005–2006.

46. Davies, S. P. The Prisoner handbook: An unauthorized companion. Boxtree: London, 2002; Fairclough, R. op. cit. 2002; Frumerman, C. N. op. cit.; Fairclough, R. (ed.) The Prisoner: The original scripts – Volume 1. Reynolds and Hearn: Richmond, London, 2005; Fairclough, R. (ed.) op. cit. 2006; Stevens, A. and Moore, F. Fall out: The unofficial and unauthorised guide to The Prisoner. Telos: Tolworth, 2007; Langley, R. The Prisoner series guide, 2nd ed. 2010; Langley, R. The making of The Prisoner. Escape, 2010; Langley, R. The Pris6ner from the inside: Plots, scripts, background. Escape, 2010; Langley, R. The Prisoner dialogue decodes. 2014.

47. Top 50 Greatest UK Telefantasy Shows Ever. SFX Collection, 22, 2005, pp. 6–57.

48. Chapman, J. Saints and Avengers: British adventure series of the 1960s. I. B. Tauris: London, 2002.

49. Graham, A. Happy birthday ITV! Radio Times, 22-28 August 2015, pp. 20–25.

50. Campbell, M. op. cit.
51. Clapham, M., Robson, E. and Smith, J. op. cit.
52. Bradbury, K. C. (ed.) Portal to infinity: An independent and unauthorized guide to BBC TV's Doctor Who. 1st Books, 2004.
53. The First 50 Years: The Results In Full! Doctor Who Magazine, 474, July 2014, pp. 62–63.

CHAPTER FOUR
Individuals and Champions

Whilst many readers will, no doubt, share the view of Gerald Kelsey, who wrote for both programmes, that "*The Champions* was more of a run-of-the-mill idea for TV than *The Prisoner*", (p. 73)[1] each series has been regarded as ahead of its time. In the case of *The Prisoner*, this is an issue to which we will return on several occasions in *Unique But Similar*. Perhaps most obviously, the prevailing mood within the *Prisoner* instalments, and the unconventional narrative methods, although innovative in their day, would seem to have much in common with significant features of some of the shows that have appeared in subsequent years. With regard to *The Champions*, Johnny Goodman, who worked on the programme as an associate producer, notes its similarity to the later *Six Million Dollar Man*,[2] and James Chapman, who, as an Open University Lecturer, may be considered to offer a more independent perspective, recognises the programme's status as "a generic forerunner of the enhanced secret agent adventures of the 1970s". (p. 188)[3] Nevertheless, a case can also be made that with its "modified humans" premise, *The Champions* belongs to the same broad tradition that gave rise to such programmes as the original television version of *The Fantastic Four* – a cartoon series based on Marvel Comics characters and made at much the same time as *The Champions*. The website *tv.com* recalls,

> The Fantastic Four gained their super powers after an experimental rocket ship designed by Reed Richards and piloted

by Reed's friend, Ben Grimm, was hit by a storm of cosmic rays on its test flight in space. When it crash landed back on earth, the four discovered that they each had gained super powers.[4]

Parallels with *The Champions* are easily drawn.

The common characteristics of one particular instalment of *The Champions* and Patrick McGoohan's series have long been identified. Robert Sellers is among those who note similarities between the two and suggests that the inspiration for the *Champions* episode *The Interrogation* "probably stemmed from the fact that, at that time, [writer Dennis Spooner] was sitting in on production meetings for *The Prisoner*". (p. 149)[5] Just as *The Prisoner* is frequently thought of as an atypical television programme, *The Interrogation* is often said to be unusual within the context of the series to which it belongs. The instalment has a disorientating, nightmarish edge to it, and indeed, various *Champions* episode guides invite the viewer to speculate on whether the events shown are really happening or simply part of a dream.[6] This interpretation is itself reminiscent of one theory that has been put forward in relation to what we see taking place in *The Prisoner*. Such a possibility was raised briefly in Chapter Two and is one to which we will return in subsequent chapters.

Most of the instalments of the Monty Berman/Dennis Spooner collaboration see agents Craig Stirling, Sharron Macready and Richard Barrett undertaking, as a team, missions on behalf of the international agency for which they operate – Nemesis. *The Encyclopedia of TV Science Fiction* explains that the special powers granted to them by a lost race living in Tibet "bound them together like triplets". (p. 87)[7] *The Interrogation*, however, diverges from the series' regular formula in several respects. There is no mission to be completed here, although details of a recent assignment are recounted and various flashback sequences included, and the episode concentrates exclusively on the experiences of only one of the team. Moreover, despite the fact that Mark Phillips and Frank Garcia refer to the programme's "globe-trotting stories", (p. 73)[8] in *The Interrogation* all the events that happen in the "here and now" take place within Nemesis headquarters. It is also notable that, in virtually all other instalments, there is little or no antagonism evident between the agents and their superior, Tremayne, yet, in *The Interrogation*, distrust and suspicion are highly apparent. Furthermore, in the closing scene, Stirling is wary of even his friend, Barrett, feeling that he offered him no help in his hour of need. Whilst many themes within this particular *Champions* instalment bear marked similarities to those of *The Prisoner*, it is in the realm of interpersonal relationships where there is a major disparity. Whereas Craig has, by this point, come to count on support from his fellow Champions, Number Six rarely expects genuine assistance from others and, unsurprisingly, he seldom receives it.

Undoubtedly, the novelty element of both *The Prisoner* and *The Interrogation* is a major factor in their appeal. *The Prisoner* has remained memorable across the decades for breaking the mould of the action/adventure television series, and the unusual nature of *The Interrogation* offers a similar attraction. Cyril Frankel, who directed ten instalments of *The Champions* including *The Interrogation*, considers it "one of the best", (p. 149)[9] and Sellers feels it is "certainly a favourite among fans". (p. 149)[10] Nevertheless, the atypical plot and location for the action arose from necessity, rather than an ambitious attempt at creative experimentation, and specifically from the need to construct an inexpensive instalment requiring only one set and just six days' work.[11]

The Interrogation resembles *The Prisoner* in that one of the regular protagonists has been kidnapped from familiar surroundings and incarcerated. Again, much of the initial action sees the hero cautiously explore his new environment. The places of confinement could scarcely be more different, however. Whereas The Village is attractive in appearance, the single room in which Stirling is being held is drab and spartan. In McGoohan's series, the real identities of those assuming the position of Number Two are not revealed. In *Many Happy Returns*, The Village's chief administrator is shown in the closing moments to be the woman we have come to know as Mrs Butterworth but even here it is difficult to believe that this is her real name. In *The Champions*, Stirling is faced with an adversary who goes unnamed throughout; in the closing credits he is identified simply as "The Interrogator". Like Number Two in *The Prisoner*, this character is clearly accountable to others and is acting on their instructions. At one point, The Interrogator is seen talking to another party on the telephone. The scene echoes comparable sequences in the *Prisoner* episodes *A. B. and C.*, *Free For All* and *Hammer Into Anvil* where Number Two reports on his progress to an unknown superior. Indeed, The Interrogator can be understood to face similar pressures to *A. B. and C.*'s Number Two – it is made clear to each that he is expected to achieve immediate results.

Sharron Macready, Richard Barrett and Tremayne do appear briefly in *The Interrogation* but the episode is basically a two-hander comparable to the *Prisoner* instalment *Once Upon a Time*. The Butler's role in the *Prisoner* story is largely that of an onlooker and assistant, although it is significant that, as the tide turns during a week of isolation, his allegiance switches from Number Two to The Prisoner. In the main, however, in both programmes the hero fights a lone struggle in a battle of wills within a highly claustrophobic environment and ultimately emerges triumphant. Again, it would seem that the need to keep a toght rein on the budget was a key consideration in the making of *Once Upon a Time*. Rupert Booth, in addition to highlighting its small cast, notes how the bulk of the filming "took place on a cost-cutting set, comprised of black drapes and stock props and dressings". (p. 180)[12] One of Roger Langley's assessments of *Once Upon a Time* would suggest that the episode was – like *The Interrogation* – prepared in some haste; he draws attention to the high degree of improvisation and the need for the lead actors to ad-lib as a result of the script being – in the eyes of production members – "much shorter than usual". (p. 83)[13] In terms of page count, however, the script is by no means the briefest in Robert Fairclough's two-volume collection,[14] although the editor notes that it includes only 30 scenes and no *Prisoner* episode consists of a smaller number.[15]

Whereas *The Interrogation* is eminently comprehensible, even to the first-time watcher, *Once Upon a Time* is oblique and demanding of the viewer. Jack Lowin, who served as a camera operator during the making of the episode, goes so far as to suggest that there was "a touch of insanity about the whole thing. The whole thing was weird."[16] For Fairclough, *The Prisoner*'s penultimate episode draws inspiration from sources as diverse as Jean Cocteau, Franz Kafka, William Shakespeare and *The Devil and Daniel Webster*,[17] while Neil McLean and David Stansfield refer to the ideas of Jung and Freud in connection with the instalment.[18] *The Interrogation* is, by comparison, much more conventional drama.

Like The Interrogator, the Number Two we see in *Once Upon a Time* resents having been allocated so short a period to apply his chosen method. Questions of personal integrity concern the captor in both instances. The reasons for Number Six's resignation arise again and again through the series and recur repeatedly in *Once Upon a Time*. The tone is set from the outset of *The Prisoner* with the first Number Two in *Arrival* explaining that it is his job to check The Prisoner's motives. In *The Interrogation*, the fact that Stirling has been entirely successful in every mission he has undertaken leads Tremayne to suspect that his allegiances are not exclusive to Nemesis but, pondering on his effectiveness, The Interrogator himself eventually acknowledges, "even a double agent doesn't get the results you get". The priorities of both Number Six and Stirling during their periods in captivity are strikingly similar. Most fundamentally, each strives to remain intact physically and mentally; they are intent on protecting their secrets, with The Prisoner revealing nothing as to why he resigned and Stirling giving no indication that his success in assignments can be attributed at least in part to the extraordinary powers he received in Tibet; in a more positive vein, each individual seeks an opportunity to escape from their situation. The three Champions and The Prisoner all possess a range of highly developed skills/abilities that distinguish them from ordinary mortals. In *The Interrogation*, we witness Stirling using his super-sensitive hearing to eavesdrop on a conversation taking place in another room and watch him employ his unnatural strength to remove the hinges from a door frame. The skills of Number Six are less immediately obvious and less pivotal to the central premise of the series.

Many of the strategies put into practice by Stirling's adversary are comparable to those used by the Village authorities. Just as, in instalments such as *Arrival* and *Many Happy Returns*, Number Six is initially permitted to believe that he can make a successful escape from The Village, in *The Interrogation*, Stirling is allowed to scent a chance of freedom if he can weaken the door of his prison. On each occasion, however, the hero's efforts are thwarted and he soon realises that he has merely played into the hands of opponents who have deliberately raised his hopes and then dashed them in order to break his spirit. In *The Interrogation*, Stirling discovers that the door conceals not a potential method of escape as he had anticipated but a solid brick wall. Other common tactics employed by the captors in both programmes include the use of drugs, penetrative questioning and the feeding of false information to the victim. The third method includes the doctoring of evidence. At one point, The Interrogator uses faked tape-recorded conversations in order to convince Stirling that he is losing his sanity, and in the *Prisoner* episode *It's Your Funeral*, Number Six is shown falsified film of dialogues between himself and previous Number Twos.

The different personas of the individual Number Twos form a striking feature of the 17 episodes of *The Prisoner* and are well recognised by Steven Ricks, who, in presenting a guide to each in turn, offers comments on their respective personalities.[19] The Interrogator, meanwhile, alternates between a friendly approach, in which he conditionally offers Stirling his freedom, and a more unsettling line of questioning, where he threatens to order Stirling's death. Furthermore, the evasive stance that The Interrogator takes early on in the episode when presented with questions from Stirling mirrors that of the Villagers in the opening scenes of *Arrival*.

The Interrogation is full of "cat and mouse" exchanges between Stirling and his antagonist. The agent gains one of his most decisive victories at the end of a role-playing scenario in which the inquisitor, in an effort to win Stirling's confidence, has taken on the guise of a contact. Suddenly, Stirling, temporarily recovered from his drug-induced disorientation, sees through the deception and spectacularly turns the tables on The Interrogator. In *Once Upon a Time*, Number Two also resorts to role-play, assuming various authority figures (i.e. father, school headteacher, master of ceremonies on graduation day, sports coach, prospective employer, magistrate and military commander) in his efforts to break The Prisoner in the isolated Embryo Room, although he, like The Interrogator, ultimately fails. Number Six's success at the climax of *Once Upon a Time* is by no means an isolated triumph. In episodes such as *Hammer Into Anvil* and *A Change of Mind*, he registers significant successes after a weak position has been turned into an attacking one. Much has been made by some commentators of the fact that, despite the various ploys used against him by the Village authorities, there are limits to the levels of danger to which Number Six is exposed. Matthew White and Jaffer Ali go so far as to suggest that a special respect and understanding that he is not to be destroyed, which derive from orders given by the ultimate authorities, "protect Number Six within The Village". (p. 151)[20] Even when making an impassioned plea to his superior that he be allowed to apply the Degree Absolute method, Number Two recognises the importance of not damaging Number Six. Stirling, too, undergoes a very considerable ordeal at the hands of The Interrogator but seldom is his life put in immediate danger. Only in time does the reason for this caution on the part of his captors become clear.

Fans of 1960s television science fiction may well be tempted to compare the relative positions of Number Six in *The Prisoner* and David Vincent in *The Invaders*. Both characters are significant thorns in the sides of powerful adversaries, yet neither is killed by their opponents. Anthony Spinner, associate producer of the first season of *The Invaders*, admits that the willingness of the aliens to allow Vincent's continued existence was a source of bemusement among the show's writers. It was, of course, necessary for the survival of the series in its originally intended form but was only really justified on the basis of what Spinner terms a "nebulous theory", i.e. if the aliens killed Vincent his death would attract too much attention. (p. 145)[21] Nevertheless, it should be appreciated that there are in the series clear instances where the aliens do indeed attempt to do away with him. Indeed, trying to murder him is one of various ploys that Bill Harry recognises are used by the aliens against Vincent; others include seeking to convince him that they intend to help mankind and framing him for criminal acts.[22]

The question of which "side" runs The Village is a longstanding debate among *Prisoner* fans. It undoubtedly forms one of the most teasing conundrums within the whole series and the issue is discussed at various points elsewhere in this book. Initially, a similar ambiguity is prevalent in *The Interrogation*. At first, we may suspect that Stirling has fallen into enemy hands and The Interrogator is working for a hostile world power. Yet, some 30 minutes into the episode, it emerges that Tremayne is party to the ordeal that Stirling is experiencing.

Indeed, Tremayne himself drugged Stirling in his own office soon after he had returned from his most recent mission.

In contrast to the enigmatic resolution of *The Prisoner*, the interrogation of Stirling ends with an unequivocal outcome. Whilst The Prisoner's flight from The Village is shown to amount to no more than a hollow victory, Stirling is not only successful in breaking free from his prison; he has done enough in the interrogation to convince his boss of his integrity. Stirling's escape owes much to an attention to detail that would have been characteristic of Number Six himself. Noticing an oddly positioned footprint on the floor of his cell, Stirling realises that he can effect an exit via a sliding panel whose controls are concealed. After a confrontation with Stirling and a consultation with The Interrogator, Tremayne rules that the result of the inquisition is "satisfactory" and, in the final scene, closes the agent's file, both literally and figuratively, even though The Interrogator has made it clear that, for him, too many matters remain unresolved. Despite the superior status of Tremayne within the Nemesis organisation, The Interrogator is by no means a submissive and unquestioning underling. The manner in which he challenges Tremayne's final decision is akin, in fact, to the belligerent insistence of the Number Two in *Once Upon a Time* that his own favoured approach must be put into operation.

In discussing episodes of *The Twilight Zone* that involve just one or two characters, Kenneth Reynolds draws attention to the demands made of the writing, directing and acting in such situations.[23] It may be argued that since *The Interrogation* and *Once Upon a Time* are around twice as long as any of the seven *Twilight Zone* episodes Reynolds cites, the standards required in these areas are even greater here.[24] Although neither the *Champions* story nor the *Prisoner* instalment features only **two** protagonists, each is still a very minimalist drama and much especially depends on the acting of those who play the main characters. In reviewing *Once Upon a Time*, James O'Neill highlights the "top performances" of McGoohan and "the always reliable" Leo McKern, who plays Number Two. (p. 269)[25] David McIntee feels that Stuart Damon's "finest moment" in *The Champions* comes in *The Interrogation*. He continues, "the viewer is certainly gripped, proving that there are imported American 'stars' who can act". (p. 25)[26]

Whilst *The Prisoner* ran for 17 episodes and formed an ongoing saga, *The Interrogation* is very much a one-off departure for *The Champions*, although the viewer may well feel that, given the power and suspense of the instalment, allied to a resolution in which The Interrogator makes clear that he is keen to resume his inquisition of Stirling at any stage in the future, a sequel later in the programme's run would have been both welcome and appropriate. *The*

Interrogation is quite unlike any other *Champions* episode and, in several respects, can be considered *The Prisoner* in miniature, with some of the most powerful themes and scenarios within McGoohan's programme reworked into the format of a more conventional action/adventure series.

References and Notes

1.   Quoted in: Phillips, M. and Garcia, F. Science fiction television series: Episode guides, histories, and casts and credits for 62 prime time shows, 1959 through 1989. McFarland: Jefferson, North Carolina, 1996.

2.   Porter, J. Johnny Goodman interview. TV Zone, 44, July 1993, pp. 8–11.

3.   Chapman, J. Saints and Avengers: British adventure series of the 1960s. I. B. Tauris: London, 2002.

4.   The Fantastic Four. tv.com. URL: http://www.tv.com/shows/the-fantastic-four-1967/ (accessed: 23 February 2017).

5.   Sellers, R. Cult TV: The golden age of ITC. Plexus: London, 2006.

6.   See, for example: Vahimagi, T. TV zone. Starburst, 4 (8) [issue 44], 1981, pp. 56–57; Fulton, R. The encyclopedia of TV science fiction. Boxtree: London, 1990.

7.   Fulton, R. op. cit.

8.   Phillips, M. and Garcia, F. op. cit.

9.   Quoted in: Sellers, R. op. cit.

10. Sellers, R. op. cit.

11. Sellers, R. op. cit.

12. Booth, R. Not a number: Patrick McGoohan – A life. Supernova: Twickenham, 2011.

13. Langley, R. The Prisoner dialogue decodes. 2014.

14. Fairclough, R. (ed.) The Prisoner: The original scripts – Volume 1. Reynolds and Hearn: Richmond, London, 2005; Fairclough, R. (ed.) The Prisoner: The original scripts – Volume 2. Reynolds and Hearn: Richmond, London, 2006.

15. Fairclough, R. (ed.) op. cit. 2006.

16. The Prisoner In-depth Tape 2. VHS video cassette. TR 7 Productions: Borehamwood, 1992.

17. Fairclough, R. (ed.) op. cit. 2006.

18. McLean, N. and Stansfield, D. The Prisoner program guide. Ontario Educational Communications Authority: Toronto, Ontario, 1976.

19. Ricks, S. The Prisoner: I am not a number! A series guide. TR 7: Borehamwood, 2000.

20. White, M. and Ali, J. The official Prisoner companion. Sidgwick and Jackson: London, 1988.

21. Quoted in: Phillips, M. and Garcia, F. op. cit.

22. Harry, B. Heroes of the spaceways. Omnibus: London, 1981.

23. Reynolds, K. The Twilight Zone: Rod Serling's wondrous land. iUniverse LLC: Bloomington: Indiana, 2014.

24. Whilst none of the seven Twilight Zone stories mentioned by Reynolds particularly resembles The Interrogation, the episode is somewhat similar to the Twilight Zone's three-man "cat and mouse" drama The Jeopardy Room. Here, too, much of the action takes place in one enclosed room; the hero is drugged and a trap is laid for him; ultimately the tables are turned so dramatically that he overcomes his adversary and escapes from his place of confinement. In both The Jeopardy Room and Once Upon a Time, the opponent is not merely defeated whilst attempting to execute his scheme – he himself is killed in the process.

25. O'Neill, J. Sci-fi on tape: A comprehensive guide to over 1,250 science fiction and fantasy films on video. Billboard: New York, 1997.

26. McIntee, D. Silver Champions. DWB, 118, October 1993, pp. 25–27.

CHAPTER FIVE
Sunshine and Shadow

The ITC press book for *The Prisoner* states unequivocally that the programme "has nothing in common with any other television series ever filmed".[1] In some ways, M. Keith Booker's analysis of "strange TV" supports this claim – the author highlights how the programme opposed the trend of American television at the time towards "Cold War spy dramas with an unproblematic anticommunist stance", was unusual in concentrating on a hero who "is constantly in the grip of forces more powerful than himself and generally fails in his efforts to overcome his foes" and refuted the usual message emerging from 1960s spy dramas that "all modern problems can easily be solved by individual effort". (p. 75) Yet, Booker also shows how *The Prisoner* is descended from the same post-modern form of television that gave rise to *The Twilight Zone* just a few years earlier.[2]

A single name readily springs to mind when each series is mentioned. The synonymity of Patrick McGoohan and *The Prisoner* is widely accepted, and Arlen Schumer writes that Rod Serling "exercised total creative control over all facets of *The Twilight Zone*, making him a true television **auteur**". (p. 22)[3] It may also be said that *The Twilight Zone*, like *The Prisoner*, defies easy categorisation. Schumer feels that labels such as "science fiction", "horror" and "fantasy" do not adequately summarise the nature of the series; he himself prefers the adjective "surreal". (p. 18)[4] Reference has already been made in this book to *The*

Prisoner's surreal characteristics and more will be said on this issue later. Schumer, meanwhile, notes the similarity between juxtaposition in *The Twilight Zone* and related concepts that emerge in surrealism as it is understood by Pierre Reverdy, who describes the form as one that involves "the bringing together of two realities which are more or less remote". (p. 21)[5] We saw in the notes that accompanied Chapter Three that *Prisoner* stalwart Terence Feely describes surrealism in very similar terms.

Tony Albarella suggests that if one term had to be selected to represent the entirety of the original version of *The Twilight Zone*, the word he would choose would be "displacement". (p. 12) The author highlights various forms of displacement that are evident in the series, one of which is displacement from society.[6] This is also, of course, a major theme within *The Prisoner*. Here the hero is **displaced** from conventional society and incarcerated in the prison that we can identify only as The Village. McGoohan himself has revealed that, even as a young child, he was intrigued by the idea of "a man in isolation", (p. 25)[7] and *The Prisoner* can be viewed as a dramatic exploration of this concept. Other significant areas of common ground between *The Prisoner* and *The Twilight Zone* may be recognised, too. In providing a breakdown of genres, themes and plot devices apparent in *The Twilight Zone*, Don Presnell and Marty McGee list some two dozen episodes that deal in some way with the loss of personal identity,[8] and this is another issue that is especially prevalent in *The Prisoner*. One particular instalment cited by the authors – the second season segment *The Obsolete Man* – would seem to share with McGoohan's series several obvious plot similarities.

Here, too, a strong-willed individual, in this case the librarian Romney Wordsworth, challenges an omnipotent, apparently totalitarian régime and ultimately, as in such *Prisoner* stories as *A Change of Mind* and *Hammer Into Anvil*, the tables are turned on the authorities so dramatically that the dominance of a seemingly all-powerful leader is brought to a very ignominious end. In *The Obsolete Man*, the victim is known only as The Chancellor and no characters other than the hero are ever named. Just as Number Six announces defiantly in *Arrival* that he will not be "pushed, filed, stamped, indexed, briefed, debriefed or numbered", Wordsworth is proud of the fact he does not fit The State's efforts to "categorise", "index" and "tag" everything. Douglas L. Howard describes The Village as a society that "demands conformity and mercilessly attempts to bend all individuals to fit into its social constructs, subscribe to its psychological norms, and to commit to its bureaucratic institutions". (p. 194)[9] These words are equally appropriate in relation to the expectations of The State portrayed in *The Obsolete Man*. According to the Starlog *Fantastic Worlds* guidebook, even the expressionist design of the huge chamber in which the first half of the action unfolds creates a sense of oppression.[10]

It would seem that just as a penny farthing is used in *The Prisoner* to represent The Village, The State in the *Twilight Zone* story may have its own insignia. A symbol appears on the The Chancellor's collar and another logo can be seen on the shirt itself. Although there are no clues in the dialogue to indicate their significance, it is sensible to assume that the design on the shirt may denote his status as a senior official and that on the collar, which can be seen on Wordsworth's collar, too, forms an emblem representing The State.

We can conclude from the totality of the *Prisoner* saga that Number Six is a man of many talents. So, too, is Wordsworth. He may be a librarian by profession but he is also a skilled carpenter who has made for himself some of the furniture in the room that he inhabits. Both Wordsworth and The Prisoner are capable of planning and implementing courses of action against authority figures that bring about spectacular victories. In *Hammer Into Anvil*, The Prisoner undermines Number Two in a systematic campaign and in *The Obsolete Man*, Wordsworth triumphs over his adversary after executing a series of well conceived moves. In the opening half of the episode, Wordsworth is the subject of a hearing to assess whether, as a librarian within a society where there are now no books, he should be declared "obsolete". Despite his inspiring speeches and, no doubt, high levels of sympathy from the viewers, Wordsworth predictably loses his case and is sentenced to death. He does, though, use his remaining time profitably. After choosing the manner of his liquidation, a privilege to which he is entitled, and asking for his demise to be broadcast via the State's television system, Wordsworth invites The Chancellor to his accommodation. It becomes apparent that Wordsworth has opted to die via the detonation of a bomb in his own room and he has locked The Chancellor in with him. In the hour immediately before Wordsworth's death, the balance of power alters considerably, in much the same way as The Prisoner gradually gains the upper hand over Number Two in *Hammer Into Anvil*. At one point Wordsworth is rebuked by The Chancellor for not facing the camera but within moments, as the official's unease escalates, the librarian chides the official when he exhibits similar behaviour. Later, The Chancellor says "they" will not allow him to remain in Wordsworth's room and be killed. Wordsworth taunts him by suggesting that by "they" he must mean The State. In so doing, the librarian has once again reversed the roles since during the earlier hearing a comment made by Wordsworth in relation to "you people" when addressing the board elicits the question from The Chancellor, "you make reference to The State?" Whereas Wordsworth ultimately accepts his fate with equanimity, an increasingly panic-struck Chancellor is reduced to a pleading, quivering wreck. Eventually, in an apparently kindly gesture, Wordsworth unlocks the door and allows The Chancellor to leave.

With the final scene of *Fall Out* repeating the beginning of the title sequence first seen in *Arrival*, the events of McGoohan's series appear to form a complete loop. The ending of *The Obsolete Man* also provides a neat circularity. Like the start of the episode, this is set in the hall where State judgements on citizens are made. Again, a hearing takes place. On this occasion, however, it is The Chancellor himself who is under scrutiny. He, too, is declared "obsolete" after field investigators have concluded that, since he has disgraced The State and proved himself a coward, he no longer has a place in society.

Television is a tool that is exploited by the authorities in both dramas. In *The Prisoner*, it forms a key element within The Village's surveillance system and, in addition, is integral to the delivery of the "Speedlearn" programme. In *The Obsolete Man*, The Chancellor welcomes Wordsworth's request that his liquidation be televised, feeling that the broadcasting of such events has a valuable "educative" effect on the population. Ultimately, however, it is the figures of authority who suffer most as a result of the use of the technology. In *Hammer Into Anvil*, The Prisoner's unexpected behaviour, some of which comes to Number Two's attention as a result of The Village's closed circuit television system, raises the suspicions of Number Two that The Prisoner is a "plant" and the pictures he sees hasten his distrust of others very considerably. In *The Obsolete Man*, the televising of The Chancellor's post-hearing meeting with Wordsworth makes the official's weaknesses plain for all to see. The conclusion to be drawn here may be that the hero of the drama is rather more adept than the society's leader at exploiting the psychological possibilities offered by the technology. For Alain Carrazé and Hélène Oswald, Number Six's "perfect knowledge of the field enables him to turn his adversaries' weapons against them". (p. 138)[11] Undoubtedly, officials of The Village and The State can be just as much victims as those they are attempting to investigate. The Chancellor is clearly most comfortable when pronouncing to his congregation from the safety of the hall where, in the words of Stewart T. Stanyard, he can stand "arrogantly behind an ominous podium, symbolizing the supposed strength of the state." (p. 34)[12] He is rather less at ease when having to deal with more spontaneous and unpredictable situations where he is not on home territory.

Matthew White and Jaffer Ali point out the speed with which the Villagers in *A Change of Mind* "take up the authoritative line as they would a cause and are quick to condemn those who do not conform".[13] (p. 90) The episode ends with Number Two fleeing from angry citizens who shout "unmutual" in chorus.

Although this more aggressive streak contrasts starkly with the Villagers' apathetic demeanour that is generally apparent in the series, in both cases the people show little evidence of any real ability, or even inclination, to think for themselves. Indeed, whilst very different, the two portrayals do adhere to the automaton-like predisposition that is highlighted in a press information booklet produced by ITC to provide answers to some of the questions that may be asked in relation to *The Prisoner*.[14] They are also consistent with McGoohan's vision that the Villagers' "souls have been brainwashed out of them".[15]

A similar lack of independent thought is prevalent in *The Obsolete Man* and here, too, there is a marked change of mood among the citizens we observe, specifically, in this case the members of The State's board that we see passing judgements. When they are asked for their adjudication on Wordsworth, the members move forward with robot-like stiffness and bark out their verdict in a harsh, expressionless monotone. Each person is similarly attired and would seem to have no individuality. All are simply instruments of The State. Just as the mob in The Village picks up on Number Six's use of the word "unmutual" and begins chanting against Number Two, so too The State's board members repeat time and time again the word "obsolete" after judgement has been passed on The Chancellor. Menacingly, they advance and surround him. Director Elliot Silverstein intended them to be "like a pack of mad dogs". (p. 210)[16] The Chancellor is manhandled and it seems that soon he will be torn to pieces. The closing narration of writer Serling, which includes a reference to "The **late** Chancellor", confirms his fate. Unlike Wordsworth, The Chancellor is humiliated and allowed no honourable death.

Given the fact that subsequent events in the series reveal that The Prisoner can never be totally free, his triumph in *Hammer Into Anvil* can be seen to amount to one favourable result within a war that cannot ever be truly won, and Wordsworth's success is clearly a pyrrhic victory. Even after Number Six has broken out of his physical prison, it would seem that the wider world and indeed his own limitations impose inescapable constraints on him. In *The Obsolete Man*, despite having the might of The State stacked against him, Wordsworth shows himself to be a stronger character than The Chancellor but he ultimately loses his life. Moreover, the society against which he was rebelling appears set to continue unchanged. By the end of the episode, The Chancellor who ridiculed him has been removed but another official has taken his place, in much the same way as one Number Two replaces another in *The Prisoner*. Moreover, as in *The Prisoner*, despite the change, the régime itself remains unaffected. It may, in fact, be argued that, by the time of *The Obsolete Man*'s closing credits, The State is in an even stronger position than it was at the beginning of the instalment since, as Peter Wolfe recognises, the events we have witnessed serve to demonstrate to citizens "that no act of heresy... goes unpunished, regardless of its perpetrator". (p. 75)[17] This perspective would appear somewhat bleaker than Serling intended, however. In a letter written to one of the episode's critics, Serling explained that one of the statements he was making in *The Obsolete Man* was that "sooner or later every dictatorship must of necessity fall because sooner or later thinking people with courage will overthrow it." (p. 413)[18]

Like The Village in *The Prisoner*, The State portrayed in *The Obsolete Man* is not named and its geographical location is never established. Wordsworth is told during his hearing that he has been under scrutiny by field investigators in his "sector" but this area, too, is unnamed. It is striking that in terms of their most readily apparent characteristics, the respective settings for *The Obsolete Man* and *The Prisoner* have been described in ways that are remarkably alike. In his opening narration for the *Twilight Zone* episode, Serling suggests that whilst the future society we will see is patterned on those of previous dictatorships, this one has "refinements, technological advancements, and a more sophisticated approach to the destruction of human freedom". It is easy to detect similarities between this situation and Adrian Page's view that The Village in *The Prisoner* offers "a futuristic scenario where social control had reached... technological perfection". (p. 58)[19]

Although there may be an inclination on the part of some viewers and commentators to position The Village according to an East/West orientation, Sue Short, like Page, thinks of the community in more abstract terms and she, too, believes that the key issue is not who is responsible for it but rather what it represents. She contends that *The Prisoner* invites audiences "to look beneath the façade of Western democracy" and assess The Village "as a microcosm of any advanced industrial nation". (p. 72)[20] Similarly, it would be erroneous to label The State in *The Obsolete Man* as "Communist" or "Fascist". It is true that Marc Scott Zicree declares unequivocally that the society in question is "neo-Nazi", (p. 208)[21] and a similar stance is taken by Albarella, who understands it to be "a slightly futuristic American society as governed by the Third Reich had Hitler's dictatorship spread and vanquished democracy worldwide". (p. 185)[22] Fritz Weaver, who played The Chancellor in *The Obsolete Man*, does not refer to the roots of the régime being Germanic but still sees the ideology being one of "fascism in the highest degree". (p. 179)[23] Likewise, J. Hoberman describes the régime that puts Wordsworth to death as one of "a fascistic superstate". (p. 151)[24] Yet, as Douglas Brode and Carol Serling observe, this is not explicitly indicated in the episode and it may be significant that The Chancellor embraces Stalin, as well as Hitler, as one of his heroes.[25] Indeed, citing The State's distinguishing features as "hatred of God, the Bible, dissidents, religious belief, books, etc.", (p. 649) Kenneth Reynolds writes, "To me, the totalitarianism portrayed... resembles Soviet Communism". (p. 298)[26] Nevertheless, Brode and Serling argue that it is "absolutists" who are the writer's target, (p. 195) and the political persuasion of The State is unimportant.[27] According to Paul Darrow, who played Avon in *Blake's 7*, a similar argument has been propounded in relation to Terry Nation's series. Darrow notes that some have interpreted the programme as "a re-evaluation of twentieth-century extremism" (p. 78), with the Federation representing any oppressive régime. It may be that of Nazi Germany or, conversely, that of Soviet Russia.[28]

For many viewers at the time when *The Prisoner* was first shown, The Village seemed such an idiosyncratic community that it was difficult to equate it with their own society. Not only were features of the modern Western world intensely magnified; new, obscure oddities were introduced. In the same way, Zicree suggests that the nature of the society in *The Obsolete Man* is so extreme viewers would not recognise it as a credible extension of their own. In Zicree's own words, "The viewer can sit at home smug and comfortable, certain that **he** would never be part of such a State." (p. 208)[29] Nevertheless, in his opening narration, Serling warns that the society depicted is one that **could** come into existence and it effectively amounts to an extrapolation of the dictatorial régimes of the past.

Another Serling drama which invests a futuristic society ostensibly very different from our own with some of the less palatable features of contemporary Earth is *Class of '99*, a second season episode of his later supernatural anthology programme *Rod Serling's Night Gallery*. In this instance, whilst assessing his students in their final examination, a university lecturer instructs them in various forms of intolerance, specifically those associated with race, class and nationality. Just as a viewer who recognises that The Village in *The Prisoner* is based on contemporary Western society may well feel a sense of shock on making this discovery, anyone watching *Class of '99* is likely to recoil in horror when it is made apparent that the "students" here are robots who have learnt their prejudices from man. In the words of Scott Skelton and Jim Benson, "We have passed our dread legacy on to the next eager generation of rote-spinning automatons." (p. 143)[30] The revelation surrounding the true nature of the learners quickly makes us rethink much of what we have seen. By the end of the instalment, we realise that the students respond to the professor's greeting at the beginning of the episode with silence and absolute stillness not merely as a result of respect for a senior; we recognise that there is no need for the tiered, solid blocks on which the students sit to be rendered comfortable and less spartan; we understand that the clinical, unemotional way that many of the answers to the professor's questions are delivered is entirely to be expected given that these "young people" are not human – they are not simply students who have been well drilled, as we might first have thought...

Number Six can be regarded as something of a rogue element within The Village and the class of 1999 includes its own individual of rather similar nature. When asked to kill another member of the group, Elkins refuses to follow the instructions given to him, questions their validity and defies the lecturer. Although an android himself, Elkins differs from his classmates in demonstrating independent thought, in much the same way as, week after week, Number Six refuses to conform in *The Prisoner*. Another episode of *Night Gallery* will be examined in greater detail in the next chapter.

Much of the first part of this chapter concentrated on a comparison of *The Prisoner* and the *Twilight Zone* episode *The Obsolete Man*. The latter is not, however, the only instalment of Serling's classic series that may bring to mind themes frequently regarded as integral to *The Prisoner*. The notion of rebellion against state-induced conformity re-emerges especially strongly in the fifth season episode *Number 12 Looks Just Like You*, written by John Tomerlin. For Hoberman, this tale "is the most insistent of anticonformist diatribes". (p. 151)[31] Here, in a hypothetical world of the future, an independently minded character refuses to submit to societal convention. In this case, eighteen-year-old Marilyn Cuberle will not accept a Transformation that will render her physically perfect and identical to much of the rest of the population. She is deemed to be "sick" by those who view her attitudes as otherwise inexplicable.

In each drama, the central protagonist is held captive in an environment which, despite its outward appearance, is effectively a prison. Short writes how, in McGoohan's series, The Village's "quaint parochialism" conceals "the machinations of a harsh totalitarian state". (p. 72)[32] The true nature of The Village does not, of course, escape The Prisoner himself; in *Free For All*, he denounces the way in which this "twentieth century Bastille" masquerades as "a pocket democracy". A comparable deception is evident in the society we see in *Number 12 Looks Just Like You*. A hospital which, in our own world, we would expect to be a place where people are **helped** forms an instrument of Marilyn's oppressors and, as Andrew Ramage recognises, here the heroine and her fellow dissidents must stay "presumably until they break down and submit to the procedure". (p. 162)[33] The Village hospital in *The Prisoner* fulfils a similar purpose; the original synopsis for the programme describes it as "a conditioning centre using the latest methods".[34]

Supporters of the ruling régime may point to how physical perfection would doubtless be welcomed by many citizens and through helping to eliminate inequality and injustice that result from physical unattractiveness and seeking to prolong life the state is acting entirely benevolently. In truth, however, the society is based on a ruthless intolerance of individuality and the "psychological adjustment" of which the Transformation is an integral part amounts to nothing less than brainwashing. In the chilling climax, after an unsuccessful attempt to escape, Marilyn loses her battle to retain her existing appearance and is "processed" in accordance with custom. Her happiness at the result of the Transformation she has undergone demonstrates that the changes which have been made to her go far beyond mere physical improvements. At the end of *Fall Out* we may be confident that The Prisoner will resume his efforts to assert his individuality, even if he has been seen to be fighting a losing struggle, but in the final scene of *Number 12 Looks Just Like You* it is clear that all of Marilyn's desire for individuality has been utterly expunged.

After witnessing the dénouement of the *Twilight Zone* episode, we can assume that Marilyn, now in her Transformed state, will be released from the hospital and reintegrated into mainstream society. There is clearly no prospect of her evading the strictures that the wider world of the future imposes, even if she should want to do so. The Village, too, is inescapable. According to McGoohan, the place is symbolic. It may be regarded as unique to each individual in that those factors which constrain us provide our personal Village and, on the most basic level, "we are prisoners of food and sleep – without either we die". (p. 6)[35]

A *Twilight Zone* instalment often compared to *Number 12 Looks Just Like You* is Serling's classic second season tale *Eye of the Beholder*.[36] According to Stanyard, this story "stands out as what many consider the best episode". (p. 34)[37] It is certainly a measure of its importance within the series that it is the only instalment featured in full in Schumer's book *Visions From the Twilight Zone*.[38] Much has been written about *Eye of the Beholder* and it is not the intention of this author to repeat what has been said already, although a brief synopsis is necessary if the reader is to appreciate any comparison between it and *The Prisoner*. In the opening moments, we are introduced to Janet Tyler, a woman who is recuperating in hospital after receiving treatment to correct an apparently hideous facial condition. This is her eleventh such hospital visit and The State does not permit any more to be made. If she has not responded to treatment on this occasion she will be transferred to a community where people of her "kind" have been "congregated". When her bandages are removed, an astonishing surprise awaits the viewer. She is revealed to be beautiful, yet her treatment is adjudged to have failed. We see that it is the doctors and nurses who actually suffer from grotesque facial abnormalities. In her efforts to escape from the hospital, Janet encounters a handsome man, Walter Smith, who is the leader of a community where she will live with "her own kind". Together, they make preparations to leave for his village.

Similarities between *Eye of the Beholder* and *The Prisoner* abound. In both cases, an individual who does not fit in finds themselves at odds with a régime that is dictatorial and unbending. However, whereas Number Six is an unapologetic rebel throughout, Janet initially speaks disconsolately of how she wants to "belong" and "be like everybody". In the later stages of the story, though, as her desperation mounts, Janet, too, denounces the régime, decrying, "The State is not God" and she challenges its right to make rules, conditions and statutes which dictate that people who are different must stay away from "normal" citizens.

The use of first names for characters is, of course, rare in *The Prisoner*, and in *Eye of the Beholder*, of the three people who are addressed by name at any point, two are the "outsiders" – Janet and Walter. In the most *Prisoner*esque moments, even the former is described by hospital personnel as Patient 307. The various medical staff we see are generally known only by their roles – "Doctor", "Nurse", etc. Just once, when a nurse is making a report on Janet, do we hear her superior referred to as Dr. Bernadi. The man who heads this society, and is seen on television praising "glorious conformity", is referred to simply as "Our Leader". The script offers no clues about who he may be. In introducing the characters, Serling chooses to describe him merely as "a big lump of bombast". (p. 295)[39] Certainly his hectoring tone suggests that he is subscribes to a similar ideology to that followed by The Chancellor in *The Obsolete Man*.

For many readers who are already familiar with *Eye of the Beholder*, it is probably the theme of physical conformity that springs to mind most quickly when they think of the episode. Yet, it is noticeable that, in his ranting speech, the Leader addresses conformity in much more fundamental terms. Only parts of the Leader's speech can be heard by the viewer as the action takes place but in Serling's script he raves to his people,

> … You recall, of course, that directionless, unproductive, over-sentimentalised era of man's history when it was assumed that dissent was some kind of natural and healthy adjunct to society… we know now that there must be a single purpose! A single norm! A single approach! A single entity of peoples! A single virtue! A single morality! A single frame of reference! A single philosophy of

government! We cannot... we must not permit the encroaching sentimentality of a past age to weaken our resolve.[40]

It is not difficult to see how similar ideas could form much of the philosophical basis behind The Village in *The Prisoner*. Perhaps even more striking, however, is the way in which the Leader's denunciation of the value of tolerance would be echoed some ten years later in the address we hear in the graduation ceremony in *Night Gallery*'s *Class of '99*. Here the assembled congregation is told: "We must recognise that many of the ancient virtues are simply weaknesses. For example, to tolerate an inferior is an act of misplaced compassion and, as such, interferes with our function as members of the society." Clearly, the importance of accepting the characteristics of others even if they differ markedly from one's own was an issue about which Serling felt strongly and he was unafraid to make his point in scripts for different television series.

Despite the Leader's uncompromising rhetoric, Janet gains sympathy from her Doctor, who at one point asks a nurse, "Why shouldn't people be allowed to be different?" even though he is aware that such thoughts could be considered treason. We can compare the way in which Janet attracts some support from the Doctor with the way in which Number Twelve allies himself with Number Six in *The General*. In both cases, personnel who would seem likely to be staunch supporters of the system and occupy trusted positions in their societies clearly have concerns of their own.

We can also draw parallels in the way Janet and troublesome citizens in The Village are subjected to "experiments". The term as used by the Doctor in *Eye of the Beholder* implies that the individual involved is little more than a research subject and Number Two's attitude in the Village hospital to Nadia in *The Chimes of Big Ben* and to The Rook in *Checkmate* is comparable. Like the Village hospital in *The Prisoner*, the medical centre we see in *Eye of the Beholder* is a place for dealing with perceived abnormalities that threaten conformity, rather than restoring patients to health.

Number Six and Janet eventually leave the places where they have spent much of the duration of the action but whereas the conclusion of *Eye of the Beholder* offers the hope of a fresh start for Janet, the closing scenes of *Fall Out* imply that The Prisoner has made little progress. Nevertheless, in each case, the individuality of the protagonist is ultimately rewarded or celebrated. Janet is not only allowed to live, despite her "flaws", but is actually given the opportunity of a better life than that which she would have experienced in the conformist society she is leaving. She is told by Walter that in her new environment she will feel a sense of belonging and be loved. Number Six, meanwhile, is praised in *Fall Out* by The President, who offers him a position of power within The Village and applauds his "private war" in which he has "revolted, resisted, fought, held fast, maintained, destroyed resistance [and] overcome coercion".

Much was made in Chapter One of Number Six's duality and this is an issue to which we will return subsequently. *The Last Flight* was one of the earliest *Twilight Zone* episodes to explore the contrasting nature of man. Here, as Brode and Serling point out, the displaced airman Terry Decker is both a hero and a coward.[41] Eventually, the protagonist is able to conquer his fears in order to save a colleague who is in mortal danger, although Decker himself perishes in the process. Decker's personality is akin to that of Charlotte Scott in the much later *Twilight Zone* episode *The Fear*. As with Decker, her façade of confidence conceals a neurotic nature. Yet, when faced with danger, she nevertheless stands shoulder to shoulder with a man she has not previously met, rather than fleeing from the threat. In the second season instalment *Nervous Man in a Four Dollar Room*, meanwhile, small time crook Jackie Rhoades is confronted by his wiser, more moral alter ego, who ultimately convinces his criminal self of the error of his ways. If the resolutions of *The Last Flight*, *The Fear* and *Nervous Man in a Four Dollar Room* are inspiring, *The Prisoner*'s climax is more pessimistic, with Number Six seemingly doomed to struggle against his own dark side for all his remaining days. This situation sharply contrasts with what Brode and Serling believe is the message to be learnt from the dénouement of *The Fear*. "All we need do to survive is embrace the best in ourselves, rather than surrender to the worst." (p. 178)[42]

Whereas the heroic and cowardly aspects of Decker and Scott co-exist as different elements within the same person's personality, in *Eye of the Beholder*, the two sides of Janet Tyler emerge in terms of how she is perceived by others. In her own society she is regarded as hideous but elsewhere she is considered entirely normal. Both here and in *Fall Out* contrast is presented in the starkest terms. In the final instalment of *The Prisoner*, Number One is revealed to be the leering, bestial element of Number Six. He is quite different from the rational, thinking man with which we have become familiar. In *Eye of the Beholder*, meanwhile, there are quite literally two Janet Tylers; different actresses play the bandaged Janet and the revealed woman. Director Douglas Heyes explains that he cast Maxine Stuart in the first half of the story "because of her voice, because her voice did not suggest a beautiful girl – it suggested a strong, harsh, realistic woman, and therefore the unveiling would be a surprise." (p. 147)[43] The revealed Janet we see subsequently was portrayed by the highly attractive Donna Douglas. The importance of the change is recognised by Brode and Serling, who comment, "By having two actresses play Janet, *Zone*'s Mirror Image is implied." (p. 205)[44] For some, such an extreme contrast was unnecessary. Indeed, Maxine Stuart herself comments, "I do feel that since this particular show dealt with conformity, they might have allowed for a less startling-looking woman and settled for reality!" (p. 331)[45]

The Prisoner is, of course, notoriously vague, and even evasive, in terms of the answers it offers to the viewer's nagging questions and, on various key issues, McGoohan has given little away in subsequent interviews. When asked by Barrington Calia in 1985 why his character resigned, McGoohan responded by avoiding the opportunity to give a specific explanation and chose to answer only in general terms.[46] *Eye of the Beholder* is similarly oblique. In his closing narration, Serling acknowledges that viewers will want to know more about the society they have witnessed. He remarks, "Now the questions that come to mind. Where is this place and when is it, what kind of world where ugliness is the norm and beauty the deviation from that norm?" Serling dismisses these questions trenchantly by asserting that they are unimportant, and maintains that his central argument is valid whether the scenario takes place "in this year or a hundred years hence, on this planet or wherever there is human life, perhaps out amongst the stars". Less fundamental questions may vex the viewer, too. Exactly who is the Leader whose speech is followed so slavishly by the hospital staff? What hold does he exercise over the citizens and how did he come to power?[47] Rather than speculate, it is perhaps more productive to understand *The Prisoner* and *Eye of the Beholder* as simply dramatised explorations of abstract societal problems and which choose to ignore the specifics of when, what, why, etc.

Readers who are particularly interested in the themes within *Eye of the Beholder* may be keen to explore the *Night Gallery* segment *The Different Ones*, in which Serling revisits many of the same ideas. The writer was most dissatisfied, however, with how his script was realised, even going so far as to call it "a piece of shit". (p. 126)[48] Anyone wishing to experience the tale as Serling intended it would be well advised to read his own short story version.[49]

The *Encyclopedia of TV Science Fiction* summarises the plot of the *Prisoner* episode *The Schizoid Man* by stating that in this instance, Number Six is the victim of a scheme by the Village authorities to convince him that he is someone else – Number Twelve.[50] Again we can detect parallels with certain *Twilight Zone* stories. As Zicree points out, the question of "Am I who I think I am?" was one that the programme would explore "many times". (p. 101)[51] The author makes this comment when discussing the first season story *A World of Difference*, in which seemingly ordinary businessman Arthur Curtis suddenly finds himself an actor in a film for which his office is a set. Similar "displacement" themes emerge in the third season instalment *Person or Persons Unknown*. Here a man wakes one morning to find that he is not recognised by any of the people who are familiar to him. Personal identity is not the only issue that links these episodes with *The Prisoner*. Zicree notes that in the case of the later story "once again we have Serling's 'fear of the unknown working on **you**, which you cannot share with others'". (pp. 280–281)[52] Such isolation also brings to mind the dimension of paranoia that is so much associated with *The Prisoner*. Perhaps the key difference is that in *The Twilight Zone* reasons for the disconnection between the hero and the reality that he understands often lie in the realm of the fantastic, whereas The Prisoner's various predicaments would seem to have been induced by conspiracies masterminded by the leaders of The Village.

For White and Ali, paranoia within *The Prisoner* is not only felt by characters within the drama. If we take the attitude that Number Six is a "plant" within The Village, then – in the authors' words – it is "as if a big trick has been played on the viewer, and it leads to one incredibly downbeat conclusion: nobody can be trusted [by us], not even the man we have come to respect for his integrity, his individuality, and his persistence against the evils of society". (p. 152)[53] We can draw parallels here between how, in some of the best crime fiction, none of the protagonists can be above the reader's suspicion. Exploring the nature of paranoia within Agatha Christie's mysteries, Mark Campbell writes, "Pick up one of her books and you will have absolutely no idea whodunit – it could be anyone. And I mean **anyone**." (p. 12)[54] Joanne Morreale writes how *The Prisoner* can provide "viewers with a cognitive 'jolt' that makes them aware of the instability of their point of view and interpretive frameworks". (p. 180)[55] If The Prisoner is truly understood as a "plant", then the scale of such "jolts" is taken to a new level.

Let us complete this chapter by taking a brief look at a *Twilight Zone* episode in which, ultimately, questions surrounding the identities of the characters who interact with the main protagonist are perhaps just as important as those concerning the nature of the protagonist himself. Like *Eye of the Beholder* and *The Obsolete Man*, Charles Beaumont's *Shadow Play* was first broadcast during *The Twilight Zone*'s second season. "Nightmarish" is an adjective often associated with *The Prisoner*. Chris R. Tame describes The Village as a "nightmare vision of life" (p. 3);[56] Carrazé and Oswald regard it as a "nightmarish prison" (p. 201)[57] and, in introducing the final episode, the synopsis provided by the *TV Times* magazine begins, "At last the end of a nightmarish adventure is in sight." (p. 425)[58] If we believe that Number Six is **actually** experiencing a bad dream and that the events we have witnessed over the course of the series repeat in a continuous cycle, we may conclude that the central protagonist is enduring a nightmare without end. The same can be said of Adam Grant in *The Twilight Zone*'s *Shadow Play*. There are, however, fundamental differences. In *Shadow Play*, Adam Grant knows that what is taking place amounts to a nightmare and is aware from the outset that the events will repeat. The episode opens with Grant being found by a court of law to be guilty of murder and sentenced to death. Convinced that what is happening is merely a recurring fantasy, he maintains that all the characters in the drama will cease to exist when he is killed and the dream ends. Grant can predict with absolute certainty the events to come. Unable to change the pattern, he is ultimately executed. The instalment finishes in much the same way as it started, with the accused man found guilty in the courtroom. On this occasion, though, the scenario takes place with different characters and only Grant remains in his previous role…

Some readers may feel that the ending of *Fall Out* should not be taken too literally. We may suspect that rather than suggesting that all the events we have witnessed will recur in identical fashion, the repetition of the first scene of the opening title sequence at the end implies only that The Prisoner will have to face the same issues again. The last few moments of *Shadow Play* indicate that there are certainly variations in the drama that repeats here. Adam Grant may be back in the courtroom but the people he must face are different in this iteration.

Ramage notes that several *Twilight Zone* stories are of a cyclical nature.[59] In some, such as *Judgment Night*, *The Howling Man*, *Death Ship* and *Come Wander With Me*, the key players appear trapped in a repeating pattern. Richard Matheson's script for *Death Ship* particularly emphasises this characteristic as, in setting down the conclusion, it calls for the reuse of "dialogue from Shot #3" (p. 204) and slightly later it instructs "Action and dialogue continues as in Shot #9." (p. 205)[60] In *Mirror Image*, meanwhile, the climax would suggest that a scenario comparable to that which we have just seen is destined to take place with a new protagonist. In *Shadow Play*, a variation on the cyclical theme arises when Grant's nightmare starts to repeat but the identities of those playing major roles in the events change. Some similarities can be drawn between this situation and the endings of the episodes *Dead Man's Shoes* and *Queen of the Nile*. Here, too, there is a mixture of constant and shifting protagonists. In the former's dénouement, the vengeful spirit of a gangster who has been murdered by an associate takes over the latest wearer of the victim's shoes and seems about to resume the vendetta against his killer. In *Queen of the Nile*, the central character – the vampire of the title – remains throughout and, in the last scene, the pattern of events that the viewer has watched begins again. On this occasion, however, a new protagonist is to become the Queen's next victim... A different form of "altered repetition" provides the climax of *Person or Persons Unknown*. After David Gurney wakens from a dream in which none of the people to whom he is normally familiar recognised him, the protagonist discovers that he himself does not know the woman who claims to be his wife. Reflecting on the nature of *Fall Out*, Steven Ricks wonders whether it should be regarded as "a conclusion" or merely "an ending". (p. 18)[61] The same question may well be asked in relation to the final moments of any of these *Twilight Zone* episodes. Rod Serling, whose *Judgment Night* formed an early, first season *Twilight Zone* episode, would return to cyclical narrative over ten years later with his *Night Gallery* contribution *Midnight Never Ends*. For Skelton and Benson, the later work, in fact, "feels very much like recycled *Twilight Zone* material". (p. 179)[62]

Many commentators and some people directly involved in making *The Prisoner* highlight how the series brings to mind images and concepts associated with the work of Franz Kafka. In broad terms, John Javna feels that the programme is "like a Kafkaesque fantasy" rather "than a standard science fiction program", (p. 48)[63] and more specific Kafka – *Prisoner* comparisons abound. As long ago as the late 1970s, Susan Nobel and Diana Goldsborough suggested that any reader wanting to pursue further the themes within *The Prisoner*'s *Schizoid Man* episode should find Kafka's book *The Trial* of interest,[64] whilst *The Prisoner Inspired* draws particular parallels between events in the same Kafka novel and the ceremonial proceedings supervised by The President of The Village in *Fall Out*. More broadly, the documentary refers to the book's elements of "surreal paranoia" and "horrific oppression" within a totalitarian state, which are, of course, key ingredients within *The Prisoner*, too.[65]

George Baker, who played the second Number Two in *Arrival*, also detects Kafkaesque overtones, with both *The Prisoner* and Kafka's work concerned with the tenuous nature of the individual's hold on reality.[66] For Lewis Greifer, Kafkaesque possibilities were evident to him as early as when he read the writers' guide for *The Prisoner*. Admitting that he found this document "just as confused as the series", Greifer suggests that the material within it could lead to treatments as diverse as Kafka-like drama or a more conventional spy thriller.[67] Greifer also contends that, under McGoohan, much of the realisation of the series was consistent with Kafka's ideas, although the programme was not in any way based on them. Greifer reflects, "Kafka really explores a man lost against social forces which confuse him, which are intangible. Some of that was in *The Prisoner* but not as an intention. It was there because Pat felt like that." (p. 168)[68]

There are, of course, many differences in perspective that are evident in the ideas of Patrick McGoohan and George Markstein respectively in relation to *The Prisoner*. It would seem, however, that **both** men were heavily influenced by Kafka. In presenting the key principles for the series, George Markstein explains, "It is Kafkaesque. We are prisoners of our environment, background, parents, education, bodies, health, society, in a world that increasingly makes little sense." (p. 64)[69] In a 1980 interview with Roger Goodman, Markstein even went so far as to admit, "I've plagiarised Kafka... Kafka played a great part in *The Prisoner*." (p. 83)[70] For Brode and Serling, meanwhile, the tone of *The Twilight Zone's Shadow Play* is, like that of *The Obsolete Man* and *Eye of the Beholder*, also "effectively Kafkaesque, [with] the entire piece... set in a surreal version of our own world". (p. 35)[71] Again, such a description would also seem to sum up highly effectively the essence of *The Prisoner*.

References and Notes

1. Reproduced in: Langley, R. (ed.) The Prisoner original 60s publicity material. 2012. Whilst it is undoubtedly fascinating for us today to examine the original publicity material surrounding The Prisoner, questions may well be asked of its authority. Roger Goodman treats it with particular caution, saying that much of it was "churned out" by "somebody in an office somewhere who had hardly seen the series" and many of the "facts" within it have been contradicted by those who had actually been involved in the making of the programme. (see Where The Secret Agent Is Whisked Away, George Markstein and The Prisoner, p. 84)

2. Booker, M. K. Strange TV: Innovative television series from The Twilight Zone to The X-Files. Greenwood: Westport, Connecticut, 2002.

3. Schumer, A. Visions from the Twilight Zone. Chronicle: San Francisco, California, 1990.

4. Ibid.

5. Quoted in: Schumer, A. op. cit.

6. Albarella, T. (ed.) As timeless as infinity: The complete Twilight Zone scripts of Rod Serling – Volume ten. Gauntlet: Colorado Springs, Colorado, 2013.

7. Quoted in: Davy, R. So who was George Markstein? In: Goodman, R. (ed.) George Markstein and The Prisoner. pandqmedia: Berwyn, Denbighshire, 2014, pp. 20–52.

8. Presnell, D. and McGee, M. A critical history of television's The Twilight Zone, 1959–1964. McFarland: Jefferson, North Carolina, 1998.

9. Howard, D. L. The Prisoner. In: Lavery, D. (ed.) The essential cult TV reader. University Press of Kentucky: Lexington, Kentucky, 2010, pp. 189–200.

10. Holton, S. and Skotak, R. Starlog photo guidebook: Fantastic worlds. Starlog: New York, 1978.

11.   Carrazé, A. and Oswald, H. The Prisoner: A televisionary masterpiece. Virgin: London, 1990.

12.   Stanyard, S. T. Dimensions behind The Twilight Zone: A backstage tribute to television's groundbreaking series. ECW Press: Toronto, Ontario, 2007.

13.   White, M. and Ali, J. The official Prisoner companion. Sidgwick and Jackson: London, 1988.

14.   Reproduced in: White, M. and Ali, J. op. cit., pp. 127–130.

15.   The Prisoner: Patrick McGoohan Interviewed By Warner Troyer – The Troyer Interview, Part Two. The Prisoner: Music, FAQs, background, episode guide, spoofs. URL: http://www.the-prisoner-6.freeserve.co.uk/troyer2.htm (accessed: 23 September 2013). Transcript of 1977 interview.

      In the same interview, McGoohan quips that the brainwashed state of the Villagers may be a result of them having watched "too many commercials". Certainly, the way that these people are manipulated is comparable to the techniques we see in the Out of the Unknown instalment Tunnel Under the World, which satirises contemporary advertising. Like The Prisoner, Tunnel Under the World also, incidentally, features a strong cyclical element within the plot.

      Further links between McGoohan's programme and the domain of advertising are apparent from the fact that in The Prisoner Program Guide, Neil McLean and David Stansfield suggest that teachers of English and Media Studies who are developing for their pupils activities centred on the programme may wish to read Vance Packard's classic monograph on advertising, The Hidden Persuaders, when exploring the concept of indoctrination – one of seven themes which the authors believe are pivotal to The Prisoner.

16.   Quoted in: Zicree, M. S. The Twilight Zone companion. Bantam: New York, 1982.

17.   Wolfe, P. In the zone: The twilight world of Rod Serling. Bowling Green State University Popular Press: Bowling Green, Ohio, 1997.

18.   Quoted in: Grams Jr., M. The Twilight Zone: Unlocking the door to a television classic. OTR Publishing: Churchvillle, Maryland, 2008.

19.   Page, A. Postmodern drama. In: Creeber, G. (ed.) The television genre book, 2nd ed. Palgrave Macmillan: Basingstoke, 2008, pp. 54–59.

20.   Short, S. Countering the counterculture: The Prisoner and the 1960s. In: Cook, J. R. and Wright, P. (eds.) British science fiction television: A hitchhiker's guide. I. B. Tauris: London, 2006, pp. 71–92.

21.   Zicree, M. S. op. cit.

22.   Albarella, T. (ed.) As timeless as infinity: The complete Twilight Zone scripts of Rod Serling – Volume four. Gauntlet: Colorado Springs, Colorado, 2007.

23.   Fritz Weaver Interview. In: Stanyard, S. T. op. cit., pp. 178–182.

24.   Hoberman, J. America's Twilight Zone. In: Schumer, A. op. cit., pp. 146–160.

25.   Brode, D. and Serling, C. Rod Serling and The Twilight Zone: The 50th anniversary

tribute. Barricade Books: Fort Lee, New Jersey, 2009.

26. Reynolds, K. The Twilight Zone: Rod Serling's wondrous land. iUniverse LLC: Bloomington: Indiana, 2014.

27. Brode, D. and Serling, C. op. cit.

28. Darrow, P. You're him, aren't you? An autobiography. Big Finish, 2006.

29. Zicree, M. S. op. cit.

30. Skelton, S. and Benson, J. Rod Serling's Night Gallery: An after-hours tour. Syracuse University Press: Syracuse, New York, 1999.

31. Hoberman, J. op. cit.

32. Short, S. op. cit.

33. Ramage, A. (ed.) Forgotten gems from The Twilight Zone: Volume 2. Bear Manor Media: Albany, Georgia, 2006.

34. Reproduced in: Langley, R. (ed.) op. cit.

35. Interview With Patrick McGoohan. In: Carrazé, A. and Oswald, H. op. cit., pp. 6–8.

36. See, for example: Zicree, M. S. op. cit.; Wolfe, P. op. cit.; Presnell, D. and McGee, M. op. cit; Ramage, A. (ed) op. cit.; Stanyard, S. T. op. cit.; Reynolds, K. op. cit.

37. Stanyard, S. T. op. cit.

38. Schumer, A. op. cit., pp. 48–97.

39. Albarella, T. (ed.) As timeless as infinity: The complete Twilight Zone scripts of Rod Serling – Volume one. Gauntlet: Colorado Springs, Colorado, 2004.

40. Ibid.

41. Brode, D. and Serling, C. op. cit.

42. Brode, D. and Serling, C. op. cit.

43. Quoted in: Zicree, M. S. op. cit.

44. Brode, D. and Serling, C. op. cit.

45. Quoted in: Albarella, T. (ed.) op. cit. 2004.

46. Talking With McGoohan. In: White, M. and Ali, J. op. cit., pp. 175–181.

47. Comparisons can be drawn between the devoted attention the hospital staff give to their Leader's speech in Eye of the Beholder and the appreciation of Number Two that is shown by the Villagers who provide likenesses of him in the various works that they submit for the arts and crafts competition in The Chimes of Big Ben.

48. Quoted in: Javna, J. The best of science fiction TV: The critics' choice from Captain Video to Star Trek, from The Jetsons to Robotech. Titan: London, 1988.

49. Serling, R. Night Gallery 2. Rod Serling Books, 2014, pp. 62–77. Reprint of 1972 work.

50. Fulton, R. The encyclopedia of TV science fiction. Boxtree: London, 1990.

51. Zicree, M. S. op. cit.

52. Zicree, M. S. op. cit.

53. White, M. and Ali, J. op. cit.

54. Campbell, M. Agatha Christie. Pocket Essentials: Harpenden, 2005.

55. Morreale, J. Lost, The Prisoner, and the end of the story. Journal of Popular Film

and Television, 38 (4), 2010, pp. 176–185.

56. Tame, C. R. Different values: An analysis of Patrick McGoohan's The Prisoner. Libertarian Reprints, 1, 1983. Reprint of 1974 work. URL: http://www.libertarian.co.uk/lapubs/libre/libre001.pdf (accessed: 23 February 2017).

57. Carrazé, A. and Oswald, H. op. cit.

58. Reproduced in: Fairclough, R. (ed.) The Prisoner: The original scripts – Volume 2. Reynolds and Hearn: Richmond, London, 2006.

59. Ramage, A. (ed) op. cit.

60. Wiater, S. (ed.) Richard Matheson's The Twilight Zone scripts: Volume two. Springfield, Pennsylvania: Edge, 2002.

61. Ricks, S. The Prisoner: I am not a number! A series guide. TR 7: Borehamwood, 2000.

62. Skelton, S. and Benson, J. op. cit.

63. Javna, J. op. cit.

64. Nobel, S. and Goldsborough, D. The Prisoner puzzle. Ontario Educational Communications Authority: Toronto, Ontario, 1978.

65. The Prisoner Inspired. VHS video cassette. TR 7 Productions: Borehamwood, 1992.

66. George Baker Interview. In: The Prisoner In-depth Tape 2. VHS video cassette. TR 7 Productions: Borehamwood, 1992.

67. Lewis Greifer Interview. In: The Prisoner In-depth Tape 5. VHS video cassette. TR 7 Productions: Borehamwood, 1993.

68. Quoted in: Rakoff, I. Inside The Prisoner: Radical television and film in the 1960s. Batsford: London, 1998.

69. Quoted in: Creator Of The Whole Fantasy: A Correspondence Between George Markstein And Roger Goodman. In: Goodman, R. (ed.) op. cit., pp. 54–72.

70. Where The Secret Agent Is Whisked Away. In: Goodman, R. (ed.) op. cit., pp. 78–95.

71. Brode, D. and Serling, C. op. cit.

Other Kafka – Twilight Zone links in relation to the two Serling episodes that have been addressed in this chapter have been made elsewhere. In recalling his plans for the climax of The Obsolete Man, director Elliot Silverstein reports that he intended "a kind of Kafka-like scene, in which [The Chancellor] was to be destroyed by a group of black-shirted Kafka figures in a Kafka-like trial". (see Elliot Silverstein Interview, Dimensions behind The Twilight Zone: A backstage tribute to television's groundbreaking series, pp. 182–83) The State portrayed in Eye of the Beholder is also deemed by Tony Albarella to be "Kafkaesque". He points to how its nature and "harsh regulations" lead to an "almost instinctive" mistrust of it on the viewer's part. (see As Timeless as Infinity: The Complete Twilight Zone Scripts of Rod Serling – Volume One, p. 327)

CHAPTER SIX
Villages and
Houses

This chapter is a revised and expanded version of an essay that originally appeared
in *The Projection Room* section of the website *The Unmutual.*

In the previous chapter, an episode of *Rod Serling's Night Gallery* was briefly
discussed. Chapter Six deals with an earlier instalment of the programme in
rather more detail. Although Scott Skelton and Jim Benson mount a robust
defence of the series,[1] *Night Gallery* has never been highly acclaimed. Indeed,
John Javna[2] and Gary Gerani and Paul H. Schulman[3] go so far as to write that it
was panned by the critics, and the view put forward in *The Encyclopedia of
Science Fiction*[4] that the show came as something of a disappointment after
Serling's classic *Twilight Zone* is widely held. Nevertheless, it included some
excellent segments. *Class of '99* is frequently regarded as one of the highlights
and another notable success was *The House*, a twenty-five-minute, season one
play written by Serling himself and based on a short story by André Maurois. In
the drama, a young woman, played by Joanna Pettet, experiences a recurring
dream which features a charming country house. On discovering the building
apparently by accident in real life, she finds it is for sale and immediately buys
it and moves in, despite the fact that she is told that the house is haunted. When
the girl experiences the manifestations for herself, a shocking revelation
emerges...

The House was first broadcast in the US on 30th December 1970, some three
years after the initial transmission of the opening episode of *The Prisoner* in
England. The two productions share several important plot similarities. Perhaps

most fundamentally, both deal with a key period in the life of a displaced person set apart from the rest of conventional society, although the starting points for the two programmes are quite contrasting. The title sequence for the British series begins with the hero resigning from a top secret post. He is kidnapped and taken to The Village, where he will be incarcerated for most of the series' duration. In *The House*, the central character, Elaine Latimer, is preparing to leave the sanatorium in which she has been recovering from the effects of mental illness. We learn very little about the circumstances surrounding the protagonists' arrivals in these closed communities. In *The Prisoner*, whilst it would appear that the hero's decision to resign has led to his abduction, the viewer is never told why he left his job or even what precisely the post involved. Similarly, in *The House*, the reasons for Elaine's admission into the sanatorium are not revealed. We may speculate that she has suffered some sort of breakdown.

There are, however, important contrasts. The Prisoner is a reluctant inmate within The Village. Elaine, meanwhile, is not keen to leave the sanatorium and is apprehensive about life beyond it. Both communities may be considered highly artificial. The "press information" booklet produced by ITC suggests that the only fun to be enjoyed in The Village is that which is "manufactured", (p. 127)[5] and Elaine's doctor tells her, "A sanatorium can be a pleasant place but there's no reality here for you. The reality comes outside." There are, though, major differences in the importance of these settings. Whereas most of the action in *The Prisoner* takes place within The Village, in *The House*, the scenes in the sanatorium are restricted to the first half of the episode.

Both The Prisoner and Elaine Latimer are portrayed as true individuals. The independence and determination of Number Six have long been celebrated by fans of *The Prisoner* and, despite the psychological problems that have clearly dogged her in the recent past, Elaine displays similar characteristics herself. References to "Miss Latimer" tell us that she is unmarried and, on leaving the sanatorium, she makes no attempt to contact any family or friends. Elaine moves into her new house alone. Like The Village in *The Prisoner*, the place in which this house is located is never named. Nevertheless, we do know that it is remote. Elaine's individuality is recognised by the estate agent, Peugot. Realising that Elaine is different from other female house buyers, he muses, "You're a woman who knows her own mind. If something appeals to you, you follow your instincts. That's good. It shows resolve and will." Even tales that the house is haunted do not deter Elaine from moving in. Peugot's attitude to Elaine shifts somewhat during the course of the programme, however, as he later implies that it is her susceptibility to suggestion that has led her to believe that the house really is haunted.

Neither The Prisoner nor Elaine is universally popular among the people they encounter. The former is variously labelled "disharmonious" and "unmutual" in *A Change of Mind*, and an elderly patient in the sanatorium takes a strong dislike to Elaine, admitting to a nurse that she "never cared for the woman". Skelton and Benson observe that the characters in *The House* are generally harsh,[6] and this elderly woman is especially unpleasant. Elaine's doctor is also somewhat less than sympathetic. He listens to her concerns about leaving the sanatorium but does not offer to extend her stay until her confidence has risen. On the contrary, he insists that the confronting of anxieties is part of ordinary life. As in *The Prisoner*, it is difficult to determine which of the protagonists in Serling's drama can be trusted. When looking round the house, Elaine quizzes Peugot about why the previous occupants left. Like many of the Villagers in *The Prisoner*, the estate agent is evasive, and he frequently responds to her questions with more of his own. Eventually, he discloses that the previous occupants, like the owners before them, believed the building to be haunted, although Peugot himself does not accept their argument. He later treats with similar scepticism Elaine's claim that she, too, has experienced hauntings within the house.

The conclusions of *The Prisoner* and *The House* would both appear to reveal that the main character of the drama has actually been responsible for the events affecting them. In the former, Number One is seen to be The Prisoner himself, whilst in the latter the ghost haunting the house is ultimately shown to be that of Elaine. If an alternative eye-catching title summarising the 17 episodes were to be given to *The Prisoner*, then *The Man Who Tortured Himself* would seem an appropriate possibility and, in the case of *The House*, *The Girl Who Haunted Herself* would be equally suitable. Nevertheless, the fact that past occupants of the building have also experienced hauntings suggests that the manifestations do not just affect Elaine.[7]

Even after the revelations surrounding the roles of the central characters in creating the situations that have been witnessed, further drama awaits the viewer. Indeed, in each production the last moments are critical and provide a final twist. In *The Prisoner*, the opening seconds of the title sequence recur, thereby implying that the hero's kidnapping will take place again. In *The House*, Elaine is disturbed by a knock at her front door and reaches the entrance just in time to watch her own car leaving the house, thus repeating events that have already been seen in the episode. Nevertheless, the mood of the two conclusions is quite different. When the clap of thunder that accompanies the title sequence of *The Prisoner* is heard once more, this may seem a somewhat ominous precursor of the events to come, although sound editor Wilf Thompson has explained that, in truth, the noise was the result of an oversight during the mixing stage of the episode's production.[8] In *The House*, a sunny, airy wholesomeness permeates the entire episode. Much is often made of the bleak and menacing tone of many of the *Night Gallery* stories. Mark Phillips and Frank Garcia believe that, whereas *The Twilight Zone* "celebrated mankind, *Night Gallery* reflected the host's darker nature". (p. 314)[9] If, however, we accept a contrasting interpretation offered by J. Hoberman, there may be greater continuity between *The Twilight Zone* and *Night Gallery* than Phillips and Garcia imply. For Hoberman, the earlier programme was "remarkably downbeat" and inspired in its viewers a "sense of skepticism". (p. 160)[10] This characteristic also provides another clear link between *The Prisoner* and *The Twilight Zone*.

The atmosphere in the *Night Gallery* story *The House* is refreshingly light, however. As Elaine herself comments, she experiences "no apprehension in the dream, no... fear or tension" and, as she approaches the house in her fantasy, she feels a sense of "peace, of serenity". Still, Skelton and Benson describe her recurring dream as a "nightmare looping into itself, to presumably be played endlessly in the mind of the lead character". (p. 64)[11] After watching the *Night Gallery* episode and the overall *Prisoner* saga, we may conclude that the events we have witnessed in **each** drama will repeat themselves in the time ahead, yet additional oddities complicate the pattern. In *The Prisoner*, a blurring of the division between the fantasy world of The Village and the real world of London is suggested by the fact that, as he returns to his home, The Prisoner's front door opens automatically and with a soft electronic buzz in a manner identical to that of his cottage door in The Village. Distinctions between the dream world and the real world are also unclear in *The House*. As Skelton and Benson note, the dream sequences are always shot in slow motion until the final scene when, at the very end, it is Elaine, now apparently awake, who is seen to move in this fashion, whilst the car leaving her house is shown in real time.[12] Certainly the "resolutions" of *The Prisoner* and *The House* may be considered to provide more questions than answers. The events are merely presented to the viewer and there is no explanatory scene to follow in which protagonists discuss the significance of what has happened and thereby offer possible interpretations to the audience. Skelton and Benson conclude, "the meaning of *The House* stays just beyond the viewer's reach". (p. 64)[13]

Since an individual seeking to explore the possible meanings of *The Prisoner* and *The House* can learn much from seeing the productions more than once, the works form durable drama for the modern DVD age. Chris Gregory writes, "*The Prisoner* appears to be an ideal 'video text', as repeated viewings reveal more and more depth in each episode... The series can be watched, discussed, reassessed and 'deconstructed' in the viewer's 'own time'." (p. 184)[14] In each production, there are features of the drama that keen fans may use as evidence to construct their own theories. Viewers may, for example, attach particular importance to the ghostliness that surrounds certain characters in the *Night Gallery* story. On meeting Elaine for the first time, Peugot seems simply to materialise and indeed director John Astin himself explains, "I had him sort of appearing from the shadows of the trees, sort of drifting in... as though he himself might have been a spirit." (p. 63)[15] In addition to the baffling closing scene which would appear to imply that Elaine is a transient figure moving between the real world and the dream world, there is other evidence to suggest that the girl may not be quite what she seems. In words that offer an early indication of Elaine's otherworldliness, the sanatorium patient who so dislikes Elaine confides to a nurse that she found her "dreamy... never walked, just sort of wafted along, like a wood sprite". The soft, flowing clothes we see Elaine wearing in the slow motion sequences at times seem to float in the air and bestow on her a wraith-like quality which adds to the general impression that the girl herself is somehow **different**.

Max Hora,[16] Chris Gregory[17] and Daniel O'Brien[18] speculate that the events depicted in *The Prisoner* can be understood simply as a bad dream. Neil McLean and David Stansfield believe that it may be assumed that The Village "is a projection of the Prisoner's own mental turmoil", (p. 10)[19] whilst Sue Short goes even further down the mental instability avenue, noting that according to one school of *Prisoner* thought, what we witness in the series may be an "elaborate delusion" resulting from a nervous breakdown. (p. 24)[20] For Steven Paul Davies, evidence in support of the dream/nightmare/hallucination interpretation can be found in the first very episode. He points to the "bizarre" nature of The Village and what goes on within it, (p. 77) and to the fact that the hero has apparently just resigned from a very stressful top secret government position.[21]

A similar theory can be proposed to rationalise the events in *The House*, especially in view of the fact that it has been established that Elaine has recently been suffering from major psychological problems. The painting that Serling shows to the audience in his opening narration may offer an advance clue. It depicts the face of the girl who comes to form the main character of the drama and this image is combined with a representation of the house into which she moves. With hindsight, the juxtaposition of the two may be thought to suggest that the whole episode takes place in the protagonist's mind.[22] In addition, Astin acknowledges that the way in which the first dream sequence is presented, with the door to the house opening only as Elaine's car leaves and the scene dissolving into a close-up of the actress's eye, implies "that she's the one in the house, that this is all playing out in her head". Astin continues, "If you're looking for a clue to explain the story, that's the clue!" (p. 64)[23]

If the whole drama is indeed viewed as simply the product of Elaine's imagination, we may read into the events both optimistic and pessimistic mental outlooks on the girl's part. Certainly, we can detect a strong aspirational dimension. Elaine finds the house of her dreams apparently through a happy accident and without carrying out any kind of extensive or systematic search for it; the quietness of the area around holds great appeal to her; the immediacy with which she makes a decision to purchase the property demonstrates a decisiveness of character that is atypical of Elaine's usual personality; she is able to buy the house of her dreams at an extremely low price; she has the financial resources to pay for the property seemingly without anxiety; the layout of the rooms is reassuringly familiar to her; she moves in swiftly (actually the same day that she views the building) and with no complications. In short, the ideal circumstances surrounding her acquisition of the house promise to provide Elaine with the kind of existence that she would **like** to enjoy. Such smooth progress is, of course, far removed from much of normal reality. Our minds may, in fact, quickly return to the early scene where Elaine's doctor tells her (and the viewer) that the encountering of problems is part of life. All too quickly, however, the façade of perfection cracks. Peugot begins to see in a more sceptical light the girl he has hitherto regarded as a strong young woman. Moreover, the persistent intrusion of the ghost and, especially, the fact that it takes Elaine's own form, may be taken to suggest that the protagonist remains highly disturbed and is not yet free of all her inner demons. The final scene of *The Prisoner* is equally bleak. If we favour the most depressing interpretation, we may conclude that the forces operating against the hero are inescapable.

If, in contrast, we take the line that most of the events portrayed in *The House* **really** do take place then in retrospect Peugot's disclosure that previous residents of the building have been driven from it by supernatural events is one of the episode's most thought-provoking plot developments. We may well wonder whether the nature of the haunting is the same for each party or whether it varies from case to case. The fact that one of the past owners and, initially, Elaine herself are unable to describe the spiritual presence in any concrete terms implies that there is some degree of commonality in their experiences. We may wonder, too, how far The Village in *The Prisoner* is subjective in nature. Although *The Encyclopedia of Science Fiction* indicates that what we see in *Fall Out* "suggests that the metaphorical prison is partly a creation of the mind itself, including the hero's", (p. 475) the book does not pursue the issue of whether the particular mental construct that we may label as "The Village" is unique to each individual or is shared by different people.[24] Patrick McGoohan has proved more helpful on this matter. In conversation with interviewer Warner Troyer he has commented, "Your village may be different from other people's villages, but we all have one." (p. 4)[25]

We can make some connections between The Village and the nature of a "hell weapon" as discussed in *Di Fate's Catalog of Science Fiction Hardware*. (p. 108) Such a weapon, it is maintained in the book, does not cause physical destruction but affects one's perception of reality. Di Fate's volume outlines how the weapon may take such diverse forms as propaganda and mind-altering drugs like hallucinogens. These are, of course, integral to systems of control in the physical Village. The *Catalog* also, however, highlights how, when activated, an advanced "hell weapon" can project illusions into the minds of others. Even if we choose to believe that The Village is actually no more than a delusion, it is probably fanciful to suggest that this has been deliberately induced by an enemy. Nevertheless, there are still parallels that may be drawn between the subjective, internal construct of The Village and the principle that a sophisticated "hell weapon" leaves each of its victims dealing with their own "reality".[26]

Whilst *The Prisoner* has become a huge cult over the last 45 years, *Night Gallery* has remained relatively little known in Britain. It was certainly given scant opportunity to make a proper impact when it was originally shown over here. In 1990, *The Encyclopedia of TV Science Fiction* reported, "ITV first screened individual episodes in 1973, but they have never been networked and the series has never been given a really coherent run, switching days, times and duration, skipping weeks and generally failing to establish a settled format." (p. 266)[27] Moreover, it was not until 2006 that a Region Two DVD boxed set embracing the pilot film and all the first season episodes (including *The House*) became available. By this time, VHS video cassette and DVD releases of McGoohan's series had been frequent.

References and Notes

1.   Skelton, S. and Benson, J. Rod Serling's Night Gallery: An after-hours tour. Syracuse University Press: Syracuse, New York, 1999.

2.   Javna, J. The best of science fiction TV: The critics' choice from Captain Video to Star Trek, from The Jetsons to Robotech. Titan: London, 1988.

3.   Gerani, G. and Schulman, P. H. Fantastic television: A pictorial history of sci-fi, the

unusual and the fantastic from the '50s to the '70s. Titan: London, 1987. Reprint of 1977 work.

4. Brosnan, J. and Nicholls, P. Rod Serling's Night Gallery. In: Clute, J. and Nicholls, P. (eds.) The encyclopedia of science fiction, 2nd ed. Orbit: London, 1993, pp. 1023–1024.

5. Reproduced in: White, M. and Ali, J. The official Prisoner companion. Sidgwick and Jackson: London, 1988, pp. 127–130.

6. Skelton, S. and Benson, J. op. cit.

7. Readers who are intrigued by The House may wish to investigate the Fear on Four radio play, Dreaming of Thee, which, especially in its early scenes, exhibits plot features that are strikingly similar to the Night Gallery instalment, although ultimately it is a much darker tale. Here a girl who has become obsessed with a recurring dream in which she approaches an unfamiliar house encounters the building in real life and is told that it is haunted by the girl herself. Thereafter, the stories diverge considerably as she dies in mysterious circumstances and, in the climax of Dreaming of Thee, her close friend would seem to suffer a similar fate.

8. The Prisoner Investigated Vol. 2. VHS video cassette. TR 7 Productions: Borehamwood, 1990.

9. Phillips, M. and Garcia, F. Science fiction television series: Episode guides, histories, and casts and credits for 62 prime time shows, 1959 through 1989. McFarland: Jefferson, North Carolina, 1996.

10. Hoberman, J. America's Twilight Zone. In: Schumer, A. Visions from the Twilight Zone. Chronicle: San Francisco, California, 1990, pp. 146–160.

11. Skelton, S. and Benson, J. op. cit.

12. Skelton, S. and Benson, J. op. cit.

13. Skelton, S. and Benson, J. op. cit.

14. Gregory, C. Be seeing you... Decoding The Prisoner. John Libbey Media: Luton, 1997.

15. Quoted in: Skelton, S. and Benson, J. op. cit.

16. Hora, M. The Prisoner of Portmeirion, 2nd ed. Number Six Publications, 1995.

17. Gregory, C. op. cit.

18. O'Brien, D. SF: UK – How British science fiction changed the world. Reynolds and Hearn: Richmond, London, 2000.

19. McLean, N. and Stansfield, D. The Prisoner program guide. Ontario Educational Communications Authority: Toronto, Ontario, 1976.

20. Short, S. Cult telefantasy series: A critical analysis of The Prisoner, Twin Peaks, The X-Files, Buffy the Vampire Slayer, Lost, Heroes, Doctor Who and Star Trek. McFarland: Jefferson, North Carolina, 2011.

21. Davies, S. P. The Prisoner handbook: An unauthorized companion. Boxtree: London, 2002.

22. Readers who are familiar with the first edition of Unique But Similar may recall how Jacqueline Abromeit's cover illustration employed comparable imagery. Here a man is seen lying prostrate on an extensive beach with a large representation of a penny farthing bicycle immediately above his head. The combining of the two images was intended to illustrate the popular interpretation that The Village and all that The Prisoner believed went on within it were actually simply a dream, a hallucination or some other product of his imagination.

23. Quoted in: Skelton, S. and Benson, J. op. cit.

24. Brosnan, J. and Nicholls, P. The Prisoner. In: Nicholls, P. (ed.) The encyclopedia of science fiction: An illustrated A to Z. Granada: St. Albans, 1979, pp. 475–476.

25. Quoted in: Nobel, S. and Goldsborough, D. The Prisoner puzzle. Ontario Educational Communications Authority: Toronto, Ontario, 1978.

26. Di Fate, V. and Summers, I. Di Fate's catalog of science fiction hardware. Sidgwick and Jackson: London, 1980.

27. Fulton, R. The encyclopedia of TV science fiction. Boxtree: London, 1990.

CHAPTER SEVEN
Sixes and
Sevens

This chapter is a revised and expanded version of an essay that originally appeared in the Spring 2009 edition (i.e. volume 38, number 105) of the journal *Foundation*.

Until its DVD release in June 2005, *The Omega Factor* was one of the BBC's hidden treasures. In the time since its original 1979 transmission, the serial has not been repeated in Britain, either by the BBC or by any cable or satellite channel, and it was never released on video cassette. In the early years of the twenty-first century, however, at least some of the mythology surrounding both *The Prisoner* and *The Omega Factor* was eroded as a result of unprecedented levels of scrutiny. In 2007, the year of the programme's 40th anniversary, a major new book analysing *The Prisoner* appeared,[1] and just 16 months earlier, the publication of a second volume of scripts meant that all were now available commercially.[2] Meanwhile, DD Home Entertainment's DVD package for *The Omega Factor* included a booklet of viewing notes, an audio commentary on one of the most effective episodes and a new documentary.[3]

John Kenneth Muir discusses at some length the notion of a "story arc", which, he suggests, sees the end of the saga taking "the plot and characters back to the beginning". (p. 171) Muir believes that *The Prisoner* exhibits this feature, as the closing shots of the finale are identical to those that started the opening instalment.[4] Piers D. Britton and Simon J. Barker argue that even the serial's individual episodes possess cyclical characteristics. They observe how each begins with the hero's abduction and, at the end of it, after all that has taken place in the previous hour, he is shown still to be trapped behind animated prison bars.[5] Pointing to Clive James's assertion that the appeal of *Star Trek* lies in the "classic inevitability of its repetitions", Chris Gregory notes how the viewer may be reassured by the thought that whatever threat is posed to Captain Kirk and the *Enterprise* crew in a particular episode, "they will – no matter how close they may seem to death or defeat – inevitably triumph against the odds". (p. 96)[6] Similarly, the *Doctor Who* plot formula stated by Andrew Cartmel, which he particularly associates with the "golden age" of the programme, concludes with the hero defeating the villain of the serial. (p. 217)[7] *The Prisoner* presents a very different form of repeating pattern. Indeed, so little real progress is made by Number Six each week that the viewer may well wonder whether the hero is doomed to spend all his remaining days in The Village.

Just as *The Prisoner* would appear to offer a perpetual loop in terms of the beginning and end of the saga, a certain degree of circularity is also prevalent in *The Omega Factor*. In the first part, *The Undiscovered Country*, journalist Tom Crane is about to begin writing an article dealing with "mind power". His work takes him to Edinburgh, where he hopes to investigate Edward Drexel, a rogue occult practitioner with a sinister past. Drexel refuses to cooperate and, apparently in an effort to deter Crane, induces an "accident" in which his wife, Julia, dies. Crane discovers in making his inquiries that he himself possesses psychic abilities and arouses the interest of the highly secret government unit Department Seven, whose brief is to examine the paranormal. Joining forces with the Department and his old friend, Anne Reynolds, Crane explores a range of incidents involving psychic phenomena over the course of the ten episodes and becomes increasingly concerned that a sinister Omega organisation is working on using the paranormal for subversive purposes. Ultimately, a key figure in Department Seven is revealed as an Omega agent. In the concluding scenes, Crane leaves Anne and the Department to return to London and is intent on resuming his career as a journalist. The most striking instance of circularity in the saga lies in the repetition of a single element of dialogue. As he says farewell to Anne at the end of the final episode, she hands him a flask of coffee, commenting, "You know how you hate that motorway rubbish." This echoes an early scene from the first episode in which, before Crane embarks on his journey to Edinburgh, Julia offers him a similar flask with an identical explanation. The repetition of the first scene of *The Prisoner* at the serial's conclusion implies somewhat ominously that Number Six's struggles are not over, and prompts Sue Short to detect in the narrative "an insistent note of hopelessness". (p. 89)[8] The dénouement of *The Omega Factor* is rather more clear cut and slightly more optimistic. After terminating his association with Department Seven, Crane makes preparations to travel to Whitehall, where evidence against the Omega organisation is apparently being prepared. Whether Crane can trust the official whom he is to meet, however, and whether any action that is taken will lead to the demise of the Omega organisation are questions which are left unresolved so as to tease the viewer further. Since one of the Omega agents has already declared that the organisation has "people in very high places", the issue of trust is particularly pertinent.

It is perhaps the hybrid nature of the two programmes that renders each so unusual and memorable. Gregory asserts that *The Prisoner* contains elements of the action-adventure, secret agent and SF genres, and addresses political, psychological and philosophical themes.[9] *The Omega Factor*, meanwhile, is dubbed "a supernatural thriller" by *The Complete Directory to Science Fiction, Fantasy and Horror Television Series* (p. 589)[10] Advance publicity for the DVD release of *The Omega Factor* claimed that the serial could be considered a precursor to *Sea of Souls*.[11] Although both programmes feature stories about the paranormal, the espionage element of *The Omega Factor* gives it an additional dimension which the later programme lacks. Most episodes of *The Omega Factor* offer fairly standalone investigations of individual cases of psychic phenomenon, yet the intrigue surrounding the possible existence of a subversive Omega organisation and the increasing likelihood that an enemy agent has infiltrated Department Seven provide ongoing plotlines that are brought to an end only in the final instalment. At this point the true reason for Julia's death is also revealed. The matter of who killed Drexel, who had been shot in darkness in the fourth episode, had been resolved just the week before. Continuing questions cement together the 17 episodes of *The Prisoner*, too. Specifically, the issues of whether The Prisoner will actually escape and of the identity of Number One maintain an essential continuity across the different instalments. These are again matters that are not concluded until the serial's final part.

The fact that ongoing questions permeate both productions enables each to be defined as an "episodic serial". As we saw in Chapter Two, John Tulloch and Manuel Alvarado specifically cite *The Prisoner*, in fact, as an example of this category of drama.[12] Nevertheless, whilst it is often suggested that Patrick McGoohan oversaw virtually every significant area of *The Prisoner*'s production, it seems that he made relatively little attempt to weave the individual stories into a single, logical and consistent narrative that progressed week by week, despite the overall unity provided by the show's fundamental questions. The lack of cohesiveness may be explained, at least in part, by the fact that McGoohan originally intended *The Prisoner* to run as a seven-part serial rather than the longer series it ultimately became. In the Goodman interview,

McGoohan concedes that most of the additional ten episodes were no more than "padding".[13] In a similar vein, Neil McLean and David Stansfield suggest that the central theme – or fundamental story – of *The Prisoner* is encapsulated in a mere five episodes (i.e. *Arrival, The Chimes of Big Ben, Many Happy Returns, Once Upon a Time* and *Fall Out*).[14] Although Bernard Williams, the first of two production managers to work on the programme, claims that *The Prisoner* "wasn't a series about a different story each week – this was a progressive series" which led towards a conclusion,[15] it is certainly true that virtually all of the instalments can be viewed in any order. Catherine Johnson goes so far as to argue that, in broad terms, there is "little or no continuing storyline running across the episodes". (p. 56)[16] Exploring development within the programme, Britton and Barker are of the opinion that, rather than the episodes building on each other, each instead rearranges "the different ideas implicit in the basic premise". (p. 116)[17] Still, in introducing the ten *Prisoner* scripts that he includes in the second volume of his two-part work that presents the totality for the series, Robert Fairclough is able to integrate, within an overall narrative, the key plot developments associated with the scripts that he has featured in the first volume when he outlines "the story so far". (p. 11)[18]

Undoubtedly, during the course of *The Prisoner*, there are fewer references to incidents in past episodes than is the case in *The Omega Factor*. According to Mark Bould, the individual *Prisoner* instalments are effectively "discrete blocks with no memory of previous episodes, or consequences in following ones". (p. 104)[19] For Anthony Davis, the lack of an integrated narrative was one of the programme's major weaknesses. He writes, "the thing that bothered me most about *The Prisoner* was the absence of any continuity between the episodes; there was no logical progression in his captors' extraordinary attempts to break him, no logical pattern to his escape bids or, indeed, to anything else". (p. 256)[20]

As many as six different writers were responsible for *The Omega Factor*'s ten instalments. It would seem that this was at least in part due to the speed with which scripts had to be prepared. Producer George Gallaccio recounts that, once the production team was assembled, work on the programme had to be done "in so much of a hurry we were throwing ideas out at writers... I would have liked to have worked more intensively with fewer writers". (p. 4)[21] Nevertheless, Andrew Pixley notes that a feature of the narrative style within *The Omega Factor* was the way in which, after sudden conclusions to episodes that appeared to leave matters unresolved, the following week characters would "comment on aspects of plotlines which had previously been left dangling". (p. 36)[22]

Despite fundamental differences in their subject matter, certain plot and concept similarities emerge across the two programmes. ESP, for example, is a theme in both. It is one of the most obvious ingredients within *The Omega Factor*, and in *The Schizoid Man* episode of *The Prisoner*, the Villager Alison is shown to have a telepathic link with Number Six. There are also similarities between *The Schizoid Man* and *The Omega Factor*'s episode *Double Vision*. In each case, the hero's opponents try to induce a mental breakdown through their use of doubles. In McGoohan's serial, as part of a plot by Number Two to make him doubt his own identity, The Prisoner comes face-to-face with his duplicate, who claims to be Number Six. In *The Omega Factor*, the double takes the form of Crane's wife, who, it has already been established, has been dead for some time. As none of Crane's colleagues accepts that it was possible for him to have seen her, Crane's opponents anticipate that their ploy will lead him to question his sanity. Both heroes emerge from the experience intact but, whereas it is apparent that Julia Crane has simply been impersonated, the methods that the Village authorities employed to create a flawless copy of Number Six in *The Schizoid Man* remain unexplained. The mystery has led to some fanciful conjecture surrounding the nature of The Village among academics and fans of the programme. Matthew White and Jaffer Ali note that the use of an apparent clone in this episode, along with various other plot oddities in the serial, has prompted some radicals to suggest that perhaps The Prisoner is being held by extraterrestrials,[23] whilst Fairclough believes that the writer of *The Schizoid Man* script, Terence Feely, "saw the Village as 'a science warp', where modern technological miracles like the creation of an exact duplicate of the Prisoner were possible". (p. 238)[24] Although no advocate of the "extraterrestrials" theory, Johnson, in highlighting the lack of scientific explanation for the advanced technology within The Village, nonetheless recognises that such hardware imbues "the visual landscape... with a pervasive sense of temporal and spatial disorientation". (p. 58)[25]

Perhaps it is inappropriate to attempt to offer any kind of convincing rationale for the presence of the unfamiliar technology we see in *The Prisoner*, since another perspective involves understanding it merely as a dramatic tool that helps to establish a situation in which the authorities are placed in a position of total power over their citizens. The programme is then able to explore what has the potential to be a classic conflict – the ultimate individual is pitted against the ultimate state.

Kenny Smith is one of the few commentators who explicitly link *The Prisoner* with *The Omega Factor*. Even he, though, observes merely that the latter may be considered the forerunner to various series that deal with the supernatural or the unexplained and "bits of *The Prisoner* [are] thrown in for good measure". (p. 6)[26] The instalment of *The Omega Factor* that perhaps most obviously brings to mind themes associated with *The Prisoner* is the fourth, *After-Image*, which forms a key episode in the overall narrative. Here Anne is kidnapped from the train on which she is travelling and encouraged to take part in what she is led to believe are experiments in sensory deprivation sanctioned by Department Seven. It quickly emerges, however, that she has been duped. Those holding her employ trickery to undermine her sense of place and time, and the conclusions she can draw about the people around her. Anne is, in fact, being subjected to a complex programme of disorientation and conditioning in which Drexel plays a prominent role.

Whereas Number Six duels with Number Two virtually every week in *The Prisoner*, Drexel scarcely merits qualification as Crane's recurring enemy in *The Omega Factor*. *After-Image* is only the second episode in which they meet and here they encounter one another for what proves to be the final time. The enigmatic Morag, meanwhile, appears in all the first five instalments. Like the Butler in The Village, Morag is never seen to speak and her silence emphasises her status as a figure of mystery.

At least one major puzzle is resolved near the end of each saga. In *Fall Out*, Number One is finally unmasked and in the penultimate part of *The Omega Factor*, it becomes obvious to the viewer that Roy Martindale, the head of the Edinburgh unit, is the traitor within Department Seven. Nevertheless, the impact of this revelation is diminished by the fact that Martindale appears to be something of a misguided idealist. Crane does not learn the truth until the last instalment. Even at the end of this concluding episode, however, Omega's plans for the discredited Martindale are left unknown. The subservience of the apparent head of an organisation to an unspecified superior is a theme that is carefully developed in both programmes. In the *Prisoner* stories *Free For All, A. B. and C.*, and *Hammer Into Anvil*, Number Two is seen talking into a red telephone to an unseen and unheard superior, and in the last two of these episodes, in particular, these conversations form a significant part in the plot. The viewer is encouraged to assume that it is Number One to whom Number Two is speaking. In episodes of *The Omega Factor* such as *After-Image, St. Anthony's Fire* and *Out of Body, Out of Mind*, Martindale is also shown talking to an unseen and unheard superior but his identity is somewhat less certain. He could be Andrew Scott-Erskine, the Civil Servant head of Department Seven who appears in the serial intermittently, yet subsequent events make clear that it could equally well be a leader of the Omega organisation. It may be significant that two telephones can always be seen on the top of Martindale's desk and, on the occasions that he talks to what could be an Omega superior, he speaks into the black receiver.

In the closing stages of each serial, a representative of the enemy organisation makes the hero a tempting offer. In *Fall Out*, The President asks The Prisoner to assume leadership of The Village or leave, and in *Out of Body, Out of Mind*, Martindale seeks to recruit Crane to the Omega organisation, promising him "an enormous opportunity... a place with Columbus, Vasco da Gama, all the great explorers... It's an offer you can't refuse." The significance of the final comment becomes evident moments later when another Omega agent asserts in a telephone conversation, "If he can't be recruited, he'll have to be disposed of." In both *The Prisoner* and *The Omega Factor*, the hero rejects the invitation and survives. McGoohan maintains, in fact, that Number Six gives little consideration to the leadership option.[27]

Details of the side responsible for The Village are shrouded in secrecy, and similarly little is learned about the nature of Department Seven and the rival Omega organisation. What is clear is that all three may be considered spy organisations of sorts. Tim Heald, in fact, goes so far as to state that Department Seven "is a front for our own dear MI5". (p. 10)[28] Let us assume for one moment that The Village is the creation of the British authorities. If we accept this argument, Alan Cox is able to draw direct parallels between *The Prisoner* and *The Omega Factor*. He comments that both deal with organised government bodies concerned with matters about which the general public know nothing, and present science fiction with a speculative political dimension.[29] Their foci are entirely different, however – the earlier series concentrates on a place where retired former agents are accommodated, whilst *The Omega Factor*'s Department Seven carries out research into the paranormal.

In the *Prisoner* episode *Do Not Forsake Me Oh My Darling*, Number Two speculates on how the mind-swapping machine invented by Professor Seltzman may enable The Village to "break the security of any nation" and in *Illusions*, the final episode of the BBC programme, Martindale is quick to recognise the implications for espionage that may be offered by the abilities of Dr Karl Bruckner, an expert in mind control, to train psychics. In the same instalment, Martindale attempts to convince Crane of the need for the Omega organisation by arguing that research into the paranormal is too important to lie in the hands of an Eastern or Western power bloc. He clearly views Omega as an independent and neutral organisation that transcends ideology. Jack Gerson's tie-in book, which adapts for prose *The Omega Factor*'s first episode and presents a new story not seen in the television series, suggests that whilst some may dub Omega's members "Fascists", they themselves believe that they are "an elite [with]... a God-given right to rule".[30]

In *The Prisoner*, the political orientation of The Village is debatable. White and Ali suggest that there are five possibilities. It may be a form of futuristic world government, or be run by the East, the West, a multinational corporation of some kind or extraterrestrials.[31] Given the fact that the clues within the show fail to present a consistent picture, there is no satisfactory answer to the question. White and Ali conclude, "In the end, we cannot know who runs The Village – and we are not supposed to. The episodes often tease us with hints here or there, but this was intended to be an enigma." (p. 160)[32] The writers' stance is supported by the reminiscences of Vincent Tilsley, who recalls that, in the brief that was given to him by George Markstein, it was made clear that the political ideology of The Village's authorities would never be disclosed.[33]

Even if both Omega and the authorities behind The Village are viewed as "the enemy", the methods that they employ are highly contrasting. The Village is, as Number Two acknowledges in the *Chimes of Big Ben* episode, an international community to which people are brought in order to extract secret information. Omega's approach is more insidious, with attempts made to infiltrate our society and to eliminate or gain control of key personnel from within. A clear rationale for the motivation behind the Omega organisation is never provided. Martindale's responses in the final episode when in conversation with others may provide some insights; otherwise it is left to viewers to develop their own understanding based on the Omega activities that they have witnessed over the ten episodes. The organisation's power structure is never revealed and only isolated operatives and agents are shown during the course of the serial. Drawing on the work of Matt Hills,[34] Johnson explains how, by refusing throughout the series to offer hard and fast answers to questions such as "Where is The Village?", *The Prisoner* provides a "perpetuated hermeneutic" that encourages speculation beyond the events seen on-screen. (p. 2)[35] A similar argument may be made with regard to *The Omega Factor* in terms of key questions like "What actually is Omega?", "Is it a force for good or does it simply strive for world domination?" and "Can the organisation ever be defeated?" Nevertheless, despite all these intangibles, The Village and Omega have corporate images reflected in their immediately recognisable logos that are seen on several occasions. The former manifests itself as a penny farthing design, and the latter an omega symbol. From time to time, these provide viewers with clues as to the nature of the enemies the heroes are confronting. Still, an air of uncertainty surrounds even the names of the two organisations and this heightens the atmosphere of menace. In *The Prisoner*, the place in which the hero is incarcerated is always termed simply "The Village", and in the BBC programme, it is mainly Crane who calls the subversive organisation "Omega".

Although various Department Seven personnel accept this name, individual Omega operatives do not use it and in the final two episodes, Martindale refers merely to "The Organisation". Gerson's book is rather more informative. Here Omega is represented as "a loose freemasonry of people concerned with manipulating power". They include "civil servants, industrialists, high ranking members of the armed forces, [and] politicians". It is an "establishment within the establishment" intent on gaining access to the information accumulated by Department Seven.[36]

Johnson[37] and Hills[38] both recognise that the issue surrounding the location of The Village is not, of course, the only major plot question left unanswered in *The Prisoner*. The latter also asks, for example, whether the hero actually escapes. Other puzzles, like why Number Six resigned and whether he is really John Drake, remain unaddressed, too. In *The Omega Factor*, the exact role of Morag, especially in relation to her apparent master, Drexel, is likewise never properly clarified. Gerson's book describes her as a "mute, lost child" who forms Drexel's "medium, whether she wants to be or not".[39] The viewer may well muse over why, then, in the fifth instalment, *Powers of Darkness*, Morag is again seen to emerge as a figure of evil when Drexel is known to be dead.

Hills highlights how, in the cases of several "cult" shows, their endlessly deferred narratives are reflected in their titles.[40] This is perhaps most apparent in *Doctor Who* (or perhaps *Doctor Who?*) Here, the very name of the programme invites viewers to speculate on the identity of the hero. Hills demonstrates how some of the overarching questions within *The Prisoner* relate to the hero's incarceration itself, such as "where and why is Number Six imprisoned?" (p. 134)[41] Initially, the significance of the title *The Omega Factor* appears to be resolved unequivocally in the first episode, when Scott-Erskine reveals to Crane – and, with him, the viewer – that the expression refers to "the ultimate potential of the human mind", which Department Seven is charged with exploring. It emerges with time, however, that the title could equally appropriately refer to the mysteries of the sinister spy organisation which is also seeking to investigate this territory.[42]

Lack of trust and a mood of paranoia are key themes within both programmes. During *The Prisoner*'s 17 episodes Number Six is reluctant to trust anyone in The Village, and throughout the saga of *The Omega Factor* Crane struggles to make his claims about the existence of a subversive organisation heard. He also learns that even the closest members of his own family are not all they seem. Crane is resentful when he discovers that his wife, Julia, and brother, Michael, have worked for Department Seven and have covered up the fact. In just the third episode, *Night Games*, Crane suspects that there may be a traitor within the Department and his relationship with the authorities responsible for the unit is uneasy throughout the serial. Crane's paranoia reaches its height in the ninth episode, *Double Vision*, in which his claim that he has seen his wife alive after her apparent death is not believed. Ultimately, in the last two instalments, Crane even begins to suspect that he has been misled by Anne. There is, in fact, some evidence that his suspicions are not groundless. In the climax of *Double Vision*, Crane discovers in Anne's flat a wig that appears to have been used by the impersonator of his late wife. Furthermore, like the treacherous Martindale, Anne is seen in *Out of Body, Out of Mind* to have on her desk two telephones, the black one of which is similar in colour to that which Martindale may use to communicate with members of the Omega organisation. Yet, the significance of this is confused by the fact that, in instalments nine and ten, only the black telephone is visible and in *Double Vision*, a call from Scott-Erskine, whose integrity seems genuine, is taken on it.

In each serial, the hero is essentially a misfit in an environment in which he is ill at ease, despite the fact that Crane joined Department Seven willingly. The Prisoner attempts to escape from The Village in the very first episode and in *The Omega Factor*, Crane talks of leaving Department Seven as early as the third part, yet it is only in the final instalment that he actually does so. In the face of little concrete evidence, in the first few episodes of *The Omega Factor* at least, viewers may well initially question how far the alleged conspiracy is simply a product of the hero's imagination. Anthony Brown, for example, is among those who wonder whether the apparent plot "might be nothing more than a paranoid fantasy".[43] As we have seen already, some enthusiasts of *The Prisoner* have taken a similar line in relation to their own programme. One such proponent is Max Hora, who reasons that the "bad dream" theory may be used to "explain the entire series". (p. 8) He queries, "Did it all really happen or was it only happening in the Prisoner's own mind?" (p. 9)[44] McLean and Stansfield also raise the possibility at various points in their episode-by-episode discussion of *The Prisoner* that the events the viewer witnesses may be no more than a product of the hero's own mind. Specifically, they invite their readers to consider this scenario in the contexts of the episodes *A. B. and C.*, *Many Happy Returns* and *Hammer Into Anvil*.[45] Roger Langley believes that it is somewhat obvious to suggest that the events of *Many Happy Returns*, in particular, may be nothing but a dream. He summarises, "No. 6 has his adventure and then wakes up in precisely the same place at the end of it all". (p. 17)[46] In another source, Langley notes that what we see in *Dance of the Dead*, too, "could almost be from a nightmarish dream". (p. 47) He recalls that at the beginning of the episode The Prisoner collapses after an especially harrowing experience at the hands of a doctor and what follows is "a surreal journey through the Village... the action seems very akin to a wild dream". (p. 47)[47] It is certainly tempting to use the "nightmare" explanation to account for some of the bewilderingly unreal sequences and other scenes in the series that would seem to defy rational explanation. For Jack Lowin, who served as a camera operator on *The Prisoner*, however, any implication that the events we witness in the series take place merely in the hero's mind amounts to "a cheat", since the programme includes sequences that do not involve Number Six at all and he would know nothing about what is happening – the action is presented only to the audience.[48]

Number Six and Crane both emerge as outstanding humans fearlessly resisting malevolent forces that appear insurmountable. Indeed, The Prisoner's talents are such that Langley is able to cite as many as 20 diverse "all round abilities" that he demonstrates over the course of the series. (p. 5)[49] White and Ali write of how his "superman aspect" becomes increasingly apparent with each episode. (p. 52)[50] Similarly, the true extent of Crane's unusual psychic powers is revealed gradually during the course of the serial. Both characters work with a remarkable zeal. Number Six is intent on maintaining his individuality, protecting his secrets, countering oppression and escaping from The Village, and Crane is driven at first by his desire to avenge his wife's death and then by his determination to expose and, ultimately, defeat the Omega organisation. Number Six scarcely weakens in his resolve to remain an individual, although near the end of the BBC serial Crane briefly contemplates giving up his struggle against Omega. A further key difference between the two heroes is that, whilst Number Six's powers are conventionally mental and physical, albeit developed to an exceptionally high level, Crane's are clearly paranormal. Moreover, Crane frequently calls on Anne for support, and has a close relationship with his psychic brother, whereas Number Six is very much an individual who is almost always alone in his struggle.

Despite all his strengths, Britton and Barker argue that Number Six is not "uncomplicatedly heroic" and note him often to be "harsh, cold, withdrawn, and antisocial", (p. 126)[51] characteristics that may be considered inevitable consequences of his aggressive individualism. Short offers a similar view, highlighting Number Six's lack of affinity with others, his attitudes of suspicion and even derision when interacting with his fellow residents and his tendency to join forces with other dissidents solely for his own benefit.[52] Bould is no more complimentary, describing him as "arrogant, misogynistic, calculating, and ruthless". (p. 219)[53] One of the most damning indications of The Prisoner's selfishness is highlighted by Alan Stevens and Fiona Moore. They observe how, in *Do Not Forsake Me Oh My Darling*, Number Six is perfectly willing to lead agents of The Village to Professor Seltzman, knowing that he will then be captured, simply so that his own mind can be returned to its original body.[54] The weaknesses in Number Six's personality are particularly important given the fact noted by Joanne Morreale that there are few other recurrent characters in the series. Thus, opportunities for the viewer to identify with anyone else are limited.[55]

When asked how he designed the character of Number Six, McGoohan has gone on record as saying that he did not create him as a hero from the outset but, as he resists the evil forces that oppose him, "he grew into one". (p. 2) McGoohan does not cite in this context particular personal qualities that render his protagonist appealing,[56] and we can perhaps conclude that any heroic status that viewers bestow upon him arises from the continual nature of his struggle against oppression, rather than engaging aspects of his personality. In this sense, we can view Number Six as an icon, rather than an actual person, and consequently it may be inappropriate to judge his character against the criteria we would employ in everyday life to assess a "good" human being. A subtle distinction is made by Daniel O'Brien; he maintains that viewers admired the protagonist without liking him.[57]

The Prisoner and *The Omega Factor* both generated considerable controversy when originally shown. Each received substantial acclaim in their early days but, as the programmes progressed, critics became infuriated and frustrated. Illustrating his argument with extracts from contemporary reviews, James Chapman writes of *The Prisoner*, "When it began it was welcomed as a bold and innovative experiment that offered a different entertainment pattern from the formulaic norms of popular television... Yet the series' refusal to provide conventional dramatic resolutions or to answer the questions it posed soon turned opinion against it." (p. 50)[58]

The attitudes of *The Daily Telegraph*'s television correspondents to *The Omega Factor* also changed considerably during the programme's two-month run. Reviewing the first episode, Ronald Hastings commented that it "made a good start last week, with plenty of atmosphere" and seemed "a good cut above other recent new series".[59] The same critic praised the "well sustained" terror in the "very creepy" second episode.[60] Thereafter, the enthusiasm of the paper's correspondents waned. Following the fifth instalment, *Powers of Darkness*, Peter Knight wrote, "This spooks and spies thriller can be very irritating, spending much of its time on the big build [up] only to provide a big let-down at the end. Half the time I seem to spend trying to work out what is going on, the rest regretting that I ever tried."[61] Assessing *The Omega Factor* just before the transmission of the final episode, Hastings adjudged that the series "has sometimes been good, sometimes disappointing (both in writing and acting) and overall can be put down as an uneven but worthwhile piece of occasional originality".[62]

The Omega Factor's delvings into the paranormal and the occult provoked fierce criticism from Mary Whitehouse's National Viewers' and Listeners' Association. Pixley reports the outcry in some detail.[63] Much of the controversy surrounding *The Prisoner*, meanwhile, centred simply on its enigmatic characteristics, although Davis does report that "some people... found the obsession with medical experiments on Number 6 verged on the sick or sadistic". (p. 257)[64]

Today, it is clear that the unusual nature of both programmes was intended to stimulate a reaction among viewers. Indeed, McGoohan has famously admitted, "I wanted to have controversy, arguments, fights, discussions, people in anger waving fists in my face... I wanted to make people talk about the series. I wanted to make them ask questions, argue and think." (p. 57)[65] In the same way, Anthony Read, who wrote *Powers of Darkness*, one of the most controversial episodes of the BBC serial, reflected in the documentary *Inside The Omega Factor*, "I didn't set out to shock... but I did set out to stimulate and to provoke thought and make people think, not just to have something cosy... washing over you."[66] Speaking in the same documentary, Eric Davidson, the director of the instalment, believes that it was the way in which the paranormal was treated, rather than simply the subject itself, that disturbed some viewers:

> I would say that we did the show... in such a way that there weren't enough big, dramatic pyrotechnics to convince the audience that this was... over the top... It was all pretty low-key. And because we were doing it in a semi-real or realistic vein or mood... I think... Mary Whitehouse had a point that 'Oh-uh. This is slightly or could be a little bit more disturbing than it should be.'[67]

The controversy surrounding *The Omega Factor* and speculation in relation to its various narrative mysteries would certainly suggest that the programme was more scary and more demanding of the viewer than might be expected of a serial whose episodes were broadcast no later than 8.10 on Wednesday evenings.[68] It should be appreciated, however, that when *The Omega Factor* was released on DVD the package was given a certificate no more restrictive than a "12".

The fact that Davidson detects a "realism" in *The Omega Factor* is perhaps not surprising given that Gallaccio used Archie Roy, a professor of astronomy at the University of Glasgow and a lifelong believer in psychic phenomena, as a "technical advisor" for the show. Roy's involvement prompted Heald to forecast when previewing the serial, "*The Omega Factor*, disciplined by his consultancy, should be impeccably authentic even if it bends one's credulity." (p. 10)[69] Such attention to plausibility renders the serial a very different type of drama from *The Prisoner*. In fact, Gregory asserts that the "impossible" circumstances that emerge in the *Many Happy Returns* episode, in particular, clearly place the programme in allegorical territory. (p. 100)[70] Johnson, however, is less comfortable with labelling *The Prisoner* unequivocally allegorical. She writes,

> In its use and disruption of the generic conventions of the action-adventure spy series, its use of a visual style designed to disorientate the subjectivity of the viewer, its bricolage of signifiers in its location, set and costume designs and its lack of explanation for the fantastic elements represented, *The Prisoner* creates a fictional world that invites hesitation between supernatural, generic and allegorical explanations for the events depicted. (p. 59)[71]

Certainly, the unconventional nature of both serials is emphasised by some bewilderingly surreal sequences. In *The Prisoner*, these are chiefly to be found in the episodes *Free For All*, *Once Upon a Time* and *Fall Out*, whilst the psychic battle to save a young student from evil forces in the climax of *The Omega Factor's Powers of Darkness* story is described by Marcus Hearn in the DVD audio commentary for the episode as "probably the most surreal thing anyone was ever likely to see on the BBC".[72] Viewers may also have been disconcerted by the way in which the focus of each programme changed remarkably during the course of the episodes. Gregory traces how, in the case of *The Prisoner*, "what purported to be a mass-audience adventure series transformed itself, before the viewers' eyes, first into a surreal political and social satire, then an intense study of psychological depths and finally into a symbolic statement of the human condition". (p. 1)[73] Although *The Omega Factor's* themes are less profound and the switch in emphasis not so marked, Brown is nonetheless able to delineate a movement away from a preoccupation with a regular villain to the wider, and much more disturbing, conspiracy plot.[74]

It is tempting to draw parallels between this shift and that evident in another 1979 BBC serial – *The Aphrodite Inheritance*. Here what started as a seemingly realistic thriller involving a murder in Cyprus became increasingly bizarre. The final episode concluded with the revelation that three of the most mysterious characters in the drama were actually modern day personifications of ancient Greek gods. Whilst this disclosure was undoubtedly earth-shattering, various clues in the preceding episodes had suggested that none of these protagonists was quite who they appeared to be. With hindsight, the fact that they were endowed with divine powers provides explanation for some of the fanciful – and even impossible – situations that we have witnessed. Rob Buckley points out that for many viewers, the true nature of the show would have come as a complete surprise, since it was not trailed as a work of fantasy or the supernatural.[75] Like Number Six, the hero of *The Aphrodite Inheritance* is intent on finding information, specifically with respect to who killed his brother and why, and in this instance, too, paranoia permeates interpersonal relationships – the viewer quickly learns that it would be unwise to trust anyone. Ultimately, though, both heroes are rewarded for their actions. Number Six's efforts to rebel are praised and he is offered the chance to lead The Village, whilst in *The Aphrodite Inheritance*, David Collier, who has behaved with honour throughout, is allowed by the gods to live and given a considerable sum of cash. Still, even after the credits roll for the final time in each show, unanswered questions remain. Buckley notes that the motivations of the gods at particular points in the story are never clarified in *The Aphrodite Inheritance*. Perhaps they were simply entertaining themselves at mankind's expense.[76] The more oblique aspects of the programme can certainly be compared with the deeper levels of symbolism within *The Prisoner*, and writer Michael J. Bird has admitted that some of his more obscure allusions were no doubt missed by first-time viewers.[77]

Few commentators would argue that Chris Carter, creator of *The X-Files*, consciously adopted the key story ingredients of *The Omega Factor* when devising his own series, yet a recurrent theme in modern reviews of the BBC serial has been the similarities between the two. Brown draws attention to how, in each production, a male leading character is prompted to investigate the paranormal by a personal loss. He works with an inquiring female scientist and both are subordinate to a boss "whose backing is less than reliable". Evidence of a shadowy, ongoing conspiracy provides an undercurrent to the individual cases that they pursue.[78] Despite the broad links with later television that are noted by Short and which have been reported in Section II,[79] it is rather harder to find more specific ties that connect *The Prisoner* with serials that followed in the programme's immediate aftermath. Writing in 2002, Chapman considered, "Its very uniqueness... makes *The Prisoner* something of a dead end in generic terms." (p. 51)[80] At around the same time, Britton and Barker also highlighted the serial's lack of "far-reaching artistic influence", (p. 95) and noted that "echoes of *The Prisoner* proved to be conspicuous by their absence. Within a short time, the still, small voice of the series was drowned out by a raucous succession of action-adventure programs epitomizing all that McGoohan had turned against". (p. 127) They concluded, "McGoohan's series might as well never have happened." (p. 127)[81] In the short and medium term, at least, it is difficult to dispute these claims, although if we accept Short's arguments the position changed somewhat in later years.

The Prisoner and *The Omega Factor* may be more highly regarded today than when they were originally shown. This perhaps leads to an assumption that **both** programmes were ahead of their time. Even so, in the *Inside The Omega Factor* documentary, Gallaccio recalls that, in the case of the BBC production, "the germ of the idea for the whole series" was inspired by a contemporary issue – the potential use of the paranormal by Russia and America for military purposes.[82] Many years earlier, an article in a June 1979 edition of *Radio Times* which discussed the real life basis of *The Omega Factor* had also indicated how research in this area by the KGB and CIA especially provided the backdrop for the programme.[83] In the same way, M. Keith Booker believes that the themes of mind control and brainwashing which pervade *The Prisoner* were "crucial concerns of the cold war", (p. 42)[84] and the fact that *The Prisoner* owed much to other real life 1960s issues is now well acknowledged.

At the time of their original transmissions, the programmes generated little spin-off merchandise yet today, the cult following surrounding *The Prisoner* has become legendary. In the 1970s, the only tie-in book spawned by *The Omega Factor* was that which has already been mentioned, and until the 2005 DVD package, published information on the programme was difficult to find. Many of the standard reference sources on SF and genre television, such as *The Encyclopedia of TV Science Fiction*,[85] *The Encyclopedia of Science Fiction*,[86] and *The Ultimate Encyclopedia of Science Fiction*,[87] do not make any mention of it. We can attribute such omissions to the possibility that in some quarters *The Omega Factor* may be regarded as a work merely of peripheral SF at most, and indeed Louise Jameson, who played Anne Reynolds in the programme, has commented that whilst she regards it as "supernatural... and other-worldly... it's not really science fiction". (p. 18)[88] Still, one may expect *The Omega Factor* to receive at least some coverage in cross-genre books devoted to "cult television". Yet, no entry for the serial is offered in either *The Rough Guide to Cult TV*[89] or Jon E. Lewis and Penny Stempel's volume on the subject.[90] As with *The Prisoner*, a revisionist assessment of *The Omega Factor* eventually gathered pace, however. The serial gained as high a position as 23 in a 2005 poll of SF fans to find the "top 50 British telefantasy shows".[91] With hindsight, an earlier indication of shifting attitudes lay in a review of the programme appearing at the beginning of the new millennium. Here the *Radio Times Guide to Science Fiction* awarded it three out of a possible five stars, describing it as "intelligent and intriguing", (p. 247)[92] and at the time of its DVD release, Marcus Hearn noted its "almost mythological status among fans of similarly-themed television programmes... the series was not forgotten by its original fans, and has become a source of intrigue for those who missed it first time round". (p. 3)[93] Some of these sentiments have been echoed by critics watching the DVDs. *Ceefax's* William Gallagher, in one of the first reviews of the package in July 2005, commented, "If you saw this in 1979 you can remember how spooky it was... the studio work is dated but it's still a slowly absorbing work."[94] David Richardson, writing in *Starburst* later the same month, was equally enthusiastic. He, too, criticised the production standards yet nonetheless considered, "the idea is alluring, the scripts are taut, the tone atmospheric".[95]

The way in which critical opinion in relation to both *The Prisoner* and *The Omega Factor* has shifted over the years is undoubtedly marked but by no means unparalleled in the history of science fiction/fantasy television. One of the most dramatic instances of a change in mass thinking is apparent in terms of the *Doctor Who* serial *The Deadly Assassin*. David J. Howe, Mark Stammers and Stephen James Walker report how this adventure was not only severely criticised by the President of the *Doctor Who* Appreciation Society when it was first shown but it also appeared in bottom place in the Society's season poll.[96] Yet, in surveys undertaken in 1991, 1989, 1987 and 1986 to determine the best *Doctor Who* story of all time, *The Deadly Assassin* attained positions as high as 14th, 11th, 12th and 11th respectively.[97] More recently, a 2014 poll found that fans rated it the ninth best *Doctor Who* serial of the 1970s.[98] A similarly spectacular change in fan reaction surrounds the Fifth Doctor story *Kinda*. This adventure, too, came last in a major season survey,[99] but the aforementioned 2014 poll found it to be the seventh best serial of the 1980s.[100] Still, it is unwise to assume that the attitudes of enthusiasts reflect the feelings of the wider population. Indeed, *Doctor Who* producer Graham Williams has gone so far as to remark that there are instances in which "fans' appreciation of a [particular *Doctor Who*] story often seemed to be the opposite of what the general public thought" (p. 111)[101]

It was not until a decade after the DVD release of *The Omega Factor* that the programme's fictional narrative was continued. In May 2014, Big Finish announced that it had signed a licence to make new audio episodes,[102] the first of which appeared in the summer of 2015. As a precursor, the same firm released an audiobook of Gerson's 1979 novel in September 2014. The paper edition was long out of print by this time and the reading, like the 2005 DVD set, brought *The*

Omega Factor to a new generation, as well as refreshing the memories of fans of the original series.

References and Notes

1. Stevens, A. and Moore, F. Fall out: The unofficial and unauthorised guide to The Prisoner. Telos: Tolworth, 2007.

2. Fairclough, R. (ed.) The Prisoner: The original scripts – Volume 1. Reynolds and Hearn: Richmond, London, 2005; Fairclough, R. (ed.) The Prisoner: The original scripts – Volume 2. Reynolds and Hearn: Richmond, London, 2006.

3. The Omega Factor: The Complete Series. DVD. DD Home Entertainment, 2005.

4. Muir, J. K. A history and critical analysis of Blake's 7, the 1978–1981 British television space adventure. McFarland: Jefferson, North Carolina, 2000.

5. Britton, P. D. and Barker, S. J. Reading between designs: Visual imagery and the generation of meaning in The Avengers, The Prisoner, and Doctor Who. University of Texas Press: Austin, Texas, 2003.

6. Gregory, C. Be seeing you... Decoding The Prisoner. John Libbey Media: Luton, 1997.

7. Cartmel, A. Through time: An unauthorised and unofficial history of Doctor Who. Continuum: London, 2005.

8. Short, S. Countering the counterculture: The Prisoner and the 1960s. In: Cook, J. R. and Wright, P. (eds.) British science fiction television: A hitchhiker's guide. I. B. Tauris: London, 2006, pp. 71–92.

9. Gregory, C. op. cit.

10. Morton, A. The complete directory to science fiction, fantasy and horror television series: A comprehensive guide to the first 50 years 1946 to 1996. Other Worlds Books: Peoria, Illinois, 1997.

11. BBC. Omega Factor. Cult TV, DVD, & lovely stuff: News, reviews & fun, 21 February 2005. URL: http://www.bbc.co.uk/cult/news/cult/2005/02/21/17166.shtml (accessed: 17 August 2012).

12. Tulloch, J. and Alvarado, M. Doctor Who: The unfolding text. Macmillan: London, 1983.

It is interesting that Tulloch and Alvarado also place the original version of Doctor Who in the "episodic serial" category. The programme is perhaps better understood as a "series of episodic serials", and in this sense is comparable to shows such as Ace of Wands, The Tomorrow People and Sapphire and Steel.

13. McGoohan, P. On the trail of The Prisoner: Roger Goodman talks to Patrick McGoohan. CD. PrizBiz, 2007. Audio recording of 1979 interview.

14. McLean, N. and Stansfield, D. The Prisoner program guide. Ontario Educational Communications Authority: Toronto, Ontario, 1976.

15. The Prisoner Behind The Scenes With Bernie Williams. The Prisoner: 35th anniversary Prisoner companion – Special edition. DVD. Carlton, 2002.

16. Johnson, C. Telefantasy. BFI: London, 2005.

17. Britton, P. D. and Barker, S. J. op. cit.

18. Fairclough, R. (ed.) op. cit. 2006.

19. Bould, M. This is the modern world: The Prisoner, authorship and allegory. In: Bignell, J. and Lacey, S. (eds.) Popular television drama: Critical perspectives. Manchester University Press: Manchester, 2005, pp. 93–109.

20. Davis, A. Patrick McGoohan talks… In: Davies, S. P. The Prisoner handbook: An unauthorized companion. Boxtree: London, 2002. pp. 254–258. Reprint of 1968 TV Times article.

21. Quoted in: Hearn, M. The Omega Factor: Viewing notes. The Omega Factor: The complete series. op. cit.

22. Pixley, A. The Omega Factor: The undiscovered country. TV Zone, 193, 2005, pp. 34–40.

23. White, M. and Ali, J. The official Prisoner companion. Sidgwick and Jackson: London, 1988.

24. Fairclough, R. (ed.) op. cit. 2005.

25. Johnson, C. op. cit.

26. Smith, K. Factored in. Vortex, 78, August 2015, pp. 6–9.

27. The Prisoner: Patrick McGoohan Interviewed By Warner Troyer – The Troyer Interview, Part Two. The Prisoner: Music, FAQs, background, episode guide, spoofs. URL: http://www.the-prisoner-6.freeserve.co.uk/troyer2.htm (accessed: 23 September 2013). Transcript of 1977 interview.

28. Heald, T. Dark secrets of Department 7. Radio Times, 9–15 June 1979, pp. 9–10.

29. Behind-the-scenes. The Omega Factor: Series One. CD. Big Finish, 2015.

30. Gerson, J. The Omega Factor: A novelisation of the TV series. 6 CDs. Big Finish, 2014. Reading by Louise Jameson of 1979 work.

It may be unwise to equate "Fascists" in this context with the extreme Right wing. The Penguin Concise English Dictionary suggests that "Fascism" has come to be used informally to mean "brutal dictatorial control", (p. 314) and certainly over the years the word "Fascist" has been employed in some quarters to describe any aggressive or authoritarian individual. It is a measure of the extent to which the term has drifted into general conversation that, in summarising the plot of the Fireball XL5 story The Robot Freighter Mystery, the Starlog Robots guidebook reports how, after hero Steve Zodiac foils a plot by the unscrupulous Briggs brothers by threatening to blow them up with a time bomb, "It is at this point that we begin to suspect that Steve Zodiac is a fascist." (p. 85)

31. White, M. and Ali, J. op. cit.

32. White, M. and Ali, J. op. cit.

33. The Prisoner in Production. VHS video cassette. TR 7 Productions: Borehamwood, 1993.

34. Hills, M. Fan cultures. Routledge: London, 2002.

35. Johnson, C. op. cit.

36. Gerson, J. op. cit.

37. Johnson, C. op. cit.

38. Hills, M. op. cit.

39. Gerson, J. op. cit.

40. Hills, M. op. cit.

41. Hills, M. op. cit.

42. It is a measure of the degree to which the mere name of a television series can inspire discussion that in his examination of Rod Serling's classic anthology series, Kenneth Reynolds devotes all of the second chapter to an analysis of what is meant by the term "Twilight Zone". (see The Twilight Zone: Rod Serling's Wondrous Land, pp. 7–12)

43. Brown, A. The Omega Factor. TV Zone, 193, 2005, p. 72.

44. Hora, M. The Prisoner of Portmeirion, 2nd ed. Number Six Publications, 1995.

45. McLean, N. and Stansfield, D. op. cit.

46. Langley, R. Portmeirion in The Prisoner and its history, 2nd ed. 2011.

47. Langley, R. The Prisoner dialogue decodes. 2014.

48. The Prisoner In-depth Tape 2. VHS video cassette. TR 7 Productions: Borehamwood, 1992

49. Langley, R. op. cit. 2014.

50. White, M. and Ali, J. op. cit.

51. Britton, P. D. and Barker, S. J. op. cit.

52. Short, S. op. cit.

53. Bould, M. Science fiction television in the United Kingdom. In: Telotte, J. P. (ed.) The essential science fiction television reader. University Press of Kentucky:

Lexington, Kentucky, 2008, pp. 209–230.

54. Stevens, A. and Moore, F. op. cit.

55. Morreale, J. Lost, The Prisoner, and the end of the story. Journal of Popular Film and Television, 38 (4), 2010, pp. 176–185.

56. Quoted in: Nobel, S. and Goldsborough, D. The Prisoner puzzle. Ontario Educational Communications Authority: Toronto, Ontario, 1978.

57. O'Brien, D. SF: UK – How British science fiction changed the world. Reynolds and Hearn: Richmond, London, 2000.

58. Chapman, J. Saints and Avengers: British adventure series of the 1960s. I. B. Tauris: London, 2002.

59. Hastings, R. Wednesday television. The Daily Telegraph, 20 June 1979, p. 35.

60. Hastings, R. Wednesday television. The Daily Telegraph, 27 June 1979, p. 35.

61. Knight, P. Wednesday television. The Daily Telegraph, 18 July 1979, p. 35.

62. Hastings, R. Wednesday television. The Daily Telegraph, 15 August 1979, p. 31.

63. Pixley, A. The Omega Factor: Dark secrets of Department 7. TV Zone, 194, 2005, pp. 34–39.

64. Davis, A. op. cit.

65. Quoted in: Hora, M. op. cit.

66. Inside The Omega Factor. The Omega Factor: The complete series. op. cit.

67. Inside The Omega Factor. The Omega Factor: The complete series. op. cit.

68. BBC. Radio Times: 1923–2009 – The Omega Factor. Genome, 2017. URL: http://genome.ch.bbc.co.uk/search/0/20?adv=0&q=Omega+Factor&media=all&yf=1923&yt=2009&mf=1&mt=12&tf=00%3A00&tt=00%3A00 (accessed: 23 February 2017).

69. Heald, T. op. cit.

70. Gregory, C. op. cit.

71. Johnson, C. op. cit.

72. Powers Of Darkness DVD Audio Commentary. The Omega Factor: The complete series. op. cit.

73. Gregory, C. op. cit.

74. Brown, A. op. cit.

75. Buckley, R. Lost gems: The Aphrodite Inheritance (1979). The medium is not enough TV blog, 7 May 2009. URL: http://www.the-medium-is-not-enough.com/2009/05/lost_gems_the_aphrodite_inheritance_1979.php (accessed: 23 February 2017).

76. Ibid.

77. The Aphrodite Inheritance. Michael J. Bird tribute website, 2013. URL: http://www.mjbird.org.uk/Aphrodite.html (accessed: 23 February 2017).

78. Brown, A. op. cit.

79. Short, S. Cult telefantasy series: A critical analysis of The Prisoner, Twin Peaks, The X-Files, Buffy the Vampire Slayer, Lost, Heroes, Doctor Who and Star Trek. McFarland: Jefferson, North Carolina, 2011.

80. Chapman, J. op. cit.

81. Britton, P. D. and Barker, S. J. op. cit.

82. Inside The Omega Factor. op. cit.

83. Heald, T. op. cit.

84. Booker, M. K. Science fiction television. Praeger: Westport, Connecticut, 2004.

85. Fulton, R. The encyclopedia of TV science fiction. Boxtree: London, 1990.

86. Clute, J. and Nicholls, P. (eds.) The encyclopedia of science fiction, 2nd ed. Orbit: London, 1993.

87. Pringle, D. (ed.) The ultimate encyclopedia of science fiction: The definitive illustrated guide. Carlton: London, 1996.

88. Quoted in: Smith, K. Omega three. Vortex, 68, October 2014, pp. 18–19.

89. Simpson, P. (ed.) The rough guide to cult TV: The good, the bad and the strangely compelling. Rough Guides: London, 2002.

90. Lewis, J. E. and Stempel, P. Cult TV: The essential critical guide. Pavilion Books: London, 1993.

91. Top 50 Greatest UK Telefantasy Shows Ever. SFX Collection, 22, 2005, pp. 6–57.

92. Fane-Saunders, K. (ed.) Radio Times guide to science fiction. BBC Worldwide: London, 2001.

93. Hearn, M. op. cit.

94. Gallagher, W. DVD reviews: The Omega Factor. Ceefax, 13 July 2005, p. 548, 4/4.

95. Richardson, D. DVD reviews: The Omega Factor. Starburst, 31 (5) [issue 327], September 2005, p. 85.

96. Howe, D. J., Stammers, M. and Walker, S. J. Doctor Who: The handbook - The Fourth Doctor. London: Virgin, 1992.

97. 1991 Doctor Who Series Survey Results. DWB, 96, December 1991, pp. 10–13.

98. The First 50 Years: The 1970s. Doctor Who Magazine, 474, July 2014, pp. 22–31.

99. Doctor Who Season Survey. Doctor Who Monthly, 69, October 1982, pp. 36–38.

100. The First 50 Years: The 1980s. Doctor Who Magazine, 474, July 2014, pp. 32–41.

101. Parkin, L. Time unincorporated: The Doctor Who fanzine archives – Vol. 1. Mad Norwegian Press: Des Moines, Iowa, 2009.

102. Big Finish. New series The Omega Factor launches! 3 May 2014. URL: http://www.bigfinish.com/news/v/new-series-the-omega-factor-launches (accessed: 23 February 2017).

CHAPTER EIGHT
The Unnamed and The Unidentified

Patrick McGoohan would not have been gratified by comparisons of *The Prisoner* and *UFO*. In the Goodman interview, Gerry Anderson's programme is, in fact, dismissed unequivocally by McGoohan as "rubbish".[1] Nevertheless, it shares a fundamental similarity with *The Prisoner* insofar as it is more likely than any of Anderson's other series, with the possible exception of *The Secret Service*, to be regarded as "enigmatic". James O'Neill describes *UFO* as "very odd", (p. 270)[2] whilst Robert Sellers considers it "arguably... the most atypical of the Anderson shows", and a significant departure from their usual pattern. (p. 186)[3] Other connections between *The Prisoner* and *UFO* come to light in the Goodman interview. McGoohan recalls that CBS's Senior Vice President of Programming, Michael Dann, was so impressed with the concept of *The Prisoner* when the show was offered to him that he agreed to buy from Lew Grade a number of other ITC series sight unseen, one of which was *UFO*. The fact that Gerry Anderson's programme was included in the package has led Brian J. Woodman to speculate that it "seems probable" that Grade was promoting *The Prisoner* "at least partly as science fiction". (p. 947)[4]

In the same way that *The Prisoner* can be understood, on a superficial level, as a tale of the attempts made by an incarcerated individual to resist interrogation and conformity, and to escape from confinement, *UFO* can be simply interpreted as a saga centred on the defence of Earth by the SHADO organisation in the face of marauding aliens. Today, the subtexts and allegorical aspect of *The Prisoner* are well acknowledged as a result of interviews with McGoohan and penetrating scholarship by fans and academics. *UFO*, meanwhile, has seldom been subjected to such rigorous analysis and some of the early efforts to scratch beneath the surface in terms of its intended meaning provoked controversy. It is revealing that, in 1987, when Chris Drake's essay *UFO: The Hidden Truth*, which could be forecast to generate heated debate, was published in the fanzine *SiG*, editor David Nightingale distanced himself from it by including a disclaimer that declared, "Whilst Chris has been given *SiG* as a platform for his thoughts, the opinions expressed are not necessarily those of the editor or a reflection of the magazine's editorial stance." (p. 17)[5] The piece, in which Drake drew parallels between Soviet aggression and the aliens in *UFO*, stimulated some lively correspondence which was published in the next edition of *SiG*.[6] Nevertheless, it would be erroneous to believe that Drake is alone in his interpretation. Some 17 years later, M. Keith Booker put forward a very similar argument, writing, "*UFO* was very much a cold war drama, and its depiction of a sinister alien threat was a rather transparent reflection of Western cold war fears of communism and the Soviet Union." (pp. 76–77)[7] This theme is pursued further by Nicholas J. Cull. He, too, comments that the aliens may be considered to constitute a "cold war enemy", and draws on the ideas of Chris Bentley[8] to highlight some of the programme's themes as "the classic stuff of 'enemy within' paranoia". (p. 201)[9] Yet, Cull suggests that *UFO* also reflects "a shifting of attitudes within the cold war", since some of the episodes raise the prospect of negotiation and can be considered to reflect "a yearning for détente and an alternative to the divided world". (p. 201)[10] Attempts to read real life events into fictitious stories can be fraught with problems, however. It is all too easy to dismiss an attempt to understand *Sapphire and Steel* in terms of the Conservative politics of the day as no more than fanciful conjecture, especially since, as the writer of the piece concedes, the show's creator P. J. Hammond has denied "that there is any direct political subtext in the programme". (p. 193)[11] Still, although the similarities that Drake, Booker and Cull detect between the real world situation and the Earth/aliens conflict in *UFO* may seem rather less obvious than those between modern society and The Village in *The Prisoner*, it may be pertinent that various commentators have asserted that the alien schemes to infiltrate human society in *The Invaders* – a programme very like *UFO* with regard to theme and one originally broadcast just a few years earlier[12] – were inspired by the perceived Communist threat to America that was at its peak in the previous decade. According *The Encyclopedia of Science Fiction, The Invaders* "belonged, in spirit, to the paranoid sf version of the Communist-spy scares of the 1950s".[13] If the aliens were intended, allegorically, to represent Communist infiltrators, it may be no coincidence that when each of them is destroyed, the being disappears in a red glow.

Direct interactions between *UFO* and *The Prisoner* have been postulated for many years. In letters appearing in *SiG* in the late 1980s, Chris Freeman[14] and Rei Honda[15] add a further dimension to the longstanding argument that the hero of *The Prisoner* may have been the victim of an extraterrestrial kidnap by suggesting that the perpetrators could be the aliens seen in *UFO*. However, as Matthew White and Jaffer Ali observe, the extraterrestrials theory is itself "on the fringe of *Prisoner* thought", (p. 159)[16] and then to go a stage further and connect two apparently very different series together in this way is bound to invite disbelief and even ridicule in some quarters. The main flaws in the stance taken by Freeman and Honda lie in the fact that, since *The Prisoner* preceded *UFO*, it is clearly unlikely that McGoohan was aware of the existence of the *UFO* aliens when *The Prisoner* was being produced and even if *UFO* was known to him it seems improbable that he would make such a close link between *The Prisoner* and a programme that obviously failed to impress him. Nevertheless, the argument of Freeman and Honda is indicative of a popular pursuit among many science fiction fans – they attempt to meld together elements from their favourite series in order to produce intriguing hybrid scenarios. Occasionally such ideas break out of fan circles and into mainstream publishing. Chris Boucher's novel *Corpse Marker*, for example, which combines aspects of *Blake's 7* and *Doctor Who*, was released under the BBC banner. This book was itself influential, inspiring Magic Bullet's *Kaldor City* range of audio dramas.[17] Noting that the appearance of *Corpse Marker* would seem to imply that the events in *Blake's 7* and *Doctor Who* can "occur in the same universe", (p. 309) Lance Parkin speculates on how these two entirely separate productions can be reconciled.[18] As I have written elsewhere with Naomi V. Hay-Gibson, there is a danger that, when new works of fiction which draw on different television series are created, the overall concoction may appear contrived and inauthentic, and it may alienate fans of the original programmes to whom the work would seem most likely to appeal.[19] Even Boucher himself concedes that crossover works like *Corpse Marker* "are awkward". (p. 169)[20]

In endeavouring to identify further ties between *The Prisoner* and *UFO*, Honda cites a series of actors and actresses who appeared in both shows – Michael Billington, Wanda Ventham, Alexis Kanner, Derren Nesbitt, Georgina Cookson, Jane Merrow and Colin Gordon.[21] Although in the later episodes of *UFO* Wanda Ventham's character, Colonel Virginia Lake, assumes a second-in-command position within the SHADO hierarchy, at times she takes on a role very similar to her function as a computer attendant in the *Prisoner* story *It's Your Funeral*. In particular, in *Reflections in the Water*, she serves as an intermediary between the computer and the commander-in-chief of SHADO operations, Ed Straker. In both cases, her superior treats with some derision the reports she offers. Honda's list of actors and actresses who can be seen in the two shows is by no means comprehensive. The names of Richard Caldicot, Conrad Phillips and Al Mancini, for example, may be added. In terms of behind the scenes involvement, lighting cameraman/director of photography Brendan J. Stafford, assistant director Gino Marotta, casting director Rose Tobias Shaw, stuntman Gerry Crampton, editor Lee Doig and camera operator Jack Lowin are among the other individuals who worked on both productions. In addition, the influential roles of David Tomblin and Terence Feely should be given particular attention. As well as serving as a producer, writer and director on *The Prisoner*, Tomblin wrote three instalments of *UFO* and directed two of them. Feely, meanwhile, wrote two episodes of *The Prisoner* and the antepenultimate segment of *UFO*. Direct links between the two programmes are not limited to personnel. Bentley points out that, in the *UFO* episode *A Question of Priorities*, a Model T Ford car is shown "driven around a Western set on the MGM British Studios backlot that had previously been seen extensively in *The Prisoner*, most notably as the town of Harmony in the *Living in Harmony* episode". (p. 108)[22]

A critical aspect of the ambiguity which characterises both *The Prisoner* and *UFO* lies in the way their emphases appeared to change during the course of their production. *The Prisoner*'s switch of direction has been noted in the previous chapter, and the more subtle shifts that can be seen in *UFO* have attracted comment, too. *The UFO Documentary* traces how the concept of the aliens developed over the duration of the series. In the early episodes, it seemed to have been firmly established that their raids on Earth were motivated by the need for human organs to replace those within their own failing bodies. Later, however, it was postulated that not only may the aliens not be humanoid but they may not even have a physical form at all, although they are clearly still capable of using their intelligence to take possession of human beings.[23] Even if this notion is accepted as a "revelation" rather than mere supposition, it would seem to raise more questions than provide answers. Alan Stevens and Fiona Moore also see a transformation over time from an alien threat that initially appears straightforward "to something much more sinister and psychological". (p. 187)[24]

Stevens and Moore further argue that, after beginning "as a fairly trashy and superficial humans-versus-aliens show", *UFO* developed, with Tomblin's involvement, "greater flights of *Prisoner*esque psychodelia". (p. 187)[25] It is striking that the three episodes which Fletcher Klimowski singles out for bearing strong similarities to particular *Prisoner* episodes were the last three instalments of *UFO* to go into production. Specifically, Klimowski comments how:

- in *Mindbender* and *Living in Harmony*, a protagonist struggles against an enemy that attacks, through hallucinations, his sense of reality;
- in *The Long Sleep* and *Once Upon a Time*, something akin to psychological flashback is used to tell the story of a character's life;
- in *Timelash* and *Fall Out*, the hero descends into an underworld in order to confront an unseen enemy and all normality is disrupted.

Klimowski draws attention, too, to the looping nature of *Timelash*, with the climax of the episode taking the viewer back to the beginning.[26] The cyclical nature of individual instalments of *The Prisoner* and indeed the whole saga has already been noted in Chapter Seven.

Some readers may well believe that one's sense of identity is as important a theme in *Mindbender* as the nature of reality. In this episode, the unusual properties of a rock planted on the Moon by the aliens lead Straker to hallucinate that his work for SHADO is no more than a scenario within a film in which he is an actor. This echoes Straker's movie boss guise, which provides a cover for his role in directing SHADO operations. The episode particularly brings to mind ideas investigated in the *Twilight Zone* story *A World of Difference* but some comparisons can also be drawn between *Mindbender* and *The Schizoid Man* episode of *The Prisoner* in that here, too, attacks on the hero's identity form a crucial part in his adversaries' attempts to destabilise him. In each instance, the individual is made to feel that he is actually someone else. Certain lines of dialogue within other *UFO* episodes may also strike a chord with fans of *The Prisoner*. In *Destruction*, for example, Straker explains that he sees the conflict between SHADO and the aliens as "a battle of wits" between the two parties. This description could equally be applied to the duel between Number Six and the Village authorities in *The Prisoner*.

"Surrealistic" is an adjective frequently employed with regard to *UFO* and *The Prisoner*. In the Goodman interview, McGoohan himself indicates that he is happier with this label than with some of the others that have been used to describe his programme.[27] In terms of *UFO*, words like "surreal" and "bizarre" are generally applied to the later episodes. Brad Newman[28] and Chris Drake and Alan Howard,[29] for example, describe the final instalments in these terms. Gerry Anderson associates the offbeat quality that ultimately became prominent to the influence of David Tomblin and director Ken Turner, who, Anderson suggests, was noted for his "zany" filmmaking.[30] Writer Terence Feely is of the opinion, however, that Anderson himself was predisposed to "lateral thinking and the surreal". (pp. 515–516)[31] If one accepts Feely's argument that surrealism is best understood as the juxtaposing of two entirely disparate objects or concepts that are never normally found together,[32] the contrast between the film company cover of SHADO and the real work of the organisation lends itself to a certain surrealism. Further strangeness results from the fact that various characters who are seen around the grounds appear completely incongruous. The viewer must assume that they are involved in the film element; if this is not the case, given the true remit of SHADO they are totally out of place.

Mark Phillips and Frank Garcia describe *Mindbender* as "the ultimate surreal adventure", (p. 515)[33] and, more specifically, the second volume in the Starlog *TV Episode Guides* series comments how this episode offers a "bizarrely disturbing look into how films mimmick [sic] real life". (p. 63)[34] Another of the more peculiar instalments is Feely's *Timelash*. There is some evidence, however, that the nature of these segments came about at least in part as a result of practical, rather than creative, decisions similar to those that preoccupied Dennis Spooner when writing the *Interrogation* episode of *The Champions* that was discussed in Chapter Four. Bentley asserts that *Mindbender* "was written as a cost-saving exercise, utilising only standing sets, studio locations, stock visual effects footage and material from earlier episodes". (p. 151)[35] A similar situation appears to have emerged with *Timelash*. Tony Barwick, who served as script editor for *UFO*, recounts how here, again, it was necessary to construct an episode that drew on only a small number of sets. As such a constraint could easily lead to a bland story, more imaginative elements had to be incorporated, and in Barwick's words, the ultimate episode "just came out of simple necessity". (p. 12)[36] In addition, there is, of course, the possibility that the offbeat orientation which was prevalent in the second half of the *UFO* saga may have arisen from the most obvious scenarios having been explored and other directions needing to be taken if the series were to continue. Ed Bishop, who played Straker, has admitted that the central premise was too restrictive and indicated that, had the series been extended into another season, the overall storyline would have had to be expanded.[37] A similar situation certainly applied in *The Prisoner*. McGoohan has acknowledged that there were only seven episodes that were completely true to the original concept, and the remaining instalments were, on occasion, stretching it.[38] This outward reach was reflected in the programme's development over time; White and Ali comment that, towards the end of the making of *The Prisoner*, ideas within The Village were becoming exhausted and an emphasis on stories set beyond its confines developed.[39]

The final episodes of *UFO* are frequently those that attract most acclaim.

Andrew Pixley's argument that the second batch of nine featured "stronger stories" is widely held. (p. 6)[40] Jon E. Lewis and Penny Stempel single out *Reflections in the Water* for particular praise, describing it as "one highlight amongst many". (p. 42)[41] In contrast, some of the last few episodes of *The Prisoner* tend to receive a less positive reaction. White and Ali find the later, less Village oriented direction "unsatisfactory", (p. 102)[42] and McGoohan himself regarded as mere fillers many of the episodes that were additional to those that he originally intended.[43]

Both *UFO* and *The Prisoner* have been described as bleak, pessimistic series. *The Encyclopedia of TV Science Fiction*, for example, notes how the former was "often edgy and downbeat in its plots and characterisation", (p. 491)[44] whilst Booker suggests that its dark tone came from the sense of alien threat that was prevalent.[45] It is certainly striking that, in *UFO*, many SHADO schemes end in failure. In just the second episode, *Computer Affair*, an effort to interrogate an alien who has been brought to Straker alive is entirely unsuccessful. In *Survival*, an attempt to capture an alien craft that has landed on the Moon also goes awry. The conclusion of *The Square Triangle* is particularly depressing. Not only have Straker's plans to take a UFO intact come to nought; it would seem that SHADO is powerless to stop a murder from taking place. There is personal tragedy for Straker, too. *A Question of Priorities* ends with the death of his son, and in the climax of *The Long Sleep*, although SHADO is able to thwart an alien plot in which a bomb explosion would cause great destruction, a girl with whom Straker has developed a strong bond of trust meets a horrible demise. All too frequently the victories gained are achieved at great cost. The loss of human life is considerable overall, with civilians as well as SHADO personnel perishing.

It is entirely possible that the very pessimism of *UFO* and *The Prisoner* provides a distinctive element that has contributed to their longstanding cult status. Isaac Asimov is in no doubt that much of the appeal of the latter lies in the inability of the hero to escape from The Village. The theme of failure, he concludes, is one to which every viewer can relate.[46] Perhaps the key question is whether, whilst watching a show ostensibly made for entertainment purposes, viewers wanted to be reminded of their own powerlessness. For Booker, *The Prisoner*'s presentation of "a world in which problems are too complex even to be understood, much less solved… probably resonated all too uncomfortably with the experience of many in its viewing audience and surely contributed to the quick demise of the series". (p. 75)[47]

Certainly, some people found unappealing the fact that, even at the climax of each instalment, Number Six appears to have made little progress. John Kruse, who was asked to contribute a script, explains that he felt the series would be "a loser" because "you end every episode on a down note... The guy is recaptured. That seems to me to be a negative and I don't like to end a script on a negative. That's really why I didn't really terribly fancy it".[48] Kruse was not alone in his reservations at the time. Ian Rakoff, who served as an assistant editor on some of the episodes and co-wrote the story on which *Living in Harmony* is based, reports that, while he was negotiating on behalf of CBS to buy *The Prisoner* for screening in the US, Michael Dann became "deeply concerned about the downbeat nature of the project", (p. 31) and asserted at one point that "the American viewing public could not go for a loser". (p. 32)[49] Given that, traditionally, the British tend to favour an underdog, audiences on this side of the Atlantic were perhaps more inclined to accept Number Six's consistent failures than were their US counterparts.

Number Six is not, of course, the only television protagonist whose efforts are thwarted on a weekly basis. For example, at around the same time but in the US, ironically, David Vincent, of *The Invaders*, encountered a similar lack of progress. *The Encyclopedia of Science Fiction* summarises, "in each episode the hero discovers and foils a new alien plot, but remains unable to convince the authorities". (p. 622)[50] For Steve Sonsky, *The Invaders* was characterised by an "utter sense of hopelessness" that made it "one of the most depressing shows that's ever been on TV". (p. 55)[51] Although Number Six and Vincent enjoy some success in terms of isolated battles, overall they are seen to be fighting a losing cause and the clear message that emerges in both *The Prisoner* and *The Invaders* is that the atypical individual will have scant success in making his voice heard in society. So often Number Six fails to achieve any real impact in The Village, and Rolf Maurer suggests in relation to *The Invaders* that the "forces of mass conformity" smother the citizen into submission. In the latter situation, the hero is unable to rouse others from their "complacent indifference to world events". (p. 78)[52] Since each is "forever doomed to struggle against overwhelming opposition", Darryl Cox likens Vincent and Number Six to the Greek mythological character of Sisyphus, who was condemned to attempt an unending task for all eternity.[53] This is by no means the only classical parallel that the programmes attract. For Lewis and Stempel, Vincent brings to mind Cassandra, the Trojan prophetess of doom.[54] Although her predictions were accurate, they were never believed. For Christian Durante, it is not preposterous to view McGoohan himself as a Cassandra of the modern age.[55] Kim Newman traces a "continuum", beginning with Aldous Huxley's *Brave New World*, in which science fiction authors warn of "how miserable everything is going to get in the future". Newman explains that works of this type satirise what was happening at the time when they are written and forecast that if current trends continue unabated issues of contemporary concern will eventually come to dominate the world. A theme integral to *The Prisoner* – the loss of individual freedom — is one of the anxieties that Newman specifically isolates. Newman makes his comments when presenting the wider context for Nigel Kneale's play *The Year of the Sex Olympics*.[56] This dystopian production was broadcast by the BBC less than six months after *Fall Out* was first shown in February 1968. Here, too, citizens are largely submissive and apathetic, whilst influential opinion-shapers are manipulative and seek to engage the people's interest through cheery promotional announcements; the language of the community that exercises power is distinctive and norms are promoted through Orwellian maxims; on a dramatic level, a rogue element challenges the status quo.

Staying with classical parallels, Section II alluded to links made between *The Odyssey* and *Many Happy Returns* made by Susan Nobel and Diana Goldsborough. The authors point to the common themes of escape, survival and return home, and invite their readers to consider whether any of the characters whom The Prisoner meets in the episode can be compared to those encountered by Odysseus.[57] *Prisoner* – *Odyssey* connections go unaddressed by Edith Hall, however, in her wide-ranging cultural history of the latter, even though she does refer in her analysis to the original versions of *Doctor Who* and *Star Trek*.[58]

In addition to acknowledging how downbeat series may fail to inspire viewers, we should recognise that, for lots of its fans, the appeal of *Star Trek*, especially, lay not in its theme of failure but, on the contrary, in its sense of **optimism**. Writing in the mid 1970s, Jacqueline Lichtenberg, Sondra Marshak and Joan Winston recalled,

> … we asked many of the show's creators a series of questions based on our thinking that the optimism of *Star Trek* – its vision of a brighter future of man, and of a world characterised by hope, achievement and understanding – was the message of *Star Trek* and one of its chief attractions. Universally, they agreed… (p. 107–108)[59]

Contrasts with *The Prisoner* could scarcely be greater.

The unanswered questions that surround much of what we witness in *The Prisoner* have led to great frustration among many viewers of the programme. In both this series and *UFO*, we learn very little about those who can be considered to constitute "the enemy". Just as, in *The Prisoner*, the fundamental issue of which "side" runs The Village remains unresolved, in *UFO* the nature and motivations of the aliens are similarly ambiguous, with discoveries in some of the later episodes seeming to contradict the evidence in earlier instalments. The aliens are never given a name. On no occasion do we hear them speak. They are always seen in their protective space suits and we find out virtually nothing about the planet on which they live. In *Close-up*, a SHADO scheme to track a UFO back to the aliens' home planet and take detailed photographs of its surface yields data that are eventually revealed to be worthless. Gerry Anderson has maintained that the lack of detail in relation to the aliens was deliberate, since to go into more depth would have resulted in the production team having to address issues arising from the revelations. He considers that a useful consequence was that an air of mystery was retained and the stories seemed more believable.[60] For some commentators, such as Booker, however, the lack of forthcoming information about the aliens helped to render them somewhat uninteresting.[61]

Part of the bewilderment of viewers watching *The Prisoner* for the first time in the 1960s arose from the fact that it ultimately proved entirely different from what they could have reasonably anticipated. The deceptive nature of the series is well understood by Robert Fairclough. He identifies how, although it was packaged as an exciting, colourful and cinematic action-adventure, the overall *Prisoner* saga would actually combine elements as diverse as Cold War paranoia, Freudian psychology, existential psychedelic fantasy and social satire.[62] Few programmes in television history have defied viewers' expectations so markedly as this hybrid. As Max Hora recognises, those who had seen *Danger Man* may well have expected some kind of straightforward follow-up,[63] especially since McGoohan played an ostensibly similar character in the two productions and the fact that he was never named in *The Prisoner* meant that there was little solid evidence to confirm that the hero was not, in fact, John Drake. Woodman points to the deceptive nature of how the show was marketed by ITC, particularly in terms of one of the trailers used. In Woodman's words, it "clearly positions the show as a spy thriller for fans of *Danger Man*". (p. 945)[64] Given that in the early days of commercial television there were fears that it would only "cater for populist taste and appeal to the lowest common denominator", (p. 86)[65] once discovered, the real nature of *The Prisoner* may well have come as a major surprise to ITV viewers. For Joanne Morreale, in truth, the show appealed to both popular and "high brow" audiences and, in doing so answered the call of the government-sponsored Pilkington Report "for programs that were challenging and controversial in both form and content". (p. 178–179)[66]

In the same way as fans of *Danger Man* would have been surprised by *The Prisoner*, many of those viewers who had grown accustomed to Gerry

Anderson's puppet series for children would have been ill-prepared for the more adult content of *UFO*. Although some of the material that was most unsuitable for children appeared late in *UFO*'s run, earlier episodes which concentrated on the break-up of Straker's marriage and the death of his son had already demonstrated that this was not a series which would simply address with live actors and actresses the same themes as *Captain Scarlet and the Mysterons*, even though common ground between the two is often identified.[67] There can be no doubt, however, that even *Captain Scarlet* was different in tone from Gerry Anderson's previous programmes. The second volume in the Starlog *TV Episode Guides* series notes that the stories were "played straight with none of the cute highjinks of the other series", (p. 31)[68] and the *Radio Times Guide to Science Fiction* highlights *Captain Scarlet's* startlingly "dark and violent" subject matter. (p. 64)[69] Much of the distinctly odd penultimate episode broadcast, *Attack on Cloudbase*, is particularly bleak. Regular protagonists are seen to die, others behave in ways that are disconcertingly out of character, colleagues quarrel and snipe, and eventually Spectrum's aerial headquarters is apparently destroyed. The instalment may, with hindsight, offer an early indication as to the more uncomfortable direction that *UFO* would take, even if normality is finally restored in a reassuring climax when it is revealed that the bizarre events have been no more than a hallucination.

Both *UFO* and *The Prisoner* were met with some unease, too, among broadcasters at the time of their early screenings. In terms of the former, according to *The Encyclopedia of TV Science Fiction*, "ITV... didn't know how to take it", (p. 491)[70] and the *Radio Times Guide to Science Fiction*, among many other sources, makes a similar claim.[71] White and Ali recount how *The Prisoner*'s Western episode, *Living in Harmony*, initially went untransmitted in the States, and they consider the arguments that surround the omission to be among seven "great debates" that preoccupy fans of the series. Whilst the authors recall that the CBS network claimed that "the portrayal of characters under the influence of hallucinogenic drugs was in violation of broadcast ethics", (p. 148) White and Ali themselves suggest that the story's allegorical parallels with issues surrounding the ongoing Vietnam conflict, coupled with its American setting, may have been the true cause of the broadcaster's concerns.[72] In addition, Neil McLean and David Stansfield draw attention to the violence prevalent in *Living in Harmony*,[73] and Dave Rogers reports that several scenes have subsequently been edited or omitted because of this aspect of their content.[74] Broadcasting interventions also affected *UFO*. In *The Long Sleep*, two characters take drugs and then act under their influence. This element and a scene which implies an attempted rape render it undoubtedly one of the most "adult" episodes of the programme. It is perhaps not surprising, then, that for its first UK transmission, *The Long Sleep* received an 11pm timeslot.[75] Chris Drake states that another episode, *The Responsibility Seat*, which included a sexually oriented scene, also received a late-night transmission slot.[76] Nevertheless, mixed messages would appear to emerge from commercial releases of *UFO*. As late as 1982, the second volume in the Starlog *TV Episode Guides* series reported that, up to the time of writing, *The Long Sleep* had been "seldom seen because of the heavy use of drugs". (p. 63)[77] Yet, just a few years later, when *UFO* was released on video cassette by Channel 5/PolyGram in the second half of the 1980s and early 1990s, the tape containing this episode was one of five in the range that received a rating no more restrictive than a "PG". More recently, however, the DVD containing this episode is the only one in the ITV Studios/Carlton *UFO* range to be given a "12" certificate. Let us contrast this situation with the treatment of *Living in Harmony* in relation to two commercial releases separated by nearly 20 years. When it appeared as part of the Channel 5 set that arrived in shops during the 1980s, the episode received the same "PG" certificate as all the other *Prisoner* episodes and, as recently as 2005, *Living in Harmony* was awarded the same rating when it formed part of De Agostini's *Official Fact File* package.

Despite all the differences between *UFO* and Gerry Anderson's previous work, some continuity with his earlier series is evident in *UFO*. Several previous chapters of *Unique But Similar* have drawn attention to how the "bad dream" theory is occasionally offered to explain the events seen in *The Prisoner*. There can be no doubt that at least part of what we witness in *UFO* also amounts to a nightmare. In the *Ordeal* episode, much of the action is a hallucination that takes place only in the mind of Paul Foster after he collapses in a sauna bath. The instalment shares strong similarities, in fact, with the *Attack on Cloudbase* story of *Captain Scarlet and the Mysterons* and, by the time *UFO* was made, dream sequences generally had a long history in Anderson productions.

In both *UFO* and *The Prisoner*, well established scenarios are combined with bizarre plot elements. The runaround, or what John Kenneth Muir terms "the roller coaster", (p. 146) has become a staple situation in SF and fantasy television. The author cites a range of instances in which it is evident, including *The Chase* in *Doctor Who*, *The Beta Cloud* in *Space: 1999* and *Headhunter* in *Blake's 7*.[78] We may argue that the classic *Outer Limits* instalment *Demon With a Glass Hand*, the *Avengers* episode *Dead Man's Treasure*, and the *New Avengers* comic segment *Emily* can be added to this list. In *UFO's Timelash*, the plot meets various criteria that Muir feels epitomise the quintessential "roller coaster". Specifically, continuing characters find themselves involved in a protracted chase within locations that are familiar to the regular viewer and are pitted against an apparently indestructible adversary. Here, however, the scenario is allied to a scheme by the aliens to freeze time and it is this situation that provides some of the most memorable images seen in the whole programme. If one subscribes to Muir's argument that the particular brand of action-adventure that *Timelash* delivers forms "the last refuge of a series running low on serious genre concepts", (p. 146)[79] again we may consider that such a story is characteristic of a series entering its final stages of production. Like *UFO*, *The Prisoner* toys with concepts that are well worn. Indeed, various elements typically associated with the genres of Western, spy and SF are apparent but these are combined with others to produce a series that is truly original. Nobel and Goldsborough catalogue the elements in *Living in Harmony* that are features of Western stories and films:

> ... the stranger who rides into a town seething with problems; the law-man who wants to turn in his badge; the gunfighter who wants to stop shooting but the world won't let him; the corrupt judge who has the town in his pay; the soiled dove in the saloon who can flutter her wings for freedom and true love. (p. 15)[80]

Ultimately, however, the Western scenario is revealed to be merely a hallucination induced by The Village's authorities. Nobel and Goldsborough imply that a certain pattern emerges in some of the later *Prisoner* episodes. They write, "Just as *Living in Harmony* comprised all Westerns, so *The Girl Who Was Death* comprises all spy-thrillers, old and new, from Poe to Conan Doyle, through Sexton Blake and Fu Manchu to modern Hitchcock, James Bond, and *The Avengers*." (pp. 17–18)[81] There is another important similarity, too. In both cases, the viewer may believe that they are watching "real" events until, in the last few moments of the instalment, it becomes apparent that all that has previously taken place is no more than a fantasy. Returning to the use of long-established scenarios, as Stevens and Moore note, the mind-swap element in *Do Not Forsake Me Oh My Darling* was hardly new, the authors themselves citing its appearance in *The Avengers*[82] – specifically it can be seen in the episode *Who's Who?* Just a few years earlier, the theme had also been addressed in the *Outer Limits* story *The Human Factor*. Nevertheless, McLean and Stansfield consider that the triple mind transfer at the episode's climax provides a "clever twist", (p. 12)[83] and it is unusual within the series to see that here the real target of the machinations in The Village is not Number Six; in this case it is Professor Seltzman.

Dating the setting of *The Prisoner* has always been a challenging task. Whilst the appearance of technology clearly far in advance of that of the 1960s may tempt viewers to hypothesise that the saga takes place at some point in the future, by which time levels of bureaucracy, surveillance and the loss of liberty have significantly escalated, and has even led to speculation in some quarters that the events take place on an alien planet, the mainstream view is that *The Prisoner* was a contemporary series addressing contemporary issues. In the Goodman interview, McGoohan himself describes the series as "a moral and social comment".[84] Programmes such as *Star Trek* and *The Twilight Zone* demonstrate that it is entirely possible to address issues of the day in settings such as a future Earth or an alien planet but this hardly appears to have been McGoohan's intention. *UFO* is more obviously set in time to come, although indications of an exact year tend to conflict. The title sequence would appear to establish the year unequivocally as 1980 and the events of *Survival* clearly take place in 1981. Yet, a 1984 wine appears in *Computer Affair*. Viewers may, however, choose to attribute this discrepancy to a continuity lapse rather than a conscious attempt to be ambiguous.

Much was made in the previous chapter of The Prisoner's less attractive characteristics. *UFO*'s Ed Straker, too, is by no means entirely likeable. Even many sources that deal with *UFO* briefly, perhaps only in passing, comment on his coldness. For example, Muir, who, essentially, is writing about *Space: 1999*, describes Straker as "obsessed and hard-nosed". (p. 6)[85] In a more detailed character study, Bill Harry notes how Straker can seem "cold blooded and ruthless" on occasion. (p. 46)[86] Helen McCarthy goes so far as to describe him as "one of the most maligned" characters in television SF. (p. 24)[87] Just as Number Six's commitment to individuality leads him into conflict with others, Straker's unflinching dedication to SHADO can render him unfeeling and insensitive. Undoubtedly, the personalities of both characters frequently veer towards the confrontational. Booker, in fact, stresses the battles that Straker, "the strong individual", must fight against bureaucratic forces in order to run SHADO as he sees fit. (p. 77)[88] Clear comparisons can be drawn here with Number Six's struggles against those forces in The Village that are intent on reducing him to a mere number.

Whilst Number Six is never able to gain the kind of freedom for which he strives, the viewer may well subscribe when watching the 17 episodes of *The Prisoner* to White and Ali's view that the hero is a kind of superman.[89] Gary Gerani suggests that he should be understood as a symbol, rather than a conventional hero, and, within the context of the series, it was not important that the character be explored "in any normal way". (p. 51)[90] Gerani's stance is consistent with the notion of "Number Six-as-icon" which was introduced in the previous chapter. This perspective makes it easier for the viewer to accept that often it seems that there is virtually nothing that Number Six cannot do. He survives intact in the face of all the schemes that are hatched against him and he even ultimately escapes from the physical Village. In *Many Happy Returns*, he constructs an effective raft, and in *The Chimes of Big Ben*, he makes a working boat. We also learn in the former episode that he himself built KAR 120C. It is clear from his plotting against Number Two in *Hammer Into Anvil* that his abilities as a spy are also formidable, although it is in *Do Not Forsake Me Oh My Darling* that we learn most about Number Six's previous life as a secret agent. Nevertheless, if the claim made by McGoohan in the Goodman interview that the hero was never specifically intended to be a spy is accepted,[91] this background detail would appear to run contrary to what McGoohan had planned. Although as recently as 2014 *Sci-Fi Chronicles* reaffirmed the conventional wisdom by stating unequivocally that even if Number Six and John Drake are not intended to be the same person, they "certainly shared the same career", with the former "clearly a resourceful ex-secret agent",[92] Alwyn Turner raises the possibility that The Prisoner could, in fact, be a scientist rather a secret agent,[93] and certain quotes attributed to McGoohan himself would support this belief. At the launch of the programme in the September 1967 press conference, McGoohan is reported to have declared, *The Prisoner* is "about a top scientist who has vital space secrets in his head".[94]

Straker appears rather more vulnerable than Number Six. In *Sub-smash*, it is revealed that he has previously suffered from claustrophobia but he is eventually successful in overcoming his demons. Despite the tendency of Number Six and Straker to show no real warmth towards many of the people with whom they come into contact, certain episodes of *UFO* and *The Prisoner* reveal that in the past they have enjoyed at least a degree of personal happiness with others. *Confetti Check A-O.K.* gives some background to Straker by, in particular, concentrating on his life with his wife, Mary, whilst *Do Not Forsake Me Oh My Darling* affords viewers an insight into The Prisoner's loving relationship with Janet Portland. These breaks with the established territory of the series have been the subject of criticism. Chris Gregory dislikes the "rather 'soppy' (and highly uncharacteristic) love scenes" in the *Prisoner* episode, (p. 142)[95] whilst, in their biography of Gerry Anderson, Simon Archer and Stan Nicholls report that another story that presented a more human side to Straker, *A Question of Priorities*, was poorly regarded by the American backers. Archer and Nicholls write, "The New York office accused Gerry of moving away from science fiction and into soap opera. No further stories of that kind were produced." (p. 148)[96] According to Nobel and Goldsborough, even in the very first episode of *The Prisoner*, before much of the "human" background of Number Six has become known, the viewer is inclined to support him, perhaps on account of the various efforts made to reduce him to a number.[97] Given the exalted position of Straker within the SHADO hierarchy, it is somewhat harder to relate to him.

Whilst Straker and Number Six frequently exhibit some of man's less attractive personality traits, other characters show important flashes of real humanity. For example, in both series protagonists who play important roles in individual episodes admit their regret for earlier actions that can be considered to constitute betrayals of trust. At the end of *The Schizoid Man*, Alison is clearly ashamed of her part in one of The Village's schemes to undermine Number Six, and in the *Flight Path* episode of *UFO*, SHADO's Paul Roper seeks to atone for passing on valuable information to the aliens. The latter character ultimately pays with his life in his attempt to redress the balance. Treachery is undoubtedly a key theme in both programmes. The Prisoner struggles throughout the series to identify those whom he can trust and, as Gregory recognises, his betrayal by women, in particular, is a recurrent plot feature.[98] In *UFO*, Roper is one of various humans who act on behalf of the aliens. Perhaps most memorably, in *Timelash*, another of the SHADO staff, Turner, the radar operator, is seen to be helping the aliens. In addition to those who make a conscious decision to betray their organisation, others fall victim to alien mind control schemes. In *Kill Straker!*, for example, Colonel Paul Foster succumbs to a hypnotic message urging him to remove the SHADO commander.

Other questions concerning trust arise in the *UFO* episode *Exposed*. In the dénouement, several individuals with whom Foster has come into contact and whom he had initially assumed were ordinary civilians are revealed as SHADO personnel, and the way in which a character whom Foster had believed to be the sister of a dead colleague is finally shown to be SHADO Operative Janna Wade is highly reminiscent of how, in surprising plot twists within *The Prisoner*, characters such as Mrs Butterworth and the personal assistant who is assigned to Number Six for the duration of his election campaign are revealed, in the final moments of an episode, to be Number Two. In addition, it emerges in other instalments that The Prisoner's old friend Cobb and the apparently trustworthy Nadia are in league with those who run The Village. Further comparisons can be drawn between *Exposed* and the *Prisoner* episode *The Chimes of Big Ben*. Here, the Village authorities and SHADO anticipate their victim's actions and stage-manage their entire experience. In *UFO*, however, trust is also explored from SHADO's perspective. In *Court Martial*, the integrity of Foster, who by this point is one of the organisation's most senior personnel, is cast into doubt when it seems that he has been leaking classified information.

The use of what may be regarded as clones forms a further common element in *The Prisoner* and *UFO*. In the former, duplicates of Number Six appear in *The Schizoid Man* and *Fall Out*, and doubles of SHADO personnel are seen in the *Reflections in the Water* episode of *UFO*. Just as The Prisoner's twin is employed in *The Schizoid Man* as part of a scheme by Number Two to weaken the hero, in the *UFO* instalment the lookalikes are central to an alien plot. The duplicate SHADO personnel, in fact, populate a replica of SHADO control. The authenticity of this copy may prompt viewers familiar with *The Prisoner* to remember how the Village authorities seek to disorientate newcomers by accommodating them in places that are identical to their homes. In *The Chimes of Big Ben*, Number Two explains to The Prisoner that the recently arrived Nadia is waking up in "an exact replica of her own room, of course".

Some commentators on *The Prisoner* have made links between The Village and Right wing ideologies. Gregory, for example, asserts, "The totalitarian society of the Village naturally has affinities with fascism", (p. 117) and suggests that the Number Two who quotes Goethe in *Hammer Into Anvil* may be "an ex-Nazi who the Village has recruited". (p. 118)[99] He also points to the resemblance between the culture of The Village and that of the Nazis, especially their dehumanising aspect. In particular, he detects parallels between Nazi principles and the way in which the leaders of The Village seek to create individuals "without self" and control their "every thought and function". (p. 118)[100] More support for the Nazi/Village link comes from the observation of Stevens and Moore that *Do Not Forsake Me Oh My Darling* deals with the forcible recruitment of a Germanic scientist.[101] Whether or not the authorities in The Village are committed to any particular ideology, the high levels of surveillance and influence exercised over the inhabitants would appear characteristic of a totalitarian state.

SHADO, too, is very controlling. It is clear from the *UFO* episode *Court Martial* that, because Earth is considered to be at war with the aliens, SHADO is run along military lines, and its leaders will stop at nothing to deliver their aims of countering the alien threat and maintaining the organisation's cover. As Cull recognises, much is made in the series of the clash between civilian and military cultures.[102] Booker highlights "SHADO's ability to pry into the lives of private citizens", (p. 77)[103] and on the basis of their own moral compasses, viewers may well have particular opinions about the extent to which such intervention is legitimate. For Newman, SHADO exhibits some "near-totalitarian" attitudes. (p. 71)[104] The question of how far the state can go in order to dehumanise and carry out surveillance on its people is part of the very fabric of *The Prisoner* and, again, the series invites a response from the viewer on the issue. Although, in *The Chimes of Big Ben*, Number Two agrees with The Prisoner's assertion that The Village is "run by one side or the other", White and Ali suggest that there is some merit in the theory that it is, in fact, a multinational corporation.[105] If this is the case and The Village lacks any kind of political allegiance then, like SHADO, it may be considered largely unaccountable and somewhat akin to the "big organisations" that were a feature of Gerry Anderson's shows in the 1960s – the World Space Patrol (in *Fireball XL5*), the World Aquanaut Security Patrol (in *Stingray*), International Rescue (in *Thunderbirds*), Spectrum (in *Captain Scarlet and the Mysterons*) and the World Intelligence Network (in *Joe 90*). Undoubtedly, The Village and SHADO share a fundamental similarity in that those running them make every effort to keep their location and even existence secret from the general public. The Village is an isolated community whose principal method of arrival and departure is via helicopter, whilst SHADO is housed beneath a film studio. Even the name SHADO (or perhaps *Shadow*?) implies that the organisation is subterranean and murky. We may say that the organisation operates in the "shadow" of its film studio cover.

Some of the techniques used by the leaders of The Village and SHADO are strikingly similar, too. In the *Prisoner* episode *Do Not Forsake Me Oh My Darling*, Number Two demonstrates to a colleague The Village's "amnesia room", in which people's memories can be erased back to any point in time the authorities choose. In *UFO* episodes such as *The Square Triangle*, *The Dalotek Affair*, *Destruction* and *The Sound of Silence*, SHADO staff either talk of or actually administer a comparable treatment that makes recipients forget their contacts with aliens and their involvement with SHADO. Whereas in *The Prisoner* we side with Number Six virtually from the outset, in *UFO* our sympathies are more likely to lie with SHADO than the "inconvenient" individuals with whom it has to deal. Even if the organisation's methods appear questionable on occasion, most viewers would accept that all must be done to defend our planet and safeguard the human race. In the words of Ed Bishop, "I guess if you analyse the SHADO set-up, it's a kind of fascist organisation with a law unto itself... answerable to no-one. Anarchic, despotic, but, somehow it was working for total good." (p. 16)[106] It is not difficult to draw parallels between this description of SHADO and Chris R. Tame's portrayal of The Village in *The Prisoner* as a "'benevolently' despotic society". (p. 3)[107]

Beyond the amnesia treatment, drugs generally figure prominently in *The Prisoner* and *UFO*, and their presence in each programme has aroused controversy. White and Ali's assertion that the official justification for the banning of the *Living in Harmony* episode in the United States was that characters were seen under the influence of drugs has already been reported, and the authors note that such substances are also a plot feature of *A. B. and C., The Schizoid Man, A Change of Mind* and *Once Upon a Time*.[108] In *UFO's Timelash*, Straker injects himself and Colonel Lake with the dangerous experimental drug X50 in order to counter an alien scheme and in *The Long Sleep*, recreational drugs are seen in use. Nevertheless, as Bentley notes, in the latter "the script took a high moral stance on the issue" and both the characters who take them "are 'punished' for the transgression". (p. 56)[109] In *The Prisoner*, too, drugs are portrayed negatively, and are frequently depicted as a tool employed by the authorities against Number Six.

White and Ali believe that, whilst *The Prisoner* is often considered "ahead of its time", it is more pertinent to view it as a product of its time, (p. 1)[110] and undoubtedly many of the themes explored within the episodes reflect actual concerns and interests of the 1960s, especially the right to individuality and the place of protest and rebellion. According to Rakoff, "*The Prisoner* was a journey to save an individual from moral decline into the anonymity of the melting community. It was the battle of the 1960s." (p. 158)[111] The basis of *UFO* is similar in that it, too, is heavily grounded in real world issues. In *The UFO Documentary*, Gerry Anderson recalls that, at the time of the programme's preparation, he was keen to capitalise on the considerable interest in UFO sightings and discussions surrounding the transplanting of organs, especially the heart. He speculated in *UFO* that the transplanting practice may be adopted by a dying alien race and their spacecraft were sent to Earth in order to collect human body parts. Anderson acknowledges, too, that his thinking surrounding the staffing of SHADO was influenced by the Women's Liberation movement,[112] and there is certainly a strong female presence in many of the key positions within the organisation. Comparisons may be drawn between this situation and the fact that, in *The Prisoner*, three Number Twos whom we see in the series are female. Nevertheless, the treatment of women in each show has also provoked criticism. The suspicion with which females are treated in *The Prisoner* was highlighted in Chapter One, whilst in *UFO*, despite Gerry Anderson's apparently forward-thinking perspective, it has been argued that, at least to some extent, attitudes were still rooted in 1960s sexism,[113] and when the programme is watched today, these date *UFO* very considerably. According to Cull, the depiction of Alec Freeman, who formed SHADO's second-in-command during the early episodes, as a ladies' man "now seems like a museum piece", (p. 206)[114] and Booker, writing from an early twenty-first century perspective, refers to the "outrageously sexist costumes" worn by the show's female characters. (p. 80)[115]

Other themes that are particularly associated with the era in which the programmes were made are addressed in both *The Prisoner* and *UFO*. White and Ali note the popularity in the 1960s of ideas involving extrasensory perception, such as mind reading and telepathy,[116] and the mental link between Alison and Number Six forms a significant element in the plot of *The Schizoid Man*. In *UFO*, concepts associated with mind power are especially apparent in *ESP*, and psychic phenomena are similarly important in instalments such as *The Cat With Ten Lives* and *The Psychobombs*. In the latter, three otherwise ordinary people are given "the ability to call on the potential of the entire universe". Subliminal techniques, especially involving advertising, were much discussed during the era in which *The Prisoner* was made, and their use in *The General*, here in the context of teaching and learning, is indicative of this topicality, whilst in the *Kill Straker!* episode of *UFO*, somewhat similar hypnotic methods are put to a more sinister purpose than mere education. In the *Champions* stories *Shadow of the Panther* and *Nutcracker*, which were made at much the same time as *The Prisoner*, subliminal techniques are, like the hypnotic process we see in *Kill Straker!*, applied as a means of mind control and psychological conditioning. Just a few years later, subliminal programming would figure prominently in the *Out of the Unknown* instalment *The Man in My Head*. As this episode's secondary themes include the suppression of individual identity and independent thought, the story may well be of particular interest to *Prisoner* fans.[117] It is a measure of the lengthy duration of the debate over the morality of the use of subliminal techniques that, in the latter half of the 1970s, McLean and Stansfield encouraged Canadian students who had watched *The General* to investigate, as a follow-up activity, the laws that were then in place in their country on subliminal advertising.[118]

In the Goodman interview, McGoohan explains how a key component in the origins of *The Prisoner* lay in concerns on the part of the authorities that people who held in their heads information about matters that were intended to remain secret could not be allowed to live out their days as they would choose, or at least not until their knowledge became obsolete. In McGoohan's own words, such people had "to be taken care of, put away".[119] The theme is extended in the *Chimes of Big Ben* episode, in which dialogue suggests that it is not just inmates who are confined to The Village. When Number Six puts to Number Two that his interlocutor is himself a prisoner, The Village's chief administrator admits, "My dear chap, of course. I know too much. We're both lifers." Although it is left unclear as to why exactly the retiring Number Two who is due for assassination by the Village authorities in *It's Your Funeral* is to be killed, it is possible that the particular knowledge he holds in his head renders him an especially significant security risk. In *UFO*, those who have had first hand contact with the work of SHADO become similarly inconvenient. This is true, for example, of Liz Newton and Cass Fowler in *The Square Triangle*, and the Dalotek team in *The Dalotek Affair*. In *Exposed*, however, the curiosity and persistence of test pilot Paul Foster ultimately lead to SHADO recruiting him as one of their own staff. In the *Kill Straker!* episode later in the series, Foster again comes under scrutiny, this time in terms of what an organisation should do in the face of subversive behaviour by a renegade member. After Foster has waged a personal campaign against Straker, he recognises that he knows too much simply to be dismissed from his post. The duel between them echoes the more ongoing struggle between The Prisoner and Number Two (or Number Two's henchmen), and the personal edge that is a feature of Foster's harassment of Straker may remind readers of Number's Six's vendetta in *Hammer Into Anvil*.

The pacing of the title sequences is characterised by a speed that we may well associate with the late 1960s. In each case, the viewer is subjected to a barrage of images, none of which remains on the television screen for more than a few seconds at most. Gregory reports that *The Prisoner*'s whole title sequence, which lasts some three minutes, consists of as many as sixty-one individual shots.[120] Whilst the opening sequence here aims to present a narrative showing the events leading up to The Prisoner's arrival in The Village, the purpose of its *UFO* counterpart is to convey some impression of the nature and range of SHADO operations. Occasionally, deviations emerge in the usual introductory material. As Bentley recognises, two episodes of *UFO* – *Confetti Check A-O.K.* and *The Psychobombs* – lack the regular opening title sequence,[121] and *The Prisoner*'s *Living in Harmony* drops the standard music and visuals. Even the title of the show is missing. In *Do Not Forsake Me Oh My Darling*, a preliminary scene is added at the very beginning, Number Six's usual introductory sparring dialogue with Number Two is omitted and unfamiliar music replaces the second part of the main theme. There is another break from the established convention in the *UFO* tale *The Square Triangle*. This instalment closes with a bleak, enigmatic scene in a graveyard instead of the usual shots of heavenly bodies and outer space.

As in *The Prisoner*, the episodes of *UFO* tend to be self-contained and may be enjoyed in virtually any order, although the use of flashback scenes in both programmes means that certain episodes are best viewed before others. In addition, further logic should be applied in *UFO*. In *Mindbender*, the SHADO pilot Conroy is killed, so this episode must really be watched after *The Cat With Ten Lives*, in which the character appears for the first time. Similarly, since *Exposed* introduces Paul Foster, other episodes in which he is seen should come later. Overall, it is difficult to understand, as coherent narratives, the entire sagas that *The Prisoner* and *UFO* present since inconsistent – and even contradictory

– clues are given at different times in relation to the programmes' key questions. If we consider one particular issue – the geographical location of The Village – Hora comments how different episodes of the programme suggest three separate possibilities,[122] and other anomalies form the fodder for many of White and Ali's explorations of the "great debates" surrounding the series.[123] Similarly, given the shift in *UFO*'s emphasis, it is hard to come to definitive conclusions regarding the nature and purpose in coming to Earth of the aliens, even though throughout its 26 episodes the programme may be understood fundamentally as a tale about the repulsion of alien invaders. As Bentley points out in connection with the episode *Destruction*, it certainly makes little sense that an alien race requiring human organs and host bodies should attempt to destroy all life on Earth as they do in that instalment.[124] In both *The Prisoner* and *UFO* the inconsistencies that emerge from episode to episode may not reduce the viewer's enjoyment of a particular tale but the discrepancies and their defiance of rational explanation limit the extent to which both programmes can be viewed as ongoing serials. In the case of *The Prisoner*, in the face of such apparent contradictions, we may well opt for a more abstract understanding. If we accept Douglas L. Howard's conclusion with regard to the location of The Village, it is in all the places suggested and none of them.[125] Our world is that of The Village. For Tame, this point is underlined in *Fall Out* by Number Six's emergence from The Village into London.[126]

Although it has always been the subject of quips by critics making unkind comparisons between the programme's human actors and their puppet counterparts in earlier Anderson series,[127] generally *UFO* is highly respected today. In the late 1980s, *The ITV Encyclopedia of Adventure* went so far as to assert that "the series is now regarded as one of the best of its genre", (p. 566)[128] and the *Radio Times Guide to Science Fiction* awards it a four-star rating.[129] Like *The Prisoner*, it has attained "cult" status and the fact that, in the years since its demise, it has been the subject of full-length books and releases on both video cassette and DVD is testimony to continuing interest in the programme.

References and Notes

1. McGoohan, P. On the trail of The Prisoner: Roger Goodman talks to Patrick McGoohan. CD. PrizBiz, 2007. Audio recording of 1979 interview.
2. O'Neill, J. Sci-fi on tape: A comprehensive guide to over 1,250 science fiction and fantasy films on video. Billboard: New York, 1997.
3. Sellers, R. Cult TV: The golden age of ITC. Plexus: London, 2006.

4. Woodman, B. J. Escaping genre's village: Fluidity and genre mixing in television's The Prisoner. Journal of Popular Culture, 38 (5), August 2005, pp. 939–956.

5. Drake, C. UFO: The hidden truth. SiG, 18, Summer 1987, pp. 16–17.

6. Lip-sync: The UFO Connection. SiG, 19, Spring 1988, pp. 10–11.

7. Booker, M. K. Science fiction television. Praeger: Westport, Connecticut, 2004.

8. Bentley, C. The complete book of Gerry Anderson's UFO. Reynolds and Hearn: Richmond, London, 2003a.

9. Cull, N. J. Was Captain Black really red? The TV science fiction of Gerry Anderson in its cold war context. Media History, 12 (2), August 2006, pp. 193–207.

10. Ibid.

11. Wright, P. Echoes of discontent: Conservative politics and Sapphire and Steel. In: Cook, J. R. and Wright, P. (eds.) British science fiction television: A hitchhiker's guide. I. B. Tauris: London, 2006, pp. 192–218.

12. An explicit connection between the series is made in: Nicholls, P. and Brosnan, J. UFO. In: Clute, J. and Nicholls, P. (eds.) The encyclopedia of science fiction, 2nd ed. Orbit: London, 1993, p. 1253.

13. Brosnan, J. and Nicholls, P. The Invaders. In: Clute, J. and Nicholls, P. (eds.) op. cit., p. 622.

14. Freeman, C. "Scarlet"/"Joe"/"UFO": Some thoughts. SiG, 18, Summer 1987, p. 10.

15. Honda, R. The UFO connection. SiG, 19, Spring 1988, p. 11.

16. White, M. and Ali, J. The official Prisoner companion. Sidgwick and Jackson: London, 1988.

17. Any reader wishing to learn more about the individual titles within the Kaldor City series should consult: Oliver, M. B. Blake's 7: The merchandise guide – Unofficial and unauthorised. Telos: Prestatyn, 2012.

18. Parkin, L. Ahistory: An unauthorised history of the Doctor Who universe, 2nd ed. Mad Norwegian Press: Des Moines, Iowa, 2007.

19. Shenton, A. K. and Hay-Gibson, N. V. The curious breed of the television tie-in. School Librarian, 59 (1), Spring 2011, pp. 15–16.

20. Chris Boucher Interview, April 2010. In: Oliver, M. B. op. cit., pp. 162–171.

21. Honda. R. op. cit.

22. Bentley, C. op. cit.

23. The UFO Documentary. VHS video cassette. Kindred: Ickenham, Middlesex, 1993.

24. Stevens, A. and Moore, F. Fall out: The unofficial and unauthorised guide to The Prisoner. Telos: Tolworth, 2007.

25. Ibid.

26. Klimowski, F. Timelash revisited. Andersonic.
URL: http://andersonic.co.uk/page6.htm (accessed: 11 December 2012).

27. McGoohan, P. op. cit.

28. Newman, B. The film and TV of Gerry Anderson. Supermarionation is Go! 1, Spring 1981, pp. 3–6.

29. Solenoid Spotlight: Tony Barwick Interviewed By Chris Drake And Alan Howard. SiG, 17, Spring 1987, pp. 10–12, 20–27.

30. The UFO Documentary. op. cit.

31. Quoted in: Phillips, M. and Garcia, F. Science fiction television series: Episode guides, histories, and casts and credits for 62 prime time shows, 1959 through 1989. McFarland: Jefferson, North Carolina, 1996.

32. Terence Feely Interview. In: The Prisoner In-depth Tape 6. VHS video cassette. TR 7 Productions: Borehamwood, 1994.

33. Phillips, M. and Garcia, F. op. cit.

34. Hirsch, D. UFO. In: Hirsch, D. (ed.) TV episode guides, volume 2: Science fiction, adventure and superheroes. Starlog: New York, 1982a, pp. 56–63.

35. Bentley, C. The complete Gerry Anderson: The authorised episode guide. Reynolds and Hearn: Richmond, London, 2003b.

36. Solenoid Spotlight: Tony Barwick Interviewed By Chris Drake And Alan Howard. op. cit.

37. Phillips, M. and Garcia, F. op. cit.

38. Interview With Patrick McGoohan. In: Carrazé, A. and Oswald, H. The Prisoner: A televisionary masterpiece. Virgin: London, 1990, pp. 6–8.

39. White, M. and Ali, J. op. cit.

40. Pixley, A. The television films of Gerry Anderson: An episode listing from Supercar to UFO, and Space 1999: part 3. SiG, 16, Autumn 1986, pp. 6–8; Phillips, M. and Garcia, F. op. cit.; Sellers, R. op. cit.

41. Lewis, J. E. and Stempel, P. Cult TV: The essential critical guide. Pavilion Books: London, 1993.

42. White, M. and Ali, J. op. cit.

43. McGoohan, P. op. cit.

44. Fulton, R. The encyclopedia of TV science fiction. Boxtree: London, 1990.

45. Booker, M. K. op. cit.

46. Asimov, I. Theodore Prisoner. In: Carrazé, A. and Oswald, H. op. cit., p. 18.

47. Booker, M. K. Strange TV: Innovative television series from The Twilight Zone to The X-Files. Greenwood: Westport, Connecticut, 2002.

48. The Prisoner in Production. VHS video cassette. TR 7 Productions: Borehamwood, 1993.

49. Rakoff, I. Inside The Prisoner: Radical television and film in the 1960s. Batsford: London, 1998.

50. Brosnan, J. and Nicholls, P. The Invaders. op. cit., p. 622.

51. Quoted in: Javna, J. The best of science fiction TV: The critics' choice from Captain Video to Star Trek, from The Jetsons to Robotech. Titan: London, 1988.

52. Maurer, R. Humanity by the numbers: A sociological look at The Invaders. In: Anchors, Jr., W. E. (ed) Galactic sci-fi television series revisited: A review of alien

invasions on television. Alpha Control Press: Dunlap, Tennessee, 1995, pp. 78–81.

53. Cox, D. Reviews & ratings for The Invaders: Edge of the 60's. IMDb, 9 August 2001. URL: http://www.imdb.com/title/tt0061265/reviews-3 (accessed: 23 February 2017).

54. Lewis, J. E. and Stempel, P. op. cit.

55. Durante, C. We are living in The Village. In: Carrazé, A. and Oswald, H. op. cit., pp. 20–22.

56. DVD Introduction. The Year of the Sex Olympics. BFI, 2003.

57. Nobel, S. and Goldsborough, D. The Prisoner puzzle. Ontario Educational Communications Authority: Toronto, Ontario, 1978.

58. Hall, E. The return of Ulysses: A cultural history of Homer's Odyssey. I. B. Tauris: London, 2008.

59. Litchenberg, J., Marshak, S. and Winston, J. Star Trek lives! Corgi: London, 1975. Chapter five of the book (pp. 106–125) explores Star Trek's "Optimism Effect" in detail.

60. Archer, S. and Nicholls, S. Gerry Anderson: The authorised biography. Legend: London, 1996.

61. Booker, M. K. op. cit. 2004.

62. Fairclough, R. (ed.) The Prisoner: The original scripts – Volume 1. Reynolds and Hearn: Richmond, London, 2005.

63. Hora, M. The Prisoner of Portmeirion, 2nd ed. Number Six Publications, 1995.

64. Woodman, B. J. op. cit.

65. Dunn, K. Do not adjust your set: The early days of live television. John Murray: London, 2003.

66. Morreale, J. Lost, The Prisoner, and the end of the story. Journal of Popular Film and Television, 38 (4), 2010, pp. 176–185.

67. See, for example: Gerani, G. and Schulman, P. H. Fantastic television: A pictorial history of sci-fi, the unusual and the fantastic from the '50s to the '70s. Titan: London, 1987. Reprint of 1977 work; Fulton, R. op. cit.; Sellers, R. op. cit.

68. Hirsch, D. Captain Scarlet and the Mysterons. In: Hirsch, D. (ed.), op. cit., 1982b, pp. 31–37.

69. Fane-Saunders, K. (ed.) Radio Times guide to science fiction. BBC Worldwide: London, 2001.

70. Fulton, R. op. cit.

71. Fane-Saunders, K. (ed.) op. cit.

72. White, M. and Ali, J. op. cit.

73. McLean, N. and Stansfield, D. The Prisoner program guide. Ontario Educational Communications Authority: Toronto, Ontario, 1976.

74. Rogers, D. The Prisoner and Danger Man. Boxtree: London, 1989.

75. Bentley, C. op. cit. 2003b.

76. Drake, C. UFO and Space: 1999. Boxtree: London, 1994.

77. Hirsch, D. op. cit. 1982a.

78. Muir, J. K. A history and critical analysis of Blake's 7, the 1978–1981 British television space adventure. McFarland: Jefferson, North Carolina, 2000.

79. Ibid.

80. Nobel, S. and Goldsborough, D. op. cit.

81. Ibid.

If we accept that Living in Harmony effectively satirises the Western genre and The Girl Who Was Death the spy-thriller, then it is appropriate at this point to compare these Prisoner episodes with the way in which Man From Atlantis presented lighthearted treatments of classic stories. Shoot-out at Land's End, for example, is a spoof of the tale of Billy the Kid; The Naked Montague is a reworking of Romeo and Juliet and C. W. Hyde is a tongue-in-cheek version of The Strange Case of Dr. Jekyll and Mr. Hyde. Stephen Kandel, who was responsible for two of these stories, has recalled that if Man From Atlantis had continued, he had plans to write further scripts in the same vein. (see Science Fiction Television Series: Episode Guides, Histories, and Casts and Credits for 62 Prime Time Shows, 1959 through 1989) A similar pattern emerged in several Doctor Who serials in the latter half of the 1970s, with Underworld deriving its inspiration from the story of Jason and the quest for the Golden Fleece, The Androids of Tara modelled on The Prisoner of Zenda and The Horns of Nimon based on the myth of Theseus and the Minotaur.

82. Stevens, A. and Moore, F. op. cit.

83. McLean, N. and Stansfield, D. op. cit.

84. McGoohan, P. op. cit.

85. Muir, J. K. Exploring Space: 1999 – An episode guide and complete history. McFarland: Jefferson, North Carolina, 1997.

86. Harry, B. Heroes of the spaceways. Omnibus: London, 1981.

87. McCarthy, H. The ultimate computer: Commander Edward Straker – A character study. SIG, 8, Summer 1983, pp. 24–27.

88. Booker, M. K. op. cit. 2004.

89. White, M. and Ali, J. op. cit.

90. Quoted in: Javna, J. op. cit.

91. McGoohan, P. op. cit.

92. Lewin, R. The Prisoner. In: Haley, G. (ed.) Sci-fi chronicles: A visual history of the galaxy's greatest science fiction. Aurum: London, 2014, p. 261.

93. Turner, A. W. Portmeirion and its creator. In: Morris, J., Turner, A. W., Eastment, M., Lacey, S. and Llywelyn, R. Portmeirion. Antique Collectors' Club: Woodbridge, 2006, pp. 26–129.

94. Langley, R. The Prisoner 1967 press conference. 2011.

95. Gregory, C. Be seeing you... Decoding The Prisoner. John Libbey Media: Luton, 1997.

96. Archer, S. and Nicholls, S. op. cit.

97. Nobel, S. and Goldsborough, D. op. cit.

98. Gregory, C. op. cit.

99. Gregory, C. op. cit.

100. Gregory, C. op. cit.

101. Stevens, A. and Moore, F. op. cit.

102. Cull, N. J. op. cit.

103. Booker, M. K. op. cit. 2004.

104. Newman, K. Doctor Who. British Film Institute: London, 2005.

105. White, M. and Ali, J. op. cit.

106. Quoted in: Drake. C. op. cit. 1987.

107. Tame, C. R. Different values: An analysis of Patrick McGoohan's The Prisoner. Libertarian Reprints, 1, 1983. Reprint of 1974 work. URL: http://www.libertarian.co.uk/lapubs/libre/libre001.pdf (accessed: 23 February 2017).

108. White, M. and Ali, J. op. cit.

109. Bentley, C. op. cit. 2003a.

110. White, M. and Ali, J. op. cit.

111. Rakoff, I. op. cit.

112. The UFO Documentary. op. cit.

113. Phillips, M. and Garcia, F. op. cit.; Sellers, R. op. cit.

114. Cull, N. J. op. cit.

115. Booker, M. K. op. cit. 2004.

116. White, M. and Ali, J. op. cit.

117. The stifling of free thought that we witness in The Man in My Head echoes what can be seen in one of the earlier, second season Out of the Unknown plays, namely J. B. Priestley's Level Seven. Here, people who have been duped into living in a self-sufficient community within a top security bunker far beneath the surface of the Earth are given alpha-numeric identifiers in place of their names, and when they speak of matters such as freedom and democracy, they are immediately subjected to a government propaganda recording. The mini-society depicted is highly routinised and access to key parts of the base is tightly controlled. The restless urges of one particular rogue individual are quelled by "treatment". Thereafter, he becomes a submissive menial. As in The Prisoner, the nature of the "side" that forms the subject of the programme is left unspecified. Oliver Wake makes various pertinent observations on this issue during the course of his review on the British Television Drama website (http://www.britishtelevisiondrama.org.uk/?p=3086) – apart from a general (who is never named and is identified only by his designation of A10), the community's leadership is unseen; a map in an operations room shows "abstract shapes and markings rather than identifiable countries" and the military

uniforms in evidence are "not clearly styled on the forces of any one particular nation". All these features endow the base with a Village-like ambiguity.

Five of the other Out of the Unknown episodes that have been mentioned in this book in connection with The Prisoner (i.e. The Yellow Pill, This Body is Mine, Welcome Home, Deathday and The Man in my Head) were produced during the fourth and final season of the programme – one of two in which Prisoner author Roger Parkes served as script editor. On a humorous note, the observant Mark Ward points out that, in the Out of the Unknown play Random Quest, one of the books attributed to the hero Colin Trafford is entitled A Change of Mind, which is, of course, the name given to Parkes's own Prisoner episode. (see Out of the Unknown: A Guide to the Legendary BBC Series)

118. McLean, N. and Stansfield, D. op. cit.

Even today, subliminal advertising is a notion that continues to intrigue and alarm. As recently as January 2015, over fifty years after it had been ruled illegal in Britain, subliminal advertising formed the subject of a significant new Radio 4 documentary – Can You Spot the Hidden Message? Although the programme did not mention The Prisoner specifically, links were made between the possibilities for thought control that some believed subliminal advertising offered and the dystopian situations that are found in fictions such as Brave New World and Nineteen Eighty-four.

119. McGoohan, P. op. cit.

120. Gregory. C. op. cit.

121. Bentley, C. op. cit. 2003b.

122. Hora, M. op. cit.

123. White, M. and Ali, J. op. cit.

124. Bentley, C. op. cit. 2003b.

125. Howard, D. L. The Prisoner. In: Lavery, D. (ed.) The essential cult TV reader. University Press of Kentucky: Lexington, Kentucky, 2010, pp. 189–200.

126. Tame, C. R. op. cit.

The notion that The Village is all around us is neatly emphasised by one of the ornaments that has been sold in The Prisoner Shop in Portmeirion. The artefact in question shows a penny farthing bicycle propped up against a sign post. One part of the sign points towards "The Village", whilst another part alerts the traveller to the fact that, in the opposite direction, they will find "Pentref" (i.e. "Village" in Welsh).

127. See, for example: O'Neill, J. op. cit.; Nicholls, P. and Brosnan, J. op. cit.; Clute, J. Science fiction: The illustrated encyclopedia. Dorling Kindersley: London, 1995; Pringle, D. (ed.) The ultimate encyclopedia of science fiction: The definitive illustrated guide. Carlton: London, 1996.

128. Rogers, D. The ITV encyclopedia of adventure. Boxtree: London, 1988.

129. Fane-Saunders, K. (ed.) op. cit.

CHAPTER NINE
The Individual
and the "Team"

According to *The Encyclopedia of Science Fiction*, a feature of British television science fiction in the 1970s was the prevalence of what they term "anxiety-ridden" series, which "reflected the fears of a society that seemed to find itself on the brink of something unpleasant". (p. 1208) The authors specifically refer to *Doomwatch*, *Survivors* and *1990* in this context,[1] although their list is by no means comprehensive. *The Guardians*, which portrayed a society of the near future in which individual freedom is stifled and order maintained by the eponymous paramilitary police force, is similarly bleak. James Chapman detects a dystopian thread within *Doctor Who* at this time, too, citing as evidence the failure of the hero to defeat his foe in the story *Genesis of the Daleks*.[2] The pessimism of this adventure is well appreciated by John Williams, who writes:

> a journalist for *The Guardian*... [noted] at the time that events were 'getting ever tougher for the Doc in the one he's bound to lose.' Not only is the Doctor on a hiding to nothing, but he struggles to impose himself on the events unfolding on Skaro, is a mere spectator for much of the action, and eventually, yes, he loses. (p. 30)[3]

The doom-laden mood extended into children's science fiction television, too – the well regarded serial *The Changes* sees people suddenly turn on technology and attack the machinery around them, with a consequent breakdown in society. It eventually becomes apparent that an ancient force has re-emerged to restore the natural balance of the world by inducing man to destroy the technology that has led him to progress too rapidly. Like *The Prisoner, The Changes* deals with the negative implications of science. There are clear similarities, as well, in the messages within the serial that relate to development and Patrick McGoohan's own views on the matter. In the Troyer interview, McGoohan reflected, "I think we're progressing too fast. I think that we should pull back and consolidate the things that we've discovered."[4] As in *The Prisoner, The Changes* finishes with some ambivalent shots, which may give rise to positive and negative interpretations. In *The Prisoner*, Number Six would seem to have escaped from the physical Village but there is clear evidence that he remains far from free; at the end of the last episode of *The Changes*, meanwhile, whilst normality has been restored, the fact that we see road traffic and trains running much as they did before would suggest that man has learnt nothing from the harrowing experience he has undergone over the ten instalments. The dénouement is, in the eyes of Alistair D. McGown and Mark J. Docherty, "inconclusive". (p. 87)[5] If man is indeed no wiser after the events, it would seem that there is no reason why they may not recur. Perhaps we have witnessed the beginning of a cycle, just as the events in *The Prisoner* appear destined to repeat. We can draw parallels, as well, between the climax of *The Changes* and that of J. B. Priestley's classic play *An Inspector Calls*. Here, too, by no means all the protagonists have changed their attitudes and clearly some need a second "jolt" to enable them to confront the consequences of their actions.

It is perhaps an indication of the limits in the extent to which viewers welcomed pessimistic science fiction that by no means all the programmes opting for a downbeat or low-key approach proved popular. Terrance Dicks recalls that, after he and Barry Letts had been invited to create an adult science fiction series for the BBC, their new drama – *Moonbase 3* – was poorly received. Dicks himself concedes, "In an excess of high-minded BBC rectitude we decided to avoid *Star Trek* type fantasy – no monsters or alien races – and go for grim realism. Reality proved too grim and the public didn't buy it." (p. 12)[6] Philip Sandifer singles out the final episode, *View of a Dead Planet*, as especially bleak in terms of its concept and tone.[7] We should perhaps interpret realism within *Moonbase 3* as not only meaning narrative plausibility; for Peter Wright the programme was also rooted in the contemporary situation. Pointing to how the series' "appeal to realism resulted in a disquieting sense of claustrophobia and isolation", he appreciates that the programme "captured the general mood of insularity felt (and often desired) in Britain during the early 1970s". (p. 297)[8]

Television's decision-makers were aware in the late 1960s and early 1970s that extreme scenarios of doom could well be met with an uneasy response from viewers and some took pains to avoid such a reaction. Alan Armer, producer of *The Invaders*, recalls that an early draft of the *Peacemaker* episode posited that the US Secretary of State portrayed was either himself an alien or working for the aliens. Executive producer Quinn Martin vetoed this element on the basis that it was "perhaps immoral to do a show that left the audiences disquieted with their government, with their sense of comfortableness with their government".[9] Similarly, a series premise put forward by Gerry Anderson when outlining an early proposal for what was to become *Space: 1999* became a matter of concern to Abe Mandell, President of the Independent Television Corporation in New York, and the man responsible for selling the show in the United States. Specifically, Anderson suggested that his new programme could see the Earth blown up. Mandell thought that the destruction of our own planet might make American audiences feel "a little insecure" (p. 20)[10] or "uncomfortable". (p. 12)[11] Anderson then dropped the idea and concentrated his attentions on a possible misfortune involving the Moon, and his series began to evolve along the lines that would become familiar to viewers of the finished product.

Given Mandell's doubts about *Space: 1999*, it is perhaps unsurprising that M. Keith Booker feels that dark depictions of the future tend not to be found in American television science fiction. Nevertheless, he does note that, in terms of early 1970s cinema, "the baleful U.S. misadventure in Vietnam, the energy crisis, and Watergate combined with growing fears of overpopulation and environmental contamination... [led to] a flurry of pessimistic, dystopian visions... including *A Clockwork Orange*, *The Omega Man*, *Silent Running*, *Soylent Green* and *Zardoz*". (p. 68)[12]

Taking a similar line to *The Encyclopedia of Science Fiction*, Jim Leach also cites *Doomwatch* and *Survivors* as series that are indicative of the depressed outlook which was characteristic of the period in Britain. He adds another to the list – *Blake's 7*.[13] The comments of other writers suggest that this series fitted the prevailing mood perfectly; *The Encyclopedia of TV Science Fiction* highlights its "gloomy vision of the future", (p. 60)[14] and *Science Fiction: The Illustrated Encyclopedia* draws attention to its "deliberately seedy, pessimistic ambience". (p. 301)[15] Una McCormack isolates two unhappy dimensions – as well as reflecting "a general disillusionment with a society gone wrong", the programme is sceptical "about the options available to those who wish to change the world around them". (p. 175)[16] For Rodney Marshall, it is too simplistic, however, to label *Blake's 7* simply as a dystopia. He suggests that other forms upon which the programme draws are political satire, comic strip action-adventure, science fiction, space opera, costume drama and Western. Marshall feels the series defies easy categorisation.[17] When he goes on to cite state surveillance, propaganda, revolution and terrorism as specific issues *Blake's 7* addresses, similarities with *The Prisoner* are brought into the sharpest relief.[18]

Survivors and *Blake's 7* are not only linked by their anti-utopian premise. In the minds of many, they will always be considered the brainchild of Terry Nation. It is his role in relation to *Blake's 7* and, in particular, the extent to which his involvement in that show may be compared with the influence of McGoohan in terms of *The Prisoner* which is of special relevance to the territory of this chapter. According to Matt Hills, the existence of a designated "auteur" is a feature of any programme that aspires to cult status. This figure, Hills argues, "acts as a point of coherence and continuity in relation to the world of the media cult", (p. 132) and may well take the form of an individual who fulfils an executive producer/creator/writer role.[19] In *The Prisoner*, McGoohan, of course, has the added status of being the series' star. In this context, McGoohan's pre-eminence is established at the beginning of the very first episode, when his name appears even before the title of the programme. The first caption we see is "Patrick McGoohan in... *The Prisoner*". Terry Nation, in relation to *Blake's 7*, is one of a handful of individuals whom Hills cites as archetypal auteurs.[20] On the most basic level, it was McGoohan and Nation who were instrumental in selling their respective series to the appropriate television company bosses. The connection between *Blake's 7* and Terry Nation is emphasised in much of the merchandising that appeared in relation to the show. Very often it bears the logo "Terry Nation's *Blake's 7*". This is true, for example, of all three novelisations, even though, in the third book, none of the scripts adapted were his.[21] Whereas McGoohan's influence on the direction of *The Prisoner* increased during the making of the programme, especially after the departure of another major key creative presence, George Markstein, and became so pronounced that Wesley Britton asserts that McGoohan "micromanaged each aspect" of the production of *The Prisoner*'s conclusion, (p. 101)[22] Nation's input into *Blake's 7* diminished. All of the first season episodes of *Blake's 7* were written by Nation but he contributed only three to each of the next two and none at all to the last. The control that McGoohan, as writer, director and star, was able to exercise over the way in which *The Prisoner* was resolved in *Fall Out* is in stark contrast to the fact that Nation was not even consulted on the final episode of *Blake's 7*.

A case can be made that, although it was made in the 1960s, rather than the 1970s, *The Prisoner* is also a product of the "anxiety-ridden" television tradition identified by *The Encyclopedia of Science Fiction*. McGoohan himself acknowledges how the series was rooted in his fears that society was becoming increasingly "numeralised".[23] Perhaps its appearance as early as 1967 is another indication that *The Prisoner* was truly ahead of its time, as director Pat Jackson[24] and commentators such as Max Hora[25] claim. An alternative interpretation is that of Steven Fielding, who views *The Prisoner* as part of the British political dystopian genre which he believes extends as far back as the 1940s.[26] Lucy Sargisson catalogues what she regards as "classic dystopian themes" that are prevalent in *The Prisoner*: "control of the individual... technology, surveillance... violence, beatings, the use of psychotropic drugs that make you change the way that you think".[27] Booker also emphasises *The Prisoner*'s dystopian characteristics, pointing to "the basic defiant-individual-versus-repressive-authority structure of the series", the use of numbers to identify citizens, the enclosed confines of The Village which create a feeling of "claustrophobic containment" and "the simultaneous video broadcasts and video surveillance". (p. 88)[28] Nevertheless, *Sci-Fi Chronicles* labels *The Prisoner* "speculative fiction" and "spy-fi" (p. 261),[29] rather than a work of dystopia, even though the series would seem to meet most of the criteria which the book indicates are characteristics of this type of story. For example, it does indeed deal with a scenario in which the society depicted is "terminally corrupt" and "unfair", and the possibility that The Village could be interpreted as "a warning" as to what our own society may become in the future (p. 546) was raised in the previous chapter.[30]

Most fundamentally, the world that is depicted in series such as *Survivors*, *Blake's 7* and *The Prisoner* is one to be feared. We may hypothesise that, in each case, even if no real prophecy is intended, many of the less attractive and most threatening features of our own situation have at least been magnified and projected into the world that forms the setting for the programme in question. Jon Abbott suggests that, in *The Prisoner*, it is the absurdities and hypocrisies of modern British life that are highlighted.[31] In both *The Prisoner* and *Blake's 7*, the privacy of the individual comes under increasing threat as intrusive technology and methods become ever more advanced. The heroes, Number Six and Blake, discover that even their dreams can be subject to manipulation. The possible Fascistic nature of The Village was addressed in Chapter Eight and we may postulate that the Federation in *Blake's 7* has a similar ideological basis. Paul Cornell, Martin Day and Keith Topping highlight the heavy use of Nazi imagery in Terry Nation's *Avengers* episode *Invasion of the Earthmen*, and observe that the inclusion of such an element forms "a common Nation trait". (p. 260)[32] Whilst it is particularly apparent in his *Doctor Who* serial *Genesis of the Daleks* and this has long been the subject of much comment,[33] Cornell, Day and

Topping single out *Blake's 7* as another Nation work in which a Nazi theme is especially prevalent.[34]

Ostensibly, a key difference between *Blake's 7* and *The Prisoner* is one of scope. Whilst the former deals principally with the oppression meted out by a tyrannical Federation that stretches across much of space, The Village is, obviously, more limited in scale. Yet, if one accepts Number Two's claim in the *Chimes of Big Ben* episode of *The Prisoner* that The Village provides a blueprint for a new order, with the whole world ultimately assuming a form much like The Village, then the conformity and coercion that we witness over the course of the series would seem destined to go unchecked. As in *Blake's 7*, there would appear to be no hiding place for the individual who is intent on freedom. This realisation is rammed home in the last minute of *Fall Out* when, as the hero approaches his London home, a hearse similar to that in evidence just before the hero was abducted moves past the camera,[35] the door of his house opens automatically in front of The Butler, thereby echoing one of the features of dwellings within The Village, Number Six is still identified on-screen as "Prisoner" and the beginning of the title sequence repeats. This conclusion would appear to reaffirm the hero's position as, to quote Alain Carrazé and Hélène Oswald, "the eternal loser". (p. 33)[36]

In *Blake's 7*, an enforced conformity is not only prevalent within societies based on planets ruled by the Federation. Similar oppression can be found on independent worlds, too. A possible conclusion to be drawn is that, just as it is clear from what we see in *Fall Out* that The Village extends beyond its physical confines, so, too, techniques characteristic of the Federation are evident elsewhere. In the episode *Volcano*, the leaders of the planet Obsidian employ methods similar to those practised by the Village authorities, namely the blocking of tendencies towards aggressive acts and regular psychological propaganda. In addition, Hower, first citizen on Obsidian, offers an analysis of man that echoes strongly some of the key themes within *Fall Out*. He comments, "every man is at war with himself. His reason is at war with his instinct. His animal and his spiritual natures clash together".

Whilst the conclusion of *Fall Out* is perhaps most significant in terms of what it pessimistically **implies** rather than actually **shows**, the final scene of the last episode of *Blake's 7*, *Blake*, is a little less ambiguous. Steven Savile goes so far as to describe it as "one of television's most downbeat series endings". (p. 22)[37] Very early on in both *The Prisoner* and *Blake's 7*, the hero indicates quite explicitly to others his aim in relation to the systems that he is opposing. In just the second episode of *The Prisoner*, Number Six announces his desire to wipe The Village off the face of the Earth and obliterate it. Blake voices a similar destructive intention, here in terms of the Federation, in *Space Fall*, when he talks of his urge to see the heart of the Federation "torn out". In *Duel* later in the first season, Blake reiterates his aim of destroying the "corrupt and oppressive" régime. Ultimately, if the events seen in *Fall Out* are to be taken at face value, Number Six is at least successful in bringing about The Village's physical destruction, even if true freedom remains elusive. Despite effecting significant victories over the course of the series, in the end Number Six in *The Prisoner* and the rebels in *Blake's 7* are seen to lose. In the final episode of the BBC series, not only is Blake killed but the demise of the Federation seems as remote as ever. Many philosophical issues have been discussed in relation to *Fall Out*; Sue Short suggests that *Blake* is also concerned with a fundamental "truth", namely that "complicity and self-interest will triumph over any altruistic ideals". (p. 210)[38]

Commentators have described the failures of Number Six on one hand and the anti-Federation dissidents on the other in very similar terms. The "insistent note of hopelessness" (p. 89) which Short detects in relation to *The Prisoner* has been reported in Chapter Seven[39] and, in the same way, *The Encyclopedia of Science Fiction* writes that, in *Blake's 7*, a mood of "doomed helplessness" comes from the rebels inflicting "mere pinpricks on the seemingly indestructible Federation".[40] Likewise, Mark Bould draws attention to the programme's "dismal tone and perpetual sense of defeat". (p. 221)[41] When asked in an interview if he thought Blake ever stood a chance of winning his war against the Federation, Chris Boucher, *Blake's 7*'s script editor and writer of nine of the episodes, admitted,

> No. I don't think it was possible. Although on occasion it was suggested that there were other freedom fighters about the place, they were never of any real threat to the Federation. So really when you came down to it, there was only Blake and his four companions, fighting alone and against overwhelming odds. (p. 10)[42]

For many viewers, *Fall Out* was something of a missed opportunity in that it did not provide the kind of answers – or indeed in some respects any answers at all – to various outstanding questions. Similar criticisms have been made in relation to *Redemption*, the opening episode of *Blake's 7*'s second season. Here representatives of the beings responsible for building the *Liberator* attempt to reclaim their property but a range of intriguing questions surrounding the circumstances that led to the ship being abandoned in space before it was encountered by the Federation prison ship remain unresolved even at the episode's conclusion. In the words of John Kenneth Muir, *Redemption* "simply does not satisfy those who want to know more about Zen [the spaceship's computer] and the *Liberator's* society". (p. 77)[43]

Although efforts were made to continue both series via other media soon after the final episodes were produced, through three *Prisoner* books appearing in the late 1960s and early 1970s and a sequel *Blake's 7* novel published in the mid 1980s, logically it is difficult to see how future television versions could pick up the shows at the point where they had been left. Each seemed to have run its course. At the end of *Fall Out*, the looping nature of the narrative that viewers had watched over 17 instalments is firmly established and in the climax of *Blake's 7*, Blake himself has been killed, the viewer has seen all but one of the other rebels shot (apparently dead) and it would seem that a similar fate may have been suffered by Avon. As *The Complete Directory to Science Fiction, Fantasy and Horror Television Series* comments, the decision not to produce a fifth season saved "someone a lot of trouble figuring a way out of a hopeless situation". (p. 136)[44] Yet, Hills recognises that both *The Prisoner* and *Blake's 7* provide "grand non-narratives". (p. 137)[45] The former leaves many questions unanswered with regard to what would have followed at the end of *Fall Out*, especially in terms of whether the events shown in the series will themselves repeat or whether it is simply the underlying issues with which the hero will again have to deal.

Even if we put aside our curiosity as to how, in broad terms, Number Six's life after *Fall Out* will unfold, there is plenty of scope for speculation on immediate concerns. As McGoohan himself points out, in the final moments, we see the door of The Prisoner's house in the real world open by itself but we are given no clues as to the reaction of the hero; does his exhilaration at escaping from the physical Village remain, at least temporarily, or does he notice that the door has moved automatically and come to a depressing realisation? McGoohan comments, "That was left in abeyance – an unfinished symphony." (p. 21)[46] Those watching the final episode have, as McGoohan intended, drawn their own conclusions. Faced with no explicit indication of The Prisoner's response to the incident, Matthew White and Jaffer Ali suggest that it is as if he **expects** the door to open much like those of houses in The Village. For the authors, this is evidence to support the argument that, throughout the series, Number Six has been living in The Village as a "plant".[47] There must be some doubt, however, as to whether Number Six is even able to see the door of his house open. It is clear to the viewers that the door swings inwards to allow The Butler to enter and then closes automatically behind him but it may argued that by this point the hero is already travelling away speedily in his car.

The most pressing question vexing fans of *Blake's 7*, meanwhile, is whether Avon has been killed. As Hills observes, "the desire to know is pointedly frustrated by virtue of the fact that the final moments of the soundtrack – a number of gunshots – play over a blacked out screen and then the end credits". (p. 137)[48] A direct link between the two climaxes is made by Jon E. Lewis and Penny Stempel, who consider *Blake's 7*'s final episode to be "the most enigmatic conclusion to a serial since McGoohan's *The Prisoner*". (p. 16)[49]

Undoubtedly part of the appeal of the resolutions of both *The Prisoner* and *Blake's 7* lies in the fact that the viewer has the freedom to construct their own "sense" from what they have seen. Faced with some of the more unpalatable truths presented by the former, the individual may choose to concentrate on the revelation that the hero has escaped from and even apparently destroyed the physical Village, although to do so and exclude other more uncomfortable evidence is clearly to misunderstand McGoohan's intention. McGoohan highlights, in fact, that The Village has **both** an external element (i.e. it is an actual place) and an internal dimension that exists within us,[50] and there is no escape from the conditions that impose on us our own personal prison. Similarly, while Anthony Brown outlines a range of hopeful scenarios that a viewer may choose to entertain in order to allow the *Blake's 7* saga to continue, he cautions that such thoughts would "seek to deny the series' unique pessimism".[51] For Gareth Thomas, who played Blake, one of the attractions of the programme was the finite nature of the overall story.[52] By the end of the series, there can be little doubt that the Federation forces have emerged victorious but it may be argued that some uncertainty surrounds the significance of this outcome. Does it represent a triumph for the forces of order or a defeat for those who strive for a better world?

Confronted with an episode which, in the words of Daniel O'Brien, abandons "all pretence of logic, sense or intelligible plotting", (p. 100)[53] many first-time viewers find watching *Fall Out* a disorientating experience, and seeing the last instalment of *Blake's 7* can also be unnerving. Reviewing *Blake* in December 1992 when it was first released on video cassette, Brown describes it as "disturbing" and "unsettling".[54] He draws particular attention to the surprising changes in Blake himself, who, initially, it would appear, has changed his allegiance, and the viewer may also be discomforted by Blake's account of the death of Jenna; the closing down of Scorpio's computer, Slave, which echoes the demise of Zen in *Terminal*; Tarrant's misreading of Blake's intentions which ultimately leads to disastrous results; and of course, the killing of four of Avon's group in a scene marked by what *The Encyclopedia of TV Science Fiction* describes as "indulgent, slow-motion savagery". (p. 61)[55] One of Brown's concluding comments, namely that this "wasn't the episode anyone expected to see", could apply equally appropriately to the last instalment of *The Prisoner*.[56] Reference has been at various points in *Unique But Similar* to the possibility that the events witnessed in *The Prisoner* may be no more than a dream. If an observation made in a *Blake's 7 Winter Special* is extended, the shoot-out in the last episode of the BBC series may be understood in similar terms. Specifically, the publication highlights how "there was no blood when some of the characters were shot and they fell in a dream-like manner". (p. 47)[57] This is consistent with the "unreal" air noted by Tony Attwood. He writes that, in the climactic moments, "time itself appears to slow down and the gun fire seems to echo endlessly". (p. 99)[58]

The hero's final, implied defeat in *Fall Out* forms the culmination of a series of successes and failures for the character over previous weeks. A similar situation arises in *Blake's 7*. An early indicator of the eventual outcome of the saga can be found in the third episode, *Cygnus Alpha*, in which Avon declares implacably that Blake is fighting a war he is bound to lose. In Section I, it was noted that much can be learnt in terms of the overall shifts in the balance of power within *The Prisoner* by exploring which battles were won by the hero and which by the Village authorities. A similar exercise can be carried out in relation to *Blake's 7*. Among the most disastrous schemes is that seen in *Pressure Point*. Here, Gan, one of Blake's original team, dies in a raid that achieves nothing, other than the discovery that the location of the Federation's Control centre is not where Blake had anticipated. The dénouement of *Gold* is almost equally depressing. Here, in an ironic plot twist, the rebels learn that their efforts have not only resulted in their acquisition of worthless bank notes but have delivered the gold that they sought into the hands of their most hated Federation opponent, Servalan.

Muir gives much consideration to the similarities of *The Prisoner* and *Blake's 7* in articulating a story arc. Attention has already been focused in *Unique But Similar* on the cycle in evidence in *The Prisoner*, and in relation to *Blake's 7*, Muir notes how, in both the first episode and the last, a dissident group is massacred by Federation security guards, a key resistance leader is killed and only one man has been seen to remain standing.[59] Further similarities between the beginning and end of the series are detected by Attwood[60] and Alan Stevens and Fiona Moore.[61] Specifically, the latter note how, in both *The Way Back* and *Blake*, the resistance is undermined by a Federation spy, whilst Attwood points to the resemblance between the Federation's Pylene 50 programme that emerges as a significant theme in the final season of *Blake's 7* and the drug-based suppression of Earth inhabitants at the very beginning of the series.

Attwood concludes, "So all in all, there has been a lot of action and a lot of deaths, but very little change." (p. 192)[62] Boucher suggests that, by the end of the final season, even Avon is starting to move in the same personal direction as Blake had before him.[63]

A series that is of a similar vintage to *The Prisoner* and which, in the eyes of some commentators, also features a pronounced iterative element is *The Time Tunnel*. However, whereas the cyclical nature of *The Prisoner* and *Blake's 7* is now widely accepted, the possibility that the events depicted in the Irwin Allen programme take place in a perpetual loop is the subject of lively debate. As long ago as the latter half of the 1970s, Gary Gerani and Paul H. Schulman recounted, "In the final episode, our two scientist heroes materialize once again on the deck of the Titanic, never to be heard from again. Viewers are left with the impression that the whole cycle [which began with an adventure on board the Titanic] will be repeated." (p. 71)[64] Yet, this interpretation is not universally supported. An alternative perspective is that the sequence which provoked it was merely a ploy to encourage viewers, through a preview, to watch a repeat of the first episode which was due to follow in the rerun to come.[65]

A fleeting form of circularity is evident in *Doctor Who*. Certainly, the sight of a policeman and a police box in the first few moments of the final Fourth Doctor serial, *Logopolis*, has stimulated considerable discussion, as it brings to mind the beginning of the series's original story, *An Unearthly Child*. That 1963 adventure starts with comparable imagery. There may be an argument that such repetition was intended to indicate to viewers that the programme has effectively come full circle and is about to be reborn with the regeneration of the eponymous hero. It is pertinent to note at this point that Chapman feels that in some ways *Logopolis* "anticipates the direction the series would take as it moved into the 1980s". (p. 139)[66] Alternatively, as John Tulloch and Manuel Alvarado recognise, the inclusion of a police box and policeman in the opening scene of *Logopolis* may be merely "a self-referencing device, relying on the institutionalised longevity of the programme to delight *Doctor Who* buffs by recalling its own origins and mythology". (p. 22)[67]

The last episodes of *The Prisoner* and *Blake's 7* proved intensely controversial. Whilst the former was denounced by many as incomprehensible, and in the words of Short, a "public uproar followed the finale", (p. 14)[68] it was the emphatic yet also enigmatic ending of the latter that bemused many viewers. *Blake's 7* producer Vere Lorrimer recounts, "By God, it did cause an outrage... the outcry really was tremendous." (p. 117)[69] For Michael Keating, who played Vila Restal, one of the rogues, the impact of the episode was heightened by the fact that it was broadcast so close to Christmas (specifically, 21st

December 1981). Keating reports how some of the letters he received after its transmission were "from people who had been out of work for months and seeing that episode just before Christmas really made them suicidal, which I felt bad about". (p. 185)[70] Nation himself was angered by how, in his eyes, the production team purposely did not let him know what was being planned. Certainly, the resolution flew in the face of Nation's own adage, "never kill anything off". (p. 273)[71] Nation's unhappiness with the climax of *Blake's 7* can be compared with George Markstein's disillusionment with the way in which *The Prisoner* ended. Just as Nation had been crucial to the early development of *Blake's 7*, Markstein had fulfilled a similar role in *The Prisoner*, and whilst Nation admitted that he "hated" those episodes that he saw in the last season and found some of the final instalment ridiculous, (p. 272)[72] Markstein has been quoted as describing the *Prisoner* episodes that were made after his departure as "an absurd pantomime". (p. 23)[73]

Much has been made in *Unique But Similar* of the fact that most instalments of *The Prisoner* are independent from one another. In contrast, the second volume in the Starlog *TV Episode Guides* series recognises that, although there were no instances where stories were billed as multi-part, many of *Blake's 7*'s episodes were "interconnected". (p. 23)[74] A substantial proportion of the second season, in fact, is concerned with Blake's quest to find and then attack the centre of Federation computer operations. It is worthwhile to take a moment to explore how this story thread, with all its various convolutions and red herrings, pans out during the season. As early as the third story of this block, the prospect is raised that Blake will attack Control on Earth, although it is not until two instalments later that such a raid is made. When it emerges that the key Federation centre is actually located elsewhere, Blake begins fresh efforts to find it. In the ninth episode of the season, Blake goes to the planet Albian in order to track down Space Major Provine, whom he believes knows the new location of Control. An encounter with Provine reveals that Control is now called Star One and it appears that its whereabouts are known not to Provine but to the cyber-surgeon Docholli. In the last three episodes of the season, the Star One strand within the narrative is unrelenting. In *Gambit*, Blake's team pursue Docholli to Freedom City but discover that he, too, is ignorant of Star One's location. They learn that the brain print of the only man with the knowledge they seek is to be found on the planet Goth. Their arch enemy Travis takes the brain print before the *Liberator* crew can reach it but the location has been memorised by the ruler's jester and they activate its articulation after speaking a trigger phrase. A possibility that Blake rejects is to take control of the Federation and run it himself. This echoes an option offered by The Village's President in *Fall Out*. He appeals to Number Six, "lead us or go". In the last episode of *Blake's 7*'s second season, it emerges that Star One has been infiltrated by Andromedans who are attempting to annihilate humanity. Ultimately, Blake cancels his plans to destroy Star One and stands shoulder to shoulder with the Federation in order to counter the alien threat. It is illuminating at this point to compare the overall sagas of *The Prisoner* and *Blake's 7* in an analogy. If we accept that both are essentially cyclical, we can think of the instalments as components within a chain that forms a circle. Yet, whilst, in *Blake's 7*, many of these pieces are linked with one another, in *The Prisoner* they remain as discrete parts.

A recurrent theme within this book has been the problem of answering precisely the question of when and where *The Prisoner* is set. Previous chapters have indicated that, whilst there may be some evidence to support the belief that the action takes place either in the future or on alien planet, by far the most likely possibility is that modern-day Earth was actually intended. In contrast, there is no doubt that *Blake's 7* is set many years hence, and thus the dystopian image presented is by no means imminent but determining a more precise date has led to conjecture. In recounting how the series was conceived, creator Terry Nation recalls explaining in a preliminary meeting at the BBC that the action was to take place in "the third century of the second calendar". (p. 7)[75] Since we can only guess at the point when such a "second calendar" was introduced, Nation's establishing statement is of little help in dating the events we witness. Attwood concludes that we may consider *Blake's 7* to be set between eight hundred and a thousand years from now.[76] This timescale is not radically different from Lance Parkin's suggestion that the events of the programme may be believed to take place in either the twenty-eighth or twenty-ninth century.[77]

In seeking to identify the long-term appeal of *Blake's 7*, Savile attaches particular importance to the theme of conflict/dissent. He recognises that, in this series, it takes both internal and external forms, with the outlaws squabbling among themselves, as well as fighting an ongoing battle against the Federation.[78] Dissent is also, of course, central to the premise of *The Prisoner*. Although this is most obviously of the external type, with Number Six never flinching in his struggles against the Village authorities, it is possible to identify an internal element, too. In *The Chimes of Big Ben*, *Many Happy Returns* and *Checkmate*, the betrayal of Number Six by characters whom he, and the viewers, have been led to believe were working with him provides an unexpected twist ending. Perhaps the main difference between the internal divisions which are depicted is that, in *The Prisoner*, Number Six's treacherous "allies" appear in only one episode and do not form regular characters, whereas in *Blake's 7*, a bond between the rebels and the viewers is forged by the former's appearance each week. On occasion, it has been argued that the inside conflicts were made too pronounced. In discussing *Orbit*, the antepenultimate episode, Muir describes Avon's attempt to murder Vila in order to save himself from certain death as "an ugly moment" and questions whether the episode goes "too far for what is essentially an entertainment". (p. 156)[79]

Comments made by McGoohan would suggest that the essence of *The Prisoner* is encapsulated in seven particular episodes.[80] We can conclude from this that the remaining ten are basically superfluous and do little to advance the overall narrative of the series. Some, such as *Living in Harmony* and *The Girl Who Was Death*, represent radical divergences from the format that viewers had come to expect, with even the seemingly obligatory Portmeirion setting entirely absent in each case, although in the final moments the viewer realises that what they have watched has formed yet another attempt by Number Two to "crack" The Prisoner. In *Blake's 7*, there are several episodes in which the Federation does not feature at all. If we assume that the basic thrust of the show is that of the ongoing conflict between the Federation on one hand and the dissidents led by either Blake initially or Avon in the latter half of the series on the other, then we may be tempted to dismiss such episodes as adding nothing to the essentials of the "real" *Blake's 7* saga. We may consider them more akin to the "exploration" type SF of series such as *Star Trek* and *Space: 1999*. This is not to imply that these instalments are worthless, however. Muir describes *The Web* as one of the "most unusual and oft-talked about" first season *Blake's 7* stories (p. 51), despite the non-involvement of the Federation.[81] Certain parallels can be drawn between this episode and *The Prisoner*'s *Living in Harmony* instalment. Just as, in the latter, the central themes of the wider series are reworked in a different setting, Muir points out that in *The Web*, the internal affairs of the planet encountered by the Liberator crew represent "a microcosm for Blake's struggle against the Federation". (p. 51)[82] Tanith Lee's *Sarcophagus* has received especially high praise from *Blake's 7* fans. Lewis and Stempel go so far as to suggest that *Sarcophagus* forms one of the best episodes of the entire series.[83] In various respects, *Sarcophagus* is as cryptic and inexplicit as many episodes of *The Prisoner*. The atypical nature of the instalment is established from the outset with a bizarre prologue nearly six minutes in length which features no dialogue and no member of the cast credited in the closing titles. We learn little in the story about the origin of the being that the *Liberator* crew encounters and, as Attwood indicates, the alien culture involved is not even named at any stage.[84] In a 1994 *Blake's 7* poll, another non-Federation episode – *City at the Edge of the World* – came as high as sixth.[85] Just as *Living in Harmony* sees *The Prisoner* operating in a completely different genre, *Blake's 7* also offers some surprising departures – *Mission to Destiny*, for example, is a one-off whodunit, with Terry Nation intending it as "an Agatha Christie story in space". (p. 250)[86] Although the murder mystery theme returns in the much later *Assassin*, in that instance there is a strong Federation involvement, with Servalan using a hired killer in her latest attempt to do away with Avon's team.

The character flaws of Number Six may well lead the dispassionate observer to wonder why so many of those who watch *The Prisoner* are naturally inclined to relate to him. A similar question can be asked in relation to fans of *Blake's 7*. Again, enthusiasts of the programme tend to side automatically with the rebels, yet, as Paul Darrow has himself admitted, his own character, who, after the disappearance of Blake at the end of the second season effectively becomes the hero, is especially unpleasant.[87] *The Encyclopedia of TV Science Fiction* notes that other rebels are also flawed: Blake becomes fanatical, Vila is spineless and Tarrant conceited.[88] Perhaps the most unpleasant character is Gan, even though he is frequently imagined to be a gentle giant.[89] If it is true, as Stevens and Moore maintain, that, after the limiter which restricts his aggressive impulses cuts out in the episode *Breakdown* we see Gan's real personality, then it is difficult to dispute the authors' assessment of him as "cunning and ruthless". (p. 48)[90] Stevens and Moore give little credence to certain evidence from the episode that may lead to a different and more kindly interpretation. At one point, Avon suggests that Gan's aggressive behaviour is the result of his defective limiter feeding "scrambled impulses" to his brain.

At various points in *Blake's 7*, the dissidents offer realistic, and less than flattering, self-assessments. Following the apparent death of Cally in the episode *Seek-Locate-Destroy*, Blake glumly notes that she was the only member of his team who was not a convicted criminal, whilst in *Blake*, Avon seems to imply that he feels his group consists only of "thieves, killers, mercenaries, psychopaths". Still, the characterisations of the rebels, and the interpersonal dynamics that exist between them, are frequently thought to form the programme's greatest strength.[91] For all the faults that are evident in Blake's personality in the later episodes in which he appears, on occasion he, like Number Six, seems something of a superman. In taking control of the *Liberator*, he alone is able to resist the craft's defence mechanism, although his imperviousness may be due to the mental conditioning he has received from the Federation, rather than any particularly special abilities. Blake also seems largely unaffected by the Curse of Cygnus that afflicts the other newcomers to the penal planet. Moreover, despite the various tensions that emerge among the seven, Blake is for the most part able to unite them into an effective fighting unit and, considering the ignominious failure that ends Number Six's escape attempt when he joins forces with fellow dissidents in *Checkmate*, Blake is arguably better equipped as a leader of men than is The Prisoner. Neither man, however, is infallible.

The experiences of Blake, Avon and Jenna as they explore the *Liberator* in the second and third episodes of *Blake's 7* to some extent mirror those of The Prisoner in *Arrival*. All the protagonists find themselves investigating, with minimal preparation, an environment that is not only alien to them but potentially lethal. In addition, just as the first two people in The Village whom Numbers Six encounters – a café waitress and a taxi driver – are evasive when asked particular questions, the *Liberator's* computer exhibits a similar trait when Avon and Blake seek to interrogate it.

In Chapter Seven, attention was drawn to The Prisoner's selfishness in using others for his own ends. The rebel movement in *Blake's 7* is by no means wholly admirable in its methods either. In the very first episode, *The Way Back*, dissidents effectively attempt to blackmail Blake into joining their cause by preparing incriminating documents which contain forgeries of his signature. The dissenters are confident that they are sufficiently convincing to implicate him in their activities. Later, in the second season story *Shadow*, Blake himself is prepared to enlist the help of an organised crime syndicate known for supplying illegal drugs, and in *Killer*, another second season instalment, Avon tries to secure the assistance of his old friend Tynus through blackmail. Avon resorts to a similar ploy in order to gain the help of the Federation academician Gerren in the later story *Games*. In the fourth season of *Blake's 7*, the rebels indulge in various acts of piracy. Bould considers The Prisoner to be "as calculating in his relationships as the Village bosses", (p. 102)[92] and, after watching a variety of dubious schemes executed by the rebels in *Blake's 7*, here, too, viewers may be tempted to conclude that neither side truly merits our support.

Instead of accepting The Prisoner's right to rebel against the Village authorities, we may take a more establishment line and back at least to some extent The Village's right to instil order and conformity. Susan Nobel and Diana Goldsborough, in fact, inquire, "What's wrong with a number? It works as well as a name", (p. 6) and the authors go on to cite a range of situations in which numbers already take the place of our names.[93] Furthermore, if, as Abbott suggests, The Village represents British society,[94] and we assume that its administrators exist to support the citizens, the viewer may well challenge the moral basis of The Prisoner's repeated attempts to undermine the Village authorities. The same attitude can be taken in relation to *Blake's 7* since, in the episode *Aftermath*, Servalan claims, "The Federation exists to protect its people." The legitimacy of the rebels' fight against it has been questioned by Michael Keating. He muses, "if you worked it out, the Federation weren't that bad. There were independent planets that seemed to get on quite happily, and we seemed to go around disturbing them". (p. 185)[95] Boucher takes a similar line, arguing that, despite all its apparent tyranny, the Federation "didn't actually touch a large proportion of the population". (p. 179)[96] The often overlooked benefits provided by the Federation, upon which millions of people depend, are outlined by Savile. He notes how its key base, Star One, controls the climates of hundreds of colonised planets, supports the navigation systems of interplanetary passenger liners and offers protection against alien invaders.[97] Even some characters in *Blake's 7* who are officially "neutral" appreciate the value of the Federation. In *Breakdown*, Professor Kayn, the neurosurgeon based on the space research station XK72, describes the Federation as the "greatest force for order in the known universe". Alwyn Turner reminds us that by no means everyone associated with the Federation is portrayed as wholly evil and cites several characters who are essentially good.[98] Nevertheless, although a severely pro-establishment stance may see Number Six as a dangerous subversive, rather than an admirable individual, and the rebels of *Blake's 7* as terrorists and not freedom fighters, for many viewers perhaps the greatest attraction of the two programmes lies in their appeal to the inner rebel in all of us. Thomas, meanwhile, feels that the question of whether Blake was a freedom fighter or a terrorist was one of the unresolved conundrums which has meant the programme continues to intrigue to this day.[99] For Darrow, the answer lay entirely with the viewer. He writes, "The good guys are the bad guys. Or vice versa. The choice is yours." (p. 71) [100]

If we do indeed assume that the dissidents in *Blake's 7* amount to what the second volume in the Starlog *TV Episode Guides* series terms "interstellar terrorists", (p. 22)[101] Savile writes that not only does this place *Blake's 7* ahead of its time, specifically in adopting a stance that would be followed by the new version of *Battlestar Galactica* some years later, but it also brings to mind in British viewers parallels with real world terrorism inflicted by the IRA.[102] This equivalence can be compared with the *Prisoner's Living in Harmony*/Vietnam situation highlighted in the previous chapter. Today, the allegorical edge to *The Prisoner* is widely accepted, so much so that even general texts dealing with television, which are not necessarily written by *Prisoner* experts, highlight it. The *Encyclopedia of Television*, for example, states, in a very matter-of-fact manner, "In many ways an allegory, the adventures within *The Prisoner* can be read as commentaries on contemporary British social and political institutions." (p. 1829)[103] It is not unusual to see elements of *Blake's 7* understood as a contemporary allegory too; Short suggests that, with a ruthless female villain leading the Federation, comparisons could be drawn with Thatcherism,[104] whilst McCormack notes how the anti-utopian themes of the programme reflect the dark economic and social times which Britain was then experiencing.[105] For anyone subscribing to these arguments, the overall conclusion is inescapable – in several ways, *Blake's 7* and *The Prisoner* were both ahead of their time and very much of their time.

The previous chapter highlighted the fact that the Village authorities and SHADO's leaders use drugs and related treatments to strengthen their position and weaken that of others whose existence may threaten them. The Federation in *Blake's 7* employs a similar strategy. The addition of suppressants to the food and water supplies of Earth inhabitants and the Pylene 50 programme on other worlds have already been noted and various other smaller scale instances in which drugs are used to maintain control can be identified. For example, in *The Way Back*, we learn that a range of treatments has been used to undermine Blake's memory of his dissident past and in *Space Fall*, he refers resentfully to his "tranquilised dreams". Again in the second story, the commander of the prison ship taking Blake and other criminals to the penal colony Cygnus Alpha orders that the highest levels of suppressants be used in the prisoners' rations to ensure that they are docile during the journey, and in the next episode the crew also dose the prisoners' air supply with a suppressant vapour. In a surprising turn of events at the end of the episode *Shadow*, it emerges that the power behind an illegal drugs trade is none other than the Federation itself. As Blake himself comments, if the Federation is to exercise total power, it must control what takes place within and beyond the law.

Drugs are not the only weapon used by both the Village authorities and the Federation against their own people. The importance of surveillance in the former context was established in Chapter Three, and discussions of life in The Village abound with references to particular spying techniques that are in evidence. Britton comments that even the seemingly ornamental statues contain eavesdropping devices and the "Be seeing you!" greeting can be interpreted as a reference to "the ever-present human and electronic watchers". (p. 102)[106] Surveillance is so much a part of the Federation-controlled Earth in *Blake's 7* that a camera designed for this purpose features prominently in the title sequences seen in the first two seasons. As Brown recognises, the message is obvious – "Big Brother is watching you. And if he doesn't like what he sees…?" (p. 18)[107] Furthermore, the first scene of the opening episode begins with a shot of such a camera. In both series, the authorities can call on brutal, distinctively attired yet individually anonymous enforcers. In *Blake's 7*, the menace of the black-clad security guards remains one of the programme's most potent images and, like the security camera, is emphasised in the title sequence of seasons one and two. Meanwhile, the Village guards evident in *The Prisoner* are considered by Tim Palgut sufficiently important to merit inclusion in his book of diagrams and blueprints.[108] In terms of civilian life, Marshall feels that faceless workers generally form a "recurring leitmotive of *Blake's 7*". (p. 257) He makes this observation in his analysis of the *Headhunter* episode, in which we meet a character who identifies himself as Technician 241. This immediately evokes memories of *The Prisoner*.[109]

In contrast to direct confrontation, infiltration is another key strategy employed by both the Federation and the Village authorities. The use of the technique is apparent from the opening *Blake's 7* episode, when Dev Tarrant, who has been accepted by the rebels as one of them, is revealed to be working for the Federation. Much later, in the fourth season adventure *Traitor*, the rebels are infiltrated by the double agent Leitz, who reports directly to Servalan. Infiltration is also seen in the last instalment, when Arlen, whom Blake thinks he has recruited to the rebels' cause, is revealed to be a Federation officer. In *The Prisoner*, the infiltration strategy is so skilfully implemented that, in *Checkmate*, Number Six recognises that a key barrier to assembling any team for mounting an escape lies in identifying whether those individuals with whom he comes into contact in The Village are guardians or potential allies. In the final episode of *Blake's 7*, the eponymous hero admits that he finds it increasingly difficult to make correct decisions in relation to supporters and enemies, and his inability to read Arlen accurately proves to be one of his most costly blunders.

In the *Voice From the Past* episode of *Blake's 7*, which was written by Roger Parkes, who also contributed the *Prisoner* instalment *A Change of Mind*, Travis infiltrates the resistance by impersonating the dissident leader Shivan, although in *Star One* Blake somewhat reverses the roles when he pretends to be Travis. The previous season, the Federation had created an android version of another dissident, Avalon, in order, ultimately, to acquire the *Liberator*. The Avalon robot is not the only double to form an important element in the authorities' schemes in *Blake's 7*. In *Weapon*, a duplicate of Blake is integral to a cunningly conceived Federation ploy. Here, however, the victim is not a regular character but a weapons specialist called Coser. Representatives of the Federation visit him with the Blake copy, knowing that Coser, thinking the Blake he sees to be genuine, will hand over a new and deadly weapon he has developed to a resistance leader he has come to regard as a hero. The Village authorities, too, employ lookalikes to deceive others. In *The Schizoid Man*, Curtis, who would appear to be a clone of Number Six, forms the cornerstone of a plot to bring about his mental disintegration. Yet, in this episode The Prisoner resorts to counter-impersonation, pretending to be Curtis during an attempted escape from The Village, and in *The General*, he poses as a committee member in order to enter the projection room and broadcast a subversive message to the people.

Both The Prisoner and Blake are treated as "special cases" by the authorities. In *The Way Back*, we learn that Blake's past as an opposition leader renders him particularly inconvenient to the administration. When it seems that he may be on the verge of rejoining the resistance, the Federation fabricate charges against him, stage-manage a trial that results in his conviction and then attempt to deport him to a penal colony. The authorities are careful to avoid eliminating him as to do so would give the resistance a martyr and provide a focus for yet more resentment against them. In *The Prisoner*, it is rare that Number Two is willing to risk Number Six's life and, on occasion, The Village's chief administrator is clearly keen to ensure that he remains physically and mentally intact. This has led some commentators to open a new debate, i.e. whether the hero did actually resign as viewers are often led to believe. White and Ali inquire as to why Number Six should receive a certain degree of "protection" within The Village unless, in reality, he is either working for Number One or is Number One himself.[110]

Whilst the dissidents following Blake and/or Avon frequently encounter the Federation's Supreme Commander and later President and total ruler, Servalan, and in the first two seasons of *Blake's 7*, Space Commander Travis, Number Six also finds himself in constant opposition to a recurring adversary – Number Two. Servalan and Travis not only provide a recognisable "face" to the Federation; they add a personal edge to the animosity, with Travis, in particular, clearly established as Blake's equivalent of Sherlock Holmes's Moriarty. Some of the more playful exchanges between Servalan and Avon, especially, often mirror the banter between The Prisoner and Number Two, whilst the paranoia that Servalan shows in *Star One* echoes that exhibited by Number Two in the *Prisoner* story *Hammer Into Anvil*. Questioning the loyalty of even her own advisers, she feels that "someone is trying to destroy the Federation from within". The real enemy, however, is Travis, who is now living as an outlaw.

The fact that the personnel who occupy Number Two's position change continually adds an unusual dynamic to *The Prisoner*. If we discount the interim Number Twos seen only in apparent flashback sequences in *It's Your Funeral*, over the course of the series some 17 different actors/actresses play the role. At first glance, the constant shifting may seem illogical – after all the greater the number of people who hold such a high office, the greater would seem the security risk, and the perennial turnover seems to sit uneasily with the importance that is attached to total secrecy in The Village. Certainly, many diverse theories have been proposed to explain the frequent changes. Chris Gregory[111] and Lez Cooke[112] maintain that each Number Two was removed after their particular scheme fails to yield the desired result, although such a reason would seem to ignore the fact that some Number Twos are significantly more successful than others. By no means all their tenures end in abject failure. For Gerani and Schulman, Number One's decision to replace his subordinate so regularly was motivated entirely by self-preservation, specifically his desire to ensure that none of his staff became sufficiently powerful to challenge his own position.[113] Evidence to support this interpretation can be found in the US publicity material for the show, which suggests that since Number One trusts no-one, his second in command will never remain in power for long.[114] Another possibility is that the rotational element was a creative production decision in order to allow different guest stars to play a high profile role within the stories. Short points to the variety that this brings to the series, and how it rendered the programme more commercially attractive.[115] This rationale has been rejected by producer David Tomblin, however. He asserts that the rapid turnover was a Village ploy designed to prevent Number Six from forming any kind of relationship with a particular incumbent and thereby exploit a possible weakness of the administrative system.[116] On a related note, George Markstein has been reported as saying that the regular leadership changes were part of the authorities' efforts to "disorientate" Number Six. (p. 9)[117] In another explanation, which strongly echoes Tomblin's argument, Markstein drew on his experience of the real world, commenting, "You butter up your bank manager for a loan over a long period of time and then, when you come to ask for the loan, there's a new bank manager and you have to start all over again!" (p. 88)[118] One of the production managers, Bernard Williams, meanwhile, puts forward yet another possibility – changing the actor or actress who played Number Two each week helped to "hook" the audience by avoiding the monotony that could result from The Prisoner facing the same adversary in every episode since each leader had a different personality and might offer a different approach.[119] A much more abstract explanation is offered by Booker. According to him, the shifts indicate "both the postmodern instability of individual identity and the constant movement towards innovation and change (as long as the underlying class structure is maintained) that is central to capitalism". (p. 89) [120] Rupert Booth offers several explanations. He, too, notes the importance of ensuring that "a strong guest role" would be available in each episode (p. 196); he recognises the need to avoid the repetition of pitting Number Six against the same adversary each week and he also sees the frequent shifts of personnel as "a comment on the bureaucratic practice of many companies and governmental organisations who would replace one operative with another from a different department... Number 6 may break one Number 2, but there will always be another to take their place". (pp. 196–197)[121]

The use of Orwellian maxims is a feature of life in The Village. In his list of "scriptures", Palgut cites a wide range. The best known include "A still tongue makes a happy life", "Questions are a burden to others; answers, a prison for oneself" and "Music makes a quiet mind." (p. 93)[122] According to Attwood, "Nothing summed up the Federation in *Blake's 7* better than its own official phrase: 'From strength to unity.'" (p. 103)[123] As with The Village and the Omega organisation, a further sense of corporate identity is forged by the Federation's distinctive logo.

Similarities are seldom drawn between *Prisoner* scenarios and the plots of individual *Blake's 7* episodes. Although Muir suggests that *The Way Back* included "a little bit of Patrick McGoohan's *The Prisoner*", he does not pursue the issue further. (p. 27)[124] We may suspect that Muir is alluding to the manner in which both Village and Federation officials single out the hero for special treatment and impose on him a programme of intensive brainwashing, and to how the action takes place in a society dominated by surveillance where nobody, it seems, can be trusted.

A more detailed comparison is made by Stevens and Moore. They detect how, in what they term the "*Prisoner*esque" *Terminal*, (p. 188) the Federation employ against Avon treatments reminiscent of those applied by the Village authorities.[125] The authors recount how, in this episode, Servalan uses psychological conditioning methods to exploit Avon's "mounting egomania and obsession" with Blake and bring him to an artificial planet where he is subjected to a drug-induced hallucination. (p. 188)[126] Stevens and Moore distinguish, however, between how, in *The Prisoner*, Number Six typically overcomes such intrusions through sheer force of personality, and the way in which Avon fails to realise that he is being led and falls victim to the scheme, so endangering himself and his crew. The authors conclude that, in *Terminal*, ideas from *The Prisoner* are both used and inverted.[127] Servalan would employ behavioural conditioning techniques again in the fourth season story *Animals* – specifically those associated with aversion therapy.

Terminal is one of many *Blake's 7* stories in which the Federation encourages the heroes to follow a particular course of action that the authorities have anticipated and, after correctly forecasting the rebels' response, ensure that a trap awaits their arrival. This pattern can be seen, for example, in *Seek-Locate-Destroy*, in which Blake is lured into returning to the site of a previous raid so as to free a captured colleague; in *Project Avalon*, where Servalan and Travis arrange for an android duplicate equipped with a phial containing a deadly plague to take the place of a resistance leader whom the Federation has taken and whom Blake is intent on rescuing; and in *Weapon*, in which Servalan and Travis lie in wait for Blake and his team. A comparable ruse is attempted by Number Two in the *Prisoner* episode *The Chimes of Big Ben*. In each case, initially the heroes fall victim to the deceptions. In *Seek-Locate-Destroy*, Blake does indeed return to the Federation complex; in *Project Avalon*, the robot is taken aboard the *Liberator*, with the crew believing that they have freed the real resistance leader; in *Weapon*, Blake falls into the trap so easily that he admits that Servalan "seemed to know every single move we were making. It's almost as if we were on strings and she was the puppeteer". At the end of *The Chimes of Big Ben*, The Prisoner not only believes that he is back in London but even starts to explain the reasons behind his resignation. Federation trickery reaches its peak in the final stages of *Blake's 7*'s last season, when, in the consecutive instalments *Gold* and *Orbit*, Servalan attempts to trap Avon. In all these episodes, though, the designs of the authorities are foiled. In the five *Blake's 7* stories, the rebels ultimately escape and in *Project Avalon*, Avon reprograms the android so that it will act against Travis and Servalan, whilst in *The Chimes of Big Ben*, The Prisoner's natural attention to detail alerts him to danger sufficiently quickly to prevent him from divulging his secrets. *Seek-Locate-Destroy*, *Project Avalon* and *The Chimes of Big Ben* are especially similar in that, in all cases, the protagonists believe at first that they have effected a successful escape.

Having considered the methods used by the authorities in both *The Prisoner* and *Blake's 7*, it would seem appropriate to explore the approaches common to the respective rebels. Whilst we may laud Number Six as the supreme individual, even he develops some alliances with others and, on occasion, he finds support unexpectedly. In *The General*, Number Twelve proves an unlikely co-conspirator, as does a former Number Two in *Fall Out*. In the same way, in the *Voice From the Past* episode of *Blake's 7*, Blake forges a union that includes a defected Arbiter General of the Federation, Ven Glynd. Both Avon and Number Six, however, discover that various friends from earlier periods of their lives are now not to be trusted. The Prisoner's former colleague Cobb is shown at the end of *Arrival* to be in league with The Village's authorities, whilst in *Killer*, Avon's "friend" Tynus proves entirely treacherous. Other betrayals, such as those perpetrated by Blake's uncle, Ushton, and Veron, the daughter of a resistance leader, are more forgivable, as they feared that harm would come to close family members if they did not comply with Federation schemes. New potential allies whose promised support would appear to offer grounds for optimism are also often revealed to be duplicitous. "Help" offered by characters such as Nadia and Mrs Butterworth in *The Prisoner* in fact leads the hero into traps, and the powerful President of Betafarl, Zukan, double-crosses Avon in the penultimate *Blake's 7* instalment. In *The Prisoner*, the deceit of Cobb is important in establishing a mood of paranoia from the very first episode, and in *Blake's 7*, it is similarly clear from the outset that the integrity of no-one can be taken for granted; those involved in the administration's conspiracy against Blake are seen to range from high-ranking officials to a humble records clerk.

In both series, the leaders who represent authority show a blind faith in technology on occasion and their misplaced reliance is exploited by their adversaries. In the *Prisoner* story *The General*, Number Two arrogantly declares that there is no question that cannot be answered by the computer which helps to deliver the "Speedlearn" programme. Ultimately, however, Number Six is able to put an end to both the scheme and the hardware itself by asking simply "Why?", thereby placing too great a demand on a machine that is incapable of working on such a level. Similarly, in the third season *Blake's 7* episode *The Harvest of Kairos*, Servalan's defeat is the result of trusting instruments and computers more than the evidence given to her by her own eyes. Snatching victory from the jaws of defeat after falling victim to yet another Federation trap, Avon's team triumph through sheer bluff, and again human ingenuity is seen to better seemingly infallible technology.

The inconsistencies in Number Six's personality which emerge over the course of the 17 episodes of *The Prisoner* have long been debated among fans. Although so often portrayed as the ultimate individual, in some instances The Prisoner becomes something of a people's champion. He attempts to liberate the Villagers at the end of *Free For All* and to prevent them suffering at the hands of the authorities in some unspecified act of terrible retribution in *It's Your Funeral*. For Gregory, Number Six's character in the latter episode is particularly problematic. He writes, "The Prisoner's role here seems to be presented slightly differently to his role in the rest of the series and his motivation – as a 'protector' of the community – is highly questionable given his continued stance of extreme individualism." (pp. 128–129)[128] O'Brien, meanwhile, juxtaposes Number Six's usual personality – "abrupt, sarcastic, scathing and downright ill-mannered" – with how in *Hammer Into Anvil* he shows a much more sensitive side to his nature when he seeks to avenge the death of a young woman who has been driven to suicide by Number Two. (p. 98)[129]

In seeking to account for such discrepancies, it is important to remember that the 17 episodes feature scripts by as many as 11 different writers and it is unlikely that any two would have an identical perception of the character of Number Six. This may also help to explain the unevenness that emerges from time to time in the portrayal of the Villagers. White and Ali feel that in *A Change of Mind*, they display a "mob mentality" which is "distinctly absent from any others". (p. 90)[130] To take this view, however, would seem to ignore the climax of *Dance of the Dead*. Here, as Chris R. Tame recounts, "in their hatred for Number 6's resolute individualism the other inmates of the Village turn on him in a mob". (p. 4)[131] According to Peter Dunn, it would be unwise to regard *The Prisoner* as a saga that presents an entirely consistent and pre-planned message which gradually unfolds over the 17 episodes. Rather, he maintains, the format provides an allegorical vehicle for the thoughts of various creative individuals.[132] If one accepts such a stance, then discrepancies from episode to episode in terms of character and motivation are entirely to be expected.

In a similar vein, David Richardson detects inconsistency in the "continuity and tone" of *Blake's 7*. He goes so far, in fact, as to assert, "show the episodes *The Way Back* and *Warlord* to a non-fan, and I suspect they wouldn't believe they even belonged to the same show".[133] As the series progresses, there is a particular lack of constancy in the personalities of Avon and Blake, although the variations in character that they exhibit can often be understood to be the result of deliberate development rather than mere "blips". Muir feels that Avon moves from "total cynicism to sudden idealism" and ultimately arrives at the same point Blake had reached in the series' first episode. (p. 174)[134] Given that, in the first two seasons, when Blake and Avon were both regular characters and their clashes were common and vitriolic, the transformation is perhaps difficult to accept. It is well known that moves to "sanitise" Avon were resisted by Paul Darrow, who played him. Darrow recalls that when, after Blake had disappeared as a regular protagonist, he was told by the production team that his own character "ought to be a little more moral", he disapproved of any such reformation, saying that he had "to be real all the way through". (p. 182)[135] Certainly, Avon's hatred of Blake appears total in the last episode of the second season, *Star One*. In one of his most impassioned speeches, Avon declaims to him,

> ... you can destroy whatever you like. You can stir up a thousand revolutions. You can wade in blood up to your armpits. Oh, and you can lead the rabble to victory, whatever that might mean. Just so long as there is an end to it. When Star One is gone, it is finished, Blake, and I want it finished. I want it over and done with. I want to be free.

When Cally interjects to point out that Avon is free now, he responds icily, "I want to be free *of him*." Blake seems genuinely shocked at Avon's clear detestation of him. It certainly seems odd that a man who has previously been shown to be so self-centred should, in the later stages of the series, take up the rebel cause wholeheartedly. In *Cygnus Alpha*, when he learns of the wealth to be found aboard the newly-acquired *Liberator* he urges Jenna to leave Blake to enjoy a life away from struggles with the Federation. It is easy in such situations to compare Avon's selfishness with that of The Prisoner when, quite voluntarily and purely for personal gain, he leads Professor Seltzman into danger in *Do Not Forsake Me Oh My Darling*.

Blake, too, undergoes a significant shift in personality. Boucher recounts how, in the final episodes of Blake's time as a regular character, he emphasised the character's fanatical aspect.[136] Earlier in the series, it was Blake's idealism that was stressed. In *Space Fall*, he regards himself as not being truly alive until "free men can think and speak" and, to him, power must be back in the hands of "the honest man". Blake's altruism extends beyond those he is aiming to help in his battle with the Federation. In *Time Squad*, his concern for aliens apparently in distress prompts him to teleport himself and Jenna into their projectile in order to investigate further. Similarly, in *The Web*, Blake is reluctant to provide Novara and Geela with the energy cells they require to free the *Liberator* from a gossamer-like structure when he discovers that they also plan to use their power to wipe out a race of beings that they consider a threat. In contrast, The Prisoner is very clearly fighting his own battle for his own purposes. By the final episode, *Blake*, the eponymous hero has changed considerably. In one scene, we see this once principled figure shoot a bounty hunter in the back. Ultimately, Blake has come to realise that it is the ends that are important, not the means.

Throughout the two seasons in which Blake is a regular character, he would appear to avoid steadfastly all romantic entanglements, although some fans have suggested that a deep emotional bond exists between him and fellow dissident Jenna. Muir, in fact, cites evidence from two episodes to support the claim that Jenna both "loves and desires" Blake. (p. 186)[137] Whilst it is clear from the events in *Hostage* that Blake feels much affection for his cousin, Inga, and there are hints of a deeper relationship between them, we learn of no real romantic history involving Blake. The position of Avon is very different, however. In the third season story *Rumours of Death*, viewers are introduced to his ex-girlfriend Anna Grant, and much is discovered about their past together. This instalment provides some of the kind of background to Avon that we learn in relation to The Prisoner in *Do Not Forsake Me Oh My Darling*.

Whereas today, *The Prisoner* is widely admired, *Blake's 7* attracts as much derision as praise in many quarters. Typically, the special effects are dismissed as unconvincing and the cheapness of the props and sets is ridiculed.[138] In an American poll reported by John Javna, several experts, in fact, cited *Blake's 7* as among the worst SF shows of all time.[139] Some years later, another especially damning assessment would come from Stephen Volk, himself a noted writer for television. Considering *Blake's 7* to be the "low point of genre TV", he commented, "I just thought it was trash from the first frames." (p. 257)[140] Darrow himself acknowledges that anyone who revisits the newspaper reviews of the series that appeared in the late 1970s "will find that there was a division of critical opinion. Some took us far too seriously. Some took us for what we were. Some dismissed us out of hand." (p. 78)[141]

If, as Chapman believes, *The Prisoner* did indeed form "something of a dead end in generic terms", (p. 51)[142] a similar observation may be made in relation to *Blake's 7*. Nearly ten years after the first transmission of *Blake's 7*'s final season, *The Encyclopedia of TV Science Fiction* adjudged that, as "an attempt to mount a serious space opera, to occupy the middle ground between the frolics of *Doctor Who* and the class of an *Out of the Unknown*", it might have been "the beginning of a new creed of television science fiction – instead it became one of the last of a dying breed". (p. 60)[143] More recently, the argument that the programme inspired few series of a similar nature has been echoed in a guide to *Blake's 7* merchandise. In an interview with Chris Boucher conducted in April 2010, the assertion was made that it was, "to date, the last mainstream, primetime, ongoing political orientated British science fiction series". (p. 167)[144]

Long before the new version of *The Prisoner* that was shown in 2009, Gregory detected a shift towards the development of the series as an "unfolding text". (p. 196)[145] Drawing on the ideas of Tulloch and Alvarado with regard to *Doctor Who*,[146] he comments how this status comes about from expanding the original "fixed text" to a wider one, with work from new creative individuals.[147] Soon after *The Prisoner* was first broadcast, three original novels were published, none of which came from scriptwriters on the series. These have now been reprinted on several occasions. Subsequently, the comic book *Shattered Visage*, new novels from Powys Media and audio plays from Big Finish have extended the overall *Prisoner* "text" yet further. *Blake's 7* has undergone similar growth. Again, shortly after the demise of the series, an original novel, *Afterlife*, arrived on the shelves of bookshops. Here, however, a more conscious effort was made to show that the work provided a natural progression from the television series. The cover of *Afterlife* proclaimed the book to be an "authentic sequel" and inside it is acknowledged that the text has been developed from an idea in evidence in two of the television episodes.[148] More recently, *Blake's 7* has expanded beyond television and the print media through two BBC audio plays and others produced by Magic Bullet, B7 Media and Big Finish. In exploring how far this new work elevates *Blake's 7* to the status of an unfolding text as the idea is understood by Gregory, it is worth noting that even when Big Finish began making new *Blake's 7* full-cast audio adventures with virtually all the original cast (i.e. Gareth Thomas, Paul Darrow, Sally Knyvette, Michael Keating and Jan Chappell), none of the six new plays that comprised the first season was authored by any of the television scriptwriters. Whilst much of the cult surrounding *Blake's 7* remains concentrated in Britain and only time will tell whether it will endure as long as that of *The Prisoner*, the continuing existence of each may well prompt the reader to accept Savile's principle that, in terms of dramatic appeal, "dissent is good". (p. 20)[149]

References and Notes

1. Nicholls, P. and Brosnan, J. Television. In: Clute, J. and Nicholls, P. (eds.) The encyclopedia of science fiction, 2nd ed. Orbit: London, 1993, pp. 1205–1209.

    Whilst it may seem tenuous to argue that the Look and Read serial Cloud Burst, which was discussed in Chapter One, also belongs to this particular sub-genre of science fiction, according to T. J. Worthington, in the offthetelly.co.uk website (http://www.offthetelly.co.uk/oldott/www.offthetelly.co.uk/index545b.html?page_id=753), it was "almost... a variant of... Doomwatch" since, in both cases, "the threat essentially [emanated] from within the planet itself".

    Links can also be detected between elements within individual Doomwatch episodes and Prisoner themes. The shortcomings of computers, for example, is an issue raised in both The General and the Doomwatch instalment Project Sahara. In addition, like The Prisoner, this particular Doomwatch story is concerned with the extent to which the lives of people who undertake work that is of interest to the security services may be investigated by those who exercise authority.

2. Chapman, J. Inside the TARDIS: The worlds of Doctor Who. I. B. Tauris: London, 2006.

3. Williams, J. Review: Genesis of the Daleks. Doctor Who Magazine, 474, July 2014, pp. 30–31.

    Genesis of the Daleks is, though, by no means the first Doctor Who serial to end disconcertingly. In The Web of Fear, some seven years earlier, we see one of the most ironic climaxes. Realising that his mind will be absorbed by the Great Intelligence, The Doctor is about to reverse the transference and move on to the attack when he is "rescued" by the well-meaning Jamie. As a result of his companion's interference, the Intelligence is merely sent into the vastness of space. From here it is, of course, free to wreak havoc elsewhere or even attack Earth again. As in Genesis of the Daleks, only the immediate threat has been averted...

4. The Prisoner: Patrick McGoohan Interviewed By Warner Troyer – The Troyer Interview, Part One. The Prisoner: Music, FAQs, background, episode guide, spoofs. URL: http://www.the-prisoner-6.freeserve.co.uk/troyer.htm (accessed: 23 September 2013).

5. McGown, A. D. and Docherty, M. J. The Hill and beyond: Children's television drama – An encyclopedia. BFI: London, 2003.

6. Dicks, T. Introduction. In: Doctor Who: The Scripts – Tom Baker 1974/5. BBC: London, 2001, pp. 12–14.

7. Sandifer, P. TARDIS eruditorum: An unofficial critical history of Doctor Who – Volume 3, Jon Pertwee. Eruditorum Press: Danbury, Connecticut, 2013.

8. Wright, P. British television science fiction. In: Seed, D. (ed.) A companion to science fiction. Blackwell: Oxford, 2005, pp. 289– 305.

9. The Peacemaker DVD Audio Commentary. The Invaders: The Believers box. CBS/Paramount, 2009.

10. Heald, T. The making of Space: 1999 – A Gerry Anderson production. Ballantine: New York, 1976.

11. Wood, R. E. Destination Moonbase Alpha – The unofficial and unauthorised guide to Space: 1999. Telos: Prestatyn, 2010.

12. Booker, M. K. Science fiction television. Praeger: Westport, Connecticut, 2004.

13. Leach, J. Doctor Who. Wayne State University Press: Detroit, Michigan, 2009.

14. Fulton, R. The encyclopedia of TV science fiction. Boxtree: London, 1990.

15. Clute, J. Science fiction: The illustrated encyclopedia. Dorling Kindersley: London, 1995.

16. McCormack, U. Resist the host: Blake's 7 – A very British future. In: Cook, J. R. and Wright, P. (eds.) British science fiction television: A hitchhiker's guide. I. B. Tauris: London, 2006, pp. 174–191.

17. Marshall, R. Blake's 7: A critical guide to series 1–4. Out There Publications, 2015.

18. While themes such as surveillance and propaganda permeate the whole Prisoner saga, terrorism and revolution are more particular to individual episodes, namely It's Your Funeral with regard to the former and Fall Out in terms of the latter.

19. Hills, M. Fan cultures. Routledge: London, 2002.

20. Ibid.

21. Hoyle. T. Terry Nation's Blake's 7. Sphere: London, 1977; Hoyle, T. Terry Nation's Blake's 7: Project Avalon. Arrow: London, 1979; Hoyle, T. Terry Nation's Blake's 7: Scorpio attack. BBC: London, 1981.

22. Britton, W. Spy television. Praeger: Westport, Connecticut, 2004.

23. McGoohan, P. On the trail of The Prisoner: Roger Goodman talks to Patrick McGoohan. CD. PrizBiz, 2007. Audio recording of 1979 interview.

24. Dixon, W. W. All my films are personal: An interview with Pat Jackson. Journal of Popular Film and Television, 39 (4), 2011, pp. 150–161.

25. Hora, M. The Prisoner of Portmeirion, 2nd ed. Number Six Publications, 1995.

26. Archive On 4: Very British Dystopias. BBC Radio 4. 15 June 2013.

27. Ibid.

28. Booker, M. K. Strange TV: Innovative television series from The Twilight Zone to The X-Files. Greenwood: Westport, Connecticut, 2002.

Even before the dystopias of the 1940s, however, authors of fiction had expressed their concern in relation to the practice of representing people via numbers. In Hard Times, which was published as long ago as 1854, Charles Dickens depicts a schoolroom scene in which young Sissy Jupe is referred to as "girl number twenty". The notes in the 1987 Penguin Classics edition indicate that this scenario may well have been inspired by a real life situation, rather than Dickens's imagination. They state, "In the Manchester Lancasterian School, the thousand children being taught in one room, with only two masters and one mistress in charge, had to be numbered off in military style." (p. 318) As in the Prisoner episode The General, there is also strong condemnation of an education system that values rote learning above all else.

29. Lewin, R. The Prisoner. In: Haley, G. (ed.) Sci-fi chronicles: A visual history of the galaxy's greatest science fiction. Aurum: London, 2014, p. 261.

30. Haley, G. (ed.) op. cit.

31. Abbott, J. The Prisoner. Starburst, 5 (4) [issue 67], March 1984, pp. 18–23.

32. Cornell, P., Day, M. and Topping, K. The Avengers dossier: The definitive unauthorised guide. Virgin: London, 1998.

33. See, for example: Doctor Who: The Twelfth Season. Fantasy Empire, Collector's Edition 2, 1983; Howe, D. J. and Walker, S. J. Doctor Who: The television companion – The official BBC guide to every TV story. BBC: London, 1998; Doctor Who: The Scripts – Tom Baker 1974/5. op. cit.; Chapman, J. op. cit.; Robb, B. J. Timeless adventures: How Doctor Who conquered TV. Kamera: Harpenden, 2009; Turner, A. W. The man who invented the Daleks: The strange worlds of Terry Nation. Aurum: London, 2011.

34. Cornell, P., Day, M. and Topping, K. op. cit.

35. In The Prisoner: The Original Scripts – Volume 2, the observant Robert Fairclough points out that differences in the number plates reveal that the hearse shown in Fall Out is not the same car that we saw earlier in the series.

36. Carrazé, A. and Oswald, H. The Prisoner: A televisionary masterpiece. Virgin: London, 1990.

37. Savile, S. Fantastic TV: 50 years of cult fantasy and science fiction. Plexus: London, 2010.

38. Short, S. Cult telefantasy series: A critical analysis of The Prisoner, Twin Peaks, The

X-Files, Buffy the Vampire Slayer, Lost, Heroes, Doctor Who and Star Trek. McFarland: Jefferson, North Carolina, 2011.

39. Short, S. Countering the counterculture: The Prisoner and the 1960s. In: Cook, J. R. and Wright, P. (eds.) op. cit., pp. 71–92.

40. Nicholls, P. and Newman, K. Blake's Seven. In: Clute, J. and Nicholls, P. (eds.) op. cit., p. 133.

41. Bould, M. Science fiction television in the United Kingdom. In: Telotte, J. P. (ed.) The essential science fiction television reader. University Press of Kentucky: Lexington, Kentucky, 2008, pp. 209–230.

42. Interview: Chris Boucher. DWB, 108, December 1992, pp. 8–10.

43. Muir, J. K. A history and critical analysis of Blake's 7, the 1978–1981 British television space adventure. McFarland: Jefferson, North Carolina, 2000.

44. Morton, A. The complete directory to science fiction, fantasy and horror television series: A comprehensive guide to the first 50 years 1946 to 1996. Other Worlds Books: Peoria, Illinois, 1997.

45. Hills, M. op. cit.

46. Quoted in: Nobel, S. and Goldsborough, D. The Prisoner puzzle. Ontario Educational Communications Authority: Toronto, Ontario, 1978.

47. White, M. and Ali, J. The official Prisoner companion. Sidgwick and Jackson: London, 1988.

48. Hills, M. op. cit.

49. Lewis, J. E. and Stempel, P. Cult TV: The essential critical guide. Pavilion Books: London, 1993.

50. Nobel, S. and Goldsborough, D. op. cit.

51. Brown, A. Once and future Blake. DWB, 108, December 1992a, p. 24.

52. Interviews. Blake's 7: Battleground. CD. Big Finish, 2014.

53. O'Brien, D. SF: UK – How British science fiction changed the world. Reynolds and Hearn: Richmond, London, 2000.

54. Brown, A. Review: Blake's 7 tape 26 – Warlord/Blake. DWB, 108, December 1992b, p. 21.

55. Fulton, R. op. cit.

56. Brown, A. op. cit. 1992b.

57. Terry Nation's Blake's 7 Winter Special. Marvel: London, 1994.

58. Attwood, T. Terry Nation's Blake's 7: The programme guide. W. H. Allen: London, 1982.

59. Muir, J. K. op. cit.

60. Attwood, T. op. cit.

61. Stevens, A. and Moore, F. Liberation: The unofficial and unauthorised guide to Blake's 7. Telos: Tolworth, 2003.

62. Attwood, T. op. cit.

63. Interviews: Chris Boucher – Script Editor And Writer. In: Attwood, T. op. cit., pp. 178–181.

64. Gerani, G. and Schulman, P. H. Fantastic television: A pictorial history of sci-fi, the unusual and the fantastic from the '50s to the '70s. Titan: London, 1987. Reprint of 1977 work.

65. See, for example: Abbott, J. Irwin Allen television productions, 1964–1970: A critical history. McFarland: Jefferson, North Carolina, 2006; Grams Jr., M. The Time Tunnel: A history of the television program. BearManor Media: Duncan, Oklahoma, 2012.

66. Chapman, J. op. cit.

67. Tulloch, J. and Alvarado, M. Doctor Who: The unfolding text. Macmillan: London, 1983.

68. Short, S. op. cit. 2011.

69. Quoted in: Nazzaro, J. and Wells, S. Blake's 7: The inside story. Virgin: London, 1997.

70. Interviews: Michael Keating – Vila. In: Attwood, T. op. cit., pp. 183–185.

71. Quoted in: Turner, A. W. op. cit.

72. Turner, A. W. op. cit.

73. Quoted in: Short. S. op. cit. 2011.

74. Hirsch, D. Blake's 7. In: Hirsch, D. (ed.) TV episode guides, volume 2: Science fiction, adventure and superheroes. Starlog: New York, 1982, pp. 22–30.

75. Nation, T. Introduction. In: Attwood, T. op. cit., pp. 7–8.

76. Attwood, T. op. cit.

77. Parkin, L. A history: An unauthorised history of the Doctor Who universe, 2nd ed. Mad Norwegian Press: Des Moines, Iowa, 2007.

78. Savile, S. op. cit.

79. Muir, J. K. op. cit.

80. Interview With Patrick McGoohan. In: Carrazé, A. and Oswald, H. op. cit., pp. 6–8; McGoohan, P. op. cit.

For many years there has been speculation as to which of the various Prisoner episodes make up the core seven. If the information given by White and Ali in their Official Prisoner Companion is taken at face value, the matter would seem to have been resolved unequivocally as long ago as 1988, when the authors boldly cited the names of the seven instalments "that McGoohan says 'really count'". (p. 122) Yet, in his biography Not a Number: Patrick McGoohan: A Life, Rupert Booth quotes his subject as saying that White and Ali had "picked their seven, but they're not my seven. They claim they're mine, but they're not." (p. 219) Booth reports, in fact, that McGoohan never revealed which episodes he believed constituted the core of the series.

John S. Smith, who re-edited Dance of the Dead (i.e. one of the seven episodes highlighted by White and Ali), has said that McGoohan "hated" the original version assembled by Geoff Foot and "asked him to throw it away. He never wanted to see it again ever. 'Put it up on the shelf,' I think he said, 'and forget about it.'" (see The Prisoner Investigated Vol. 1) In view of McGoohan's low opinion of the first version, it seems astonishing that he would ever accord "core" status to Dance of the Dead, in particular.

81. Muir, J. K. op. cit.
82. Muir, J. K. op. cit.
83. Lewis, J. E. and Stempel, P. op. cit.
84. Attwood, T. op. cit.
85. Blake's 7 Series Survey. DWB, 125, April 1994, pp. 12–13.
86. Quoted in: Turner, A. W. op. cit.
87. Interviews: Paul Darrow – Avon. In: Attwood, T. op. cit., pp. 181–183.
88. Fulton, R. op. cit.
89. See, for example: Harry, B. Heroes of the spaceways. Omnibus: London, 1981; Fulton, R. op. cit.
90. Stevens, A. and Moore, F. op. cit.
91. Javna, J. The best of science fiction TV: The critics' choice from Captain Video to Star Trek, from The Jetsons to Robotech. Titan: London, 1988; Fulton, R. op. cit.; Savile, S. op. cit.; Wright, M. Blake's 7. In: Haley, G. (ed.) op. cit., p. 329.
92. Bould, M. This is the modern world: The Prisoner, authorship and allegory. In: Bignell, J. and Lacey, S. (eds.) Popular television drama: Critical perspectives. Manchester University Press: Manchester, 2005, pp. 93–109.
93. Nobel, S. and Goldsborough, D. op. cit.
94. Abbott, J. op. cit. 1984.
95. Interviews: Michael Keating – Vila. op. cit.
96. Interviews: Chris Boucher – Script Editor And Writer. op. cit.
97. Savile, S. op. cit.
98. Turner, A. W. op. cit.
99. Interviews. op. cit.
100. Darrow, P. You're him, aren't you? An autobiography. Big Finish, 2006.
101. Hirsch, D. op. cit.
102. Savile, S. op. cit.
103. Berger, A. A. The Prisoner: British spy and science fiction series. In: Newcomb, H. (ed.) Encyclopedia of television, volume 3 M–R, 2nd ed. Fitzroy Dearborn: New York, 2004, pp. 1829–1830.
104. Short. S. op. cit. 2011.
105. McCormack, U. op. cit.

Similar arguments have been advanced in relation to Terry Nation's earlier series Survivors. Speaking in the Goodbye Great Britain 75-77 instalment of the BBC documentary programme The 70s (BBC2, 13 October 2013), presenter Dominic Sandbrook argues that Survivors reflected the "pessimism" and "paranoia" of a

Britain which, at the time, was "stalked by calamity" and where "power was up for grabs". In outlining the plot of the second episode, Genesis, Sandbrook comments that whilst Survivors may have been presented as "escapist fantasy", for many viewers "the threat of a militant union leader seizing power in a Left wing coup was all too real".

106. Britton, W. op. cit.
107. Brown, A. Around the galaxy in fifty seconds. DWB, 108, December 1992c, pp. 18–19.
108. Palgut, T. The Prisoner: The Village files. Titan: London, 2003.
109. Marshall, R. op. cit.
110. White, M. and Ali, J. op. cit.
111. Gregory, C. Be seeing you... Decoding The Prisoner. John Libbey Media: Luton, 1997.
112. Cooke, L. British television drama: A history. British Film Institute: London, 2003.
113. Gerani, G. and Schulman, P. H. op. cit.
114. Reproduced in: Langley, R. (ed.) The Prisoner original 60s publicity material. 2012.
115. Short. S. op. cit. 2011.
116. The Prisoner Investigated Vol. 1. VHS video cassette. TR 7 Productions: Borehamwood, 1990.
117. Langley, R. The Prisoner who's who? 2012.
118. Where The Secret Agent Is Whisked Away. In: Goodman, R. (ed.) George Markstein and The Prisoner. pandqmedia: Berwyn, Denbighshire, 2014, pp. 78–95.
119. The Prisoner Behind The Scenes With Bernie Williams. The Prisoner: 35th anniversary Prisoner companion – Special edition. DVD. Carlton, 2002.
120. Booker, M. K. op. cit. 2002.
121. Booth, R. Not a number: Patrick McGoohan – A life. Supernova: Twickenham, 2011.
122. Palgut, T. op. cit.
123. Attwood, T. op. cit.
124. Muir, J. K. op. cit.
125. Stevens, A. and Moore, F. Fall out: The unofficial and unauthorised guide to The Prisoner. Telos: Tolworth, 2007.
126. Ibid.
127. Ibid.
128. Gregory, C. op. cit.
129. O'Brien, D. op. cit.
130. White, M. and Ali, J. op. cit.
131. Tame, C. R. Different values: An analysis of Patrick McGoohan's The Prisoner. Libertarian Reprints, 1, 1983. Reprint of 1974 work. URL: http://www.libertarian.co.uk/lapubs/libre/libre001.pdf (accessed: 23 February 2017).
132. Dunn, P. Review: Decoding The Prisoner. The Unmutual. URL:

http://www.theunmutual.co.uk/reviewsdecoding.htm (accessed: 23 February 2017).

133. Richardson, D. Producer's notes. Blake's 7: Mirror. CD. Big Finish, 2014.

134. Muir, J. K. op. cit.

135. Interviews: Paul Darrow – Avon. op. cit.

136. Interviews: Chris Boucher – Script Editor And Writer. op. cit.

137. Muir, J. K. op. cit.

138. See, for example: Fulton, R. op. cit.; Clute, J. op. cit.; Fane-Saunders, K. (ed.) Radio Times guide to science fiction. BBC Worldwide: London, 2001.

139. Javna, J. op. cit.

140. Worlds Of Their Own: A Round Robin Interview. In: Savile, S. op. cit., pp. 254–272.

141. Darrow, P. op. cit.

142. Chapman, J. Saints and Avengers: British adventure series of the 1960s. I. B. Tauris: London, 2002.

143. Fulton, R. op. cit.

144. Chris Boucher Interview, April 2010. In: Oliver, M. B. Blake's 7: The merchandise guide – Unofficial and unauthorised. Telos: Prestatyn, 2012, pp. 162–171.

145. Gregory, C. op. cit.

146. Tulloch, J. and Alvarado, M. op. cit.

147. Gregory, C. op. cit.

148. Attwood, T. Terry Nation's Blake's 7: Afterlife. Target: London, 1984.

149. Savile, S. op. cit.

CHAPTER TEN
Fight and
Flight

The previous chapter opened with the observation that various 1970s British science fiction television programmes were of the "anxiety-ridden" type. Several featured less than perfect societies and/or communities that had emerged from a global disaster. Although American, rather than British, the TV series of *Logan's Run* displays both these characteristics. Here the society in question has arisen in the aftermath of a devastating nuclear war and it, too, is deeply flawed. Domes have been constructed to ensure that inhabitants are protected from the dangers outside and the seemingly perfect life that people now enjoy has been brought about through computer control. By the time the series opens in the year 2319, inhabitants of the City of Domes have been conditioned to accept that when they reach their 30th birthday they must enter "the great sleep" and submit to the ceremony of Carousel. The City's propaganda maintains that they will be renewed and live again in another body. There are, however, sceptics who distrust what they are told and seek to escape to the world outside. These "runners", who are denounced by one of those who is charged with apprehending them as "sick", aim to find a mythical refuge called Sanctuary, where people can live out their remaining days in peace and freedom. The series concentrates on the adventures of two such runners – Logan and Jessica – who, having made their escape from their city, join forces with the android REM (an acronym for Reclective Entity – Mobile).

One of the most striking immediate similarities between *The Prisoner* and *Logan's Run* lies in the fact that in both productions characters are known by numbers. At least in the City of Domes, though, people are allowed first names, too. Reference is made, for example, to Logan Five, Jessica Six and Francis Seven. Much of Number Six's dissidence in *The Prisoner* would seem firmly rooted in moral and philosophical principles, whereas the rebels in *Logan's Run* are intent on countering a much more serious problem – that of enforced premature death at the age of 30. The 1967 novel from which the television series derives its original inspiration presents an even more draconian society. In the book, written by William F. Nolan and George Clayton Johnson, citizens are not permitted to live past 21. In both The Village and the City of Domes, inhabitants are given every opportunity to live happily as long as they follow the diktats of the authorities. Apart from the governing Elders and those who have the task of pursuing the runners, few citizens seem expected to undertake any real work in the computer-controlled future world. In The Village, meanwhile, although we see people fulfilling such roles as shopkeepers, doctors, maids and painters, many would seem to be in league with the authorities and no work is apparently required of those who, like Number Six, harbour secrets. According to the narration heard at the beginning of the first episode of *Logan's Run*, "living [in the City] is unending joy. Every wish is granted. Every sensual dream is realised." These pleasures are offered at a high price, however. Whilst Villagers in *The Prisoner* are merely required to surrender their secrets, in *Logan's Run* the City dwellers must submit to Carousel. Viewers may well take issue with the more oppressive aspects of control in The Village but even some of these may seem fairly minor when we learn that life within the City of Domes is based on a fundamental lie – the Carousel ceremony results in death, not rebirth as the authorities claim.

Freedom of thought is rare among denizens of the City of Domes and The Village. In *The Prisoner*, the automaton-like responses of the Villagers are perhaps most apparent in *Free For All*, in which the people form easy targets for manipulation in the hands of the Village authorities when an election takes place. We are told in the scene-setting voice-over of *Logan's Run* quoted above that the world to be portrayed has been designed by computers. Since so many of the inhabitants seem entirely passive and unquestioning, we may almost conclude that the breed of man which has emerged since the nuclear holocaust has been developed by these computers in their own image. Indeed, in the first episode, the human – machine distinction becomes blurred when one of the City's Elders talks about "reprogramming" Logan and Jessica for their own ends. Further references to such reprogramming in the episodes *Capture, The Innocent, The Judas Goat, Carousel* and *Turnabout* serve to emphasise the point.

The manner in which *The Prisoner* reflects real life 1960s concerns has been a significant theme within *Unique But Similar*, and *Logan's Run* is similarly grounded. Series star Gregory Harrison highlights how the central premise arose from the ageism of modern society. With youth forming a characteristic that was highly prized, there was a mood during the era in which the programme was made that life "over the age of 30 wasn't anything worth living". (p. 177)[1] Harrison also recalls that, in 1968, just a few years before the series, the film *Wild in the Streets* had presented a situation in which the US government was taken over by a group of young adults. Harrison maintains that *Logan's Run* was essentially a science fiction version of the film's central concept.[2] The clearest indication of the real world roots of the series can be found on the opening page of the original *Logan's Run* novel, which begins, "The seeds of the Little War were planted in a restless summer during the mid-1960s, with sit-ins and student demonstrations as youth tested its strength."[3] It is an indication of the importance of student unrest during the decade that in *The Prisoner: The Official Fact File*, the subject is one of 17 addressed in a section devoted to the world of the 1960s that shaped the programme.[4]

A further indication of the prevailing mood of the day can be found in Aaron Spelling's *The New People* – a late 1960s ABC Television series that offered yet another portrayal of a youth-dominated society. Here a group of American college students find themselves marooned on an island after their plane crashes. The instalments are devoted to the various philosophical issues that are raised in the fledgling community which forms. Mark Phillips and Frank Garcia explain how, as with *Logan's Run*, the context of the show should be understood in real world terms. Specifically, they highlight that the basis of *The New People* was rooted in "during the turbulent 1960s, when many young people were questioning their government and its power over them". (p. 219)[5]

Contemporary anxieties about overpopulation were also transplanted into the futuristic setting of *Logan's Run*. According to one of the Elders in the first episode, the main reason for the extermination of citizens at the age of 30 is the fact that the City of Domes can sustain only a finite number of people. As in *The Prisoner*, surveillance features prominently – those who support the status quo are heavily reliant on technology in order to find out about escape attempts. The *Prisoner* themes of surveillance, oppression, conformity and dissidence are often thought to be timeless, and the concern of *Logan's Run* with overpopulation is another ongoing real world issue, certainly in Britain. In August 2013, whilst the second edition of this book was in its early stages of preparation, the BBC website reported that figures just released by the Office for National Statistics indicated that more babies were born in the United

Kingdom in 2011–12 than in any year since 1972, and the associated population growth in the UK was higher than anywhere else in the European Union. Inevitably, these revelations led to anxieties regarding the pressure that the increase would place on resources and services such as schools.[6]

A key difference between *The Prisoner* and *Logan's Run* is that although in both cases the adventures of a rebel (or group of rebels) provide the central focus, in the latter the protagonists are mainly intent on what might be regarded as "defensive" actions, namely escaping their pursuers and finding safety in Sanctuary. In contrast, like the heroes and heroines in *Blake's 7*, Number Six fights against the authorities very directly, in addition, of course, to attempting to protect his secrets and escape from The Village. It is this multiplicity of aims that gives rise to the different *Prisoner* story types that have been outlined in Section I. For scriptwriter Lewis Greifer, The Prisoner's various agendas were the source of considerable confusion. What, he wonders, was **actually** Number Six's main purpose, and indeed that of the other Villagers?[7] In *Logan's Run*, flight and safety are firmly established as the protagonists' priorities. Although in *Carousel*, Logan briefly entertains hopes of inspiring a mass revolution, ultimately he never finds himself in the position from which he can make the rallying call he envisages. David Gerrold points out one of the intrinsic problems inherent in any series whose characters' principal concern is that of flight. He suggests that it is all too easy for the protagonists to be seen as cowards in these circumstances and it is difficult to inject constant running with any degree of heroism. Gerrold recognises, however, that the scenario changes if the characters are striving to reach a particular place or a search of some kind is involved.[8] In *Logan's Run*, this greater sense of purpose was provided by the quest for Sanctuary.

Logan is initially a member of the establishment and changes sides. Like his friend Francis, at the beginning of the programme he is a Sandman whose function lies in hunting down and eliminating runners. He is not, then, a natural counterpart of Number Six, who rebels against the Village authorities virtually from the outset. In turning against the masters he has hitherto served and assisting an existing rebel, Logan, at least in the early part of the first episode, is somewhat reminiscent of Number Twelve in *The General* or the Number Two we see in *Fall Out*. A case can be made for arguing that when we first meet her Jessica is closer to Number Six in that she is already a rebel. By playing on Logan's uncertainties, she is able to persuade him to join her and it is Jessica who leads in their escape into the world beyond the domes. Although she is aware of Logan's doubts surrounding the nature of rebirth in the City, it would seem that Jessica has not made any attempt to involve him systematically in a way comparable to how The Prisoner purposely recruits fellow dissidents in *Checkmate*. Logan and Jessica are simply brought together by circumstance when the Sandman is assigned to kill the girl while she and another runner are trying to make their escape, and her impassioned plea resonates with him. Nevertheless, Logan quickly emerges thereafter as the real hero of the series. His natural suspicion and curiosity about the world around him are reminiscent of Number Six's free-thinking traits and he uses these characteristics to good advantage on various occasions.

Each week The Prisoner pits his wits against Number Two, and Logan and his party face their own recurring adversary in the form of Francis. Assigned by the Elders to return Logan and Jessica to the City so that they can testify at Carousel and denounce running, Francis is promised a place on the Council, and thus continued life after 30, if he is successful. John Kenneth Muir highlights how Francis is cast in the role of "the Hapless Pursuer" – "a dedicated military man who attempts to catch the hero... every week", (p. 61) and thus fulfils a similar function to Travis in *Blake's 7*.[9] Comparisons can be drawn between the Sandmen and those forces responsible for maintaining order in *The Prisoner* and *Blake's 7*. In each of the three series the authorities can call on the unequivocal support of unmistakably clad enforcers. Francis declares instinctively in the first episode of *Logan's Run* that Sandmen "don't question the order of things". His words are equally applicable to the guards we see in the two British series.

The contrast between the right of the state to control and the individual's right to freedom is fundamental to *The Prisoner*, and a similar tension is reflected in a philosophical exchange between Logan and Francis in the third episode, *Capture*. Their conversation leads to the conclusion that whilst the premature death of citizens in Carousel may serve the needs of the City, it is clearly not in the best interests of the people themselves.

In both programmes, the hero is immensely valuable to the authorities, who, for much of each series, are keen that he remains alive and in a reasonable state of health. In such episodes as *Free For All*, *The Schizoid Man* and *Dance of the Dead*, it is established that limits exist with regard to the treatment that should be meted out to Number Six, although the reason for this caution does not become apparent until the last instalment. In *Logan's Run*, it is the prospect that the hero will issue a public statement declaring that Sanctuary does not exist and that running is futile which makes his continued existence so attractive to the Elders. Nevertheless, in *Carousel*, it becomes clear that Logan will be put to death once his propaganda value has been exploited to the full.

The leaders of the City of Domes do not pin all their hopes of capturing

Logan on Francis and his team of pursuers. In *The Judas Goat*, they resort to the ruse of impersonation, despatching an impostor to masquerade as the escaped runner Hal 14 and win the confidence of Logan's party. There are obvious parallels between the City Council's use of the Hal 14 lookalike as a false friend to trap Logan and Jessica and the way Number Two calls on various duplicitous individuals in his schemes against Number Six in *The Prisoner*. In *The Judas Goat*, the treachery is made possible through the exploitation of technology that endows another of the Council's trusted Sandmen with the exact physical appearance of Hal 14. Impersonation is also, of course, a tactic adopted by the authorities behind The Village – Curtis's efforts to unsettle Number Six by pretending to be him in *The Schizoid Man* were referred to in the previous chapter. An important difference is that in *The Judas Goat*, the viewer is shown the means by which the transformation of Sandman Joseph Eight is achieved, whereas after watching *The Schizoid Man* we remain uncertain as to whether Curtis is a natural born double of Number Six, an altered human or a clone that has been deliberately created.

Whilst much of the action in *The Prisoner* takes place inside The Village, a lot of that from the second episode onwards of *Logan's Run* is set beyond the City of Domes. The nature of the society within the City and the relationship between it and Logan's group became less prevalent issues as the programme ran. Indeed, they fade as themes considerably after the first instalment and in some episodes references to the way of life in the City of Domes are no more than occasional. From the second segment onwards, Francis provides the clearest personification of City of Domes authority but in eight of the last 13 instalments even he does not appear. Nevertheless, actor Randy Powell is featured in the title sequence of each of these episodes.

According to the Starlog *Robots* guidebook, "What started as an intelligent commentary on a perverted system of societal organization soon sadly degenerated into yet one more variation of *The Fugitive*, and became nothing more than an extended chase melodrama." (p. 96)[10] Very quickly, episodes of *Logan's Run* began to adhere to the long established format in television science fiction whereby, in undertaking their quest, the regular characters encounter a different – and frequently hostile – culture each week. Certainly, like the society that exists in the City of Domes, many of the civilisations encountered by Logan's party are seriously flawed. In various instances within *Logan's Run*, the heroes can be considered to face a kind of "double dystopia" – in fleeing from their own imperfect future world, they find themselves encountering another where the way of life provides further peril. As Phillips and Garcia point out, for much of the time, if the fugitives are not being captured, chased or threatened, they find themselves having to rescue others.[11]

One episode that will strike a particular chord with *Prisoner* fans is *Fear Factor*. In this instalment, people with independent and inquiring minds are "treated" to make them accept the values of the society's leaders. Here, however, the aim lies in creating a master race, somewhat similar to that envisioned by the Nazis, rather than simply a community of docile citizens. We can also draw parallels between the plot of the *Prisoner* episode *A. B. and C.* and the dream analysis theme in the *Futurepast* segment of *Logan's Run*. In both cases, dreams bring danger to the hero. Within this context, Number Two attempts to use the machinery and drugs available to him in order to manipulate The Prisoner into divulging the reason for his resignation; in *Futurepast* Logan and Jessica confront their deepest fears in the dreams they experience and if the intensity of the dreaming progresses beyond a particular point this can result in death.

In several episodes of *Logan's Run*, the heroes either escape or leave after effecting an improvement in the society, sometimes by helping to bring about some form of justice. Logan occasionally emerges as peacemaker. In *Half Life*, he is able to unite two opposing factions – the Positives and the Castouts, and in *Stargate*, he raises the possibility of cooperation between alien invaders and the human Timon. Overall, the series is very similar to *The Fantastic Journey*, which had been shown on television only months earlier.[12] Here a group of travellers lost in the Bermuda Triangle and intent on returning home moves from one time zone to another, coming into contact with disparate civilisations and experiencing a series of weekly adventures in the process.[13] Two of the episodes – *Children of the Gods* and *Riddles* – deal quite specifically with problems that arise in youth-dominated societies.[14] Thematic similarities are perhaps not unexpected in view of the fact that several individuals worked in a significant capacity on both *The Fantastic Journey* and *Logan's Run*. They include producer Leonard Katzman, associate producer William O. Cairncross, story editor D. C. Fontana and writers Michael Michaelian and Katharyn Michaelian Powers.

By providing Logan's party with a different culture to investigate each week, those responsible for the programme were able to offer a considerable diversity of themes through scenarios that incorporated such elements as exploration by aliens (in *The Collectors* and *Stargate*), extrasensory perception (in *The Innocent*), time travel (in *Man Out of Time*), a murder mystery (in *Crypt*), mind control (in *Fear Factor*) and even a haunted house (in *Night Visitors*). The adventures embracing these ingredients did little, however, to bring the travellers closer to their ultimate goal. We have considered more than once already in *Unique But Similar* how some of those episodes beyond Patrick McGoohan's intended seven deviated from the essence of *The Prisoner*.

According to Greifer, part of the wide range of the stories' content resulted from the fact that in order to go beyond reworkings of the obvious "escape" scenario, writers like himself sought to explore more oblique issues.[15] Robert Fairclough, in fact, notes how, after a spate of early stories that dealt in some way with attempts by The Prisoner to escape, the series was saved from repetition by diversifying "into areas such as interrogation (*Once Upon a Time*), psychology (*The Schizoid Man*), assassination (*It's Your Funeral*), social satire (*A Change of Mind* and *The General*), the subconscious (*A. B. and C.*) and paranoia (*Hammer Into Anvil*)". (p. 465)[16] We can attribute the variety in *Logan's Run* to a similar need to move away from all too limiting "party on the run" situations.

In Chapter Seven, attention was drawn to the cyclical nature of many *Prisoner* episodes. Some instalments of *Logan's Run* exhibit a similar characteristic, although in these instances the heroes are at least able to make good their escape. In the opening instalment, with REM's help, Logan and Jessica free themselves from the clutches of a group of excessively solicitous androids intent on serving any humans with whom they come into contact but at the end of this encounter Francis is apprehended by one of the robots that welcomed Logan and Jessica. It is clear that Francis will face the same problem as his predecessors in terms of effecting an escape. In the much later episode *Night Visitors*, after the runners have freed themselves from the forces of darkness which inhabit a sinister house, in the final scene we see a curtain at the window of an upstairs room twitch, thereby confirming that the shadowy occupants have not been defeated and lie in wait for the next unsuspecting travellers…[17]

One of the most highly acclaimed *Logan's Run* episodes is *Man Out of Time*. It is, in fact, regarded by Dave Golder as the best instalment in the series.[18] The plot concerns David Eakins, a scientist from the twenty-second century, who travels two hundred years into the future in order to learn more about – and ultimately prevent – the events that led to the nuclear war. If the holocaust is averted, however, Logan's party will cease to exist. Ultimately, not only is Eakins unsuccessful in his mission; the time travel machine that he and his team have developed quickly emerges as "the ultimate weapon", since its use allows world leaders to be killed before they become important. Rather than helping to prevent the war, the time machine ironically becomes one of its principal causes when an enemy power makes the first strike in order to stop Eakins's side from using it.[19] As in *The Prisoner*, the positive and negative aspects of science are shown in stark terms. There are parallels to be drawn, too, between the time machine we see in *Logan's Run* and the "time tilting" device featured in the *Outer Limits* story *The Forms of Things Unknown*. Here again, such technology is seen to have good and bad effects. Tone Hobart, the creator of the time tilting equipment, recognises the benefits it can bring through returning to life loved people from the past but when it also resurrects the evil Andre Pavan, Hobart realises the damage it may cause and ultimately decides that it must be destroyed.

The Prisoner's encounter with Number One in *Fall Out* may be construed as a comment on the "duality" of man. Here the rational, intelligent character whom we have come to regard as the hero confronts his more sinister, bestial alter ego. The *Half Life* episode of *Logan's Run* can be interpreted as another treatment of this theme. In their quest to create a perfect society, the people encountered by Logan's party in this instalment "process" each member of their group so as to create two separate entities – one inherently good and peaceful, the other more aggressive – and in the "civilised" society only the former is retained. Nevertheless, just as in *Fall Out* the two sides of The Prisoner come into contact with one another, Jessica's positive and negative personas meet in *Half Life*. The message from *Fall Out* would seem to be that we are always constrained by our own weaknesses. Noreen Ackland, one of the episode's editors, summarises what she believes to be the intended meaning by saying, "we're all prisoners within ourselves. We're a prisoner to our own being."[20] It would appear that *Half Life*, meanwhile, is telling us that both peaceful and aggressive elements are needed inside each of us if we are to be truly human. The title of the episode would seem to reinforce this message. In *Stargate*, we meet more doubles, when aliens create replica bodies of Logan and Jessica, which they intend will be inhabited by their own kind. Parallels between this situation and the plot of the *Doctor Who* adventure *The Faceless Ones* discussed in Chapter Three quickly spring to mind.

There may also be a religious connection between *Logan's Run* and *The Prisoner*. In the former, Jessica wears an amulet around her neck and uses it in the first episode to open a door in the City of Domes that ultimately leads to the world beyond. Since we learn in *Capture* that runners before Jessica have worn amulets of a similar design, we may wonder whether its shape is somehow emblematic of the fugitive movement, in much the same way as a penny farthing represents The Village in *The Prisoner*. It is tempting to equate the cross-like pattern of the runners' amulets with the crucifix so often associated with Christianity. If we accept the explanation of Norma West, who appeared in the *Dance of the Dead* episode of *The Prisoner*, that McGoohan intended the "Be seeing you!" salute to modelled on the sign of the fish used by the early Christians,[21] then *Logan's Run* and *The Prisoner* may share a theological link. It should be noted, however, that when asked if certain aspects of *Fall Out* had a religious basis, McGoohan has emphatically denied this to be the case.[22]

Similarities can certainly be detected between the second episode of *Logan's Run, The Collectors*, and *The Prisoner* in that both are very much concerned with manipulation, the nature of reality and, in particular, the possibility of hallucination. We can, of course, question whether The Village has any actual physical existence at all and in *Living in Harmony* it is clearly apparent that much of what we have witnessed has taken place only in Number's Six's mind. In *The Collectors*, meanwhile, the heroes are made to **think** that they have reached Sanctuary as part of a test by aliens to determine their suitability for their purposes. At another point in the episode the aliens use the same techniques to try and convince Logan that he is back in the City of Domes. *The Collectors* bears comparison with the *Prisoner* instalment *The Chimes of Big Ben*, too, in that trickery on the part of others lies at the heart of the protagonists' misconceptions. Moreover, in both *The Collectors* and *The Prisoner*'s *Arrival*, the characters meet friends from the past who are not all they appear to be. In the latter, Number Six's former colleague Cobb is shown to be in league with those who run The Village and in *The Collectors*, Jessica's fellow runner Martin is revealed to be no more than a hallucination himself.

Psychological games form an important theme within the eleventh *Logan's Run* episode, *Carousel*. Here Logan is shot with a "memory warp" dart by representatives of the latest culture that is faced by the fugitives. As a consequence, he has no recollection of his time as a runner and he is soon returned to the City of Domes by Francis. The authorities persuade him to testify against Sanctuary and he is asked to address the Assembly before Carousel. Parallels can be drawn between the truth test Logan undergoes and that administered to Number Six by the Labour Exchange Manager in *Free For All*. In the latter, however, the "test" is clearly part of a major brainwashing procedure implemented against Number Six. A scenario in which a previously rebellious hero is apparently transformed into a much more submissive figure also emerges in the *Prisoner* episode *A Change of Mind*. Like Logan in *Carousel*, Number Six undertakes to make a public statement of support for the authorities. Ultimately, however, this proves to be a ruse and it is clear that by the later stages of the instalment The Prisoner has recovered his true personality sufficiently for him to concoct a plan that involves denouncing the system he has been expected by his adversaries to champion. In *Carousel*, Logan has similar intentions but is unable to put them into effect.

Ultimately, Sanctuary proves elusive to Logan, Jessica and REM. Although it seems briefly in *The Collectors* that they may have found it, by the end of the episode it is clear that their hopes had been based on an illusion and the three friends must begin their quest for Sanctuary once more. This realisation is comparable to how at the end of the last episode of *The Prisoner*, we see that despite having escaped from the physical confines of The Village complete liberty would still seem an unachievable goal. As McGoohan himself asserts unequivocally, "Freedom is a myth." (p. 4)[23] After watching Logan's party struggle in vain over the course of the series to reach Sanctuary, and finding little concrete evidence of such a place, viewers may conclude that Sanctuary at least in its physical form may be unattainable as well. This may lead us to wonder whether Sanctuary is best conceptualised somewhat differently – as a state of mind, perhaps. Such a hypothesis extends a notion introduced in *Half Life* by the "processed" Jessica. In conversation with Logan, she claims, "Sanctuary lies within each of us. All we need is the key." Nevertheless, to use this principle to explain the nature of Sanctuary across the whole series may be to elevate *Logan's Run* to a philosophical level that was never originally intended.

References and Notes

1.	Quoted in: Phillips, M. and Garcia, F. Science fiction television series: Episode guides, histories, and casts and credits for 62 prime time shows, 1959 through 1989. McFarland: Jefferson, North Carolina, 1996.

2.	Ibid.

3.	Nolan, W. F. and Johnson, G. C. Logan's run. Buccaneer: Cutchogue, New York, 1999. Reprint of 1967 work.

4.	The Prisoner: The Official Fact File. De Agostini, 2005–2006.

5.	Phillips, M. and Garcia, F. op. cit.

6.	BBC. More UK births than any year since 1972, says ONS, 8 August 2013. URL: http://www.bbc.co.uk/news/uk-23618487 (accessed: 23 February 2017).

7.	Lewis Greifer Interview. In: The Prisoner In-depth Tape 5. VHS video cassette. TR 7 Productions: Borehamwood, 1993.

8.	Javna, J. The best of science fiction TV: The critics' choice from Captain Video to Star Trek, from The Jetsons to Robotech. Titan: London, 1988.

9.	Muir, J. K. A history and critical analysis of Blake's 7, the 1978–1981 British television space adventure. McFarland: Jefferson, North Carolina, 2000.

10.	Hefley, R. M. and Zimmerman, H. Starlog photo guidebook: Robots, 2nd ed. Starlog: New York, 1980.

11.	Phillips, M. and Garcia, F. op. cit.

12.	The Fantastic Journey was first broadcast in the USA between February and June 1977 and in Britain between March and May 1977, whilst the equivalent dates for

Logan's Run are September 1977–January 1978 (USA) and January–April 1978 (Britain).

13. Much was made in Section I of the importance of avoiding speculation in which it is claimed that a certain work may have had a significant effect on a particular television production or itself been influenced by the predecessor to a major degree. The entry for The Fantastic Journey which is found in the first edition of the landmark Encyclopedia of Science Fiction: An illustrated A to Z serves to underline how frequently such inferences are made. Here John Brosnan hypothesises that the idea underpinning The Fantastic Journey was "probably inspired by Fred Hoyle's novel October the First is Too Late". (p. 208) Tellingly, however, when, fourteen years later, the second edition of the Encyclopedia appeared, this statement had been toned down to the suggestion that The Fantastic Journey's premise was "perhaps inspired" by the Hoyle story. (p. 405)

Chapter Seven referred to how The Prisoner dealt with the confrontation between the ultimate individual and the ultimate state. Other fundamental conflicts are explored in The Fantastic Journey. We see, for example, struggles between all powerful elites and their downtrodden underlings (in Atlantium), between youths and adults (in Children of the Gods), between militarists and the pacifist travellers (in Dream of Conquest), between religious fanatics and the rationalist travellers (in An Act of Love), between men and women (in Turnabout) and between good and evil (in The Innocent Prey). Typically, these episodes end with some form of resolution – usually a settlement or defeat for the aggressors – but The Prisoner, despite some mini-triumphs, seems destined to fight a battle that is without end.

14. Any reader who wants to explore further ways in which science fiction/fantasy television programmes up to 1987 have addressed youth oriented societies may benefit from watching the Star Trek episodes Miri and And the Children Shall Lead and the Kolchak instalment The Youth Killer.

15. Lewis Greifer Interview. op. cit.

16. Fairclough, R. (ed.) The Prisoner: The original scripts – Volume 1. Reynolds and Hearn: Richmond, London, 2005.

17. Night Visitors ends in a very similar way to the Fantastic Journey episode Funhouse. Since Night Visitors was written by the man who had produced The Fantastic Journey, parallels between the two stories may not be completely unsurprising. In Funhouse, too, the travellers ultimately escape the "peril of the week" without it being vanquished and it is clear that the next visitors to the area will face the same danger.

18. Golder, D. Second run. SFX Collection, 32, 2007, pp. 66–67.

19. Significant similarities are evident between the Man Out of Time episode of Logan's Run and the 1972 Doctor Who serial Day of the Daleks. In the latter, too, a group of

well intentioned humans on Earth use a time travel device in the hope of preventing a war that will have terrible consequences and, again, their actions set in motion the very events they are intent on avoiding. At the beginning of Chapter Nine reference was made to a dystopian thread within 1970s Doctor Who. In fact, three years before the story mentioned in that context, Day of the Daleks provided a particularly bleak portrayal of the future. Here the wars that result from the destruction of a peace conference lead to a Dalek take-over of Earth. According to David J. Howe and Stephen James Walker, in Doctor Who: The Television Companion, this serial presents one of only two scenarios in the original version of Doctor Who in which an alien invasion of our planet has actually succeeded. Nevertheless, unlike Man Out of Time, Day of the Daleks ends on a note of optimism, as it is made clear that the alien invasion can be prevented. Hopes for peace do not lie in The Doctor's hands, however; they reside in the fate of the conference that will take place after the climax of the final episode.

20. Noreen Ackland Interview. In: The Prisoner In-depth Tape 3. VHS video cassette. TR 7 Productions: Borehamwood, 1992.

21. White, M. and Ali, J. The official Prisoner companion. Sidgwick and Jackson: London, 1988.

22. The Prisoner: Patrick McGoohan Interviewed By Warner Troyer – The Troyer Interview, Part Two. The Prisoner: Music, FAQs, background, episode guide, spoofs. URL: http://www.the-prisoner-6.freeserve.co.uk/troyer2.htm (accessed: 23 September 2013). Transcript of 1977 interview.

23. Quoted in: Nobel, S. and Goldsborough, D. The Prisoner puzzle. Ontario Educational Communications Authority: Toronto, Ontario, 1978.

CHAPTER ELEVEN
A Village Like No Other and a School that is Different.

"Everything seems so perfect but really everyone's watched, controlled, doing what we decide". Those words could easily have been spoken by a conspiratorial Number Two to a new colleague in one of the episodes of *The Prisoner* but they are actually part of a speech by Martin Smith, the teenage hero of the children's serial *Codename Icarus*, written by Richard Cooper. Let us begin this chapter by taking a moment to consider the broad plot similarities between this five-part BBC drama and Patrick McGoohan's series. In each production, an individual with exceptional talents leaves conventional society and undergoes a prolonged period of life in an idiosyncratic community with its own norms and conventions. The leaders are virtually all-knowing and advanced surveillance systems miss little of importance. For those inside, contact with the world beyond is not permitted. Uncomfortable with what is required of him and with how the oppressive community is run, the disaffected hero rejects this society and makes an unsuccessful attempt to flee. For much of his time in the community, he fights a lone battle. Support from his fellows frequently proves either non-existent or less than reliable, although, eventually, he is able to leave with help from others. In deciding to go, the hero declines an invitation to take up a position of great importance which is offered to him by one of the society's leaders. In the final episode, the mastermind who exercises supreme power in the community stands revealed. Ultimately, the hero opts to return to regular society but knows that the consequences of his decision pose their own challenges. He would seem to face a difficult future…

Whereas The Prisoner is kidnapped from his home and taken to The Village, Martin Smith voluntarily enters the school Falconleigh, which has been established by the shadowy Icarus Foundation. Since Martin, an adolescent mathematical genius, is ridiculed and unappreciated in his own school, it would seem that he has little to lose by making a new life elsewhere. Even though Martin's decision to go to Falconleigh is his own, he, like The Prisoner, has been "targeted". Through using his school's computer to complete a series of mathematical challenges, Martin has come to the attention of the head of Falconleigh, John Doll, who persuades Martin to join him. It is not long before, as the *Curious British Telly* website points out, the serial offers some "complex investigations into the concept of free will and choice",[1] and similarities with *The Prisoner* in this regard are quickly evident.

The education system is represented unsympathetically in both *The Prisoner* and *Codename Icarus*. Lewis Greifer has explained how, at the time when he wrote the script for *The General*, his children were taking their O and A Levels. Whilst they were very receptive to studying from information, they resented the focus on rote learning for examinations which had led to the development in schools of what Greifer terms a "sausage grinder" mentality.[2] In the eventual episode, the author's low regard for teaching methods that promote such learning by heart, rather than curiosity and understanding, is obvious. In *Codename Icarus*, only one scene takes place in a conventional classroom. Here Martin is bullied and belittled by an overbearing teacher who is quick to sneer at his young pupil and reluctant to make any effort to empathise with him.

The cosmopolitan nature of The Village is demonstrated in the first *Prisoner* episode, and subsequent instalments emphasise further that residents are from many parts of the world. In the BBC serial, it is firmly established that the Icarus Foundation has founded schools similar to Falconleigh in various locations across the globe. Thus the international reach of those responsible for Falconleigh and The Village is plain.

When Martin begins his time at Falconleigh and is assigned his own room, Doll helps him to settle in by giving him the opportunity to select his own furniture from a catalogue. We will remember, of course, how the transition into Village life for new inmates in *The Prisoner* is eased by the authorities accommodating them in exact replicas of their own homes. Significantly, a girl who becomes one of Martin's few friends in Falconleigh, Sue Kleiner, spurns the accepted practice within the school by refusing to choose her furniture from the catalogue. Although we generally learn little about the other adolescents at

Falconleigh, in much the same way that we discover hardly anything about many of the other inmates in *The Prisoner*, it is obvious from Sue's display of self-assertiveness that Martin is not the only pupil here who can think for themselves and we can draw certain parallels in this sense between Sue and *Prisoner* characters like the old man with the stick in *Checkmate*. Women in *The Prisoner* are frequently portrayed with little depth and, overall, Sue scarcely fares better in *Codename Icarus*. She is the only female character in the serial and, as the *Curious British Telly* website notes, even she "seems rather redundant as she's mostly relegated to acting as a feed for working out Martin's mood".[3]

Just as it quickly becomes evident that The Village is a community unlike any other, oddities soon emerge in relation to Falconleigh. This is a school with no academic terms, and holiday entitlements – if there are any – are not taken by the pupils. There is a squash court but this is never seen used for sport. Rather, it is the usual venue for battles of will between pupils and those in positions of authority at Falconleigh. The squash court is thus an arena for games of a rather more sinister kind than we might expect. In contrast to the usual situation in schools, Martin is referred to as "Sir" by Farley, his teacher, who, in turn, expects Martin to address him by surname. Doll himself requests that Martin know him as John, Jack or Jacko. At Falconleigh, it is the teachers who learn from the pupils. Alistair D. McGown and Mark J. Docherty describe these role reversals as "bizarre" and "almost perverse". (p. 157)[4] Nevertheless, the fact that on one occasion Martin is rebuked for listening to his radio whilst Doll is trying to talk to him reminds us that, even at Falconleigh, at least some of the values that underpin traditional schools remain evident.

When Number Six undertakes his early explorations of The Village his exchanges with others are awkward and a similar uneasiness is apparent in *Codename Icarus*. One of the first fellow pupils Martin meets is evasive when he asks her name and is reluctant to discuss her work, declaring that the school's leadership feels that such conversation would "waste energy and discourage invention". Whereas The Village can be seen as an exaggerated reflection of our own society, Falconleigh is quite different; it is clearly an unusual academy for adolescent geniuses. Initially, it would seem that Martin is free to leave whenever he wishes. There are no insurmountable physical barriers and no security staff patrol its boundaries. Yet, when Martin attempts to go, he is thwarted. Those who manage Falconleigh employ an effective combination of drugs, hypnosis and other forms of psychological conditioning to maintain the status quo – techniques very similar to some of those adopted by the Village authorities against not only Number Six but other inmates, too. For example, in *Checkmate*, such conditioning is instrumental in the authorities' efforts to bring both The Rook and The Queen under their control. In *Codename Icarus*, a key weapon in the leaders' armoury lies in convincing Martin that he is admired and valued at Falconleigh, whereas in the wider world he would either be mercilessly exploited or be treated as an outcast. In truth, Martin has good reason to be fearful of the life beyond Falconleigh. In the final episode, British intelligence personnel treat him as bait in a trap in order to bring the Icarus Foundation into the open. Although Martin is very much the hero of the serial, in this instance it is clear that he is subservient to a higher purpose. A similar pattern emerges in the *Prisoner* story *Do Not Forsake Me Oh My Darling*, where Number Six is used by the Village authorities as a pawn in their efforts to trace Professor Seltzman.

It is obvious from the outset what is required of Number Six in *The Prisoner* – he is expected to disclose certain information about why he resigned from a top secret post. In *Codename Icarus*, only gradually does it become apparent that the calculations undertaken by Martin will ultimately result in the development of a deadly quark bomb. Already, the work of Falconleigh's pupils has been employed by the Icarus Foundation to pioneer a method of destroying new missiles that are being tested by the British military. Like The Village, Omega and *Blake's 7*'s Federation, the Icarus Foundation is frequently seen represented through a distinctive insignia, and at the end of episode one, this plays an important part in alerting viewers to the fact that it is the work of pupils attached to the Icarus Foundation that has been responsible for the anti-missile system we have witnessed in action.

Before long, Martin becomes suspicious of the purposes of those behind Falconleigh. If he were to adopt an attitude of passive acceptance, like many of the Villagers in *The Prisoner*, it would seem possible that he could become happy in his new environment. Certainly in the first half of the serial, Sue seems perfectly settled in the school. At one point, she confides wistfully to Martin, "I don't know what I'll do when I finish at Falconleigh. Anywhere else would be terrible." Martin, in contrast, is soon questioning and independent. Like Number Six, Martin does not enter into any romantic relationships; even he and Sue seem no more than close friends. At one point, after they have made plans to escape together from Falconleigh, Sue reneges on their agreement. Although it is clear that she has not deliberately betrayed him and she is as much a victim of the school's mind control strategies as Martin is at other points in the serial, it is easy for *Prisoner* fans to draw comparisons between her decision to stay and some of those situations in McGoohan's series that point to the untrustworthiness of women.

A feature of the Village environment in *The Prisoner* is the way in which the gaiety and carnival-like atmosphere that is so often evident changes to nightmarish menace in moments. Similar switches are apparent at Falconleigh when the victim is subjected to Icarus's mind games. In the first, Farley shifts without warning from addressing Martin with great respect to dismissing him as a "freak", a "guttersnipe" and a "working class yobbo who can't even string two words together and make sense". Rob Buckley highlights Martin's slow degeneration "into a pale wreck" during the course of these mind games.[5] Number Six also, of course, undergoes a considerable ordeal in The Village. Although various methods are used by authorities in their attempts to break The Prisoner's spirit, the verbal games of "cat and mouse" between Number Six and Number Two form a frequently recurring scenario. Comparable scenes in *Codename Icarus* involve confrontations in the Falconleigh squash court between Martin and Farley. Indeed, for *Prisoner* fans, the spartan appearance and claustrophobic atmosphere of this place will, no doubt, be felt to echo the nature of the Embryo Room in *Once Upon a Time*.

We may well ponder as to the fate of those inmates within The Village who do accede to Number Two's wishes. The state of Dutton, whom we see in *Dance of the Dead*, may offer some clues. Viewers are also left uncertain as to the sanctions that are taken against pupils at Falconleigh who either fail to cooperate or are unable to deliver work of the calibre that the Icarus Foundation seeks. Doll is less than forthcoming in satisfying Martin's curiosity about the previous occupant of the room that has been allocated to him. All Martin is told is that the boy proved a "disappointment" and his early promise went unfulfilled.

Although in *The Prisoner* Number Two remains ignorant throughout of the reasons for Number Six's resignation, beyond this it seems there is very little about The Prisoner that is unknown to The Village's leaders. It is an indication of the depth in which his life has been investigated that in *Arrival*, Number Two is aware that The Prisoner eats two eggs with his bacon for breakfast and in *The Chimes of Big Ben*, Number Two discovers from Number Six's file that at the age of 15 he was "top of his class in woodwork". Similarly, in *Codename Icarus*, the mastermind behind Falconleigh announces proudly that he is familiar with every detail of Martin's work.

Both Number Six and Martin are regarded as "special cases" by the leaders of the communities. It is made clear at the climax of the final episode of *Codename Icarus* that Martin, through his calculations that will lead to the creation of the quark bomb, represents the culmination of all of the Foundation's endeavours. Even before this revelation, it is apparent that Martin commands special respect at Falconleigh. Earlier in the same instalment, the supreme power behind the Icarus Foundation commands that, whilst the other youngsters may leave, Martin, who by this point has escaped, must be returned to the school.

One of the key strategies employed by the Village authorities in *The Prisoner* is the infiltration of the community by supporters of the régime. Consequently, Number Six is frequently at a loss to determine whom he can trust. This issue also arises in *Codename Icarus*, although here in the wider world rather than in Falconleigh. Over the course of the five episodes, we learn that either members of the Icarus Foundation or sympathisers of it have become an integral part of the fabric of Britain's security services and possibly even the government. Andy Rutherford, a naval intelligence officer who seeks to find out more about the goings-on at Falconleigh, discovers that one of his most trusted contacts is entirely treacherous. Infiltration is also, however, a weapon that is used against Falconleigh since when Rutherford launches a rescue mission to free Martin, he poses as a new teacher at the school after kidnapping Farley. In both *The Prisoner* and *Codename Icarus* schemes by apparently well-meaning outsiders lead to circumstances which eventually result in the hero being returned to the community from which he has tried to escape. In *Many Happy Returns*, despite what would seem to be efforts to help Number Six by British intelligence officers, The Prisoner finds himself back in The Village at the end of the episode and after being liberated from Falconleigh by Rutherford, the psychological conditioning that Martin has received compels him to go back to the school.

Whereas there has been much debate about where and when *The Prisoner* is set, it is beyond dispute that *Codename Icarus* takes place in contemporary Britain, specifically that of the early 1980s when the programme was made. Like the ITV series, it deals with contemporary concerns. The background of the Cold War is common to both productions, and the theme of the arms race is especially prevalent in *Codename Icarus*. The Cold War distrust between nations and the computer that Martin is seen to use at his school in the opening episode are probably the elements that date the serial most obviously. Given the time in which *The Prisoner* was produced, it is perhaps inevitable that some viewers would immediately ask whether The Village is a community that has been established by the "East" or the "West". Yet, as we have seen, the truth may well be that it belongs to neither camp. In time, we learn that Falconleigh, too, bears no allegiance of this kind. The sophistication of *The Prisoner* is such that, once we have watched the totality of the programme's 17 episodes, we may feel that any resolution which associated The Village firmly with one particular power bloc would be rather too facile and the same may be said of any comparable revelation about Falconleigh in *Codename Icarus*. Ultimately, viewers discover that the Icarus Foundation is the brainchild of an individual who aims to sell to both sides the developments that have been made possible by his young scholars. Whilst viewers may empathise with his distrust of both the East **and** the West and applaud his desire to return the money that is made to the young people who study in the Icarus schools, his hope that he can keep the men of power in his own power, "making them sweat in a dance of fear" inevitably leads to the conclusion that he is something of a megalomaniac. Chapter Eight drew attention to the argument that there are close connections between The Village and Fascism and, with the aim of the Icarus Foundation lying in creating a technocratic society run by scientific experts, it is not difficult to make comparisons between this form of elitism and certain Nazis doctrines. We can also draw parallels between Icarus's flawed technocratic aims and McGoohan's personal belief that the modern scientific world "imprisons" and "engulfs" the individual. (p. 1)[6]

In both The Village and Falconleigh the protagonist who has been seen to exercise day-to-day leadership is shown not to be the holder of ultimate power. In *The Prisoner*, Number Two's subservience is evident at various points in the overall saga as he converses with a superior but the identity of this leader remains unknown until, of course, the last episode. In *Codename Icarus*, after John Doll has introduced himself as the man who runs Falconleigh, for much of the first half of the serial viewers accept him as the person who wields the greatest authority within the school. Although dialogue in the last three episodes reveals that Doll is little more than an Icarus employee himself, an unexpected disclosure is still to come at the very end. Just as the fact that The Prisoner himself is shown to be Number One will amaze those seeing *Fall Out* for the first time and who are unaware of what will take place in the episode, so the revelation that the Icarus Foundation is the creation of German scientist Edward Froelich is designed to elicit a reaction of surprise. Froelich has appeared at various points in the serial already but has not been properly identified and early on, in particular, he has been presented as a rather more modest character. In the second episode, Froelich, in fact, describes himself as a mere "technician". At the beginning of the third instalment, Froelich arrives at Falconleigh by helicopter, thus inviting comparisons with the way in which many senior officials are brought to The Village in *The Prisoner*.

Like *The Prisoner*, *Codename Icarus* is very much concerned with the moral dimension behind the use of science. There are striking similarities between dialogue from *Do Not Forsake Me Oh My Darling* (reported in Chapter One) and a significant exchange in the final instalment of Richard Cooper's serial. Musing on the nature of science, Sue says, "The atomic bomb was terrible but the original research – splitting the atom – that's led on to so much – energy which may save the world one day. It's not the actual knowledge that's bad it's just…" Martin's brother completes her train of thought: "It's just what the rest of us do with it." This is one of several dialogues in the last two episodes that emphasise the ethical issue at the heart of the serial. According to Buckley, although the significance of such discussions might be "mostly wasted" on an audience of children, the underlying theme was "ultimately the show's raison d'être".[7] McGown and Docherty imply that they feel the moral questions raised in Cooper's serial are given too high a profile, as they are critical of the limited degree of exciting drama in the serial. They write, "Heralded primarily as an action thriller, it actually contains very little in the way of action or thrills." (p. 157)[8] Nevertheless, *Codename Icarus* does include such significant "thriller" elements as kidnapping, impersonation and a car chase. The balance between the different aims underpinning *The Prisoner* has also drawn criticism. James O'Neill, for example, writes that *Fall Out* "is nearly all allegory and no plot", (p. 269)[9] whilst Chris R. Tame feels that realism was sacrificed for symbolism which, on occasion, was ambiguous.[10]

Three of the programmes examined in *Unique But Similar*, namely *The Prisoner*, *Look and Read: Cloud Burst* and *Codename Icarus*, explore to a significant degree the use and abuse of science. The fact that, chronologically, *The Prisoner* was the first of these may lead some readers to imagine that McGoohan's series was an innovator in addressing the theme in a television series. Such a viewpoint would be ill-advised, however. Indeed, *The Avengers* episode *The Positive Negative Man* was presenting its own treatment of the issue as *The Prisoner* was first being shown in Britain. Here, while one scientist explains to Steed the potential of "broadcast power" in providing energy for cars, aircraft and even entire cities, a renegade former colleague is exploiting its high voltage possibilities for murderous purposes. Moreover, the *Outer Limits* episode *The Forms of Things Unknown*, which was briefly mentioned in the last chapter in relation to the good and bad effects of time travel, was first aired in the US as early as May 1964 – over three years before *Arrival* was seen in Britain.

For all his status as the hero of *Codename Icarus*, Martin, like Number Six, is by no means a wholly appealing character. As Buckley comments, he is "arrogant", "mean" and treats even Sue "with disdain".[11] Martin is clearly not a boy who is easily satisfied. He is a misfit in the school he attends at the beginning of the first episode; then later, at Falconleigh, whilst the other pupils generally seem to accept the régime, he resents the strictures that are imposed, as well as objecting on moral grounds to the nature of the work he is undertaking. How far his reactions establish Martin as a genuine individual and rebel in the mould of Number Six and how far he is simply a victim of his own teenage angst is debatable. Just as the last scene of *The Prisoner* would seem to suggest that the hero must fight his old battles again, so after the ending of

Codename Icarus we know that Martin must once more face the suspicions, labels and injustices of the mainstream education system if he is to realise his undoubted potential and achieve his aim of putting science to use for noble purposes. Indeed, it is revealing that one of the motivations behind Martin's temporary return to Falconleigh in the final episode was his fear that the more conventional alternative was no better. M. Keith Booker suggests that although a key theme within *The Prisoner* is Number Six's dogged persistence in attempting to escape from The Village, the wider world is portrayed in such harsh terms that there is "a significant doubt in the series whether that return is even worthwhile". (p. 82)[12] Viewers of *Codename Icarus* may well be equally uncertain as to where Martin's best interests would be most effectively served.

References and Notes

1. Codename Icarus. Curious British Telly, 24 October 2015. URL: http://www.curiousbritishtelly.co.uk/2015/10/codename-icarus.html (accessed: 23 February 2017).
2. Lewis Greifer Interview. In: The Prisoner In-depth Tape 5. VHS video cassette. TR 7 Productions: Borehamwood, 1993.
3. Codename Icarus. op. cit.
4. McGown, A. D. and Docherty, M. J. The Hill and beyond: Children's television drama – An encyclopedia. BFI: London, 2003.
5. Buckley, R. Lost gems: Codename Icarus (1981). The medium is not enough TV blog, 12 February 2010. URL: http://www.the-medium-is-not-enough.com/2010/02/lost_gems_codename_icarus_1981.php (accessed: 23 February 2017).
6. Quoted in: Nobel, S. and Goldsborough, D. The Prisoner puzzle. Ontario Educational Communications Authority: Toronto, Ontario, 1978.
7. Buckley, R. op. cit.
8. McGown, A. D. and Docherty, M. J. op. cit.
9. O'Neill, J. Sci-fi on tape: A comprehensive guide to over 1,250 science fiction and fantasy films on video. Billboard: New York, 1997.
10. Tame, C. R. Different values: An analysis of Patrick McGoohan's The Prisoner. Libertarian Reprints, 1, 1983. Reprint of 1974 work. URL: http://www.libertarian.co.uk/lapubs/libre/libre001.pdf (accessed: 23 February 2017).
11. Buckley, R. op. cit.
12. Booker, M. K. Strange TV: Innovative television series from The Twilight Zone to The X-Files. Greenwood: Westport, Connecticut, 2002.

CHAPTER TWELVE
Two Struggles Against
Oppression

In Chapter Eight, it was noted that first-time, 1960s viewers of *The Prisoner* who were expecting to see some sort of conventional follow-up to *Danger Man* would have reacted to the true nature of the programme with surprise, in much the same way as people familiar with Gerry Anderson's Supermarionation productions may well have been taken unawares by the more adult oriented and hard-hitting *UFO* which followed. Another drama that provoked considerable shock among those watching was the 1987 Television South (TVS) serial *Knights of God.* Alistair D. McGown and Mark J. Docherty feel that for parents used to settling down to family dramas on a Sunday afternoon, this "harsh futuristic drama" was a marked diversion from the norm. (p. 202)[1] Disquiet was not, it would seem, limited to viewers. The *Encyclopedia of Science Fiction* reports that *Knights of God*, like *UFO* before it, "caused jitters among ITV network bosses". In this instance, they were "worried that the serial might prove too gritty for family viewing in its Sunday teatime slot". (p. 215)[2]

It is a measure of its uncompromising substance and style that although the serial goes unmentioned in the *Very British Dystopias* radio documentary that was referred to in Section II, *Knights of God* could quite justifiably have been addressed in the programme. Presenter Steven Fielding explains that dystopian stories deal with fears for the future, and often reflect the anxieties of the time when they were written, especially in terms of challenges to democracy.[3] *Knights of God* meets these criteria as effectively as many of the works featured in *Very British Dystopias*. Issues such as the north-south divide and unemployment are raised by one of the characters when establishing the background to the situation that is in place as the serial opens, and these were very much matters of concern when the programme was made. *Knights of God* portrays the events in Britain after a Civil War has been fought in the year 2000. Such turmoil could not easily be dismissed as fanciful speculation by contemporary audiences – just a few years before the serial's production, the real life riots in places such as Brixton, Toxteth and Handsworth had shocked the nation. The programme postulates the scenario that, by 2020, the royal family has been deposed, the whereabouts of the rightful King of England are unknown and a new ruling order, the eponymous Knights of God, is in control. The régime does not, though, go unopposed. Like *The Prisoner*, *Knights of God* is concerned with the classic dystopian conflict of the strong state against the rebellious individual. However, whereas for much of the time Number Six fights a lone battle, here we see groups of dissenters taking on the oppressors, and we know that pockets of resistance exist in various parts of the country. Parallels with *Blake's 7* are difficult to escape, especially as Gareth Thomas played a prominent dissident in both series and in each case the will of the establishment is enforced by forbidding, black-clad guards.

Chapter Nine outlined two of the ways we can interpret the status of Number Six. At one end of the spectrum, he can be regarded as a noble campaigner for freedom, at the other a malignant non-conformist. As far as the Village authorities are concerned, he is, to quote Alain Carrazé and Hélène Oswald, the "eternal spoilsport". (p. 91)[4] The rebels in *Blake's 7* can also be viewed as dangerous subversives, and the resistance fighters in *Knights of God* may be understood in comparable terms. Although viewers are likely to sympathise with these oppressed people, the most militant of them are dismissed as "terrorists" by the founder and leader of the Knights, Prior Mordrin. Nevertheless, one of the dissidents, young Gervase Edwards, who forms the hero of the serial, is, in time, initiated into the Knights of God order. We can draw parallels here with the way in which, in *Fall Out*, Number Six is offered a position of power within The Village. Even when faced with these opportunities, however, both characters still take every chance to assert their individuality, with The Prisoner rejecting the invitation of leadership and Gervase challenging his superiors through insubordination and threats to desert.

Many commentators emphasise the quaint charm of The Village and it is not unusual to see the place compared to establishments long familiar to us. M. Keith Booker suggests that it "looks precisely like a theme park", (p. 87)[5] and *The*

Encyclopedia of Science Fiction detects parallels between The Village on one hand and holiday resorts and old people's homes on the other.[6] Indeed, George Markstein has described The Village as "a sort of miniature Butlins". (p. 90)[7] Yet, the intrusion of high technology, especially in terms of surveillance equipment, is frequent. There is a similar juxtaposition in *Knights of God*. Much of the technology we see in the TVS serial is concentrated in the hands of the ruling régime, and, in this context, closed circuit television cameras, computers, weaponry and communications systems figure prominently. The Knights' control room is especially impressive in terms of the technology in evidence, even if, on occasion, its roots in the era in which the serial was made are obvious. Helicopters play a significant role in both *The Prisoner* and *Knights of God*. In the former, they provide a key means of moving people to and from The Village. Indeed, since much of the surrounding area is consumed by mountains and the sea, many other forms of transport are problematic. In *Knights of God*, helicopters fulfil this function, too, and they are also frequently seen deployed for the pursuit and apprehending of rebels.

The very basic way of life led by the masses in *Knights of God* may well remind viewers of the simple existence we associate with the people in John Christopher's *Prince in Waiting* trilogy of novels for youngsters. Lillian Biermann Wehmeyer comments that the language, dress and customs apparent in these stories are reminiscent of feudal Britain.[8] Whereas much of the world of The Village would seem entirely alien, various aspects of life in 2020 are instantly recognisable to us. Whilst the sport of kosho that we see in *The Prisoner* emphasises the strangeness of this other place, the fact that squash is played by certain members of the Knights of God order affirms that this future society is not totally different from our own.

The writer of *Knights of God* was Richard Cooper, who, just a few years earlier, had been responsible for *Codename Icarus*. The scale of the two dramas is different, with the 1981 BBC work mainly devoted to the experiences of one particular boy in one particular school, i.e. Falconleigh, and *Knights of God* dealing with the fight for control of a whole country but there are certain continuities of theme in relation to coercion, indoctrination and mind control. Like The Village in *The Prisoner*, the "education and retraining camp" to which Gervase is sent is actually a place of incarceration and here, too, we see various acts of rebellion. They range from petty insolence towards authority to escape breakouts. Similar in look and austerity to a war-time concentration camp, the education and retraining centre is also employed for brainwashing, and Prior Mordrin uses drugs to implant in Gervase's head the post-hypnotic suggestions that he must destroy the reputation of his father, condemn what he stands for and eliminate Mordrin's greatest enemy, who is orchestrating all the resistance against the order. Mind control is, of course, equally important in *The Prisoner*. However, whereas Number Six typically overcomes any such incursions into his mind through his own strength of personality, in *Knights of God* it is Gervase's devotion to the girl Julia that enables him to survive intact. In this instance, it is clear that love does indeed conquer all.[9] This is in contrast to the argument presented in the last episode of *The Prisoner*. Here The Butler and Numbers Two, Six and Forty-eight make their violent escape from The Village as we hear The Beatles's song *All You Need is Love*. The juxtaposition of the sight and sound messages would seem to suggest that there are times when love is not all that is needed – on the contrary, in the Goodman interview, Patrick McGoohan points out that situations arise when armed confrontation can effectively "clear the air" and return the situation to "square one".[10]

Beyond the use of drugs and indoctrination, we can see further parallels, at a range of levels, between the Knights' strategies for maintaining control and those of The Village's leaders. In broad terms, control of the mass media is an important feature of both régimes. In *The Prisoner, The Tally Ho* newspaper forms a mouthpiece for the Village authorities, whilst *The Order* fulfils a similar function in the TVS serial. With regard to more specific tactics, in the *Prisoner* episode *Do Not Forsake Me Oh My Darling* Number Two releases the hero in the expectation that he will lead Village pursuers to Professor Seltzman. In *Knights of God*, too, captors are willing to free the hero physically in order to perform an act that would strengthen their position, namely to weaken the rebels by eliminating a major threat to those ruling the country. Number Two's scheme achieves the desired result as, ultimately, Professor Seltzman is traced and brought to The Village but Mordrin's designs are thwarted.

Just as Number Two has at his disposal the not inconsiderable might of all The Village's resources, so Mordrin is backed by the Knights' military power. Mordrin is not, however, immovable and, like the Number Two we see in *Hammer Into Anvil*, over time he shows himself to be suspicious and obsessive. "I trust no-one," Mordrin admits to a close colleague in episode nine and by the last but one instalment he is clearly highly unstable. There is no evidence in *Hammer Into Anvil* that any of his inferiors are **actually** plotting against Number Two but it may still be questionable to label him "paranoid" in the purest sense; after all, Number Six does carry out a vendetta against him. As Susan Nobel and Diana Goldsborough point out, "the persecution was real." (p. 17)[11] *The Encyclopedia of TV Science Fiction* shows how the essence of *The Invaders* can be summed up by "the graffiti cliché: 'Just because you're paranoid, doesn't mean they're **not** out to get you.'" (p. 187)[12] This saying can usefully be employed in relation to Number Two in *Hammer Into Anvil* as well. There may be no Village-wide conspiracy here but Number Six is from the outset of the episode intent on breaking him. Similarly, in *Knights of God* there is a determined attempt by the Head of State Security – the manipulative Brother Hugo – to undermine and eventually unseat Mordrin. The major difference is that in *Knights of God* the threat lies within the order, whereas in *The Prisoner* the perpetrator is one of the dissidents.

In the closing stages of each programme, a shock revelation is made in relation to the hero's personal identity. Just as Number One is unmasked as The Prisoner, in *Knights of God* Gervase is ultimately shown to be the rightful King of England. With hindsight we can see why it was so significant in *The Prisoner* that Number Six be treated as a special case, and, in the same way, we eventually understand why Gervase's father, Owen Edwards, told the boy as early as the opening moments of the first episode that it was vital that he lived. The importance of Gervase is a theme that recurs throughout the serial. After the shock disclosures, though, the mood of the conclusions is quite different. *The Prisoner* would seem to end pessimistically, whilst the climax of *Knights of God* sees a new king on the throne and the hope of a fresh start. Still, as in *The Prisoner*, there is something of a cyclical element here, as the country has effectively returned to the position that was in place before the Civil War of 2000. As if to emphasise this development, the Union Jack flag is returned to a place of honour.

Gervase and The Prisoner can both be considered somewhat self-destructive individuals, although for very different reasons. In *Knights of God*, Gervase's negative state of mind is induced by Mordrin's drugs and hypnosis – Gervase is conditioned to destroy the King of England whom he finally discovers to be himself. It is quite easy to see how such Mordrin's psychological tampering could result in either suicide or a mental breakdown for Gervase. In *The Prisoner*, we may well ask ourselves why, if he is truly in charge of The Village, Number Six allows himself to experience the various ordeals that he undergoes during the course of the series. Matthew White and Jaffer Ali suggest that his aim may have been to test the security of The Village.[13] Following this "rational" line of argument, however, means understanding *The Prisoner* purely in dramatic terms when the relationship between Number Six and Number One is actually a much more abstract issue concerning the nature of man. Again, it is appropriate to consider the Martin Buber quotation that was alluded to in Section II – "It turns out that the answer is given on a different level from that on which the question [in this case 'Who is Number One?'] was formulated." (p. 202)[14]

In both programmes, there is a strong quest element. For much of *The Prisoner*, Number Six is intent on pursuing information and freedom. He seeks to engineer or otherwise exploit every possible opportunity to escape but at the end of *Once Upon a Time*, he makes it clear after emerging triumphant from his Degree Absolute ordeal that his immediate priority lies in learning the identity of Number One. This concern is consistent with ideas within the original synopsis used to outline the essential premise of *The Prisoner*, the document draws attention to Number Six's unceasing efforts to discover the truth, specifically in relation to why he is a captive and who is holding him.[15] In *Knights of God*, meanwhile, Gervase, after becoming separated from Julia, first seeks to find her. Then, from the tenth episode onwards, he concentrates on locating the deposed King of England with the aim of re-establishing him on the throne. In both series, the hero's quest to find a particular person culminates in an unusual form of self-discovery. Speaking in the final episode, one of Gervase's allies tells him, "The King had to be found within yourself". We may say that the *Knights of God* narrative would be incomplete without such a self-discovery. In the same way, Number One had to be found within The Prisoner if McGoohan's message about the nature of man was to be established. Moreover, McGoohan himself has argued that since *The Prisoner* was an allegorical series, it must have an appropriately allegorical ending in terms of the identity of Number One.[16] The revelation surrounding Gervase's real status is not the only *Knights of God* plot twist which centres on the identity of a key protagonist. In an earlier development, it emerges that Mordrin's own father is himself a prominent dissident.

Commentators such as White and Ali suggest that The Village may be viewed as the product of some kind of unified world power.[17] Nevertheless, Number Two's comment in *The Chimes of Big Ben* that, one day, he would like to see the whole world patterned on The Village template implies that the community which becomes increasingly familiar to us over the 17 episodes is, at this stage, something of a prototype. An alternative interpretation is put forward by Roger Langley, who tentatively postulates that the place where Number Six finds himself at the end of *Many Happy Returns* could be similar to The Village "which No. 6 left but... a different one. Maybe there are Villages like this all over the world." (p. 16)[18] On a more abstract level, Langley points to how The Prisoner's place of incarceration may also be understood as a metaphor for our own "global village". (p. 16)[19] The thoughtful viewer may wonder how far the model of government we see in *Knights of God* may extend. Might similar movements arise in other parts of Europe or indeed in other continents? Or perhaps, if it had been given the opportunity to do so, the régime portrayed in the programme might have expanded beyond Britain.

We saw in Chapter Eight how, for some writers, The Village may be deemed to be Fascist in nature. Links are often made, too, between Right wing ideologies and the Knights of God order. Indeed, in seeking to offer a succinct summary of the programme's content, *The Complete Directory to Science Fiction, Fantasy and Horror Television Series* suggests that "Nazi priests in charge of Britain" would constitute a fair description. (p. 417)[20] No doubt some readers will note parallels between the Knights' emblem of two crossed swords and the Nazi swastika, although, in truth, the former is probably equally likely bring to mind the Communist hammer and sickle motif. What is clear is that whilst the penny farthing design often seen in *The Prisoner* is so ambiguous and esoteric that McGoohan has had to explain its significance on more than one occasion,[21] there can be little doubt that the crossed swords pattern which is ubiquitous in *Knights of God* evokes images of conflict and military might. Despite the links highlighted in Chapter Ten between the "Be seeing you!" salute and the early Christian sign of the fish, it is unlikely that even those readers who attach particular importance to the connection will be able to detect a coherent religious theme within *The Prisoner*. According to White and Ali, "many observers have interpreted [*The Prisoner's*] religious symbolism and themes in a variety of… contradictory ways". (p. 171)[22] The Knights of God régime, meanwhile, is avowedly anti-Christian, as well as anti-monarchist. In the second episode, a leading member of the establishment denounces Christianity as a "religion for slaves" and "weaklings". The reference to God in the Knights' name may be designed to bestow on the order a certain respectability but it does not impress the Archbishop of Canterbury, Thomas Armstrong, who, in episode eleven, speaks bitterly to Gervase and Julia about how the Knights have "perverted" the meaning of the word.

At several junctures in *Unique But Similar* the point has been made that, in the eyes of various people, and indeed in those of McGoohan himself, *The Prisoner* was overlong. It is revealing, in fact, that when the new version of the series was broadcast in 2009, only six episodes were made. Section I suggested that, essentially, each of the seventeen instalments in the original series presents a treatment of one of only three main scenarios – endeavours by The Prisoner to escape, efforts by him to subvert Village schemes or his attempts to remain intact in the event of plots against him. Lewis Greifer feels that there was a distinct tendency among scriptwriters to fall back on the first plot type.[23] Piers D. Britton and Simon J. Barker find certain aspects of *The Prisoner* "remorselessly repetitive", (p. 97)[24] and we may well form the opinion that scope for the creation of situations which were fundamentally new within the confines of the programme's format was limited. For McGown and Docherty, *Knights of*

God was also too protracted. They point to the frequency of scenes that involved "much gallivanting across tough country landscapes and battle after battle with the rogue freedom fighters". (p. 203)[25] Just as McGoohan would have preferred *The Prisoner* to take the form of a tighter, seven-part mini-series,[26] McGown and Docherty would have liked to have seen *Knights of God* as a shorter, ten-part serial.[27] Some of the various twists and turns within the narrative are typical elements of the action and adventure genre but they may also remind *Prisoner* fans of key developments within the 1960s programme. The way in which, at the end of episode seven, Gervase is captured by another group of dissidents after a misunderstanding is reminiscent of how fellow would-be escapee The Rook delivers The Prisoner into Number Two's hands in *Checkmate*.

Notwithstanding the criticism of their respective lengths, both programmes are often lauded as lavishly produced. The magazine *SFX* goes so far as to describe *Knights of God* as "wonderfully epic", (p. 122)[28] and *The Complete Directory to Science Fiction, Fantasy and Horror Television Series* praises it as "expensive and ambitious". (p. 417)[29] It has been reported, in fact, that the thirteen-part serial cost as much as a million pounds to make.[30] The profile of the programme was certainly raised considerably by a strong cast that included John Woodvine, Patrick Troughton and former *Prisoner* actor Nigel Stock. Whatever the motivation behind the decision to change Number Two's identity each week, there can be no doubt that it enabled a host of well known actors and actresses to play major roles within *The Prisoner*, with the result that the overall cast of players is as impressive as that in *Knights of God*. Yet, whilst *The Prisoner* has become a major cult, largely as a result of the absence of both repeat screenings and commercial releases on video cassette or DVD *Knights of God* tends to be forgotten today.

References and Notes

1. McGown, A. D. and Docherty, M. J. The Hill and beyond: Children's television drama – An encyclopedia. BFI: London, 2003.
2. Fulton, R. The encyclopedia of TV science fiction. Boxtree: London, 1990.
3. Archive On 4: Very British Dystopias. BBC Radio 4. 15 June 2013.
4. Carrazé, A. and Oswald, H. The Prisoner: A televisionary masterpiece. Virgin: London, 1990.
5. Booker, M. K. Strange TV: Innovative television series from The Twilight Zone to The X-Files. Greenwood: Westport, Connecticut, 2002.
6. Brosnan, J. and Nicholls, P. The Prisoner. In: Nicholls, P. (ed.) The encyclopedia of science fiction: An illustrated A to Z. Granada: St. Albans, 1979, pp. 475–476.

7. Where The Secret Agent Is Whisked Away. In: Goodman, R. (ed.) George Markstein and The Prisoner. pandqmedia: Berwyn, Denbighshire, 2014, pp. 78–95.

8. Wehmeyer, L. B. Images in a crystal ball: World futures in novels for young people. Libraries Unlimited: Littleton, Colorado, 1981.

9. Knights of God is not the only science fiction television series from the pre-1988 era covered in this book that has provided a treatment of the way in which love can offer freedom. In The Fantastic Journey, which was briefly mentioned in Chapter Ten, the regular characters search for the mythical place of Evoland (or perhaps Everland?) which, they have been led to believe, will provide them with a route back to their own time and place. Story editor D. C. Fontana has commented, "Drop the 'and' and it's love spelled backwards." (quoted in: Science Fiction Television Series: Episode Guides, Histories, and Casts and Credits for 62 Prime Time Shows, 1959 through 1989, p. 85)

10. McGoohan, P. On the trail of The Prisoner: Roger Goodman talks to Patrick McGoohan. CD. PrizBiz, 2007. Audio recording of 1979 interview.

11. Nobel, S. and Goldsborough, D. The Prisoner puzzle. Ontario Educational Communications Authority: Toronto, Ontario, 1978.

12. Fulton, R. The encyclopedia of TV science fiction. Boxtree: London, 1990.

13. White, M. and Ali, J. The official Prisoner companion. Sidgwick and Jackson: London, 1988.

14. Quoted in: Carrazé, A. and Oswald, H. op. cit.

15. Reproduced in: Langley, R. (ed.) The Prisoner original 60s publicity material. 2012.

16. Six Into One: The Prisoner File. Channel 4. 16 January 1984.

17. White, M. and Ali, J. op. cit.

18. Langley, R. Portmeirion in The Prisoner and its history, 2nd ed. 2011.

19. Ibid.

20. Morton, A. The complete directory to science fiction, fantasy and horror television series: A comprehensive guide to the first 50 years 1946 to 1996. Other Worlds Books: Peoria, Illinois, 1997.

21. See, for example: Talking With McGoohan. In: White, M. and Ali, J. op. cit., pp. 175–181; McGoohan, P. op. cit.

22. White, M. and Ali, J. op. cit.

23. Lewis Greifer Interview. In: The Prisoner In-depth Tape 5. VHS video cassette. TR 7 Productions: Borehamwood, 1993.

24. Britton, P. D. and Barker, S. J. Reading between designs: Visual imagery and the generation of meaning in The Avengers, The Prisoner, and Doctor Who. University of Texas Press: Austin, Texas, 2003.

25. McGown, A. D. and Docherty, M. J. op. cit.

26. McGoohan, P. op. cit.; Interview With Patrick McGoohan. In: Carrazé, A. and Oswald, H. op. cit., pp. 6–8.

27. McGown, A. D. and Docherty, M. J. op. cit.

28. Timeline: Britannia Rules The Airwaves. SFX Collection, 22, 2005, pp. 106–129.

29. Morton, A. op. cit.

30. Fulton, R. op. cit.

CHAPTER THIRTEEN
The Incarcerated Individual, the Boy Hero and the Whitehall Mandarin – Their Common Tactics of Subversion

Although at first sight comparisons between Gerry Anderson's last major puppet series of the 1960s, a programme that has been described by James Chapman as "surely the most enigmatic television series ever made" (p. 49)[1] and a BBC situation comedy from an entirely different era may seem tenuous, there is no doubt that individual episodes of *Joe 90*, *The Prisoner* and *Yes, Prime Minister* share some remarkable plot similarities. Connections between the first two programmes have, in fact, been made for many years. As long ago as 1983 David Nightingale considered that the *Joe 90* episode *Three's a Crowd* had "a strong flavour of *The Prisoner* running through it". (p. 19)[2] Nightingale does not elaborate on his observation but any reader familiar with *The Prisoner* and the *Joe 90* episode will notice clear parallels, too; in both narratives, attempts are made to exploit the vulnerability to women of one of the regular characters. An attractive female poses as a friend in order to extract secret information in each instance. This chapter, however, concentrates on a different instalment of *Joe 90* – specifically, one described by Stephen La Rivière as "downright bizarre". (p. 185)[3]

Identifying the key theme within the *Prisoner* story *Hammer Into Anvil*, Ian Rakoff writes that it deals with "the power of suggestion and other psychologies". (p. 186)[4] These words can be applied equally justifiably to the *Joe 90* adventure *See You Down There* and to *Man Overboard*, the opening part of the second season of *Yes, Prime Minister*. In each case, one of the main characters with whom the regular viewer has grown very familiar conducts a campaign stronger in style than in substance to undermine the position of a high profile figure. In two of the programmes, the perpetrator is the eponymous hero. Another comparison is offered by Matthew White and Jaffer Ali. They detect similarities between The Prisoner's behaviour in *Hammer Into Anvil* and that of Iago in Shakespeare's *Othello* – both are intent on planting "the seeds of betrayal" but, unlike Iago, Number Six's campaign is justifiable; (p. 96) he is intent on righting a wrong.[5] The parallels between *Othello* and *Hammer Into Anvil* are also discussed in *The Prisoner: The Official Prisoner Fact File*.[6]

In both *The Prisoner* and *Yes, Prime Minister* the paranoid state of the victim is established from the outset. In the former, Number Six becomes aware of Number Two's fragile disposition when his reaction to a telephone call from his superior betrays his insecurity, and in *Yes, Prime Minister*, Cabinet Secretary Sir Humphrey Appleby is familiar with the personal anxieties of Jim Hacker from his previous experience of working with him.[7] When he explains to a colleague an emerging plan he is conceiving to dupe the Prime Minister, the colleague retorts that "only someone in an advanced state of paranoia" would fall victim to it but Sir Humphrey has already recognised that Hacker distrusts entirely any subordinate who appears to be gaining sufficient popularity in either the party or the country to be able to challenge his position and he exploits this unease skilfully so as to set in motion a scheme of subterfuge. As one of Sir Humphrey's allies comments, "the higher the office, the higher the level of paranoia". In *Joe 90*, however, there is less on-screen evidence in the early part of the story to suggest that the victim will be such a vulnerable target for the deception that will follow. The plot seems to be based merely on a "hunch" of Shane Weston, the commander-in-chief of the World Intelligence Network's London office.

The motives of the perpetrators differ very significantly. In *Joe 90*, the plot devised by Weston and implemented by Joe is conducted to bring to book the ruthless businessman Ralph Clayton, who has been using some highly questionable tactics against other companies. Although in strict terms he can be said to be operating within the law, Professor McClaine has no doubt that what he is doing amounts to "out-and-out fraud". WIN's concern is by no means entirely altruistic. One of the latest firms suffering from Clayton's unscrupulous behaviour is Leto Machine Tools, which supplies specialised components to the World Intelligence Network. Whilst Joe is backed in his crusade by the might of the WIN organisation and the local police force, in *Yes, Prime Minister* the plot to discredit the Employment Secretary is hatched by Sir Humphrey alone, although he gains willing support from his predecessor, Sir Arnold Robinson. Since Sir Humphrey's machinations are principally aimed at preventing the adoption by the government of a policy proposed by the Employment Secretary which Sir Humphrey knows will be unpopular with the military, comparisons can be drawn between his campaign and that of WIN – the priority in each case is to stop the subject's current actions and effect a return to "normality". As he considers it difficult to offer convincing political and strategic reasons for rejecting the proposal, Sir Humphrey's plan to discredit its advocate is based on his belief that the best opportunity to undermine the initiative is "to play the man instead of the ball". In *The Prisoner*, however, Number Six's campaign has a much more personal edge. When the hero becomes aware that Number Two's torture of a young Villager has resulted in her suicide, he promises to avenge her death and, in a reversal of the usual scenario within *The Prisoner*, his subsequent efforts form nothing less than a bid to "break" Number Two. His battle is effectively a vendetta. *Hammer Into Anvil* and *See You Down There* begin with very similar threats made by those who feel a strong sense of injustice with regard to the conduct of the character who can be seen as the "villain" of the story. In *Joe 90*, Harris, owner of the latest business to suffer at Clayton's hands, forecasts somewhat ominously to Clayton, "One day you'll realise that you just can't trample on people. You'll learn", and after disturbing the merciless interrogation of Number Seventy-three that leads to her death, The Prisoner responds to Number Two's angry interjection, "You shouldn't have interfered, Number Six. You'll pay for this," with the cold riposte, "No, you will."

The most startling similarity shared by all three plots is that each is based entirely on a set of ruses. Clayton is not affected by any hallucinogen; The Prisoner is not a "plant" introduced by The Village's authorities to test security as he pretends – he merely provides a credible impersonation of such an agent, and the Employment Secretary has no desire to unseat Hacker. Few actual lies are told. Yet, the campaigns are executed so convincingly that they are entirely successful, with the victim assembling in his own mind various pieces of evidence which, taken as a whole, would appear to present a compelling picture of loss of control, treachery and subversion. The most fundamental untruth arises in *Joe 90* as Professor McClaine states quite unequivocally that Clayton has been given a hallucinogenic drug via his tea. The incidents that affect Clayton immediately after this claim has been made are so fantastic that he becomes genuinely convinced that he is "seeing things" and ultimately agrees to halt his dubious business practices in order to receive a non-existent antidote. At the end of *Hammer Into Anvil* Number Two is clearly a broken man and offers his resignation to his superiors. A similar fate befalls the Employment Secretary. Sir Humphrey's victory may, however, be short-lived since, with its original advocate having left his post, Hacker is keen to press ahead with the policy which Humphrey has tried so hard to thwart and asks that it be discussed as the first item on the agenda in the next meeting of Cabinet. A significant difference in the outcomes of the three campaigns is that the victim learns the truth in *See You Down There* but even here Clayton does not find out for himself. Near the story's climax, he is told by Professor McClaine that no hallucinogenic substance has been administered. Hacker and Number Two remain entirely oblivious to the nature of the trickery.

Whilst White and Ali argue that the tactics employed by The Prisoner against Number Two in *Hammer Into Anvil* are very much in the tradition of those that have been seen in *Danger Man*,[8] *Yes, Prime Minister* creators Jonathan Lynn and Antony Jay suggest that Sir Humphrey's abilities are reminiscent of those of "a master magician" – he "could conjure up very good arguments out of thin air". (p. 11)[9] *Joe 90*, meanwhile, accesses a variety of brain patterns that enable him to exploit the skills of a great trumpet player, a leading power backpack operator and the world's best mimic in the WIN scheme to destabilise Clayton.

Both Clayton and Hacker initially respond with disbelief to the early phases of the campaigns of subversion. When Clayton is informed by Professor McClaine, who is posing as one of the businessman's tea staff, that he has swallowed a hallucinogenic pill he reacts with incredulity and orders McClaine to leave his office. Similarly, when Sir Humphrey begins to imply gently that the Employment Secretary may be looking to challenge Hacker's position, the Prime Minister is at first bemused. As the three plots intensify, however, in each case the victim's position is undermined by well-meaning subordinates who inadvertently become accomplices in the campaigns. In *Joe 90*, Stewart and Evans, two prominent members of Clayton's board, unwittingly help to bring about his psychological disintegration; in *Yes, Prime Minister* the Chief Whip's caution and unwillingness to give a categorical denial that a leadership coup is being planned when Hacker discusses the matter with him lead to an escalation of the Prime Minister's fears; in *The Prisoner* the reports of a laboratory technician, the Director of Psychiatrics at the Village Hospital and the bandmaster, which fail to reveal further information on what Number Two suspects, convince him that various members of The Village are involved in a "conspiracy" against him. With increasing paranoia taking hold of each victim, colleagues begin to doubt the mental stability of their leader, who, in time, comes to question the loyalty of his closest aides and ultimately calls on them to resign. Even the Supervisor, the hitherto trusted henchman Number Fourteen and the ever-faithful Butler are dismissed by Number Two. In *Man Overboard*, the removal of the Employment Secretary is, of course, the whole aim of Sir Humphrey's machinations.

Humour figures prominently in all three episodes. Since *Yes, Prime Minister* is itself a comedy, this is entirely to be expected. It is interesting, however, that whilst *The Prisoner* is often regarded as a highly cerebral programme that asks deep philosophical questions about the nature of man and society, James O'Neill describes the *Hammer Into Anvil* instalment as a "black comedy". (p. 269)[10] Robert Fairclough highlights the "dry humour" of the episode, (p. 77) much of which is directed against Number Two. Specifically, Fairclough draws attention to how The Prisoner's Morse code message translates as "pat-a-cake, pat-a-cake, baker's man" and his dummy bomb is a cuckoo clock.[11] The casting of Patrick Cargill, who is today probably best remembered for his role in the comedy programme *Father, Dear Father*, further emphasises the humour of the episode. As in *The Prisoner*, impersonation is a major theme within *See You Down There*, with Professor McClaine and Shane Weston both posing as Clayton's tea staff and Sam Loover masquerading as a policeman. Weston also assumes the guise of a doctor at one point. Much of the comedy within the story emerges from these surreal situations. Even the victim himself is not free from impersonation or at least alleged impersonation. In *Hammer Into Anvil*, The Prisoner pretends that someone on the telephone has been claiming to be Number Two in order to pass on false instructions to him, and in *See You Down There*, Joe mimics Clayton's voice, again on the telephone and again to pass on false instructions, in this case to Stewart and Evans.

The most direct acknowledgement of the influence of *The Prisoner* on the *Joe 90* instalment is the "see you down there" salute and catchphrase used by the WIN officers at the end of their visits to Clayton. As Chris Bentley observes, it is clearly based on the "Be seeing you!" farewell from *The Prisoner*.[12] In both programmes, the message is ambiguous and the custom in *The Prisoner* has been the subject of considerable speculation among fans and commentators. One possible explanation was reported in Chapter Ten. Initially, the "see you down there" phrase in *Joe 90* might seem to deal obliquely with Clayton's fate in the afterlife should he continue with his ruthless business methods but Professor McClaine explains in the final moments of the episode that "down there" is a reference to reducing Clayton to his hands and knees.

Although of all the episodes of *The Prisoner* it is the *Hammer Into Anvil* instalment that would appear to be most closely aligned to *See You Down There*, psychological warfare is a feature of the relationship between Number Two and Number Six throughout the series. Indeed, the pretence surrounding the way in which Joe and his colleagues attempt to convince Clayton that he has just ingested a hallucinogenic drug echoes the way in which the Village authorities lead Number Six to believe erroneously that he has undergone an operation to pacify him (in *A Change of Mind*), is actually Number Twelve (in *The Schizoid*

Man), and has made an effective escape from The Village (in *The Chimes of Big Ben*). The mental games of "cat and mouse" reach a peak in *The Prisoner*'s penultimate episode, *Once Upon a Time*, in which the hero turns the tables on his adversary in decisive fashion. Similarly, much of the appeal of *Yes, Prime Minister* and its predecessor, *Yes Minister*, lies in the ongoing sparring between Hacker and Sir Humphrey, with each registering personal victories during the course of the programmes' life spans. Summarising the outcome of *The Tangled Web* – the last episode of *Yes, Prime Minister* broadcast – Graham McCann writes, "This time, Sir Humphrey had been thwarted. The next time, one suspected, Hacker would probably be the one to lose out. That was how it had always been. That was how it would always be." (p. 283)[13] In *See You Down There*, however, the duel between Clayton and WIN is very much a one-off, with the former making his only appearance in the series.

Over the last 30 years, in particular, *The Prisoner* has been the subject of much scholarly scrutiny. As was indicated in Section II, various critical essays which highlight similarities between the show and other creative works appear in *The Projection Room* section of the website *The Unmutual*.[14] Comparative investigation forms a major theme within fan appreciation of many programmes, in fact, and in *The Discontinuity Guide*, the identification of specific links between each of the original *Doctor Who* serials and other texts forms a significant component of the book.[15] Much less attention, however, has been directed towards making connections between Gerry Anderson's series and other scenarios, and Chapter Eight outlined how one of the wider comparisons that has been attempted met with controversy. It is also very difficult to determine the true extent to which the plot of one episode of a particular television programme has been influenced by a preceding instalment of a different show but, as this chapter and others within the book have aimed to demonstrate, it can nevertheless be illuminating to explore the different ways in which programmes of quite contrasting types have employed similar basic scenarios. A final instance in which *The Prisoner* and another major television series exploit the same plot situation will be examined in the last chapter.

References and Notes

1. Chapman, J. Saints and Avengers: British adventure series of the 1960s. I. B. Tauris: London, 2002.
2. Lip-sync: S.I.G. Letters. SiG, 7, Spring 1983, pp. 18–20.
3. La Rivière, S. Filmed in Supermarionation: A history of the future. Hermes Press: Neshannock, Pennsylvania, 2009.

4. Rakoff, I. Inside The Prisoner: Radical television and film in the 1960s. Batsford: London, 1998.

5. White, M. and Ali, J. The official Prisoner companion. Sidgwick and Jackson: London, 1988.

6. The Prisoner: The Official Fact File. De Agostini, 2005–2006.

7. Much has been made in Unique But Similar of the fact that we never learn which "side" is holding Number Six in The Village. In Yes Minister and Yes, Prime Minister, meanwhile, the party allegiance of Jim Hacker is not revealed. Indeed, seldom is the name of any political party even mentioned. Antony Jay and Jonathan Lynn point out in The Yes Minister Miscellany that politically, Hacker is "placed firmly in the centre of the… spectrum" (p. 8); the name of his headquarters – Central House – is an amalgam of Conservative Central Office and Labour's Transport House, and during his election night count Hacker is shown with a white rosette. The motivation for ensuring that Hacker could not be clearly identified with the Right or the Left did not lie in any attempt to portray the politician as an enigmatic figure, however; the writers were simply keen to avoid allegations of party bias.

8. White, M. and Ali, J. op. cit.

9. Lynn, J. and Jay, A. (eds.) Yes Prime Minister: The diaries of the Right Hon. James Hacker – Volume II. BBC: London, 1987.

10. O'Neill, J. Sci-fi on tape: A comprehensive guide to over 1,250 science fiction and fantasy films on video. Billboard: New York, 1997.

11. Fairclough, R. The Prisoner: The official companion to the classic TV series. Carlton: London, 2002.

12. Bentley, C. The complete Gerry Anderson: The authorised episode guide. Reynolds and Hearn: Richmond, London, 2003.

13. McCann, G. A very courageous decision: The inside story of Yes Minister. Aurum: London, 2014.

14. The Unmutual: The Projection Room – The Prisoner Compared. URL: http://www.theunmutual.co.uk/projection.htm (accessed: 23 February 2017).

15. Cornell, P., Day, M. and Topping, K. Doctor Who: The discontinuity guide. Doctor Who Books: London, 1995.

CHAPTER FOURTEEN
The Journey that Never Was... Another Weapon in the Armoury of Deception

The previous chapter explored an episode that was atypical of *The Prisoner* series in that the instalment was devoted, virtually from start to finish, to a plan devised and executed by Number Six to strike a blow against The Village's leadership. It is far more common, of course, for episodes to concentrate on schemes by the authorities to break The Prisoner. This chapter is devoted to one such instance, which bears a strong resemblance to a deception conceived and then put into practice by the IMF team in the original series of *Mission: Impossible*. In both the *Prisoner* episode *The Chimes of Big Ben* and the first season instalment of *Mission: Impossible* entitled *The Train* a charade involving a lengthy journey takes place and is designed, ultimately, to ensure that the victim discloses certain important information whilst under a misapprehension, having been lulled into a false sense of security.

The plot of the *Mission: Impossible* episode is convoluted and, if a comparison with the *Prisoner* story is to be made, a few moments must be taken to recount it. Dan Briggs, leader of the Impossible Missions Force, is charged with ensuring that Deputy Premier Milos Pavel does not succeed the current Prime Minister, Ferenc Larya, as leader of Svardia. Larya, who has little time left to live, favours Pavel as his country's next head of state since he expects him to continue his own democratic policies. Nevertheless, the IMF fears with good justification that, once he is in power, Pavel will actually establish himself as a dictator and crush any opposition mercilessly. The scheme that Briggs formulates to prevent Pavel from taking over in Svardia is ingenious. Essentially, it involves convincing Larya that he must travel by train to Bern for a life-saving operation. Pavel and his military supporter, General Androv, are persuaded to accompany him. The journey ends in an apparent crash, which would seem to result in Pavel and Androv being taken to a hospital for medical attention. When they are told that Larya has been killed in the accident, they plot how Pavel's tyranny of Svardia will begin. The whole drama surrounding the journey, the crash and its aftermath has, however, been faked by the IMF and, unbeknownst to the plotters, the dialogue between Pavel and Androv is being watched and overheard by Larya, who now realises the former's unsuitability to succeed him and quickly withdraws his support.

In both *The Train* and *The Chimes of Big Ben*, the simulated journey is merely a ruse to bring about the perpetrators' real aim. With regard to screen time, the relative prominence given to the journeys is very different. As the title of the instalment implies, in the *Mission: Impossible* adventure, the scenes on board the carriage and the various accompanying deceptions form a very lengthy part of the episode and, in fact, constitute almost a third of the instalment's total length, whereas The Prisoner's apparent escape from The Village to what he initially believes to be London occupies less than seven minutes.

It is only when the victim has seemingly arrived at their destination that the most important event in each overall narrative takes place, with the final moments of each episode unfolding in a convincing mock-up of a building. In what he first assumes to be the familiar London office of his superiors, Number Six begins to confide the reasons for his resignation. Once he hears Big Ben finish its hourly chimes he realises, however, that he cannot have reached London as he had anticipated because the clock's chimes match the time shown on a watch given to him in what would appear to be Poland and there should be an hour's time difference between the two places. It is a measure of the extent to which the whole episode is constructed around the last few moments that the writer of *The Chimes of Big Ben*, Vincent Tilsley, recalls how the idea that the Village authorities would create some kind of facsimile of the London office formed his first thought when he was conceiving the episode. He then worked backwards to develop the story, and comments modestly that the revelation surrounding the time and The Prisoner's watch formed "a fairly obvious bit of commonplace plotting... It doesn't take much to think that one up".[1]

Although Number Six's explanation for resigning goes unfinished as he ceases his speech once his suspicions are aroused, according to *The Prisoner: The Official Fact File*, the statement that he does provide, i.e. that his resignation was "a matter of conscience", constitutes "the most information that he ever reveals about himself and his motives". (The Episode Guide, p. 12)[2] Steven Paul Davies, however, maintains that the "one serious answer" Number Six gives to the question of his resignation is to be found not in *The Chimes of Big Ben* but in *Once Upon a Time*, when he answers simply that he resigned "for peace of mind". (p. 147)[3]

In *The Train*, with Larya apparently dead, Pavel and Androv feel at liberty to discuss the former's plans for Svardia. Here, the victims fall for the IMF deception completely, whilst it is The Prisoner's attention to detail that enables him to see through the charade to which he has been subjected and, ultimately, preserve his secrets. The fraudulence of the hospital and the office settings is clearly established in the final moments of each episode. On suspecting trickery, Number Six angrily pulls out cables to silence a tape recorder that is playing traffic noises and opens the building's double doors to discover he is still in The Village; once Pavel has incriminated himself, the IMF team push aside what appears to be the wall of a room within the hospital to reveal that the whole area is little more than a set of the kind that would be used in the making of a film.

The fact that what we have assumed to be a genuine office is no more than a replica comes as a major shock to both The Prisoner and the first-time viewer but the hospital's true nature is less of a surprise to the watching public. This reflects a marked difference in the mode of storytelling used in the two productions. In *The Train*, viewers are granted a "god's eye" perspective. As well as seeing the events which the victims of the stratagem experience, we are able to watch the work of the IMF team in establishing the charade. We observe, for example, how, during the "journey", agents switch the points of the track so that the train can be shunted into a warehouse, how a film is used to show the passengers scenery that would be evident on a genuine journey, how rockers recreate the movement of a train even when the carriage is otherwise stationary and how sound recordings of air brakes and train whistles are played to add auditory authenticity. Some of these methods are strikingly similar to those employed to stage the make-believe railway journey shown in the *Avengers* episode *The Grave-diggers*. Here, however, Sir Horace Winslip, who insists on eating his meals at home in a simulated moving carriage, is little more than a bumbling, railway-mad eccentric; the IMF's agenda is rather more serious – they are concerned with the fate of a whole country.

Whilst in *The Train* and *The Grave-diggers* viewers are witnesses to the deception that surrounds the "journey", in *The Chimes of Big Ben* we are not only left in the dark just as much as is The Prisoner; it would seem that we are also deliberately misled. Chris Gregory maintains that the images of lorries, cranes, ships and aeroplanes, which are clearly designed to indicate to the viewer that a journey is really taking place, "are in many ways amongst the strangest in the series". (p. 73)[4] Gregory suggests that these shots may either amount to flaws in the narrative or form "subjective" images, representing what Number Six **imagines** is happening. This line of reasoning quickly returns us to the theory that The Village and the events that we see within it themselves amount to no more than a dream or hallucination, since, as Gregory recognises, if the images depicting transport are to be regarded as "subjective", "then other assumptions of 'realism' with regard to what we see on the screen must be called into question" too. (p. 74)[5] Alan Stevens and Fiona Moore find the transport shots less puzzling, suggesting that the Village authorities could easily have arranged for the would-be escapees to be "driven/flown etc around the countryside for a while". (p. 54)[6] Irrespective of which interpretation is favoured by the reader, it is clear by the end of the episode that The Prisoner has been the victim of a scheme by the Village authorities and certain other scenes within the episode begin to make more sense. In particular, we can now understand why various escape preparations made by Number Six and Nadia, and indeed the beginning of the homeward journey itself, are allowed to proceed when they could easily have been prevented.

Although, in the final analysis, the plan by the Village authorities to trick Number Six fails, a viewer who is familiar with the dénouement and is watching the episode again may feel that, for much of the time, it seems that The Prisoner has fallen into the trap entirely. In *The Train*, meanwhile, there are several occasions when it appears that Pavel and Androv will learn the truth. A selenium rectifier is at one point in danger of burning out before another can be fitted. If this happens, the sound effects so pivotal to the deception will be silenced and the ruse exposed. Also, Androv becomes suspicious when no carriages other than his own are in evidence but quick-thinking Rollin Hand, the master of disguise who is assigned the task of supervising events on the train by answering questions and heading off potential problems, is able to salvage the situation by offering a sufficiently convincing explanation.

Infiltration is a key theme in both *The Train* and *The Chimes of Big Ben*. Like Hand, Larya's doctor and nurse are both acting on behalf of the IMF. Similarly, in the *Prisoner* story, Nadia is introduced into The Village specifically to win Number Six's confidence, present herself as a fellow dissident and, in time, take on the guise of a willing accomplice in an escape attempt. In both cases, substantial teams lie behind the trickery. Briggs can command the support of any members of the IMF whom he considers suitable and indeed at the beginning of the story, we watch him select the operatives for this particular assignment with care, whilst in *The Chimes of Big Ben*, the scheme to ensnare Number Six is backed not only by the Village authorities but also by men whom The Prisoner trusts as his superiors in the Intelligence services. It is possible, too, that the whole arts and crafts competition, which has given Number Six the opportunity to construct the components for his boat, has been staged for his benefit.

If one key difference between *The Chimes of Big Ben* and *The Train* is the extent to which the two schemes are ultimately successful, another lies in the nature of the victim. In the former, he is the series' hero, whereas in the latter, he is the villain of the story. Nevertheless, it is possible to present a case that, even in *The Train*, the target is something of a misguided patriot, rather than totally evil. At one point in the segment, Pavel claims to Androv that he is sickened by the prospect of the killing to come and says he regrets there is no other way to rid Svardia of her enemies than to put his opponents to death. Pavel justifies his actions by claiming, "the decay goes too deep. It must be cut away". Patrick J. White suggests that his misgivings make Pavel unique within the series – he is

> ... the only *Mission* opponent to ever express any qualms over his dastardly plans... As IMF strategies grew more and more ruthless, it became obvious that to present the heavies as anything less than 100 percent evil was a sympathy-engendering mistake. Pavel's musings were the first and last of their kind. (p. 101)[7]

Perhaps the most unpleasant character in *The Train* is not Pavel but Androv, who chuckles at the thought that Svardia's jails will soon be emptied when their occupants are executed, and does not dispute the Deputy Premier's accusation that he **relishes** killing.

Although the personality of Pavel differs from that of the usual kind of adversary faced by the IMF, in other respects *The Train* may be considered a quintessential *Mission: Impossible* episode and it adheres rigidly to the show's standard story formula. According to James Chapman, a "minimalist" strategy was employed throughout the series in this context, with the plot reduced to a set of clearly definable "moves":

> ... the leader of the IMF is presented with a mission by an unknown voice on a tape; he assembles his team and briefs them; an elaborate deception is plotted to discredit an enemy; the deception is put into practice with members of the IMF team playing out their

assigned roles; an unforeseen circumstance jeopardises the deception but is averted through improvisation; the deception is completed successfully, whereupon the IMF team packs up and leaves. (p. 57)[8]

Virtually all these elements are evident in *The Train*.

Robert Fairclough reports how, although *The Chimes of Big Ben* was the fifth episode of *The Prisoner* filmed, it was only the second broadcast.[9] Several writers have suggested that it should actually be seen later in the series.[10] Nevertheless, it may be said that the viewer's surprise at the unexpected ending is heightened when the instalment is shown so early in the sequence. If it is watched later and the viewer has already witnessed the failed escape attempts featured in *The Schizoid Man*, *Many Happy Returns* and *Checkmate*, the final twist may be undermined by the fact that, with each passing week, one may be starting to accept that Number Six will never free himself from The Village. The unsuccessful escape scenario certainly had some novelty value in the early episodes, however. Isaac Asimov admits that he reacted with disbelief when "Theodore Prisoner", as he terms him, did not liberate himself from The Village by the end of *Arrival*, and Asimov remained convinced that he would manage to do so in the next instalment,[11] which, in both Britain and the US, was indeed *The Chimes of Big Ben*.[12] Similarly, it seems reasonably plausible at this point in the series that Number Six should trust Nadia. Subsequently, The Prisoner will become increasingly aware that the use of women to betray or deceive him forms a recurrent strategy practised by the Village hierarchy. If Nadia were to appear in one of the later episodes, we would expect Number Six to have learnt from his experiences and be less willing to accept her as a co-conspirator.

Alwyn Turner comments that "the stasis of stalemate" dominates *The Prisoner*. He elaborates, "those in authority over The Village want to know why he resigned, which [Number Six] refuses to reveal, while he seeks to escape his confinement, which they do not allow". (p. 103)[13] The prevalence of this pattern is particularly apparent from the table provided in Section I, which offers an episode-by-episode breakdown of the hero's fortunes. It may be argued that *The Chimes of Big Ben* is a microcosm of the series' recurrent emphasis on the silence of Number Six and his inability to flee. Here The Prisoner thwarts a scheme intended to lead him to disclose his secrets but cannot effect an escape. The overall outcome of *The Chimes of Big Ben* is debated by Susan Nobel and Diana Goldsborough, who summarise that it may be regarded variously as a success for Number Two, a triumph for The Prisoner or "merely a draw", depending on one's viewpoint. (p. 7)[14] A more unequivocal resolution emerges in *The Train*, with the IMF team gaining a resounding victory for democracy and the free world. Nevertheless, it is unfortunate that an innocent party has to be a victim of the deception. In both the *Mission: Impossible* episode and *The Chimes of Big Ben*, the hopes of the targeted individual are aroused and, in the final minutes, shattered but in *The Train*, so, too, are those of Larya, who spends a considerable part of the story under the misapprehension that successful surgery will restore his health. The scene in which he learns the truth and realises that there will be no life-saving operation for him provides the instalment with one of its most poignant moments. It is made all the more moving by the stoicism he demonstrates when he hears the news.

The Train was something of a trendsetter in the history of *Mission: Impossible* as the essential plot would be reworked within the programme's framework on several future occasions. According to White, it is the first instalment within the series "to employ the false journey, a famous *Mission* trademark, in which a subject is led to believe he is in transit when, in fact, he isn't moving at all. Later episodes would vary the vehicle, from truck to airplane to submarine". (p. 100)[15] The frequency with which the central concept within *The Chimes of Big Ben* has emerged in fiction is also noted by Stevens and Moore. Specifically, they write, "The whole idea of a building or office being mocked up in order to convince a spy that he is not where he thinks he is, is a stock feature of a number of post-war spy thrillers, most famously *The Ipcress File*." (p. 52)[16] Perhaps, then, we should scarcely be surprised that this scenario, a faked journey that ultimately delivers the protagonist to the key destination and similar methods of executing the deceptions, such as the use of sound recordings and blinds to prevent the intrusion of evidence that will arouse suspicion, can be found in the episodes of two major television series. What is maybe more unexpected is the fact that the productions that have been discussed in this chapter were first shown within just a few months of each other. *The Train* was originally transmitted in the US in March 1967, and the initial broadcast of *The Chimes of Big Ben* took place in Britain during October of the same year. Another indication of the popularity of the basic concept in the latter half of the 1960s is provided by Fairclough, who sees parallels between the plot of *The Chimes of Big Ben* and that of the *Man in a Suitcase* episode *Brainwash*. Fairclough reports, "broadcast the same week as *The Chimes of Big Ben*, [the *Man in a Suitcase* instalment] features its anti-hero McGill imprisoned in a fake country house inside a warehouse". (p. 42)[17]

Much has been made in *Unique But Similar* of the common ground shared by *The Prisoner* and *The Invaders*, and the latter's episode *The Believers* features a ploy comparable to that which we have seen employed in *The Chimes of Big Ben*. In this instalment first broadcast in December 1967, the aliens find after kidnapping David Vincent that their first strategy aimed at ensuring that he discloses certain information ends in failure. They then use another technique – they move his unconscious body to a mock-up of a hospital room and, as he recovers, lead him to think that he has been freed as a result of an apparent raid by the US military. The Invaders hope that if he is convinced that he is now in safe hands, he will feel able to speak freely. Like Number Six in *The Chimes of Big Ben*, however, Vincent sees through the deception, in this case almost at once.

The final episode of *Captain Scarlet and the Mysterons – The Inquisition –* presents another late 1960s instance in which a hero who has been captured by aliens is encouraged, whilst his sense of place is disrupted, to reveal particular information that he is intent on maintaining secret. In this case, a drugged Captain Blue is instructed by an interrogator, who claims to be a Spectrum intelligence officer, to reveal his organisation's cipher code in order to prove his identity after he has apparently been missing for three months. It ultimately emerges that Blue's inquisitor is actually a Mysteron agent and what the Captain had assumed to be Cloudbase control room is really no more than a replica within an otherwise empty building. Blue, like Vincent, is saved from succumbing to the scheme by his instinctive scepticism. The "cat and mouse" theme involving a captured regular protagonist and a hostile antagonist is reminiscent of the *Champions* episode *The Interrogation*. In both instances, we see flashback sequences and the "here and now" action takes place virtually entirely in a very limited area. The main difference is that in the dénouement of *The Interrogation*, we learn that it is a fellow member of Nemesis, rather than an enemy agent, who has been questioning Stirling.

The Train and *The Chimes of Big Ben* have been the subjects of enthusiastic reviews. White believes that the fake journey plot "was probably never better used [in the *Mission: Impossible* series] than here, where it is fresh, well detailed, and convincing", (p. 100)[18] and Davies asserts, "Polls in fanzines reveal [*The Chimes of Big Ben*] to be one of the most popular [*Prisoner*] episodes." (p. 81)[19] Nevertheless, in the eyes of various commentators the credibility of each story suffers as a result of the gullibility exhibited by the victims of the deceptions. Acknowledging that the script for *The Train* is dependent on a fundamental fallacy, the director of the instalment, Ralph Senensky, concedes, "It is impossible to look at a projection screen and not know that it's a projection screen." (p. 100)[20] Gregory, meanwhile, criticises the extreme improbability of the escape attempt of Nadia and The Prisoner, highlighting how unlikely it would be for them to evade The Village's surveillance devices so easily and how they are able to hide themselves in crates that will be delivered to London.[21] In addition, Stevens and Moore draw attention to the "whacking great convenience" that one of Nadia's resistance colleagues is waiting for the escapees' arrival on the beach at the very time when they actually appear. (p. 52)[22] This in itself should arouse Number Six's suspicions, the authors maintain. Yet, any viewer who is willing to suspend their disbelief whilst watching the two episodes is amply rewarded.

References and Notes

1. The Prisoner in Production. VHS video cassette. TR 7 Productions: Borehamwood, 1993.
2. The Prisoner: The Official Fact File. De Agostini, 2005–2006.
3. Davies, S. P. The Prisoner handbook: An unauthorized companion. Boxtree: London, 2002.
4. Gregory, C. Be seeing you... Decoding The Prisoner. John Libbey Media: Luton, 1997.
5. Ibid.
   Gregory's argument that the transport pictures indicate what Number Six imagines is happening can also, of course, be used in various other contexts to counter Jack Lowin's view – outlined in Chapter Seven – that the "dream" explanation is "a cheat".
6. Stevens, A. and Moore, F. Fall out: The unofficial and unauthorised guide to The Prisoner. Telos: Tolworth, 2007.
7. White, P. J. The complete Mission: Impossible dossier. Boxtree: London, 1996.
8. Chapman, J. Saints and Avengers: British adventure series of the 1960s. I. B. Tauris: London, 2002.
9. Fairclough, R. (ed.) The Prisoner: The original scripts – Volume 1. Reynolds and Hearn: Richmond, London, 2005.
10. See, for example: Nobel, S. and Goldsborough, D. The Prisoner puzzle. Ontario Educational Communications Authority: Toronto, Ontario, 1978; White, M. and Ali, J. The official Prisoner companion. Sidgwick and Jackson: London, 1988; Fairclough, R. The Prisoner: The official companion to the classic TV series. Carlton: London, 2002.
11. Asimov, I. Theodore Prisoner. In: Carrazé, A. and Oswald, H. The Prisoner: A televisionary masterpiece. Virgin: London, 1990, p. 18.
12. White, M. and Ali, J. op. cit.
13. Turner, A. W. Portmeirion and its creator. In: Morris, J., Turner, A. W., Eastment, M., Lacey, S. and Llywelyn, R. Portmeirion. Antique Collectors' Club: Woodbridge, 2006, pp. 26–129.
14. Nobel, S. and Goldsborough, D. op. cit.
15. White, P. J. op. cit.
16. Stevens, A. and Moore, F. op. cit.

17. Fairclough, R. op. cit. 2002.
18. White, P. J. op. cit.
19. Davies, S. P. op. cit.
20. Quoted in: White, P. J. op. cit.
21. Gregory, C. op. cit.
22. Stevens, A. and Moore, F. op. cit.

Epilogue

Although for decades there has been much written about the novelty and originality of *The Prisoner* and indeed such comments continue to be made to this day, *Unique But Similar* has demonstrated that many plot elements inherent in the individual episodes and wider themes within the overarching narrative are apparent in other television productions that appeared either before 1967 or in the 20 years that immediately followed the programme's first transmission. Whilst some of *The Prisoner*'s more futuristic ingredients inevitably bring to mind aspects of particular works of science fiction, other components would seem to transcend genre and are as likely to be found in programmes rooted in the here-and-now – and even in situation comedies – as they are in speculative dramas set in outer space or time to come. As no doubt all of us can relate to *The Prisoner*'s fundamental issues with regard to individuality, freedom, dissidence, manipulation and oppression, whether our scale of reference is based on concrete personal experience or a more abstract, philosophical framework, many ideas within the programme can be said to achieve a certain universality and it is thus scarcely surprising that they can be detected in a wide range of creative works elsewhere, even though most of those which have been scrutinised in *Unique But Similar* were produced at a time when *The Prisoner* was often considered no more than an eccentric, one-off television experiment that was to a large extent unsuccessful. We may well smile to ourselves as we recognise in other contexts the particular dilemmas Number Six faces or the methods that he or his adversaries employ. On occasion, the technologies we see are unfamiliar and may even seem somewhat fanciful but the motivations of those using them are likely to be instantly identifiable.

APPENDIX:

The Works Examined

The Twilight Zone was a 156-episode anthology series created by Rod Serling and originally broadcast by CBS in America between 2nd October 1959 and 19th June 1964.

It is currently available on DVD.

The Train was a first season episode of *Mission: Impossible* written by William Read Woodfield and Allan Balter and originally broadcast by CBS in America on 18th March 1967.

It is currently available on DVD as part of the package *Mission: Impossible 1 – The First TV Season.*

The Faceless Ones was a six-part, fourth season *Doctor Who* serial written by David Ellis and Malcolm Hulke and originally broadcast by BBC Television between 8th April and 13th May 1967.

It no longer exists in its entirety within the BBC archives. The soundtrack, however, is currently available on CD and the two surviving episodes can be found in the DVD package *Doctor Who: Lost in Time.*

The Interrogation was an episode of *The Champions* written by Dennis Spooner and originally broadcast by ITV on 29th January 1969.

It is currently available on DVD as part of the package *The Champions: The Complete Series.*

See You Down There was an episode of *Joe 90* written by Tony Barwick and originally broadcast by ITV on 23rd February 1969.

It is currently available on DVD as part of the package *Joe 90 Collector's Edition.*

UFO was a 26-episode ITC series produced by Gerry and Sylvia Anderson and originally broadcast on ITV between 16th September 1970 and 1st April 1971.

It is currently available in the form of a two-volume DVD package.

The House was a first season episode of *Rod Serling's Night Gallery* written by Rod Serling himself (based on a short story by André Maurois) and originally broadcast by NBC in America on 30th December 1970.

It is currently available on DVD as part of the package *Night Gallery: The Complete First Season*.

Cloud Burst was a ten-part *Look and Read* serial for schools written by Richard Carpenter and originally broadcast by BBC Television between 24th September and 3rd December 1974.

It is not available on DVD.

Children of the Stones was a seven-part HTV serial written by Jeremy Burnham and Trevor Ray and originally broadcast by ITV between 10th January and 21st February 1977.

It is currently available on DVD.

Logan's Run was a 14-episode series created by Ivan Goff and Ben Roberts and originally broadcast by CBS in America between 16th September 1977 and 16th January 1978.

It is currently available on DVD.

Blake's 7 was a 52-episode series created by Terry Nation and originally broadcast by BBC Television between 2nd January 1978 and 21st December 1981.

It is currently available in the form of a four-volume DVD package.

The Omega Factor was a ten-part BBC Scotland serial created by Jack Gerson and originally broadcast by BBC Television between 13th June and 15th August 1979.

It is currently available on DVD.

Codename Icarus was a five-part serial written by Richard Cooper and originally broadcast by BBC Television between 8th and 22nd December 1981.

It is currently available on DVD.

Knights of God was a 13-part TVS serial written by Richard Cooper and originally broadcast by ITV between 6th September and 6th December 1987.

It is not currently available on DVD.

Man Overboard was a second season episode of *Yes, Prime Minister* written by Antony Jay and Jonathan Lynn and originally broadcast by BBC Television on 3rd December 1987.

It is currently available on DVD as part of the package *Yes, Prime Minister: Series Two.*

SCRIPT
DOCTOR

The Inside Story of **Doctor Who** 1986-89

by Andrew Cartmel

"There are worlds out there where the sky is burning, and the sea's asleep, and the rivers dream. People made of smoke, and cities made of song. Somewhere there's danger, somewhere there's injustice, and somewhere else the tea's getting cold. Come on, Ace — we've got work to do!"

Andrew Cartmel was the script editor on **Doctor Who** from 1986 to 1989. During his time on the show he introduced the seventh Doctor and his companion Ace (Sylvester McCoy and Sophie Aldred) and oversaw forty-two scripts written by eight writers new to the series.

With a clear mission to bring proper science fiction back into **Doctor Who**, he formulated what was later termed 'The Cartmel Masterplan', re-introducing the mystery to the character of the Doctor as the series celebrated its twenty-fifth anniversary and beyond.

Script Doctor is his memoir of this time based on his diaries written sometimes on set and sometimes not even in the diary itself but on the back of scripts. Illustrated with 32 pages of photographs, many of them not published before, this is a vivid account of life in the **Doctor Who** production office in the late eighties.

ISBN 978-1-908630-68-1

THE

WORZEL

BOOK

by Stuart Manning

When a former Time Lord swapped time and space for the mystery of the countryside, one of children's television's most unusual personalities was born. Jon Pertwee's portrayal of the anarchic scarecrow Worzel Gummidge won him a new generation of viewers and would become his most enduring character.

The Worzel Book traces the journey of Scatterbrook's scarecrow, from the days of early radio and the novels of Barbara Euphan Todd, through to the hit ITV television series and its eventual resurrection in New Zealand.

This is the untold behind-the-scenes story of a much-loved TV classic, featuring over 40 new interviews with cast and crew, including Geoffrey Bayldon, Jeremy Austin, Bernard Cribbins, Barbara Windsor and Lorraine Chase, illustrated throughout with over 200 photographs in black and white and colour, many previously unseen.

ISBN 978-1-908630-60-5

DRAMA AND DELIGHT

THE LIFE AND LEGACY OF
VERITY LAMBERT

by Richard Marson

For five decades, the name Verity Lambert appeared on the end credits of many of Britain's most celebrated and talked about television dramas. She was the very first producer of **Doctor Who**, which she nurtured through its formative years at a time when there were few women in positions of power in the television industry. Later, she worked within the troubled British film business and became a pioneering independent producer, founding her own highly-successful company, Cinema Verity.

Within her profession, she was hugely respected as an intensely driven, sometimes formidable but always stylish exponent of her craft, with the stamina and ability to combine quantity with quality. Many of her productions have had a lasting cultural and emotional impact on their audiences and continue to be enjoyed to this day.

But who was the woman behind all these television triumphs and what was the price she paid to achieve them?

Combining months of painstaking research and interviews with many of Lambert's closest friends and colleagues, *Drama and Delight* will capture the energy and spirit of this remarkable woman and explore her phenomenal and lasting legacy.

ISBN 978-1-908630-33-9

ALSO AVAILABLE FROM **MIWK PUBLISHING**

A PECULIAR EFFECT ON THE BBC

by Bernard Wilkie

Bernard Wilkie is a pioneer in the world of visual effects. Along with Jack Kine he co-founded the BBC's Visual Effects Department in 1954. Between them they worked on many BBC productions to list, including *Doctor Who*, *Out of the Unknown*, *Quatermass*, *Monty Python's Flying Circus*, and *Some Mothers Do 'ave 'em*. Bernard passed away in 2002, having written this book in the late 1990s.

A Peculiar Effect on the BBC is his previously unpublished memoir that looks back on his career as a whole, covering each programme in detail with a light, but still educational, and often cautionary tone.

Whether it's trying to make a smoke gun, encase an Ice Warrior in a block of ice, create a Loch Ness Monster or simply come up with a way of presenting a photo collection on screen utilising only one studio camera, Bernard and Jack rose to the occasion – often choking, soaking and terrifying their colleagues in the process. And almost all of these effects had to be done live – the pressure was on!

Foreword by visual effects designer Mat Irvine and afterword by visual effects designer Mike Tucker.

ISBN 978-1-908630-61-2

DIRECTED BY
DOUGLAS
CAMFIELD

by Michael Seely

Douglas Camfield is still regarded as a master of his craft; a television director whose career spanned twenty years and 163 productions. He worked on many popular and groundbreaking series of their day, including **Doctor Who**, **Blake's 7**, **The Nightmare Man**, **The Sweeney**, **Van der Valk** and **Z Cars**, not to mention many long since forgotten and lost productions.

Camfield passed away in January 1984. He was 52.

Towards the end of his life, he recreated the past with the romantic chivalry of **Ivanhoe** and tales of honour in African deserts with **Beau Geste**. His productions frequently topped the ratings charts, including his final serial, **Missing From Home**.

Adopted by an army family, he chose television over the military, and rose from the cutting room floor to become one of the new wave of BBC directors, determined to prove the potential of the medium and take it further away from its roots in theatre and radio and into cinema.

Told with help from his friends and family, *Directed By Douglas Camfield* is the story of a man who commanded the love, loyalty, respect and commitment from his cast and crews, how he overcame seemingly insurmountable hurdles, including his health, and who took risks with his career in order to achieve his goals.

ISBN 978-1-908630-16-2

JAUNT

AN UNOFFICIAL GUIDE TO
THE TOMORROW PEOPLE

by Andy Davidson

Shape-changing robots, military masterminds, ITV technicians – it's a deadly universe out there, but the Tomorrow People are here to help.

The Tomorrow People are man's next step up the evolutionary ladder: Homo superior. From their secret base deep below the streets of London, they offer hope of a better future for the human race as members of the all-powerful Galactic Federation.

Jaunt follows **The Tomorrow People** from its origins in the creative melting-pot of 1970s children's television to a worldwide hit. It revisits them in the 1990s for some light-hearted **Avengers**-style action and returns a decade later for a series of bold, challenging audio plays.

Homo superior has been with us for forty years, and **Jaunt** chronicles the phenomenon that is again preparing to return to our screens in a big-budget US adaptation.

Jaunt includes exclusive interviews with series creator Roger Price, producer Ruth Boswell and the Tomorrow People themselves – Nicholas Young, Peter Vaughan Clarke, Elizabeth Adare, Mike Holoway and Misako Koba.

With an introduction from Roger Price, **Jaunt** also features the complete script of the unmade ninth series adventure *Mystery Moon*.

ISBN 978-1-908630-23-0

All Memories Great & Small

by Oliver Crocker

Based on the bestselling books by James Herriot, **All Creatures Great & Small** remains one of the BBC's most popular television programmes ever produced.

Released as part of the 100th birthday celebrations for the real James Herriot, Alf Wight, *All Memories Great & Small* is an ideal companion to the series. Every episode is accompanied by exclusive memories, thanks to 60 new interviews with cast and crew. Stars Christopher Timothy, Robert Hardy, Peter Davison and Carol Drinkwater are joined by dozens of guest stars and members of the production team, many of whom have never shared their memories of making this television classic before. Tributes are also paid by family members of those no longer with us.

This book is also packed with insight into all 90 episodes, including original synopses, credits, production and transmission dates, viewing figures and dozens of previously unpublished behind the scenes photographs. There is also a foreword from Rosie Page, daughter of Alf Wight, the real James Herriot.

"A must for all Herriot fans... This is a very worthy addition to James Herriot's centenary year." Rosie Page, daughter of Alf Wight

ISBN 978-1-908630-32-2

TOTALLY TASTELESS

THE LIFE OF JOHN NATHAN-TURNER

by Richard Marson

Totally Tasteless: The Life of John Nathan-Turner tells the story of the most controversial figure in the history of **Doctor Who**.

For more than a decade, John Nathan-Turner, or 'JN-T' as he was often known, was in charge of every major artistic and practical decision affecting the world's longest-running science fiction programme.

Richard Marson brings his dramatic, farcical, sometimes scandalous, often moving story to life with the benefit of his own inside knowledge and the fruits of over 100 revealing interviews with key friends and colleagues, those John loved to those from whom he became estranged. The author has also had access to all of Nathan-Turner's surviving archive of paperwork and photos, many of which appear here for the very first time.

This new edition includes a new chapter covering the period from the book's inception to its release and beyond, as well as a number of previously unpublished photographs.

ISBN 978-1-908630-65-0

www.miwk.com/

www.facebook.com/MiwkPublishingLtd

www.instagram.com/miwkpublishing/

www.twitter.com/#!/MiwkPublishing